Strindberg in Inferno

Strindberg in Inferno

GUNNAR BRANDELL   *Translated by Barry Jacobs*

Harvard University Press, Cambridge, Massachusetts, 1974

FOREWORD *by Evert Sprinchorn*

It is a remarkable fact in the history of the theater that two major creators of the modern drama wrote in minor languages and came from what their contemporaries regarded as the fringe of civilization. Ibsen was a Norwegian and Strindberg was a Swede; but together, these rivals "made the Scandinavian Peninsula," as Bernard Shaw put it, "the dramatic Capitol of Europe." By the mid-1890s Ibsen, bent on conquering the world, had overwhelmed Germany and was infiltrating France. The Germans bowed down before Ibsen's genius and proclaimed that "the light today comes to us from the North." In Paris, however, his triumphal march was slowed by the xenophobic French critics and by his Swedish rival. In the 1894–1895 season Strindberg became the most discussed foreign dramatist in the City of Light, outshining even Ibsen. When Strindberg's *The Father* was performed, a Paris magazine published a cartoon of the climactic scene in which Strindberg's tormented captain throws a lighted kerosene lamp at his wife. The captain looks very much like Strindberg, and beneath the cartoon is the caption: "The light today comes to us from the North."

As the furor died down, Ibsen resumed his march of triumph,

while Strindberg, to the consternation of friends and relations, ignored the theater and devoted himself to experiments in the transmutation of the elements. He appeared to have left the field of battle to fight the demons within his own mind. As one of the spoils of battle Ibsen at this time added to his collection of paintings, mostly Renaissance oils, the fine portrait of Strindberg done by Christian Krohg. Ibsen chose to call it "The Outbreak of Madness," and to William Archer, surprised to see Strindberg's face in Ibsen's study, the Norwegian master explained, "I rejoice in that portrait. I think he looks so delightfully mad."

It was common talk in the Scandinavian community that Strindberg was indeed mentally unbalanced, and as his fame spread to other countries during the twentieth century, the image of him as the mad writer, suffering for his art and undisciplined in the creation of it, became so firmly impressed in the public mind that psychiatrists felt free to write monographs diagnosing his insanity; Freud, without having read him, could describe him as suffering from "grave mental abnormality"; and handbooks and literary manuals, without adducing any facts, could state flatly that Strindberg had been confined for a while in an asylum, implying that he was certifiably and clinically mad.

This image of Strindberg as the obsessed artist, teetering on the brink of madness and frequently falling in, was fashioned largely by Strindberg himself and embroidered by his enemies. As a young man, Strindberg liked to think of himself as the romantic artist creating in a frenzy, at one with nature and the cosmos and at odds with civilization and society. When he abandoned his childish illusions about man and God and recognized the impermanence of truth and the hollowness of ideals, he wanted the rest of the world to share his disillusionment and loss of faith. In a novel called *The Red Room* he pictured Stockholm through his journalist's eyes, with its fatuous politicians, derelict actors, and bohemian painters. The vividness of the picture and the breathless vigor of the prose stamped the work as the product of the most talented writer to arrive on the Swedish literary scene in a generation. After its publication in 1879 he wrote a series of satiric sketches under the title *The New Kingdom,* in which no public institution was spared and most of the public figures were recognized. He became the idol of the rebellious young and a terror to the pillars of society.

But iconoclasts have a way of falling before the very temples they attack, and in 1884 Strindberg found himself in court facing charges of blaspheming against the state religion, on the basis of tasteless remarks made in one of his short stories about Jesus as a rabble-rouser and about the comparative merits of commercial and Communion wine. The Queen of Sweden and her feminist friends were determined to destroy this too clever young man who made sarcastic remarks about their religion, who was apparently in league with the socialists, and who insisted that sexual indulgence was the basis of a happy marriage and that sexual abstinence was psychologically and physically harmful. Worst of all, he ridiculed Ibsen, god of the feminists. It was not to be borne, and the Queen saw to it that the government prosecuted him for the only crime with which he could legally be charged: blasphemy. Pitted against the government, the shy Strindberg retained the sympathy of the liberal-minded and defenders of freedom of speech, by whom, when he was acquitted, he was hailed as a David.

But he knew that he had lost. The Philistines could destroy him simply by turning their backs and closing their doors, which they proceeded to do. Though only in his mid-thirties, he saw his career as a writer drawing to an end. He composed his memoirs in six volumes, made a valiant effort to recapture his public with a humorous novel about Swedish fishing folk, witnessed the dissolution of his marriage, and was abandoned by his publisher. In 1892 he moved to Berlin, where he became the center of a bohemian circle. From there he drifted to Paris, hoping to capitalize on the fame that a production of *Miss Julie* at Antoine's avant-garde theater had brought him. But after a year of notoriety, during which he vied with Ibsen for the attention of the intelligentsia, he disappeared from public view, leading a hermit-like existence and living off benefactors who were willing to invest in his wayward genius.

No serious critic questioned his genius. His prose had rejuvenated the Swedish language; his stories and novels had inaugurated a new era in Swedish cultural history; his plays were the only ones written by a Swede that could be compared with those of Ibsen. In 1890 he was to Swedish literature what Hemingway, Faulkner, and O'Neill together were to American literature in the 1930s. But he was hated, as no Swedish writer had been before him and as no writer in America has ever been. He was reviled in the press, denounced from the pulpit, spat at in the street. He may have invigorated Swedish literature with the power of his prose, but that prose had corrupted Swedish youth with its call for sexual license. He may have created the most powerful roles in the Swedish theater, but he had polluted that theater with the pathology of *The Father* and the obscenity of *Miss Julie.* He may have united the nation in admiration of his art, but he had divided that nation into an upper and a lower class and set them warring against each other. When he disappeared into the beerhalls of Berlin and the cafés of Paris, many Swedes rejoiced inwardly at his downfall; and when rumors of his madness reached their ears, they took satisfaction in knowing that their God had visited a condign punishment on this brilliant prince of darkness.

The story of his life might have ended here. It would have formed a fine moralistic chapter in the history of Swedish literature: the rise and fall of August Strindberg. The last lines could have offered a glimpse of the once promising writer, now seedy, unkempt, impecunious, ashamed to be seen where he might be recognized, shuffling beggar-like along a Paris street to his little room, where among his crucibles he seeks in vain for the Philosopher's Stone that will transmute matter and transform his life. His hand, bleeding from psoriasis, scribbles some alchemical nonsense on a piece of paper and stuffs it into a bag filled with a thousand such papers, the last works of a burned-out mind. Finis.

But Strindberg's life was to prove even more exemplary and dramatic. Out of those thousand notes kept in his Green Sack the vision of a new world began to take shape. Out of his trials and tribulations a new soul was formed. Out of his inferno an artist was reborn. What seemed like madness and incoherence to those who knew only part of Strindberg's activities in the 1890s was only the chaos of a mind exploring new frontiers, absorbing ideas from all directions, and taking years to sort out what it had discovered.

Not until a number of years after Strindberg's death in 1912 did a few Swedish scholars realize that the inferno years constituted something more than a religious conversion from a materialistic atheism to a creedless mysticism. And not until 1950 did Gunnar Brandell bring clarity to those confused years by assembling all that was known about the influences affecting Strindberg from without and all that could be inferred about his inner psychological development. Since 1950 more information has of course come to light, but Brandell's study remains fundamentally sound, still the best guide to those years of anguish and discovery that Strindberg later regarded as the most intensely exciting of his life. By reading Brandell, one can share in the richness of those years, for he reveals how out of Strindberg's broken life came a new form of art.

In 1897 Strindberg published the autobiographical novel *Inferno,* a strikingly original work. It deeply impressed Ibsen. Now when visitors noticed Strindberg's portrait, Ibsen explained, "It hangs there to keep watch on me; he is my mortal enemy," or, "I cannot write a line without that insane man staring at me with his crazy eyes." A year later Strindberg sent Ibsen a copy of *To Damascus,* the play that marks a turning point in the history of dramatic technique. What Ibsen thought of it is not known. But he read it while at work on *When We Dead Awaken,* and after completing that play, he said that if he were to return to the old battlefields, he would "appear with new weapons and in new armor." Ibsen wrote nothing more, his writing career ending with the century. The new weapons and new armor were forged by other artists, chief among them being Strindberg—Strindberg the dramatist, Strindberg the novelist, Strindberg the essayist, Strindberg the painter, Strindberg the poet of alchemical formulas and free association.

In 1924 O'Neill avowed that Strindberg was "the precursor of all modernity in our present theatre." This statement is even more true today than it was fifty years ago, when less was known about the course of the modern theater and still less about Strindberg.

PREFACE *by Barry Jacobs*

August Strindberg (1849–1912) saw the world in terms of conflict: class conflict, the battle of the sexes, the warfare between
stronger and weaker brains, the struggle between titanic heroes and
cosmic forces. Behind this perception lay deep inner conflicts, which
he first perceived as external. At all periods in his career he was
guided by this sense of conflict. Indeed, his literary career may be
said to have developed from it. One of his earliest inner conflicts, a
religious crisis that he underwent in adolescence, resulted in his
rejection of evangelical pietism and his acceptance of the liberal uni-
tarianism of Theodore Parker. This "conversion" placed him at odds
with his family. Later, when he was a student at Uppsala between
1867 and 1872, he resisted his father's demand that he renounce his
dream of becoming a writer and choose a more practical vocation.
His brief career in the mercantile world, as editor of an insurance
trade journal, gave him an insight into dishonest business practices
and economic exploitation, while the revolutionary works that he
published in the early 1870s provoked the disapproval of the literary
establishment. These experiences prompted him to take arms
against oppressive social institutions: the family, big business, the

press, the upper classes, the church, and the state—all of which became his targets in the novel that finally established him as an important literary figure in Sweden, *The Red Room* (1879). Much like Ibsen, Strindberg at this period hoped to lay the "ghosts" of outmoded ideas and institutions, and he quickly became one of the leaders of the so-called "Realistic Breakthrough," the literary movement that dominated the 1880s in Scandinavia.

Strindberg was happy and much in love when he married Siri von Essen in 1877—shortly after her divorce from his friend Baron Carl Gustav Wrangel—but he was soon to become embroiled in the turbulent debate surrounding Ibsen's *A Doll's House* (1879), Bjørnsen's *A Gauntlet* (1883), and other modish works dealing with feminism. The antifeminist position that he took probably did little in the long run to ensure his own domestic tranquillity. In *Sir Bengt's Wife* (1882) he appeared in the guise of a liberator who wished to free people from the unrealistic and romantic notions about love that often make them unwilling to accept the everyday annoyances of marriage. When he continued this role in a series of "case studies" entitled *Married* (1884), the book for which he was brought to trial for blasphemy, he turned his criticism directly on Ibsen's Nora, charging among other things that her marriage failed, not because it prevented her from being herself, but because she could not face reality. In other words, he now seemed to feel that her most serious problems were internal and psychological.

By this time he had begun to lose interest in social issues and was moving toward the ethical nihilism of Schopenhauer and Hartmann, whose pessimistic philosophies he had found attractive in the early 1870s. Moreover, he had borrowed Max Nordau's idea of the intellectual superman and begun to see the world in terms of two opposing types: the few "great" intellects (or stronger brains) and the masses of "small" intellects (or weaker brains). Women, in his estimation, belonged to the latter category, and he amassed a good deal of evidence to demonstrate their biological inferiority, from which he argued that the feminist movement was a sign of mass regression. These ideas ultimately served to isolate him from many of his fellow naturalists. At the same time, having become increasingly interested in psychology, he now found the problems of the individual psyche more interesting than external social and political conflicts. Indeed, in his autobiography *The Son of a Servant* (1886), he examined the patterns of external conflict in his life in an attempt to discover why he was torn by so much inner strife. One suggestion was that some of his problems stemmed from the social gap between his parents: while his mother's "slave blood" (he exaggerated) made him sympathize with the lower classes, his legacy from his solidly bourgeois father made him identify himself with the upper classes. Although this analysis hardly explained fully his complex psychological makeup, it showed that he had arrived at a profounder understanding of the relation between external oppositions and inner unrest. This approach, in turn, generated new literary themes, which soon appeared in his work. In 1877, when he wrote both *The Father* and the autobiographical novel entitled *A Madman's Defense,* his love for Siri had degenerated into obsessive jealousy, and he suspected that she was spying on him and wanted to have him committed to an asylum. Both of these works deal quite openly with his psychological reaction to the conflicts in his dissolving marriage, a reaction that led him toward a tragic vision of life.

One of the assumptions shared by most naturalists was the absolute necessity of freeing man from the dead hand of the past, including such illusions as "God" and such crippling codes as "Christian morality" and its attendant preoccupation with sin and guilt. In *The Son of a Servant,* Strindberg described his participation in this effort and gave his psychological and egocentric formula for the new ethics that would free man from guilt: "Never do anything that you will regret and never regret anything that you do." Although he had in some measure achieved a tragic sense of the inevitable downfall of the superior individual, this formula is too simple to inform a tragedy, perhaps because it is curiously lacking in moral perspective. Ibsen was one of the first "naturalists" to realize that man cannot live without illusions, as he suggested in *The Wild Duck* (1884), and Strindberg soon discovered that to avoid regret does not eliminate guilt. His new intellectual and psychological orientation had led him to think of conflict between individuals in terms of what he called "psychic murder," a process by which the "small" or weak people become vampires, totally lacking in moral awareness, and their superior adversaries become innocent victims. But—to borrow one of his own metaphors—guilt lurked even in the seams of the garments in which he clothed these ideas. In two of his important naturalistic tragedies, *Miss Julie* (1888) and *Creditors* (1890), he raised the question of guilt only to find that he could not deal with it. Miss Julie rejects the idea of easing her own burden of guilt and resigns herself to bearing the consequences of her actions, while Tekla, the psychic murderess in *Creditors*, flatly denies her guilt by appealing to a concept of determinism. Her former husband, who appears as her moral creditor, explains that she is "Without guilt but not without responsibility. Guiltless before Him who no longer exists, responsible to (herself) and to (her) fellowman." This solution rings hollow, perhaps because it seems incapable of generating the kind of inner conflict appropriate to tragic suffering. Thus, Strindberg's only answer to the tragic dilemma of the superior heroes he created in the 1880s was a paradox: their very strength causes the strong to succumb to the weak, because their superior ethical sense prevents them from engaging in the unscrupulous tactics of their opponents. This paradox also lies at the center of the novel *By the Open Sea* (1890), which Strindberg published shortly before his divorce from Siri. The book deals with an intellectual superman, Inspector Borg, whose conflict with smaller minds drives him into isolation, whereupon he loses his identity altogether and finally commits suicide.

In 1892 Strindberg moved to Berlin and gave his friends to understand that he had abandoned literature for science. In 1893, when he married the young Austrian journalist, Frida Uhl, his literary career seemed at an end. His second marriage was no happier than his first, and after a severe psychotic attack in August 1894, he left Frida and took up residence in Paris, where during the next two years he continued his "scientific" experimentation and underwent four more nervous crises of mounting intensity. At this time he wrote almost exclusively in French. On August 23, 1896, when he thought that he was on the road to recovery and was planning his next autobiographical work, *Inferno,* he wrote to his friend Torsten Hedlund that it was to have the same theme as *By the Open Sea:* "The downfall of the individual when he isolates himself; salvation through work without honor or gold, duty, the family—consequently—woman—the mother and the child." This description, however, had little to do with the book Strindberg actually wrote, in French, the following spring. That he could not write another work like *By the Open Sea* was a function of the fact that the mental crises he had just undergone had added a moral and religious dimension to his outlook that was lacking before. In his laboratory and in the Paris zoo, the Jardin des Plantes, he had discovered the hand of the Creator and thereby found his way back to a religious view of the world. Having done so, he was forced to abandon the paradox of the stronger individual in favor of a moral enigma, which he was soon to explore in such great dramas as *To Damascus* (1898) and *A Dreamplay* (1902). His imperfect tragic vision of the 1880s had been transformed into a far more profound understanding of the problem of suffering.

In this painstaking analysis of Strindberg's moods and ideas during the 1890s, Gunnar Brandell unravels the complex development that Strindberg underwent between *By the Open Sea* and *Inferno* and assesses the personal mythology and brilliant new literary style that emerged in *To Damascus.* Some of the most important documents dealt with here—"The New Arts," "Graveyard Reveries" (here translated as "In the Cemetery"), *Inferno,* and *Jacob Wrestles*—have been translated by Evert Sprinchorn and are available in his volume entitled *Inferno, Alone and Other Writings.* Sprinchorn's witty and informative introduction to that volume provides the best possible introduction to Brandell's subtle reconstruction of Strindberg's Inferno crisis, so that in referring the reader to it, I feel exonorated from the necessity of recounting many of the details of Strindberg's life during those years. I shall content myself with a few words about two of his closest friends in the period.

Strindberg's most important letters during the 1880s, when he was regarded as one of the leading writers in Sweden, were addressed to noted literary figures: Verner von Heidenstam, Ola Hansson,

Georg and Edvard Brandes, Friedrich Nietzsche. In the 1890s, after he had retreated from the literary world, his two chief confidents were otherwise obscure persons who shared his interest in mysticism. One of these, Leopold Littmansson (1847–1908), had become a close friend of Strindberg's in 1872, when they both belonged to the bohemian circle that used to assemble in a private room at Bern's Restaurant in Stockholm—the same circle that Strindberg immortalized in *The Red Room*. In those days Littmansson, a clever violinist, was a poor bank clerk, but later he became a musician in Paris and made an advantageous marriage. He was comfortably settled in Versailles when Strindberg reestablished contact with him in June 1894, shortly before his first crisis. Because Strindberg tried to keep Littmansson fully abreast of his psychic development during the ensuing crises, their correspondence plays an important part in Brandell's reconstruction of Strindberg's inner conflicts. Strindberg's other close friend during this period was a recent acquaintance, Torsten Hedlund (1855–1935), who was an affluent publisher living in Gothenburg. Their correspondence began in July 1891 when Hedlund, a Theosophist, having thought that he recognized a number of theosophical ideas in *By the Open Sea,* wrote to Strindberg to ask his opinion of Madame Blavatsky. In the years of poverty and mental anguish that constituted Strindberg's Inferno crisis, Hedlund not only served as a sounding board for his new ideas, but also became Strindberg's chief material benefactor and spiritual guide.

In preparing this book for translation, Brandell made a few excisions and many additions, so that this English version amounts to a revised edition of what has become a standard work on Strindberg. I am pleased to have been instrumental in bringing it to a wider audience. Here and there, I have augmented both the text and the notes with information the author found it unnecessary to provide for his original audience. In carrying out this project, I was faced with the problem of translating the many utterances of Strindberg's that Brandell adduces in the course of his analysis. Although some of the works frequently cited are already available in English translation, others—including Strindberg's letters and his "scientific" works—are not. Therefore, in the interest of preserving unity of tone, I have translated all citations from Strindberg myself. Since Brandell identified all such citations in the body of his text by referring to John Landquist's standard Swedish edition of Strindberg's works, which is presumably unavailable to readers of this translation, I saw fit to eliminate these references from the translation. However, I have tried to date all statements made by Strindberg in letters, so that the interested reader may consult the full text in his collected letters, *Strindbergs Brev,* edited by Torsten Eklund.

In citing works written in Scandinavian languages, I have not bothered to reproduce the original title in the text, and I have tried to choose the most commonly accepted English titles for Strindberg's works, some of which are known by at least two titles in English. Such is the case, for example, with *En dåres försvarstal,* which has appeared as both *The Confessions of a Fool* and *A Madman's Defense,* and with *I havsbandet,* which has been published as *In the Outer Skerries* and *By the Open Sea.* In all such cases I have selected the more accurate English title. Strindberg's untranslated works presented greater difficulties, as in the case of *Kvarstadsresan,* a peculiarly Swedish coinage of Strindberg's, which I have called *Embargo Journey.* In the case of works written in Latin, German, or French (including the many French works by Strindberg), I have tried to supply the original title in parentheses after the first citation of the translated title. For famous and influential works, like Flaubert's *The Temptation of Saint Anthony* or Schopenhauer's *The World As Will and Idea,* only the familiar English titles are given; for obscure or untranslated works, like Jollivet-Castelot's *La vie et l'âme de la matière,* I have retained the original title, supplying a translation in parentheses after the first citation. I have not tried to translate the fanciful Latin titles that Strindberg chose for some of his scientific works, such as *Antibarbarus, Sylva sylvarum,* and *Hortus Merlini,* nor have I tampered with the title of the work that he named for the Paris zoo, *Jardin des Plantes.* Unless otherwise indicated in the notes, I am responsible for all translated material in this book.

It only remains to express my gratitude to the people who have been in a position to aid and instruct me during the completion of

xviii *Preface*

this project. I am deeply indebted to Professor Krister Stendahl of
the Harvard Divinity School for helping me find English equivalents
for the many technical theological terms in certain parts of this
book. Through discussions of difficult passages, Brita K. Stendahl
and Professor Sven Linnér have helped me immensely with the problem of trying to convey something of Strindberg's complex literary
and epistolary style. François Rodriguez and Professor Jean Gourgue
have generously aided me by explaining the stylistic curiosities in
many of the French passages that Brandell cites, and Dr. John
Moore of Montclair State College has corrected my translations from
the German and translated many of the German citations. Finally, I
wish to thank Virginia LaPlante of the Harvard University Press,
whose editorial ability has made this translation much more readable
than it would otherwise have been.

CONTENTS

one   *Introduction and Background*   *1*

two   *The Inferno Psychoses*   *66*

three   *Jacob Wrestles*   *98*

four   *A New Cosmos*   *160*

five   *Toward a New Poetics*   *222*

Notes   *279*

Description   *314*

Bibliography   *325*

Index   *331*

Strindberg in Inferno

O N E *Introduction and Background*

When August Strindberg abandoned literature in 1892 and turned to science and "alchemy," he was one of the most famous literary naturalists in Europe. With publication of the first part of *To Damascus* in 1898, he emerged as the creator of an exciting new dramatic style that bears a resemblance to expressionism, surrealism, and even to drama of the absurd. During the interval he had experienced mounting anguish, which culminated in 1895 and 1896 in a series of psychotic attacks. In *Inferno* (1897) he gives a detailed analysis of the torments he had suffered and describes the new outlook on life he had achieved as a result of this crisis. Since the marked change in his literary style after *Inferno* reflects his new outlook, an understanding of this crisis is immensely important for the study of his works.

Strindberg preferred to think of his Inferno crisis as leading to a conversion, and he called his new religious insight "confessionless Christianity." His biographers and critics have been unable to agree on this evaluation. One authority, Axel Herrlin, regards the Inferno crisis as "a return to an outlook which had by and large been his center of gravity during the greater part of Strindberg's preceding life. It was a *regression,* but not a conversion." [1] Martin Lamm, a truly innovative scholar of Strindberg, rejects this interpretation and asserts instead that the Inferno crisis was "a conversion, one of the most thoroughgoing known to our literature." [2]

This way of posing the problem would seem too limited. It is not a disjunctive question of either/or, but a coordinate one of both/and. Moods, attitudes, and even ideas from Strindberg's earlier life played a large part in the Inferno crisis; but it still resulted in a new attitude, partly because he found himself in a new psychological situation, partly because at this point in his life he worked out his moral and religious problems with much more intensity than ever before. The Inferno crisis entailed both a review and a reevaluation of Strindberg's entire life, and through this crisis the moral aspect of existence, an alternative that had frequently confronted him before and which he had just as frequently rejected, gradually came to dominate his outlook on life.

To determine the meaning of the Inferno crisis, one should regard it as one in a series of religious crises that Strindberg underwent and as a link in the continuing process of his pyschic development. The sketch of Strindberg's development before the Inferno crisis presented here as both background and introduction to the crisis itself is by no means intended to capture the whole of Strindberg, but only the side of him that faced religious and moral problems and was characterized by guilt feelings and anxiety.

In an article entitled "Mysticism—For the Time Being" (1887), Strindberg connects his childhood faith with a deep-seated feeling of insecurity, manifested primarily in his fear of the dark. At first, his mother had protected him against all the dangers that the darkness might conceal, but later—when he had learned to pray—the concept of God afforded him "a vast calm," which he equates with the strength that his mother had formerly given him. "God," he states, could "combat all evil powers."

One hardly needs to take these statements literally. They coincide all too clearly with the widely held naturalistic concept of religion as a function of the savage's fear of unknown powers. [3] However, one cannot help reflecting on the striking resemblances between Strindberg's childhood religion, as he describes it here, and certain characteristic ideas that he held during the Inferno period (1894–1897). Like the young Strindberg's God, the Jehovah who dominated his conversion in the 1890s was closely connected with evil powers.[4]

"Diables noirs" or "evil spirits" are among Strindberg's favorite expressions, and he uses these terms to convey different meanings. In a letter to Carl Gustav Wrangel on October 7, 1875, he seems to be thinking of Saul when he speaks of the "spirits" that possess him. In short, he uses the word to mean psychic obsessions. In "Mysticism—For the Time Being" he uses the same terms to characterize a primitive, critically conceived animism. Later, during the psychotic attacks that comprised his Inferno crisis, he allows these and similar expressions to assume a number of different and vacillating meanings.

One cannot be certain that "evil powers" meant the same thing to Strindberg when he was recalling his childhood as they did later when he was describing the neurotic anxiety states that seem already to have been familiar to him during childhood. Yet it is obvious that he somehow connected these anxiety states with religious experiences—not in such a way, however, that he necessarily fled from anxiety to religion.

Close examination of Strindberg's accounts of his childhood shows, moreover, that far from emerging exclusively as a protection, religion itself was somewhat terrifying to him. In the above-mentioned article, he speaks of "the god of fear and sacrifice—he only protected those who were good and obedient to their parents." Then he adds: "The latter was less appealing to me and was unnecessary, for I was so frightened by my father that I would never have dared to disobey." In *The Son of a Servant* (1886), Strindberg imbues the church and cemetery of St. Clara with a mood of ghostliness and horror, which—as Martin Lamm points out—was always closely associated with his religious experiences.[5]

Religion triggered his moods of anxiety, but was also capable of dispersing them. In an enlightening episode, which occurs in both *The Son of a Servant* and "Mysticism—For the Time Being," Strindberg explains how he alleviated his terror of religion by means of a religious act. When he was eight years old and was boarding with a sexton's family in the country, he and some of his companions once played in the church, where they ran up onto the lectern in the count's pew. The lectern came loose, and his friends all fled. At first he was paralyzed with fright, but he fell down at the altar and prayed to God for help in fixing the broken lectern. Thereupon he received new power and easily hammered the wood back into place with the aid of one of his shoes.

It is not difficult to find the prototype for this God of Strindberg's, who filled him sometimes with terror, at other times with confidence. He harbored similarly ambivalent feelings for his father. Many times he affirmed that he feared his father, and in his old age still maintained that he had always thought of his father as "an inimical power." The other component of his filial feeling, a combination of admiration and trust, is somewhat more difficult to pin down. But Torsten Eklund is doubtless correct in maintaining that essentially Strindberg "fostered a strong respect and admiration for the power and authority incarnated in his father." [6] The most illuminating passage that Eklund cites in this connection from *The Son of a Servant* reveals that a few kind words from his father had dispelled Strindberg's grief and guilt feelings after his mother's death. Speaking of himself in the third person (as he does throughout the book), Strindberg writes, "He had gained a friend, a powerful, intelligent, virile friend, whom he admired."

Strindberg regarded his father as the incarnation not only of the authority to judge and punish, but also of the ability to shield and protect. According to *The Son of a Servant,* during childhood Strindberg viewed existence as a pyramid of increasing powers: his place was at the bottom; next came his brothers, his mother, his father, the landlord's deputy, the general, the police, and the king; and at the top was God. God was the most powerful of all—he "must necessarily be higher than the king." By being identified with the role of the father, Strindberg's childhood God acquired the Janus-like character of being both terrifying and benevolent—like the patriarchal Jehovah—a stamp that was to characterize him ever afterward.

This does not mean, of course, that one should think of the Jehovah whom Strindberg worshiped during the Inferno period either as a direct reproduction of Carl Oskar Strindberg or of Strindberg's childhood God. The only connection between his childhood experiences and his adult religious ideas lay on the emotional plane. Even when the godhead and the father figure played no demonstrable role for him, Strindberg needed (or was inclined) to subordinate himself to others in the same way that he had done with his father. Furthermore, such people were always superior to him in one way or another, either in social rank or in authority. One glimpses this process at work, for example, in his relations with Carl Gustaf Wrangel and with the noted Norwegian writer Bjørnstjerne Bjørnson.

Most significant in this respect, however, was Strindberg's attitude toward G. E. Klemming, his superior when he worked at the Royal Library (1874–1882). Among other things, this relationship provides a further glimpse of Strindberg's tendency to connect authoritative people with his image of deity. Strindberg adverts to this relationship several times, and an accent of awesome respect always creeps into his voice when speaking of Klemming. In "The Battle of the Brains" (1886), he reports that he trembled so visibly whenever he approached the "great, famous man" (who is clearly Klemming) that he was asked, "Are you suffering from an ague?" In "Shortcuts" (1887), he remarks that Klemming "seemed omniscient and just, mild and devastating—like the Almighty." In the same work, Strindberg includes a fictional version of an episode that he later recounted directly in *A Blue Book* (1907). On certain days Klemming was "like a blindman" and could not read the old manuscripts with which he customarily worked. "One day he placed a medieval codex in a nearly undecipherable hand before me and half in jest asked me to read it. Although I had never made a study of medieval handwriting, I read it at once." According to his own account of the matter, Strindberg became Klemming's "medium" and was thereby enabled to accomplish feats of which he would otherwise have been incapable—exactly like the boy in the church at Ådala who received added power by praying at the altar.

In "Shortcuts," he refers to Klemming as "the head of Zeus."

During the Inferno period, when Strindberg sometimes saw a head of Zeus in the configuration of wrinkles on his pillow, he thought he "was in rapport with his deceased teacher." It is clear, moreover, that he always associated Klemming with the more benevolent powers who he thought were guiding his destiny at this time. Indeed, Strindberg believed that Klemming could actually serve as their substitute. Describing the nocturnal manifestations of the spirits or powers that plagued him during the crisis, he writes: "I noticed certain mischievous features that were reminiscent of him; and one night I remember that I called into the darkness: Is it ———? since the whole masquerade was in his style, that is, it was like his benevolent but teasing manner. Of course, I got no answer, but the impression remained: a mixture of dreadfully desperate seriousness, and in the middle of it all a friendly smile, comforting, forgiving, protecting—just as he was during his lifetime when he overlooked my rogueries."

The father was the prototype of all the powerful, condemning, punishing, and directive authorities that Strindberg alternately submitted to and opposed throughout his life. A reasonable explanation for the strength of his opposition is that it was a function of a powerful state of anxiety coupled with a strong guilt complex. The moral authority of society—first incarnated for him in his father—was much too demanding for August Strindberg when he was a child. He strained himself by bearing this moral burden, and despite his efforts to be "good and obedient," he constantly suffered from a guilty conscience. In *The Son of a Servant,* he describes how his surrogate, Johan, wavered "in constant fear that some fault would be discovered." It is also with reference to his childhood experiences that Strindberg first expresses the idea that was to play an important role for his undirected guilt feelings during the Inferno crisis: "Life was a penal colony where one paid for crimes committed before birth, and therefore the child was never free from remorse."

This oppressive awareness of guilt demanded relief. But his criticism was not originally directed against the moral norms themselves, but against their representative, his father. Strindberg accepted the moral obligations, but took revenge by proving that his father was himself unable to measure up to those standards. Following a process that psychoanalysts have often described,[7] Strindberg's critique of his father began—as Eklund points out—in the name of the very principles that the father had inculcated in him.[8] The famous story of how little Johan had been wrongfully accused of drinking part of a bottle of wine proves that his father was unjust. The account of Johan's alleged theft of screws from carriages (when in reality he had simply found them in the street) shows that the father's "love of truth" had forced the son to tell a lie. "Vague doubts about 'other people's' love of truth awakened in the child and led at this time to a fresh wave of counterattack"—is the way that Strindberg describes the development of his own perfectionist and hypercritical attitude. Here, too, one can trace a direct line of development from his childhood experiences to the Inferno period. In *Jacob Wrestles* (1897), where Strindberg takes the cosmic powers to task and complains of their pettiness and favoritism, he relies on the same sort of casuistry that he had earlier used when noting his father's imperfections.

His tendency for self-torture had the same origin. Indeed, psychologists have frequently emphasized the connection between self-torture and strong guilt feelings.[9] In his autobiography, Strindberg recounts that, as a child, he hid whenever any pleasure was in the offing, or he stood at the end of the line whenever there were treats for the children. Self-torture was Strindberg's form of overcompensation, making up for his deeply felt incapacity to live up to common moral obligations. Instead of feeling that he was the "worst" of all, he became "better" than others by means of this deliberate deprivation. In *The Son of a Servant,* Strindberg himself analyzes this process:

By-passed! With all the bitterness of someone who has been left out, he goes out into the garden and hides in an arbor. He feels like the least important of people, the last, the worst. But he does not cry now. Instead he feels something cold and hard like a steel skeleton rising within him. And after critical appraisal of the entire group, he finds that he is more honest than any of the others, because he did not eat a single berry out in the berry patch, and thus—bang! Next came the false conclusion—because he was

better than the others, he had been overlooked. Result: he considered himself better than the others. And he experienced a strong sense of pleasure
from having been overlooked.

Eklund maintains that this need for self-torture was the basis of
Strindberg's "enormous capacity to portray the infernal, the dismal,
and the oppressive in his works." [10] When this capacity reached its
culmination during the Inferno crisis, which in turn resulted in his
conversion, Strindberg clearly regarded his dark moods as a sort of
expiatory suffering. He expresses pride in his misfortunes, regarding
them as marks of special favor; he feels "better" than others when he
is suffering and compares himself to Job. But in *The Son of a Servant,*
Johan, the leading figure, seems already to have assumed an attitude
that was reminiscent of Job's: "He was so proud of this latest reminder of his cruel fate that later in the evening he had to boast
about it to his brothers."

For information concerning Strindberg's early childhood, one is
largely dependent on his autobiography. Of course, it is not certain
that the image appearing there is exact, even though Strindberg set
out with the resolution to be completely objective and impartial.
For obvious reasons, it does not contain sufficient material to give a
complete picture. Yet the childhood reminiscences of Strindberg's
sisters, to which one generally turns in order to confirm the thesis
that Strindberg painted his childhood "all too darkly," were written
even later than *The Son of a Servant* and therefore cannot be considered to be essentially more faithful to reality than is his autobiography. In any case, their only importance is that they allow one to
evaluate the objective correlative of Strindberg's childhood moods,
not the moods themselves.

Despite the uncertainty inherent in the documents, it is probable
that even during his childhood, anxiety played an important role for
Strindberg. Furthermore, it is likely that much of what was later to
characterize his attitude toward God was already established in his
childhood milieu, particularly by means of his relationship to his father: his mixture of fear and confidence, his stubborn insistance on
asserting his rights, his contentiousness, and his need for self-

torture. Anxiety and guilt feelings can be regarded as the lowest common psychological denominator of these phenomena.[11]

Strindberg's religion during his childhood was centered around the father-God figure. "My thoughts about God," he writes in "Mysticism—For the Time Being," "included the idea of an infinitely strong man, from whom I borrowed power by means of prayer. Strangely enough, it was also true that I never prayed to the weak, tortured Christ." When Strindberg reached the age of puberty, his religiosity assumed a new aspect, which can be called the "Christ phase" or the "maternal phase." Women—his mother in particular—were instrumental in promoting his experience of Christ.

The description that Strindberg gives of his mother in *The Son of a Servant* is generally regarded as having been distorted by the basic sympathy he felt for his father, who played the thankless role of breadwinner for the family. Both here and elsewhere, however, Strindberg lays strong stress on his dependence on his mother. Though he perhaps did not grieve for her very deeply when she died, later on he certainly felt the need of a mother and sought a replacement for her. "This feeling of longing and desolation connected with his mother remained with him throughout his life. Had he entered the world too soon? Was he perhaps not fully developed? Why was he so firmly tied to his mother?" (*The Son of a Servant*).

Most of the critics who have studied Strindberg's early development have no doubts concerning the answer to Strindberg's question. They speak, as Eklund does,[12] of the fact that his "need for tenderness" had been thwarted, partly because his mother had no time for him while she was alive, partly because she died when he was so young. As a psychological term, the "need for tenderness" is a portmanteau concept. One of its meanings, however, is particularly relevant to Strindberg's religious development. As he explains in *The Son of a Servant,* his mother represented Providence for her children. Despite the fact that she was "the public prosecutor," she always "comforted, soothed and calmed us, after father had administered punishment." Johan fled to her "to obtain comfort and mercy, but seldom justice." His father punished; his mother forgave. Her role in Strindberg's childhood development was to counterbalance the strict moralism of his father. In her he found something that transcended the relation between guilt and punishment; she was not just, but she was comforting. However, he states that she did not really gain his respect because she herself was not above tattling. This statement is not surprising in view of the powerful impression made on Strindberg by paternal strictness, which he had accepted with one side of his nature. Whenever he was not criticizing his father, Strindberg harbored great respect for him. His mother represented the gospel; his father stood for the law.

The religious terms are germane here. During the evangelical resurgence that was just beginning in the 1860s, Strindberg's mother acquainted him with a milder form of Christianity than he had known in his earlier childhood. He has described his father as "a sort of theist," who would rather read Archbishop Wallin's romantic and majestical sermons than go to church. In other words, his father does not seem to have been actively interested in religion. His mother, in contrast, "ran after Olin and Elmblad and Rosenius— three prominent evangelists—and had friends who brought her copies of leading evangelical publications of the day, *The Pietist* and *The Voice of the Dove.*" Later, when she was sick, she often spoke to Johan "about religion and other serious matters." Always atoning for the children herself, she showed Strindberg the way to a kind of religion that centers around atonement, and the only legacy she left him when she died was the cult of Christ.

According to *The Son of a Servant,* Strindberg's own pietistic period began in the autumn of 1862, soon after his mother's death. Religion clearly served him as a substitute for his mother. He says in his autobiography that he grieved for his mother "hardly a quarter of a year." Direct personal grief was thus succeeded by a period during which he turned to Christ for the same reason that he had formerly turned to his mother.

At that time, his growing awareness of sexuality provided a new and more powerful object on which to focus his persistent guilt feelings. Of course, the connection between sexuality and the perception of guilt is also a permanent feature of the Christian cultural ethos. When Strindberg learned to masturbate, he became involved in the struggle between sexual drive and guilt repression that was to become—in varying forms—a recurrent theme in his life. The beginning of this struggle was one of the questions that actively engaged his attention later on. His first version of the story (which appears in *The Son of a Servant*) was considered tendentious by Strindberg himself. In that version, he claims that his first experience of masturbation did not constitute a turning point in his spiritual life and that it was not until later, when he read "Dr. Kapff's notorious pamphlet," that he was seized by feelings of anxiety and sought comfort in religion. He corrects this account in *Jacob Wrestles,* where he writes: "The fall—fall indeed!—was immediately followed by feelings of remorse, and I can see myself in my nightshirt, sitting at the table with the prayer book before me, in the faint light of the summer dawn. Feelings of shame and remorse, despite my complete unfamiliarity with the nature of the sin. Innocent, because I was unaware, and yet guilty. Seduced, and later a seducer myself; anguish followed by recurrence; doubt in the validity of my accusing conscience." [13]

It was perhaps natural that Strindberg should seek help in pietistic devotion. The brand of piety known as "Herrnhuter" or "Moravian" Pietism had survived during the period of Enlightenment theology; and when the new evangelical awakening was brought to Sweden in the middle of the nineteenth century by George Scott and C. O. Rosenius, its most ardent supporters were found among middle class circles in the capital—the class to which the Strindberg family belonged. Moreover, the family had long been connected with the evangelical movement: Samuel Owen (whose widow was Strindberg's paternal aunt and lived in C. O. Strindberg's house) had in his day belonged to the group that had worked through Scott to introduce Methodism into Sweden. His mother's religious interests have already been mentioned. His stepmother brought similar religious leanings into the Strindberg household. Strindberg writes that she read Gustaf Beskow's works and "leaned toward evangelicalism." In his autobiography he emphasizes the fact that he and his stepmother tried to outdo each other in the practice of piety. His brother Axel also seems to have participated in this competition.

The person who did the most to reinforce Strindberg's propensity for pietism, however, was Edla Heijkorn, who was fifteen years older than he and whom he discusses in *The Son of a Servant* in the chapter entitled "First Love." In a confession that he made in his old age, he reveals that she was the person from whom he learned the most during his youth: "She was not without faults, but she only taught me what was right and what was good; she wanted me to 'be better than she was,' and she led me toward pietism, which she favored, but could not adhere to herself" (*Posthumous Papers*). From what he states in *The Son of a Servant,* it would appear that although she was ahead of him in theoretical matters, he exceeded her in seriousness and in consistency. He became "her conscience," and she became his theological guide. It is not unlikely, moreover, that the role she played served as a substitute for his mother. In general terms, Strindberg certainly denies that he was seeking a mother figure in her, but he nonetheless admits that she mothered him and that such behavior "affected him deeply."

As a matter of fact, it is a pity that this vital episode is only partially elucidated by the available source material. Strindberg's correspondence with Edla Heijkorn is not extant, and his disclosures about her in *The Son of a Servant* are rather vague. The same is true of his statements about the nature of his pietistic religiosity. When Strindberg wrote his autobiography, he was decidedly hostile to the pious adolescent he had once been, and his treatment of this period of his life generally maintains an ironic, caviling tone. By way of illustration, he includes the little religious essays he wrote at the time, but they provide few criteria for any judgment concerning the exact nature of his "pietism."

According to Strindberg, this inclination to pietism was only a manifestation of the acute consciousness of guilt or sin, awakened in him by the practice of masturbation. "Bankrupt on earth—he was to die at twenty-five, after his spine had disintegrated and his nose had fallen away—he sought heaven" (*The Son of a Servant*). Evangelical preaching, with its tendency to focus on Christ, pushes the idea of atonement into the foreground. According to Strindberg, "Rosenius looked like peace itself and radiated heavenly joy. He admitted that he certainly was a thoroughly wicked sinner, but he said that Jesus had purified him and that now he was happy" (*The Son of a Servant*). The young Strindberg clearly sought this same happiness, this "peace in Jesus," whenever he was beset by feelings of terror and remorse. In later years, when Strindberg looked back on his interest in pietism, he called it a "shortcut." Seen against the background of fear of the law which had been instilled in Strindberg by his environment, pietism does appear to have been a psychological "shortcut" for him—by means of religious awakening, his anxiety would disappear miraculously: "As it was described, conversion was supposed to happen like a flash of lightning and be followed by the certainty that one was God's child, and thus one would have peace."

One gathers, however, that Strindberg never did experience a certainty of salvation, for he concludes: "Nevertheless, Johan had not experienced the workings of grace, and he was troubled." Instead of liberating him from anxiety, his religion tended to become an expression of his "melancholy." [14] Thus, he seized upon the pessimistic traits in "Jesusism" and agreed that "the world was a thoroughly execrable place," but failed to accept the optimistic counterbalance to this view. The pessimistic nature of his religion is very apparent, for example, in three essays that he wrote in French in 1864, which were later included in *The Son of a Servant*. The first one is designed to prove that human life is "a life of pain." The second argues that the only "happiness" that one can find without salvation is illusory. The third one treats the theme that "egoism directs all of our actions." Christianity, as Strindberg understood it, is not very far from philosophical pessimism, which he was later to embrace. In fact, in his old age he readily spoke of Schopenhauer as a disciple of Christ.

In this melancholy one can perhaps trace the influence of Rosenius. Even though this evangelist seemed to Strindberg to be a happy person, the revival that he led nonetheless had a trace of gloominess about it. Moreover, it was in the school of evangelicalism that Strindberg first developed the pessimistic attitude to life that constitutes a perceptible undertone in most of his works.

But the influence of Rosenius does not suffice to explain the special character of Strindberg's pietism. Its fundamental melancholy derives from the fact that he never dared to trust in forgiveness, in the efficacy of atonement. A concomitant feature of this refusal to accept one of the basic tenets of Christianity was the fact that throughout Strindberg's religious development up to the time that he completed *Inferno,* Christ played a subordinate role for him. Christ appeared powerless in comparison with the imperious and punitive God who ruled the universe. The relationship can be expressd in another way: the maternal side of Strindberg's religion never took precedence over the paternal side. Even in religious matters, Strindberg wanted to settle his disputes man-to-man, without losing his independence. "Can God forgive? Yes, if He can punish us first," he wrote in a draft of *Jacob Wrestles.* [15] His stubborn refusal to relinquish his conviction that crime always provokes punishment was the factor that prevented Strindberg from ever becoming a genuine "pietist." [16]

Of course, this factor did not prevent pietism, which was Strindberg's first conscious religion, from having a marked effect on his religious development in other respects. Although the revival in the mid-nineteenth century was, to a great extent, a revival within the Swedish Lutheran church, the idea of congregation diminished in importance as a consequence of the emphasis placed on being "Christian on one's own initiative." Over the various Christian communities loomed the faint hope that someday all true Christians, regardless of creed, would be united. Toward the end of his life, when Strindberg was once again desirous of becoming a "pietist," he assumed the same slightly ambivalent relation to the church. Although he was not inimical to the church, he considered that outward forms were unessential. Ecumenical toleration came naturally to him, and this attitude was later reinforced through his acquaintance with the works of Theodore Parker.

This liberal element in the evangelical movement was connected with a principle that gradually led to open opposition to the church—the principle of life before doctrine. Strindberg shared this position, which was inextricably bound up with all his activities. It is banal to observe that, for Strindberg, life and doctrine coalesced. Even during his periods of atheism and interest in social reform, theoretical convictions as such were not central to his thought. His first concern was to shape himself and his life so that they conformed to his principles, to become a "new man" or a "superman."

This observation is especially relevant to his purely religious attitudes. In a letter written during the 1870s, for example, Strindberg gives a definition of religion that has a strongly pietistic ring: "What do we mean by religious belief? Not one's acceptance of certain teachings, but rather his transformation into something better— to such an extent that he is no longer the person he was!" During the Inferno crisis he still tended to suppress theoretical matters in discussing religion. Even though Strindberg might have reached a similar position without going through a pietistic phase, one must nonetheless stress the fact that he first encountered this subordination of doctrine to life as the conscious goal of the "pietists," and that he was attracted by this very feature: "Tired of school books, which had no living water to give, since they did not deal with life, he found more nourishment in a religion that found constant application in daily life" (*The Son of a Servant*).

His pietism was gradually superseded by Parkerism—this time it was an older male friend and not a woman who was Strindberg's mentor. At the same time, Strindberg acquired a taste for diversions that he had formerly considered sinful. Parker loosened the moral bonds that were the legacy of his middle-class background. According to *The Son of a Servant*, the first time that Johan failed to attend church, he did so "to defy both his father's command and the voice of his own conscience." The problem, as explained farther on, was "not to do anything one would regret, or else not to regret anything that one did!" During Strindberg's pietistic period, he had tried the former approach; he tried the latter during his Parkerian phase. It was a radical attempt to cancel out entirely the concept of life that had been imprinted on his mind by his upbringing, and this attempt was clearly a part of his conscious opposition to his father. According to one scholar, Parker was "completely foreign to the feeling of guilt, and sin, and anguished responsibility before God and could not understand it." [17] This American optimist clearly moved within an entirely different conceptual world from that which Strindberg had formed under the influence of the situation in his parental home. Thus, it is with good reason that in *The Son of a Servant* Strindberg characterized the experience of reading Parker as an "emancipation." Strindberg's Rousseauan idealism and his ideas of social reform can be traced back to the liberating influence of Parker. These ideas inform the entire period that he later denied during the Inferno crisis, when once again he consciously made guilt a central concern, thereby returning to the pattern of ideas that had dominated his childhood and early youth.

For these reasons, a consideration of Strindberg's Parkerism and his neorationalism falls outside the framework of this study. In *The Son of a Servant,* however, Strindberg indicates that his liberation was not total. Johan's last words in his decisive conversation with the engineer are: "But I still have regrets! I regret doing what is right, for it would be wrong to play the hypocrite in these old heathen temples. My new conscience tells me that I am right, and my old one says that I am wrong. I can never be at peace again!" What is interesting here is the "conscience" that Strindberg calls his "old" one. It represents the conceptual world that is in part primitively Christian and revolves around the question of guilt. For a long time, this "old conscience" was to lead a subterranean life before it finally struggled back into the central place in his thought: "His new self rose up against his old one, and they lived in disunity, without being able to be separated, like an unhappy husband and wife, for the rest of his life."

A few years later, when Strindberg came into contact with the moralizing impulse that proceeded from Kierkegaard, it became apparent that his attempt to eradicate his "old self" had been unsuccessful. First, he read Ibsen's *Brand.* It made a powerful impression on him, and he naturally applied its message to himself. But *Brand* did not give rise to any moral crisis, because Strindberg—as shown by *The Freethinker* and *in Rome* (both written in 1870)—reinterpreted Ibsen's ethical idealism to make it congruent with his own striving toward liberation. In Brand's demand for personal integrity Strindberg read an injunction to be uncompromising, partly in religious opposition in the Parkerian vein, partly in fulfillment of his artistic vocation.

The first time that he read Kierkegaard, in the autumn of 1870, Strindberg seems to have been affected in a different way. According to his autobiography, this was a time of agitating conflicts of conscience. During that September, *In Rome* was performed at the Royal Dramatic Theater, in Stockholm, but despite the fact that "his boldest wish was thereby fulfilled," Strindberg reacted with repugnance and self-reproach—just as he was to turn away from the theater world a quarter of a century later after the première of *The Father* in Paris. Then the unfavorable reviews of *In Rome* and *The Freethinker* appeared. Strindberg was stung by the critics' remarks and felt "the same agony that he imagined a criminal would suffer" (*The Son of a Servant*). In order to rehabilitate himself, he plunged immediately into the composition of *Blotsven,* a play about a Swedish king during the late Viking period. But a few weeks later when his friend Josef Linck criticized that play at a meeting of the Runic Society (a club for young poets to which they both belonged), he became so depressed that he burned the manuscript. In *The Son of a Servant,* at the end of the chapter devoted to these events of the autumn of 1870, Strindberg describes the hysterical crisis accompanied by thoughts of suicide that overwhelmed him at this time.

Even before Linck criticized him, however, Strindberg had experienced doubts about his vocation. In a letter to his cousin, Johan Oscar Strindberg, he writes that he found *Blotsven* execrable: "I have doubts about my vocation—perhaps I ought to become a schoolteacher—perhaps this vocation to be an author is nothing but a figment of my imagination!" (Oct. 8, 1870). According to *The Son of a Servant,* he had already experienced such a change of heart by the time he attended the première of *In Rome* in September. He thought that the play was stupid and vain and that "his portrayal of the son's relation to his father was cynical." In writing this drama about Bertel Torvaldsen, Strindberg had asserted his own poetic vocation in conscious and emphatic opposition to his father's demand that he devote himself to academic studies instead of to writing. In the letters he wrote immediately after his return to Uppsala in the autumn of 1870, Strindberg declares his firm resolve to settle down to his studies. In September, he writes to his cousin, "I am studying like a fiend and intend to take my degree soon, provided that I do not take my own life first." Somewhat later he reports that he is "studying for the new doctor's degree" (apparently the licentiate in philosophy, which was instituted in 1870) and that he will write to his father concerning the project. These resolutions did not lead to any significant results. Instead, Strindberg threw himself into the composition of *Blotsven,* and thus arose the conflict between "vocation" and "duty" that engaged him during the autumn of 1870.

Strindberg's reading of Kierkegaard became a factor in this moral conflict, as he roundly asserts in *The Son of a Servant,* and one must probably accept the influence as real, even though he did not write anything about it to his cousin. Nor is it difficult to understand the role that Kierkegaard played for Strindberg. At this time, Strindberg thought of "vocation" as referring partly to his poetic mission, partly to his religious mission, that is, to his work in the interest of promoting Parkerian liberalism. The ideology behind this double vocation was aimed entirely against his father's authority. As far as one of its components was concerned, the poetic vocation, his father's wishes left him with a clear alternative: he could either continue studying for a degree or leave the university and become a schoolteacher—in either case he would be doing something useful. But whereas Strindberg finally agreed to bow to his father's will and renounce his poetic mission, he could find no real terms of surrender on the religious and moral plane. It was here that Kierkegaard's teachings came to his aid by providing him with an alternative. Kierkegaard's strict, strongly moralistic interpretation of Christianity represented the exact opposite of Parker's and carried Strindberg back to the Old Testament religious milieu he had lived in before his rationalistic "emancipation."

It is quite likely that Kierkegaard's primary importance in Strindberg's conflict derived from his moral, not his religious, message. In *The Son of a Servant,* Strindberg maintains that such was the case and plainly wishes to make one believe that at the time of his first acquaintance with Kierkegaard, he was not aware that Kierkegaard was a theologian. The student essay that Strindberg wrote in 1871 shows that his chief borrowings from the Danish thinker were arguments against the aesthetic point of view. This essay bears witness to the deep impression Kierkegaard had made on him. He writes:

> You must read *Either/Or.* You will read the first book and feel a sword go through your soul. You will read the second and doubt so profoundly that you will be shaken to your deepest foundations and you will feel all of the pains of hell. Then you will read . . . what, indeed? his *Training in Christianity?* I do not know, for I myself am in the midst of the battle, but I do not believe that I can get any further by reading—I can only struggle forward toward—what? another question mark!—toward "personality" Kierkegaard calls it. What is it, then, that Kierkegaard wants? I hardly think he knows that himself. But what he does not want is disbelief, irreligiousness, levity. And his eternal service is that he has crushed Hegel's empty pantheism. Kierkegaard wants—sincerity!

According to his autobiography, Strindberg found that the demands of duty in *Either/Or* were "the categorical imperative" in new, more refined dress. "After reading *Either/Or,* he felt sinful." But, as already shown, the demands of duty and a sense of sin were also part of the framework of Strindberg's religious experiences during his childhood and youth. He could hardly have avoided the suspicion that this road would lead him back to pietism or to the old-fashioned Christianity of his childhood.[18]

Nearly two years later, Strindberg—under the influence of Georg Brandes—had arrived at a different concept of Kierkegaard. According to these typically Strindbergian turns of phrase, Kierkegaard is now "the old man, who is conservative because he does not understand the new and therefore fears it," and his teachings are "Christianity's last cry for help before she goes down for the last time." This view, however, did not prevent Strindberg a few months later from taking Kierkegaard into his good graces once more, after he had entered into a period of depression. "He is terrible! But he drags one along with him in the dance of death! He is just the man for me!" Strindberg's "new" self continued to be pitted against his "old" self, and this deadlock was still in effect in 1884, just before Strindberg wrote a long short story entitled "The German Lieutenant." In a letter he wrote to Jonas Lie at the time, he discusses "the ethical sense of duty" in Kierkegaard's terms, but in the short story his new moral outlook, which is reminiscent of Parker and Rousseau, gains the upper hand.[19]

Strindberg probably always read Kierkegaard from time to time. *The Instant* (1855), for example, is among the works that he crossed out in an auctioneer's catalogue of his books in 1883, because he did not want it to be sold.[20] Brandes' book on Kierkegaard appears in the same catalogue. Finally, this Kierkegaard mood plays a palpable role in his Inferno crisis.

It is difficult, however, to assert that Kierkegaard exerted a continuous influence on Strindberg. Although detailed examination of the works Strindberg produced during the 1870s shows various traces of his ideas, Kierkegaard clearly did not provide a firm foundation for Strindberg's views during any extended period. Instead, Strindberg used Kierkegaard's works in situations where he thought he needed them, that is, during periods of depression, which were usually accompanied by religious and moral conflicts.

For this reason, Strindberg continued to employ Kierkegaard's formulas for the rest of his career, but only when he found himself in situations that induced a state of mind similar to the one he had experienced in 1870, when he first came across Kierkegaard's works. Whenever he seemed to be confronted by one of the more serious periods of his life, that is, when he was more concerned with ethics and religion, he was prone to speak of the "Choice," the "Vocation," the "Leap," and the like—as he did, for example, in Switzerland in 1884 (just before the *Married* trial), and then again during the initial stages of the Inferno crisis. Here is a characteristic passage from a letter he wrote to an old friend, Leopold Littmansson, in 1900: "What is wrong with your nerves? Is it your psyche that is bothering you, as in my case? . . . A 'vocation' in life? A 'choice'? Old Søren Kierkegaard curved nerves with a horse remedy! The choice and the vocation!" These expressions capture the very essence of the crossroad situation.

Kierkegaard showed Strindberg the dialectical possibilities in his own being. In the essay written during his student days, Strindberg

employed Kierkegaard's method of presenting various positions by
inventing a dialogue. Later on, he frequently acted in the conviction
that his being contained possibilities that had not yet been exploited. When he was converted to atheism, and when he later reverted to belief in God during the Inferno period, he did so partly as
an experiment: he decided to assume one point of view and see where
it led when put into practice. The "experimentation with points of
view" points back to Kierkegaard and his "stages on life's way."

Strindberg can hardly be said ever to have achieved a total view of
Kierkegaard's philosophical and religious system, and he often used
phrases from Kierkegaard in quite another meaning than they had in
the original contexts. But emotionally, he was fully capable of feeling at home in Kierkegaard's conceptual world. His "old" self corre-
sponded to what was "reactionary" about Kierkegaard. Here he encountered a sense of original sin that was as strong as his own and a
"casuistic" relation to a fatherlike God—concepts that were in perfect agreement with those he had held since childhood. Toward the
end of his life, Strindberg announced that "Kierkegaard with his
confessionless Christianity has once again become my banner" (*Talks
to the Swedish Nation*). This is not quite accurate, for during all of his
religious periods other elements—pietistic and pessimistic—were
united with those taken from Kierkegaard. The most interesting
thing about this statement is the phrase "once again." Thus, in
1912 Strindberg did return to Kierkegaard, but he had returned to
him repeatedly in the past, and even his first experience of Kierkegaard was a return—to the moralism of which his father had been
the first guarantor.

Kierkegaard maintains that the paradox of religious faith expressed in the phrase "Credo quia absurdum" is complemented by
another paradox. Faith is also paradoxical from the moral point of
view. It is offensive to the moral outlook of the natural man. Kierkegaard preaches about "the edification implied in the idea that as
against God we are always in the wrong." For this reason, his God
acquires the awful aspects of an Old Testament God, which is especially apparent in the famous treatment of the testing of Abraham in
Fear and Trembling. Strindberg's dependence on an Old Testament

concept of God, particularly during the initial stages of the Inferno crisis, can be traced back—at least in part—to Kierkegaard.

Kierkegaard adopts motifs from Enlightenment and Romantic critiques of religion, but he radically changes the conclusions they reached. His religion has most of the characteristics for which Christianity has been criticized—irrationality, primitivism, inhumanity—and according to him, because of these features alone can it be considered true Christianity. It will later appear that Strindberg's Inferno struggle involved a similar vacillation between criticizing religion and accepting it. This ambivalent attitude is particularly evident in *Jacob Wrestles*. Furthermore, although he enumerated a series of objections (in the form of a defiant logomachy with God) that can be directed against the Christian belief in a thoroughly benevolent Providence, his struggle nonetheless ended with the admission of defeat. When Strindberg felt himself driven toward religion against his will—against his intellect—he followed Kierkegaard's schematization of conversion.[21]

For Kierkegaard, man meets his God not only with feelings of fear and trembling, but also with defiance. In this matter, one can readily see the connection between Kierkegaard and the Promethean impulses expressed so impressively in the works of the radical Romantics, especially those belonging to the school of Byron. Strindberg picked up these impulses from both sources. The interest shown by all these poets in the figure of Job emphasizes this connection even more strikingly. Shelley has a posthumous fragment about Job, and during the Inferno crisis the Book of Job was among Strindberg's most important sources of edification. In Kierkegaard, the Job figure occurs as a prototype in many powerful passages in *Repetition,* which inspired the accusations that Strindberg leveled against the cosmic order in both *Inferno* and *Jacob Wrestles:*

Woe to him who devours the widow and the fatherless and defrauds them of their inheritance, but woe also to him who would slyly defraud the afflicted of the momentary consolation of relieving the oppression of his heart and "contending with God." Or in our time is godly fear so great that the afflicted man does not need what was customary in those old days? Does one perhaps not dare to complain before God? Is it now godly fear that has become greater, or fear and cowardice? Nowadays people are of the opinion that the natural expression of sorrow, the desperate language of passion, must be left to poets, who as attorneys in a lower court plead the sufferer's cause before the tribunal of human compassion. Further than this no one ventures to go. Speak therefore, O Job of imperishable memory! Rehearse everything thou didst say, thou mighty advocate who dost confront the highest tribunal, no more daunted than a roaring lion! There is pith in thy speech, in thy heart there is godly fear, even when thou dost complain, when thou wouldst justify thy despair against thy friends who rise up like robbers to assault thee with their speeches, and even when incited by thy friends thou dost tread their wisdom under foot and despise their defense of the Lord, accounting it the finite shrewdness of a veteran courtier of a worldy-wise minister of state. Thee I have need of, a man who knows how to complain aloud, so that his complaint echoes in heaven where God confers with Satan in devising schemes against a man.

Complain! The Lord is not afraid, He is well able to defend Himself, but how might He be able to speak in His defense if no one ventures to complain as it is seemly for a man to do? Speak, lift up thy voice, speak aloud, God surely can speak louder, he possesses the thunder—but that too is an answer, an explanation, reliable, trustworthy, genuine, an answer from God Himself, an answer which even if it crush a man is more glorious than gossip and rumor about the righteousness of providence which are invented by human wisdom and circulated by effeminate creatures and eunuchs.[22]

Even when Strindberg was very young, sexual experiences awakened strong guilt feelings in him. For this reason, it is not surprising that he made a clear distinction between the sexual and the erotic. As a consequence of this split, his infatuations always resembled a sort of spiritual and nonsensuous Madonna worship. In both *The Son of a Servant* and *A Madman's Defense* (1887–1888) Strindberg emphasized the irrational element in his youthful attitude; at the same time, he perhaps exaggerated his Platonism in order to make himself appear to be the innocent victim of the designs of depraved women. By the middle of the 1880s, however, he regarded himself as having outgrown the role of Joseph, and he spoke contemptuously of "the Satan-worshipping despair of the post-Romantics, who saw in woman a means of salvation, an angel." The historical reference is, of course, completely accurate. Strindberg grew up in a milieu where these problems were much more beset by taboos than they are now and in which the official attitude toward sex was marked by the somewhat shabby idealism that informs midnineteenth-century poetic style—the style of what is called "Signature poetry" in Sweden. He was influenced by these circumstances, and he was not alone in his dilemma. But for him this was not simply a modish attitude, as he pretended when he wrote *The Son of a Servant.* It lay much deeper. Through such books as *The New Kingdom* (1882) and *Married* (1884), Strindberg—more than anyone else in Sweden—liberated the younger generation from their strict moral heritage and conventional idealism. But although he became a liberator of others, he was never able to free himself from his sexual fears that had persisted since youth. During the 1880s, when he was advancing a completely different program, these fears still played an important part in his life. In every woman he always hoped to see something of a mother, a Madonna, a reconciler—until disappointment took over and provided him with terms denoting roles diametrically opposed to these.

If one consults Strindberg's early correspondence, one finds that his talk about "spiritual Madonna worship" is often well justified in the case of his earliest erotic attachments. In 1874 and 1875, Strindberg had a love affair, which is said to be reflected in the figure of Kristina in the poetic version of *Master Olof* (1876) and is also glimpsed in *The Red Room* (1879). In *The Son of a Servant,* he portrays this relationship as being predominantly sexual. In a letter to the Wrangels, he gave what was possibly a more accurate account of it, but this part of the letter was later clipped out. It appears from his correspondence, however, that Strindberg found the relationship tedious and tried to free himself from it on at least two different occasions, which are separated from each other by a year of discontent. The maneuver he employed was fairly characteristic of him: he invented a new love for himself, one that was purer. In the first letter dealing with this fictional new love, written to his journalist friend Gustaf Christiernsson in the spring of 1874, he speaks of a "soul that has not been mistreated or sullied by the world" and says that he trusts his new feelings "because they are of a quite different nature." On the second occasion—when he finally succeeded in making the break—he proceeded in exactly the same manner, except that this time his infatuation was with a real person. Turning to youthful memories, he focused on his sisters. They had a friend, Elisabeth, whom he now began to love from a distance. In a love letter that he wrote to her in episodes between April 20 and May 24, 1875, he recalls seeing her when he was a child, and he calls to mind the fact that she displayed a maternal attitude that appealed to him: "She had a little sister whose mother she had to be—the poor children had lost their mother. She never tired of her or grew angry with her. She would always make peace between the other children—." Her mission in his life would be to effect reconciliation, he declares in accents that have a religious ring: "A sword has pierced my soul. God has sent her to save a life. This is my ardent belief and to maintain this belief I have dared what I have dared!"

That the living counterpart of this idealized figure was a married woman contributed to Strindberg's feeling that the "affair" implied a degrading kind of slavery for him. Even years later, it still weighed heavily on his conscience. Of course, this episode can hardly have been known to a very large segment of his public, especially not during the period when he was living in France and writing in French, but in the draft of an unfinished work in French (dated 1893 by his close friend, Carlheim-Gyllensköld), he still felt called upon to defend his honor in drastic terms. He claims that he never "seduced another man's woman"; he was only "an unmarried youth who had been ruined by a married whore." [23] Shortly after this episode, when he began to frequent the home of the Wrangels, Strindberg became involved in a triangle of exactly this sort. And later, he was extremely eager to defend his honor in this case, too. Indeed, *A Madman's Defense* is at least partly intended to prove the correctness of a conclusion drawn by Strindberg in a letter to his eldest brother, Axel, around the same time: "In W's affair, my role was particularly honorable—and I saved the children, the mother—and by assuming the guilt—even W. himself, who was having an affair with his cousin" (May 8, 1887).

When the drama was played out, Strindberg was not so certain of his guiltlessness. To cast his eyes upon Siri Wrangel was forbidden

to him from the very beginning, for not only was he her social infe-
rior, but he also regarded her husband as his friend and protector. For
a long time, he tried to find another love object to whom he could
transfer his feelings, and he played his part so intensely that he must
have half-believed in it himself. Consequently, he considered his
friendship for the baroness to be "pure." In *A Madman's Defense,*
Strindberg describes how he arranged an altar in his room dedicated
to the secret cult of his "Madonna with child." A letter to the
Wrangels confirms this statement: "I bought a tea-rose and some cut
flowers. I cleared off the table in my garret and made a little arbor or
an altar—which was it?—and there I placed her picture—my image
of the Madonna—and then I lit four large wax candles in front of my
Madonna and prayed" (Aug. 8, 1875). A letter he wrote to the
baron before the break also betrays an enthusiastic cult of friendship:
"I felt how pure I was in your presence and could never find it sinful
to love thus—and I loved you both—I could never distinguish between you in my thoughts—I always saw you together in my
dreams" (March 24, 1876). After their mutual declaration of love,
he wrote to Siri that his love was spiritual; he wanted to "show the
world an example of a case of adultery that was not adulterous"
(March 12, 1876). She was not to be his mistress, as he explained to
her somewhat later: "When I write, I want to be grown-up. Otherwise, let me be your little child. And you could not believe how
much I love you—with all of my being—as a mother, a sister—
anything you like, but not as a mistress! Let me be your child, but
do not hate me for it" (April 13, 1876). Then their fall became a
fact, and soon thereafter Strindberg explained with great—all too
great—emphasis that his beloved had not been sullied by their affair: "No, you have showed me that angels exist, even among human
beings, and that just because they are human beings, their wings do
not fall off, even though they touch the earth. Have you ever
watched a swallow when a storm is approaching? She sweeps the
gravel, but she rises when the weather clears!" He gives her "the kiss
of peace, the pure and holy kiss" and receives her "into that invisible
fellowship that we—we who suffer, we who strive—have formed
here on earth" (May 3, 1876).

In spite of everything, Strindberg and Siri held on tightly to the theory of pure love. A month later he speaks in contrite tones: "Believe me, when the intoxication that we abhor—but bow to—has passed, our love will once more become as great and as wonderful as it formerly was! I think that lovely time is already returning!" In the French draft of a novel that dates from roughly the same time, he suggests to Siri that he intends to write about "the difference between friendship and love." Its conclusion is to be the same as the one reached in his letters to her during this period: "_Sens moral:_ there is a love that is not sensual and that is not consummated and does not wish to be consummated in marriage. Notice the fine distinction between the legitimate love of the husband (who desires) and the lover (who desires nothing, but is no less guilty in the eyes of the world)." [24]

When Strindberg wrote _A Madman's Defense_ in 1887–1888, he no longer believed in this troubadour morality, and in one dithyrambic chapter he refers to "the intoxicating minutes of satisfied love" as "the joy of life, the only joy that makes our despicable lives worth living." Even though at this point he has revised the actual events, elsewhere he still seems to represent them correctly. After describing the experience of sensual love, he begins the next chapter abruptly: "She is certain of my love now and misuses it." In the same chapter, one glimpses an idea that was later to wield great power over Strindberg: that Siri was deceiving him with her former husband. To a certain extent, his correspondence confirms the fact that he suspected her of infidelity. At the end of May 1876 (that is, in the same month when their relationship became adulterous, thereby justifying everyone's suspicions), Strindberg wrote a letter to Siri in which his jealousy is ill-concealed:

Every time you see your child, you—my wife—will be affronted by a crude person. You will leave the scene with less strength, less self-respect. He will be permitted to interfere in our destinies—he will scratch out every word I wrote in your soul—You will—and you will have to—hear him defile me without raising your voice in my defense. —His embrace is warmer than mine. His eyes are more constant, and his soul more intimate.

You will miss all of these qualities in me. You will compare what you have with what you have lost, and in the end you will curse me!

According to *A Madman's Defense,* Strindberg is supposed to have harbored suspicions about Siri's character from the very time that these decisive events took place—indeed, from the moment that he first became conscious of his sensual desire for her. Later, of course, these suspicions found ghastly expression in the novel about his marriage, *A Madman's Defense.* Although Strindberg kept his suspicions to himself for a while, the above letter suggests that his account of his attitude to her is probably correct.[25] In view of the powerful guilt feelings that sexual activity always seems to have induced in him, it is understandable how he could have held two diametrically opposed attitudes toward her at the same time. When one is laden with guilt feelings, the natural reaction is to attempt to transfer the guilt—or a large part of it—to someone else. If Siri was the sort of "angel" that he wanted to pretend she was, then he would be no more than a contemptible seducer; if the opposite was the case, however—if she was shabby enough to let Wrangel flirt with her— then Strindberg would be the relatively innocent one, who had been "ruined by a married whore," just as he had been in his previous love affair.

Naturally, psychoanalysts have fixed upon the fact that Strindberg's treatment of love in *A Madman's Defense* wheels abruptly between two poles, "Madonna" and "slut." [26] For them, it is easy to discern behind this polarity the childhood situation in which the child appeals to the mother for tenderness, but feels deceived by her because of her intimacy with the father. It is extremely difficult to assess the probability of such a reconstruction of the circumstances, since this case concerns a historical personality and a real situation. Therefore, the extant material—and not a psychological theory— must be one's point of departure.

That Strindberg himself was very close to such an interpretation is hardly open to debate. Even if Freud had never formulated his theory about the Oedipus complex, Strindberg's analysis of his own situation in *A Madman's Defense* would have naturally linked him with a similar syndrome. In describing his attraction to the Wrangels, for example, he emphasizes the fact that his first visit to their home seemed like a repetition of experiences from his childhood. He states that they lived at number 12 Norrtullsgatan. According to Strindberg, this was the house in which he had watched his mother die and seen her replaced by a stepmother, but he has retouched the facts, for his mother died in the house next door, number 14.[27] When he rang the doorbell, he continues, Carl Gustaf Wrangel opened the door—instead of his own father, whom for a moment he had expected to see. After Siri had left, he and Wrangel entered the deserted apartment, as they would enter "into the presence of the dead," and they did so "in a state of mournful intimacy," which suggests the understanding that had sprung up between Strindberg and his father after his mother's death. Moreover, at one point Strindberg asks himself if the religious veneration he feels for Siri does not derive from the influence of his childhood memories. After posing this question, he stresses the fact that he tends to identify Siri with his mother and implies that this is an important factor in their relationship. This identification is most strikingly expressed in the famous exclamation: "Is there anything abnormal about this instinct? Am I the product of some whim of nature? Are my feelings perverse, since I find such pleasure in possessing my mother? Is this the unconscious incest of the heart?" (*A Madman's Defense*).

Nor is *A Madman's Defense* the only book in which Strindberg invokes this theory about the significant role played by the mother image in his erotic life. One might naturally suspect that he distorted the situation when he put it into a novel, but even in his more objective autobiography, *The Son of a Servant,* he interprets his erotic activity according to this theory. In this work, he states again and again that whenever he longs for a "pure" love, the image of his mother comes to mind. Speaking of his infatuation for his sister, "Elisabeth," he writes: "And when he saw his sisters, the eldest of whom resembled their mother, he had such a pure feeling for these young women that he thought that all feelings for other women were impure." [28] In another place in the same work, he describes how in his early youth he had suffered from pangs of conscience after dedicating a licentious poem to a girl whom he was courting: "Thus her love for him had been pure, and he had only wished to possess her. How crude! How vulgar! How could he have been so vile as to believe that a barmaid could not love innocently? Why, his own mother had been in the same social class as this girl. He had insulted her. For shame!" (*The Son of a Servant*).

With this context in mind, one can find an explanation for Strindberg's erotic attitudes without even looking for it. Seen in this light, both his preliminary appeal to the conciliatory aspect of his mother and his subsequent guilt-laden disappointment appear to be successive phases in an ineluctable sequence of events. If he originally regarded his father as the incarnation of the moral code of society—the order with which Strindberg found himself most frequently at odds—then he turned to woman so that she could "reconcile" him with the social order. For this attempt at reconciliation to succeed, the love had to be "pure," since nothing awakened Strindberg's guilt feelings more powerfully than sexual activity. To break sexual taboos made all reconciliation impossible. These motifs reappeared during the Inferno period in a concentrated form, which corresponds exactly to the sentiment expressed by Strindberg in a letter to Siri in the spring of 1876: "Now there is only you and I—and God!"

This background suffices to demonstrate that Strindberg's erotic experiences were, if not the only, at least one of the most consistent means of awakening his guilt feelings. Of all the neurotic crises and fits of depression that afflicted him during the 1870s, his nervous attack on the island of Kymmendö in 1873 and the other one connected with his trip to Dalarö in 1875 are the most important. In both cases, erotic conflicts played an important role.

In the summer of 1873, Strindberg thought that he was faced with economic catastrophe. A bank loan came due at the same time that he was required to pay the costs of printing *The Swedish Insurance Journal,* of which he was then the editor. He fell ill with "gastric fever" and experienced hallucinations: "A voice outside him cries 'guilty' and a voice within echoes the cry. In debt to the national bank! A terrible creditor, a whole nation. He had consumed the people's money and deceived their representative. He tried to defend himself by saying that the eleventh of July was never out of his mind, that he had sent in his payment, that he had never wished to deceive anyone! It did not help. He was possessed by his tor- mented conscience" (*The Son of a Servant*). When he recovered, he went to Dalarö, where he met a fellow-student. On the way back, he wanted to commit suicide by scuttling the boat, as he later arranged for the hero to do in *By the Open Sea* (1890). But this incident did not end the crisis. When he returned to Kymmendö, the housekeeper was alone in the cottage. She comforted him. "For three days, they lived together like a married couple, alone in the house, and Johan felt himself coming back to life. An invisible bond grew up between them, and since she had been the only person to sympathize with him during his illness and was now both amiable and tender, he clung to her" (*The Son of a Servant*). When she deserted him, he suf- fered a fresh attack. In a frenzy, he stalked out into the forest. Un- able to find consolation in the beauty of nature, he seized a stick and brought down branches all around him. Finally, he climbed a pine tree by the shore, sat there like a horseman, and imagined that he was pitted against the cuirassiers of the waves and the monitors of the skerries.

For a long time, Strindberg believed that he had suffered an at- tack of insanity. Writing to Wrangel two years later, he described the Kymmendö experience as a prelude to the Dalarö attack—"I preached out there and had my fits—when I was suffering from my illness!" (Oct. 7, 1875). He also used part of the Kymmendö experi- ence when describing the incipient mental breakdown of Lieutenant von Bleichroden in "The German Lieutenant" (1884). But by the time he wrote *The Son of a Servant,* he had decided that the episode was altogether too well-written to pass for the work of an insane person: "He had invented it—that's all there was to it."

Like the Kymmendö episode in 1873, the trip to Dalarö in 1875 recurs as a motif in both "The German Lieutenant" and *By the Open Sea.* In order to escape from the love that Siri von Essen had kindled in him, Strindberg attempted to flee to Paris, but he soon regretted

this decision and forced the pilot to set him ashore on Dalarö. Here
he planned to commit suicide, but he wished to die in such a manner
that he would have the opportunity of seeing his beloved once more
on his deathbed. With this purpose in mind, he did all that he could
to induce pneumonia and then took to his bed. All these actions, of
course, are common reactions of hysterical flight. In addition, he
took refuge in religion. In an agitated letter written from his
sickbed on Dalarö to Carl Gustaf Wrangel, Strindberg reports that
"the Lord has smitten him" and that "spirits have driven him out
among the trees." He considers himself insane. People point at him
and watch him closely. But the pastor of the island's congregation
has given him hope that he, Strindberg-Saul, is not completely lost:
"Behold, Satan has demanded thy soul so that he might sift it like
wheat—but I have delivered thee, he said! That was a millionth of a
drop of comfort." God has never answered him, he reveals, but he is
still prepared to throw himself into the arms of God, or of Christ—
"the sacrifice is to believe in the absurd—it is my faculty of reason,
that is to say, my pride, that must be sacrificed." He feels like a
vanquished rebel, a Jacob who has struggled with God and admits
his defeat: "I have revolted against God—I have blasphemed—like
Jacob, I have struggled against Him—But no one cried out Saul!
Saul! Even so, my hip is lame" (Oct. 7, 1875).

These statements already contain a system of attitudes and symbols that is strongly suggestive of those accompanying the Inferno
crisis. Furthermore, it is obvious that these symbols and attitudes
are drawn largely from literary sources. The whole letter is written
in the fragmentary, romantic style that Strindberg loved at the
time, and the situation—the priest by the bedside of the haunted
blasphemer—has several literary analogues. One thinks first, perhaps, of Byron's *Manfred,* a work that had made a profound impression on Strindberg.[29] In that play, the hero repudiates the abbot's
admonitions in the last scene and, all alone, fights his last battle
with the evil spirit. Strindberg was not so steadfast—at least not according to the account he gave to Wrangel—but in *By the Open Sea*
he rearranged the episode in order to make the posture of romantic
defiance more strongly evident.

A kind of Manichean religious system gradually developed from these and similar youthful crises. Although this religion turned up constantly in varying forms during the crises in Strindberg's later life, it reached its fullest development during the greatest of these, the Inferno crisis. It shall be referred to here as Strindberg's "crisis religion." [30]

States of neurotic anxiety always incited Strindberg to counterattack. Feeling that he was at war with the cosmic order, he would redistribute the moral burden in such a manner that his own guilt appeared to be the fault of the cosmos. Not Strindberg, but God was to blame for making such a damned mess of the world. This kind of projection was a characteristic feature of his crisis religion. It could take various forms: a pessimistic form—the world is ruled by an evil power; a dualistic form—powers of good and of evil are pitted against one another; an essentially monistic form—the world is ruled by a beneficient power, although lower, demonic powers exercise a limited influence. But these nuances, which as a matter of fact are often difficult to distinguish from each other, appear to have been relatively unimportant. Whenever his situation seemed unbearable, Strindberg defended himself by resorting not to doctrines, but to mythological representations.

This sort of Manicheism is a metaphysical expression of the Romantic attitude of defiance. One finds counterparts to it nearly everywhere in *Sturm und Drang* and Romantic writers—from Goethe to Viktor Rydberg. The religious content in these fantasies varies sharply. Strindberg was, of course, acquainted with *Ormus and Ariman* by the greatest of Swedish Romantics, C. J. L. Almquist (1793–1866), who uses the Persian myth as a spiritual envelope for the same kind of opposition to society shared by *Sturm und Drang* writers and by left-wing Romantics. He had read Victor Hugo, whose Titanism has a lyrical tone of blasphemy and revolt. But in the passionate outbursts that he found in Kierkegaard's *Repetition* he had encountered a much more serious expression of the idea that a personal evil power rules the world. Perhaps by this time he had already been impressed by Kierkegaard's lines describing how "God confers with Satan in devising schemes against man." [31]

Strindberg's need to feel that he was struggling against a more powerful opponent, was suffering innocently, and was defying authority had been established in childhood. Because it satisfied this need, Romantic Manicheism appealed to him as a form of religion. There is probably no reason to disbelieve his assertion in *The Son of a Servant* that he labored with such concepts quite early in life. But his Manichean crisis religion does not appear in any very clear form in the autobiography, until he begins describing his experiences on Kymmendö in 1873, where he reports on Johan's state of mind:

Because of his sickness, which had turned his brain inside out, Johan could not keep all his thoughts in order. Thus, old ideas rose within him. Even if he had never invoked God, he had never eliminated the possibility that God was the originator of the universe. He sought a cause for all his misfortunes, and since religion had taught him to seek all things outside of himself, rather than within, he conceived of an evil god, who controlled human destiny. Old memories of Ormuz and Ariman rose up, and soon his system was complete. It seemed so simple to him: this world of lies, of deceit, and pain must be ruled by an evil power, to whom the Supreme Being had granted power. Thus he struggled against the Evil One, and God—the principle of Good—sat by and looked on, with his hands folded. This fever religion lingered with him for a long time and was a sort of comfort, since it relieved him of responsibility for the difficulties he had fallen into for lack of foresight.

This "fever religion" was not his own invention. In fact, one can point more or less confidently to the source that had inspired him. One cannot be certain that he was yet acquainted with Byron's *Cain,* but he already knew and admired *Manfred,* which according to *The Son of a Servant* appealed to him because he, too, was "a person who was dissatisfied with heaven and with heavenly rule." In the second act of *Manfred,* the hero is confronted with the demonic hosts whose power on earth is said to be increasing. They are the "Fates" and "Nemesis," who afflict the earth with evil, and their ruler is Ariman, "Prince of the Powers invisible."

The philosophy of Eduard von Hartmann, whose work Strindberg became acquainted with in the winter of 1872–1873, served to amplify the impulses he received from Byronic pessimism. In *The Son of a Servant,* Strindberg emphasizes the fact that Hartmann's system did not strike him as new or revolutionary. It was simply a corroboration of his old suspicions: "Then it was true—what he had so often imagined—that everything was a humbug!" In the philosophy of pessimism he thought that he recognized the ancient myth of the tree of knowledge, which he interpreted with the words, "conscious life is pain." Its view that all things are vain, which was also the main tenet of Christianity, had long informed his own world view. His consciousness of this "was the secret of his life; for when he could not admire something, become attached to something, or live for something, he thought to himself that he was simply too intelligent to let himself be duped."

Although in the passage that follows this statement, Strindberg seems to be presenting the point of view he had held at the time of writing *The Son of a Servant,* in the few sentences cited here he seems to have succeeded in capturing the original eclectic and ambiguous nature of his pessimism. Its basis was the pietistic *contemptus mundi* of his youth, which he had later fused with impulses received from Romantic Manicheism and pessimistic philosophy. Although Strindberg's statements suggest that he made a subjective interpretation of Hartmann's philosophy, he uses such vague terms in characterizing his views that they could with equal justice be regarded as a paraphrase of the famous opening monologue of *Manfred:*

> Sorrow is Knowledge; they who know the most
> Must mourn the deepest o'er the fatal truth,
> The Tree of Knowledge is not that of Life.
> Philosophy and science, and the springs
> Of Wonder, and the wisdom of the World,
> I have essayed, and in my mind there is
> A power to make these subject to itself—
> But they avail not: I have done men good,
> And I have met with good even among men—
> But this availed not: I have had my foes,
> And none have baffled, many fallen before me—
> But this availed not: —Good—or evil—life—
> Powers, passions—all I see in other beings,

Have been to me as rain unto the sands,
Since that all-nameless hour. I have no dread,
And feel the curse to have no natural fear,
Nor fluttering throb, that beats with hopes or wishes,
Or lurking love of something on the earth.[32]

Similarly, Romantic Manicheism is fused with a Schopenhauer and Hartmann-like pessimism in the *Epilogue to Master Olof* (1877), which provides the most essential evidence available concerning the nature of Strindberg's crisis religion during the 1870s. He himself was aware of the connection between this epilogue and his later religious views. Indeed, he even pointed out that this "mystery play" anticipates certain ideas that became important to him during the Inferno crisis, and he added a translation of it to the French edition of *Inferno*.

In this epilogue, the highest power in the universe is represented by the "Eternal One," who is both passive and remote. Subordinate to him are an evil power—called God—and a good power—called Lucifer. These two opposed forces contend with one another over the fate of man, but the evil god gains the advantage: he is the world's immediate ruler, and he holds men in check by endowing them with the reproductive instinct. Lucifer, the speaker of truth, unsuccessfully attempts to enlighten men about the meaninglessness of life and to "teach them to die."

Commenting on this epilogue in *The Son of a Servant,* Strindberg states that here he had "formulated the pessimistic world view." Although scholars have usually assumed that he was referring in general terms to the pessimistic philosophers, they have been unable to agree on which of these philosophers he is most likely to have meant. Whereas Martin Lamm makes a strong case for Hartmann and opines that Strindberg had "transported Hartmann's metaphysics into his *Epilogue*," Torsten Eklund strongly urges Schopenhauer's role and regards the work as an "allegorical re-creation of Schopenhauer's metaphysics." [33] But it seems pointless to continue this discussion further, for to do so would presuppose a philosophical precision that Strindberg seldom bothered to achieve. For that matter, one need not limit "the pessimistic world view" exclusively to Scho-

penhauer and Hartmann. Besides philosophical elements, Strindberg's own pessimistic world view included strains of Manichean
religiosity that are nearest to those found in Byron.

Nor are these diverse elements incompatible. Although Schopenhauer is more bitter and less defiant than Byron, the emotional reg-
ister of his philosophy is reminiscent of Byron's. Schopenhauer's
anthropomorphic tendency also permits him at times to speak in
mythological terms about the will as a personal, evil power.[34] But
the faithful disciple of Schopenhauer and Hartmann always understands that such expressions are purely allegorical. Pessimistic philosophy did not emerge as mythology, and the principles it depended on were not only impersonal, but were also supposed to
conform to the laws of nature.

Strindberg's mythology in the *Epilogue* is not primarily an allegorical concept, however. Lamm, who emphasizes this fact, feels that
Strindberg "was really governed by some sort of belief in demonology, according to which the world is controlled by powers that not
only are inimical to man, but are downright evil—a belief that used
to haunt him during his periods of depression." [35] If Lamm is right,
then the ideas that Strindberg obviously borrowed from pessimistic
philosophy—such as his concern about the role of the "will to live,"
the fear of death, and the reproductive instinct in life—appear to be
somewhat less central to his thought than is generally admitted. In
other words, Strindberg merely transformed Schopenhauer's and
Hartmann's assertions about the meaninglessness of existence into
articles in a bill of indictment brought against the ruler of the universe.

In *The Son of a Servant*, Strindberg explicitly states that the *Epilogue* was directly based on concepts that arose from the religious
crisis he underwent while involved in the conflict between Siri and
Gustav Wrangel. "During that stormy year, when he had been in
great mental anguish, his alternate childhood belief returned to
him. According to this belief, both good and evil powers are at work
in the universe, and this view resulted in a dualism with two gods:
God and the Devil, as they are called in Christian teaching, but
when he saw the world so dark, he could not believe that the devil

had yet been vanquished." Thus, the evil God in the *Epilogue* was both a "way of explaining the universe" and, intermittently, an intuitively sensed, personal reality.

At the time that he wrote the *Epilogue,* external circumstances may have helped to make this belief in a "ruling devil" more immediate to Strindberg. In the spring of 1876, Siri's marriage with Carl Gustav Wrangel was dissolved, and in January 1877 their daughter died. The following May Siri's mother, Betty von Essen, died. "Two dead and so many wounded in order to satisfy a woman who is not worth an old pair of shoes," Strindberg exclaims in *A Madman's Defense.* This time, however, he was probably not so certain of his own innocence. Before the child fell ill, Strindberg had tried to console Siri for the separation from her daughter that would necessarily occur when she remarried by availing himself of one of Kierkegaard's favorite themes: "Rest assured that He no more demands this sacrifice of you than he did of him [Abraham] —He only wishes to test you—to chasten you—to see if you are worthy!" (May 3, 1876). After the child's death, these words acquired a dreadful significance for him. Finally, Siri and Strindberg were married on December 30, 1877, and about a month later Siri gave birth to another daughter, who died within two days.

The "Prologue" to *Faust* is one of the closest literary analogues to Strindberg's *Epilogue.* Equally important, however, as Eklund points out, is Byron's *Cain,* which Strindberg had probably become acquainted with both directly through the text and indirectly through Brandes' account in *Main Currents in Nineteenth Century Literature.* [36] The mythological configuration is identical in both dramas; that is, in both works the Christian God represents evil and Lucifer stands for the good. One difference is that Strindberg places the Eternal One above the two contending powers. According to comments in *The Son of a Servant,* he did so because he was unable to escape from the idea of God as a "lawgiver." During the Inferno crisis the same tendency appears: "God in nature" is not quite the same as the God who directs Strindberg's personal destiny. In other words, two different paths of speculation lead Strindberg to distinguish between God as Creator and God as Providence.

The Romantic Satanism that Strindberg encountered in poets like Byron was transmitted to *fin-de-siècle* poetry by writers like Barbey d'Aurévilly and Baudelaire.[37] In the middle of the 1890s, when Strindberg became acquainted with similar ideas in the works of Huysmans and the Occultists, he felt that he had been ahead of his time, and in 1894 he wrote to his friend Leopold Littmansson: "Do you remember how we anticipated the whole current *fin-de-siècle* movement and even Satanism way out there on Kymmendö? Do you remember 'Strindberg's Religion' with Satan as the ruler of the world!" (July 1894). He was not completely unconscious of the real historical situation, however. In one of the drafts of *Inferno,* he cites Byron's "sorrow is knowledge" and refers to *Cain.*

When he wrote *Inferno,* Strindberg demonstrated a detailed knowledge of the history of belief in the devil. Though some of this information was garnered from the countless "occult" works that he studied in the 1890s, he had already laid the foundations of this historical insight into Satanism back in the 1870s, when at his own request he was given the task of writing an article entitled "The Devil" for the first edition of the *Nordisk Familjebok,* a standard Swedish encyclopedia. For this purpose he borrowed various works on magic and the occult from the Royal Library in 1876. The material he used in his article for the *Nordisk Familjebok* was probably also suggested by a much more accessible source, namely, Viktor Rydberg's popular *Medieval Magic*—a work that Strindberg immersed himself in once again during the Inferno crisis.[38]

The character of Jacques in *The Secret of the Guild* (1880) appears as a sort of retrospective survey of Strindberg's crisis states during the 1870s. Jacques is simultaneously brutal and extremely weak-willed. In matters involving crime and treason he can act resolutely, but in his weaker intervals he falls into states of apathy and thinks he is being haunted by an invisible person who is always at his side. He unresistingly allows himself to be influenced by his surroundings and repeats words spoken by other characters in the play. Stories about murder and bloodshed exercise a particularly fascinating effect on him. Viewed in the context of literary history, this figure clearly

appears to be a product of neo-romanticism; and one ought to bear
in mind that shortly before Strindberg wrote this play, he had studied the *Contes fantastiques* of those two Hoffmann imitators, Emile
Erckmann and Alexandre Chatrian.

As is the case with many romantic heroes and villains, the explanation for Jacques's spiritual unrest lies in a crime committed in the
past. Among Strindberg's favorite writers, both Byron and Kierkegaard openly hint at the existence of a sinful secret in their own
lives. In this play, however, Strindberg deals not with individual
but with family guilt. The original transgression was committed by
Jacques's father, but the ensuing curse haunts Jacques as powerfully
as it did his father. By swearing falsely, Jacques repeats his father's
crime, but this very repetition ultimately cancels the former crime
by serving as both a punishment and a means of atonement. Jacques's melancholy and his evil inclinations also function to reduce
his father's debt, for as Jacques observes, "that crime was so great
that it took two of us to atone for it."

Many scholars have noted this syndrome. In order to explain
Strindberg's "curious doctrine of vicarious suffering," some, like
Herrlin, have referred to Linnaeus' notes on *Nemesis;* others, like
Eklund, have pointed to Schopenhauer's doctrine of atonement.[39]
Both these explanations appear doubtful, however, because of a
statement that Strindberg made in a letter to Eugène Fahlstedt in
the spring of 1875: "Whoever comes into contact with me or my
family is lost!" (April 18, 1875). As far as one can tell, at that time
Strindberg was still unfamiliar with Linnaeus' *Nemesis Divina* and
with the works of Schopenhauer. In other words, even before he discovered analogous ideas in these authors, he imagined that some sort
of guilt was hanging over him and the members of his family. One
can imagine that he had long been familiar with notions of this sort.

Strindberg could have stumbled across this idea of family guilt in
many of the romantic works that he studied during the 1870s. It is
already present, for example, in the earliest Romantic "tragedy of
fate," Friedrich-Ludwig-Zacharias Werner's *Der vierundzwanzigste Fe-
bruar* (1810), and it is frequently exploited in the works of Hoffmann and subsequent writers. In Kierkegaard, Strindberg had en-

countered a staging of the Romantic "crime in the past," which must have been especially stimulating to his imagination. Kierkegaard himself was a tormented and demonic figure, making mysterious allusions to a dark point in his own past. But his concept of the interrelation between crime and punishment transcended his own existence. The "great earthquake" in his life was the discovery that his father had once cursed God. This was the crime that had made Mikael Kierkegaard's life one long penance, and it provided Søren with an explanation for his own melancholy. When *The Secret of the Guild* was written, Brandes had already published his book on Kierkegaard, in which he examines these broodings thoroughly. He writes: "To Kierkegaard, it seemed as if the consequences of his putative offense could—in one way or another—be inherited. His early training and discipline in religious matters had so prepared his mind for superstition that the idea that his family had incurred God's wrath quite naturally suggested itself to him." [40] Strindberg's Jacques describes his position in similar terms: "I believe that crime grows in the blood, like soot or rust, and that things will never be well until it breaks out. I believe that one inherits these feelings the same way that one inherits debts. Haven't I ever told you that I sometimes believe that my father committed some crime in his youth for which he was not punished?"

Strindberg probably became acquainted with Linnaeus' notes on *Nemesis* in the middle of the 1870s. This work, as Nathan Söderblom, Herrlin, and Lamm have pointed out, [41] made a powerful impression on him and captured his imagination, particularly during his great crises. In this work he encountered a concept of family guilt that had the same legalistic Old Testament basis as the one he had found in Kierkegaard, but at the same time Linnaeus' concept included a number of concrete observations and images from life that must have appealed to his taste for the factual.

Later, however, when Strindberg adopted Linnaeus' ideas, he gave them a highly subjective interpretation. In his own essay entitled "Nemesis divina," written in 1887, Strindberg maintains that "like all prominent personalities, who after great struggles have risen to places of honor in life and who gaze back in astonishment at the difficulties they have overcome, so too Linnaeus thought that he was under the powerful and special protection of a god. From that premise, he concluded that the same god who protected him must also crush his enemies." But such, of course, is not the line of thought that Linnaeus develops in his notes on *Nemesis divina*. For him, crime must sooner or later lead ineluctably to punishment, and he never claims that he or anyone else is under the special protection of a just God. The only thing that the two ideas have in common is the concept of a God who directly intervenes in human life. True to his habit of imagining events in personal categories, Strindberg gives Linnaeus' idea an egocentric interpretation and pushes it in the direction of the magical.

The two turning points in Strindberg's life were the crisis precipitated by the scandal following publication of *Married*—when Strindberg was tried for blasphemy and acquitted (Nov. 17, 1884)—and the Inferno crisis. The former led him into atheism; the latter brought him back to a belief in God. Taken together, they frame his naturalistic and pessimistic period, which lasted barely a decade. Although this period will not be treated here, it is clear that the events of 1885, after the tension generated by his fear of imprisonment had pushed him into a mental crisis, are indispensable to an understanding of the Inferno crisis, for if one wishes to gain a clear picture of how Strindberg returned to religion, one must also elucidate the main features of the opposite process, when he heaved the concept of God overboard.

From a psychological point of view, Strindberg's decade as a literary naturalist coincides with his period of marked paranoia. Strindberg's personality type, up to the *Married* crisis, was primarily hysterical in nature. After the Inferno crisis, he developed schizoid tendencies, which manifested themselves primarily in an introverted autism. The intervening period was marked by the emergence of paranoid tendencies. Obviously, this distinction cannot be applied to his case with a high degree of precision. But however approximate these terms might be, they are an aid in characterizing the dominant type in each of these periods.

During Strindberg's paranoid period, struggle was the central concept in his thought. Wherever he looked, he saw battle—in literature, politics, and science, in the relations between friends and between married couples. He felt that he himself was constantly armed for a battle that had fronts on every side. His wakeful suspicions were as active during chance meetings with strangers as in the daily company of his wife. He was constantly engaged in sleuthing and analyzing clues, and he sought hidden causes behind the most banal happenings.

Apparent logic was as characteristic of the paranoid associations he made between events as was their lack of contact with reality. Now more than ever Strindberg prized his critical, restlessly working faculty of reason; he aimed at achieving a thoroughly rational world view. But at the same time, he often had the feeling—one to which he himself attested—that reality was eluding his net of deductions. In his battle with the feminists, in his long discussions of "persecution," and in *A Madman's Defense* one encounters the same phenomenon: Strindberg making a frenetic effort to prove something that finally, despite all his syllogisms, escapes him. He never quite reaches certainty; he whips himself on from one argument to another, without finding the final, decisive one.

His delusions of persecution, his extreme jealousy, and his consciousness of his own superiority are the most striking features of this attitude. These phenomena are closely allied. Strindberg thought he was being persecuted precisely because he was a superior being. At the same time, he depended on his "stronger brain" to nullify the attacks against him. All these motifs were concentrated in "the battle between the sexes." Strindberg feared that his wife was engaged in intrigues against him, and he counterattacked by adducing evidence of her culpability in past situations. "Jealousy" was part of the strategy in his battle for liberation. Here, too, it is apparent that the focal point of Strindberg's conflicts may be found in his erotic life.

External circumstances contributed to the development of Strindberg's paranoid attitude. During the first half of the 1880s, his situation changed radically. He became a well-known, respected author, but he was even more controversial than he had been at the end of the 1870s. This development reached its culmination in 1884 when he was tried for writing in *Married* that the Eucharist was "that infamous deception enacted with Högstedts Piccardon wine (at 65 öre the quart) and Lettström's corn cakes (at one crown the pound), which the priest maintained were the flesh and blood of that rabble-rouser, Jesus of Nazareth, who was executed 1800 years ago." This was too much for the authorities to bear. At the time he experienced fully the glamour as well as the terror of being the unchallenged cynosure of public attention. He later wrote to his theosophical friend and benefactor, Torsten Hedlund: "You know, during and especially after the *Married* trial, when the whole Swedish nation hated me, I felt as if I were part of a magnetic storm that sometimes pressed me down to the earth, sometimes gave me enormous power through its influence" (July 11, 1896). From then on, he was quite prepared to interpret all utterances and gestures, both in Sweden and in the rest of Europe, as directed against him personally, and he completely disregarded their real meaning. Any recognition that might come his way appeared to him to be due tribute to his greatness and importance; adverse criticism he equated with acts of revenge.

Furthermore, during the better part of this period, Strindberg chose to live abroad, mostly in Switzerland and France, where he felt freer and where, separated from his friends in Sweden and only sporadically aware of their activities through letters, he had no possibility of checking the facts and therefore could not make any realistic judgments about the great "Strindberg battle." This period of foreign residence may also have nourished his paranoid tendencies in another way. In foreign countries, Strindberg felt that he played "the foreigner's role of the man who is outlawed, the interloper who can expect nothing in another country, who barely receives simple justice" (*The Son of a Servant*). Despite his large vocabulary, particularly in French, he had trouble speaking foreign languages; consequently, his "tongue-tie" (aphasia) was an even greater handicap than it had been in Sweden. One of his favorite ideas at the end of the 1880s was that isolation leads to insanity, which is most likely to take the form of delusions of persecution. This opinion was not solely the product of his lucubrations, as one of his letters to the Norwegian writer Jonas Lie shows: "My isolation in Switzerland became corrosive; I thought I was being persecuted, and I spied treachery all around me—nothing but foes lying in wait for me" (April 30, 1885).

As Lamm maintains, however, the decisive factor in this development was the *Married* trial in 1884, and one must look to the circumstances of this case in order to find the deepest causes for Strindberg's change of attitude. When he was notified of the summons, he was seized by anxiety. It is well known that only through the intervention of his publisher, Karl Otto Bonnier, was he finally induced to appear in court. Raised against him was the hand of social authority threatening punishment. As one might expect, this menacing situation aroused the same feeling of terror that had informed all his earlier manifestations of defiance toward the authority of his father, of society, and of God. When he was caught breaking the law, his first impulse was to hide.

Whereas Strindberg had been in a happy and idyllic mood in 1883 while writing the first of his two collections of stories entitled *Married,* the indictment pronounced against him in 1884 fell upon an author who sensed his own culpability in the affair and felt that he had gone too far by speaking so openly about sexual matters and so boldly against religion. According to *The Son of a Servant,* after he had finished the first collection, he went to his wife "to be scolded" because he felt "so terribly contrite." He thereupon made her promise not to read the book. But a little further on he writes that she had already "forgiven" him for the first part of *Married.* In a letter to Jonas Lie before the trial he reveals: "I struck my own wife. It was a personal sacrifice that I had to make." [42] Only by referring to these events can one understand the following outburst in the otherwise studiedly cheerful *Embargo Journey* (1885), the book where Strindberg gives his own account of the indictment and trial: "I am suffering because I struck a blow. I suffer intensely, but I have no right to regret what I have done! It was the most important blow of all. It had to be. If only I had managed to avoid being the executioner—.

Forward, onward, over corpses and cries! That's the way it has to be! I did my duty, and yet! I was in the right, and yet!"

The ideas of demonism that Strindberg had resorted to during earlier crises once again took possession of him, as can be gathered from a few of the episodes he relates from the time of the trial. According to *Embargo Journey,* he was sought out in his hotel by a peculiar person, who in great agitation accused him of destroying his enemies by means of sympathetic magic. Although Strindberg received these accusations with apparent irony, he actually was deeply interested in them. Somewhat later, he sent a list of his dead enemies to Bonnier, adding that there were people who thought that he had "done them to death by means of magic." Similar ideas appear in the short story entitled "Shortcuts," based on an actual seance Strindberg had attended, in which his surrogate, Dr. Billgren, attends a strange spiritualistic seance at which different religious factions struggle over the possession of Strindberg-Billgren's soul. Behind this story can also be glimpsed "the Zeus head," Klemming, who was Strindberg's former superior at the Royal Library. Naturally, Strindberg exposes the whole seance as humbug in the story, but certainly he could not have been unmoved by the horrible prophecy concerning him that appears in the text—unless, of course, this quotation from the Book of Psalms was his own addition to the account of the seance: "Behold, he travaileth with iniquity, and hath conceived mischief, and brought forth falsehood" (Ps. 7:14).

Because he had used his wife as a model for some of the characters in the first part of *Married,* Strindberg's conscience was bothering him even before the trial. She was one of the people he had "wounded" or "struck." During the trial he was more or less consciously forced to revert to his old trajectory between ideas of anxiety, imagined guilt, and punishment, which had always been associated with the erotic sphere of his life. This reversion resulted in an increasingly fierce campaign against his wife, the stages of which are marked by the story "The Breadwinner" (in the second part of *Married*), by *The Father,* and by *A Madman's Defense.*

When his suspicions about his wife's infidelity were once again awakened, Strindberg characteristically returned to the ideas that he had nurtured during the stormy period just before his marriage. The first clearly paranoid manifestation of Strindberg's "jealousy" occurs in an episode in *A Madman's Defense,* based on events that took place during his stay in Grèz in 1885. Strindberg maintains that his "now famous monomania" first became fully evident at that time. In all probability, the chronology in *A Madman's Defense* is reliable on this point. A letter that he wrote to his friend Isidore Kjellberg, a newspaper editor, on October 1, 1885, appears to represent his first attempt to engage his circle of friends in his own investigations of Siri's infidelity. He had already read Ibsen's *The Wild Duck* during the trial, but at that time it had not reminded him of his own situation. In Grèz, however, he read it once again and discovered that it was about his marriage with Siri. In this play, he found indirect corroboration for his suspicions that Siri had become Wrangel's mistress after she ceased to be Baroness Wrangel, and he thought that he had also discovered proof that their first daughter, who died when she was two days old, had really been Wrangel's child. From many statements that Strindberg made at different periods in his life can be seen his eagerness to clear himself of all accusations of immorality in the Wrangel affair. The myth that he reads into his own life from *The Wild Duck* is designed to place him in a redeeming light, to make him appear the innocent victim of the evil designs of other people. If all this was true, Strindberg would be free of all obligations to Siri and of all responsibility for the death of the child who had been born a bit too soon after their wedding.

The psychological key to Strindberg's obsessive jealousy is to be found in the introduction to *A Madman's Defense,* where he tells of falling sick from "overexertion," growing weaker, and then appealing to the maternal side of Siri's nature because he burns "with the desire to relieve himself of his imagined guilt by means of a full confession." But his pangs of conscience also give rise to a desire to justify himself. Point by point, he enumerates the wrongs with which he has reproached himself, and he finds that they are unjustified. But he does not stop there—perhaps "a crime has been secretly committed in these mists, in which I have been moving like a shadow for years!" Thus, Strindberg postulates the existence of a transgression on Siri's part, because otherwise he himself would be the guilty one. "I shall die if I do not find out! Either a crime has been committed in the dark, or else I am insane. I have no choice but to bring the truth to light!"

By means of his defensive paranoia, Strindberg succeeded in bringing about everything that he had not already effected by his hysterical outburst and his attempts at flight. After he wrote *A Madman's Defense,* his marriage did move toward dissolution. One might wonder whether Strindberg entertained any suspicions about the legitimacy of his other children, or if he later retained the belief that his first wife had deceived him. There is nothing, so far as I know, to indicate that the suspicions he voices in *A Madman's Defense* survived the composition of that work. After the divorce, his paranoia had served its purpose and therefore became superfluous.

These ideas of jealousy are so closely allied with ideas of persecution that they would seem to have the same origin. Although Strindberg's delusions of persecution were directed mainly against his wife, whom he suspected of wanting to commit him to an institution, they also spilled over into the literary and political areas of his activity. The connecting link between these two emotions was the "league of women," which he suspected of conspiring with his wife to effect evil plots. Clearly, this league was at bottom only a multiple exposure of Siri and her friends in Strindberg's imagination. Strindberg could not in good conscience take action against Siri, unless he was convinced that she was persecuting him. The very word "defense" or "speech for the defense" (försvarstal) in the title of his book about their marriage suggests the degree to which he imagined that she was persecuting him. Indeed, Strindberg usually justified his literary attacks on people who were very close to him by arguing that he had acted only in self-defense.

It has often been pointed out, of course, that most of the people who aroused Strindberg's suspicion were those to whom he was in some way indebted. The intriguers who he imagined were conspiring against him were actually the very friends who were doing everything they could to help him. But the case is not always so simple;

that is, instead of being confined solely to his friends, his suspicions wandered aimlessly from one person to another, especially during the 1890s. The consistent factor in his reactions, however, was an unfailing connection between guilt feelings and ideas of persecution. Strindberg's need to feel that he was being persecuted arose only in situations in which he was also beset by feelings of remorse.

Time and again Strindberg asserts the existence of a psychological connection between feelings of remorse and indebtedness and delusions of persecution, but the connection was apparent to him only when he was evaluating other people. Thus, he exclaims in one of his early letters to his eldest brother, Axel: "Or is it your guilty conscience that makes you afraid to encounter your imagined enemies face to face!" (Dec. 24, 1876). In *A Madman's Defense,* he describes Siri's morbid fear of being poisoned, and he is quick to draw a conclusion: "What was it if not guilty conscience preying on her?" Her instincts of self-preservation, he continues, "force her to fabricate a story that then acquires the contours of reality, and this story finally shields her from her guilty conscience." He was unable to apply this insight to himself until the Inferno crisis had reached its final stage. Until then, he carried on a vigorous polemic against the idea that he himself was suffering from "delusions of persecution," even though he was able—in the midst of his period of greatest agitation—to give an exact diagnosis of the situation of a paranoid, as in the statement from a letter to Hedlund: "But if a person has committed a small crime and is afraid of the consequences, then this miserable wretch easily gets the idea that the person he has wronged is pursuing him. And if such is not the case, then he is suffering from 'persecution mania' and can finally end in a madhouse, which he instinctively seeks as a place of refuge. Or else he wants to annul the testimony of the person he has wronged by having him declared insane" (May 17, 1896).[43]

By the beginning of 1884—when Strindberg moved to Switzerland—his theistic notions had once again become a reality for him. "The Creator had popped up again for him in Switzerland; when confronted with the glorious specimen of Creation in which He manifested himself, he could find no other explanation" (*The Son of a Servant*). But the concept of God was inseparable from ethical demands; and from Italy he wrote to Jonas Lie: "No, no. During periods of mental anguish, one is simply not satisfied with protoplasm. And in my isolation in Ouchy I have fought out cruel battles within myself. The ethical—the sense of duty—creeps forth, and one advances toward his martyrdom" (March 11, 1884).

The "cruel battles" mentioned here are more fully described in the short story entitled "The German Lieutenant," which Strindberg wrote in April 1884. After Bleichroden, the German lieutenant in the story, has permitted the execution of some *francs-tireurs*, he is seized by a feeling of self-reproach, which finally leads to a mental breakdown; but when he abandons pessimistic philosophy in favor of Rousseau, he finds peace. Strindberg asserts in this story that the conscience is partly artificial, partly natural, and that one should obey only the voice of the natural conscience.[44] At the nondenominational religious service attended by Bleichroden, he learns about "Christianity's simple teachings: to love thy neighbor as thyself, to be patient and tolerant, and to forgive one's enemies." At this point Strindberg rejects the God of the Pentateuch, the avenger who punishes the children to the third and fourth generation. In other words, Parker, supported by Rousseau, has once again superseded Kierkegaard and the religion of Strindberg's childhood; Strindberg's "old" self has been vanquished by his "new" self.

This period of optimism forms the background of Strindberg's *Married* crisis and his subsequent conversion to atheism. For a while he believed that reconciliation with God was possible. He felt that he had extended his hand to seal a union with the world order and had asked his old enemies to forgive him. But the trial came as a rebuff, and it found a writer who had already grown accustomed to posing problems on the religious plane. His optimistic belief in God was associated with his own hope for reconciliation; when that hope failed, he hastily swung around to an attitude of enmity, suspicion, and atheism.

In *The Son of a Servant,* Strindberg gives an account of his conversion to atheism in the chapter entitled "He Becomes an Atheist." Here he associates his conversion with a stay at Luc sur Mer on the

French coast in July 1885, a dating of the experience that coincides with one that he gives in a letter to the sociologist and politician Gustaf Steffen (March 21, 1886). But he also mentions the "fantasy of God, which he has long since buried," since it had received "one blow after another" during the first half of the year 1885. This change of attitude is chronologically framed by the *Married* trial and by the first manifestations of his "obsessive jealousy" in August 1885.

Just as he was to do later during the Inferno crisis, Strindberg now used his crisis state as a means of capturing the imagination of the young. Most members of the new generation of writers were atheists or agnostics. As revealed in *The Son of a Servant,* Strindberg had by this time become acquainted with the work of Robert Ingersoll and with Tolstoi's *My Religion;* the latter work excited his particular admiration. Finally, he found "confirmation of his own ideas in a little story by a young Swedish writer who demonstrates—more by subjective groping than by objective proof—the inadequacy of the concept of God." He was referring to Oscar Levertin's story, "At the Eleventh Hour," which appeared in the collection entitled *Conflicts* (1885).

Although the first two of these "influences" ought to be seen in close connection with Strindberg's Parkerian optimism, Levertin's argument comes closer to Strindberg's real atheism, as described in *The Son of a Servant.* In Levertin's story, a sea captain named Hedenborg, who once got into a fight with a stranger in a foreign port, has lived ever since that experience under the pressure of feelings of remorse, for he supposes that he was responsible for another man's death. When he learns, after ten years of suffering, that his antagonist escaped unscathed from the adventure, the scales seem to fall from his eyes and he suddenly rejects his belief in God. He cannot believe in a merciful God who does not want to help man, but he does not want to believe in a despotic God who has no interest in helping man. Thus, Levertin formulates the classical objection to belief in the Christian God; that is, he shows that suffering in the world repudiates the idea of a God who is both omnipotent and wholly beneficent. In Strindberg's case, the argument is more crassly personal. When he saw his enemies fulminating against him during the *Married* trial and discovered that he was being treated unjustly, then "he slowly arrived at the notion that the world was governed by powers that are quite different from a loving, personal God." This change was characteristic of Strindberg. The problem of theodicy always occupied a central place in his religious speculations, but the evil he had in mind was primarily the evil to which he himself was subject. During the trial, his relation to God was a "personal acquaintance," a sort of contract; when he was disappointed, he broke the contract, terminated the acquaintance.

What Strindberg says about Levertin's atheism is also true of his own: it is a conviction arrived at mainly by means of subjective groping. He reveals that when he was in economic distress, he began to reflect on the question of whether or not he had been right in sacrificing his own and his family's security for the sake of his "idealistic" convictions. The answer was no, but how could he—given his upbringing and his disposition—have acted otherwise? "Thereupon he began to doubt the existence of a beneficent Providence, who directs everything for the best and who can alter human destiny." When he saw on every side of him people who were motivated by egoism, his doubt increased. He points to the partisan battles after the death of Victor Hugo and to the advance of reactionary literary and political forces in Scandinavia as examples of what he means by "egoistic motives." "From all of this confusion it gradually became clear to Johan that everything was really the product of the ego that simply had to be promoted, and in the course of a searching self-inquiry he came to the same result—although he was none too happy to admit it as long as all the others—the furies and the hangmen—maintained, and could actually lead other people to believe, that they acted out of love."

Only after he has reached this point in his moral self-examination does he look to Creation as a whole. Then he finds that development on the planet Tellus follows no apparent rational plan. But unlike other atheists or agnostics, he also turns against evolutionary optimism. In their idea that the world is changing for the better, he discerns a "liberal theology" and the remnant of the doctrine of dithe separation and approaching divorce, these defenses no longer had any function to perform. But for Strindberg, a change of attitude always implied a change of outlook as well. Thus, *By the Open Sea* is a work in which naturalism and the rational approach to life clash with strains of magic and religion. At this point, Strindberg partly returns to the romantic world picture he had cherished in his youth.

These features are not very striking. Strindberg himself seems to have been more or less unconscious of them. After finishing the novel, he described its theme in a letter to Ola Hansson: "The persecution of the strong individual by the Weak, who instinctively hate the Strong. Isolated, persecuted from above and below, his mind falters and goes to pieces bit by bit" (June 13, 1890). On the whole, this is exactly the way the book has been interpreted: a portrait of a Nietzschean struggle, tinged with tragedy. This interpretation appears to correspond to the novel that Strindberg wanted to write when he began *By the Open Sea,* the working title of which was "The Master." But the structure of the completed work—particularly in the later chapters—is considerably more complicated than the book he described to Hansson. Lamm is justified in calling it "one of Strindberg's most contradictory works." [47] Here I shall only indicate some of the motifs that conflict with the novel's programmatic support of positivism and of the idea of intellectual aristocracy.

At first, critics regarded *By the Open Sea* as the most conspicuous expression of Strindberg's "Nietzscheanism." But subsequent scholarship, particularly the work of Eklund, makes it clear that the ideology represented by Inspector Borg in *By the Open Sea* is essentially different from the philosophy of the mature Nietzsche. Even though the atmosphere occasionally recalls Nietzsche, it really derives from a positivistic and pessimistic outlook that is more likely to suggest Max Nordau and Schopenhauer. Nietzsche's philosophy certainly did not exert any profound influence on this work. Even as a human type, the novel's decadent hero is an intellectual aristocrat completely unlike Nietzsche's instinctively self-assured superman. The Nietzschean features here comprise colorful elements in a different kind of conceptual framework. [48]

Strindberg's outlook, however, contains one other element that has been more or less overlooked: Romantic Titanism. As earlier scholars have shown, the young Strindberg was enchanted by the examples of cosmic self-awareness that he found in the strong men of the *Sturm und Drang* and the Romantic movement, and he was deeply impressed by the defiant bearing that this feeling of self-awareness occasioned. By letting Inspector Borg struggle not only against human beings but also against nature, he dips back into the conceptual world of his youth. Borg's relation to nature expands into a titanic struggle, a superhuman feat. When Strindberg's hero is turned loose on nature with hoe and spade and transforms the barren skerry into an Italian cemetery, he feels that he is nature's enemy, "something of a Titan, who was assaulting Creation, correcting the Creator's crude scrawl, dislocating the axis of the earth so that the south moved slightly northward." But when the work is finished, terror breaks loose: his titanic revolt can also call down punishment on him, and the white gulls make him think of "the two black ravens that had come from heaven to bear his soul to hell." In various places—as in the description of Borg's navigation of the small boat in Chapter One, and in the section about the captive whistle bouy—one gets the impression that in his encounters with nature the inspector is facing half-personal forces, enemies with whom he must engage in combat.

From Nordau and Nietzsche, Strindberg sought the way back to a Romantic conception of the world. The work that exerted the strongest influence on his treatment of the titanic theme in *By the Open Sea* was clearly Victor Hugo's *Les travailleurs de la mer*. The theme of Hugo's novel is man's struggle against nature, which has all the earmarks of a personal test of strength. Hugo feels that man will reshape nature. "The world, the work of God, is the sketch from which man works." Gilliatt's struggle out on the cliff becomes titanic, acquires a hint of revolt and blasphemy. In one place, Hugo charges that man's power over nature approaches "impiety." He adds—using the same line of thought that Strindberg used in his description of the inspector's titanic struggle—that man's desire to be able to move the earth's axis and to create an eternal spring in the world is no more than a dream.[49]

The accents of terror and crime in the Titan theme emerge even more clearly in the short story entitled "The Silver Marsh," which is based on Strindberg's experiences from the summers of 1890 and 1891, both of which he spent on the island of Runmarö. The hero of the story is a "curator" (his Swedish title indicates that he is something like the curator of a museum) and a hunter, who fearlessly takes up the struggle against the marsh that has given rise to many folk superstitions. But the marsh proves to be guarded by "jealous powers," and the curator does not succeed in his undertaking. First, he has trouble finding his way to it. Only by turning his coat inside out—a practice which, according to folk belief, will aid people who are lost—does he manage to find the right road. The first time that he fishes in the marsh, unpleasant omens give him an uneasy feeling: a great black woodpecker cries shrilly, and a gust of wind causes his boat to lurch. The following summer, when the curator returns to the island alone, he unveils the secret of the marsh by first inspecting some inscriptions on a flat piece of rock that have apparently been made by lava: "CVII," he reads, and 107 is the atomic weight of silver. Despite the fact that there have been more and more mishaps on the island, he goes out with rock drills and dynamite to drain the marsh and discover its secret, but he is hindered by the fish. Finally, his idea that the marsh contains a wealth of silver dissolves like a mirage, and he leaves the island.[50]

The Hugoesque Titanism in *By the Open Sea* and "The Silver Marsh" links Strindberg's crisis religion of the 1870s with his Inferno crisis. In the novel, the concept of God appears only as a fleetingly glimpsed "empirical way of explaining things to his searching mind," but there is a straight line of development from Inspector Borg's titanic struggle on the skerry to Strindberg's own concept of himself during the Inferno years as Jacob struggling with God. A statement made by Strindberg in a letter to Leopold Littmansson in 1894—that is, before his genuinely religious development had begun—underscores the connection. Strindberg had experimented with thunder, not perhaps without thinking of Prometheus' theft of fire. This theme turns up in the second part of *To Damascus* (1898). Of the experiment, he writes to his friend: "Two years ago on the island of Dalarö, I put a lightning rod in a tree and had the conductor attached to my desk. I still have the report that I wrote up after a thunderstorm, when I stood with the wires in my hand and my watch on the desk! Jacob struggling with God!" (August 14, 1894).

Strindberg's consciousness that he was fighting against a stronger power gave his attitude of defiance a special coloring. During his period of struggle in the 1880s, he clung fairly consistently to the idea that the "Strong" must finally succumb to the "Weak," in sharp contrast to Nietzsche. If one wishes to find a literary counterpart to this tragic concept of the superman, one should perhaps choose Schopenhauer, whose notion of intellectual aristocracy is very similar to Strindberg's: "Every hero is a Samson: the strong man succumbs to the intrigues of the weak and the many: if he finally loses patience, he utterly crushes both them and himself; or else he is only a Gulliver among the Lilliputians who by dint of their enormous number ultimately overwhelm him in spite of everything." [51]

This is exactly what happens in *By the Open Sea* and "The Silver Marsh." The curator in the latter work leaves "his last visiting card at some sort of asylum," an outcome that clearly should be taken as the punishment he deserved for probing into nature's forbidden secrets. Inspector Borg likewise approaches mental destruction, but at the last minute he averts total defeat by committing suicide. The final chapter, which describes the inspector's degeneration, is among the most complicated and difficult passages in the entire body of Strindberg's work.

That both Nietzsche and Strindberg's friend, the Swedish painter Ernst Josephson, succumbed to mental illness around this time may have had something to do with the description of the inspector's total breakdown. Moreover, the impressions that Strindberg gathered from the psychological literature he was studying at the time may have contributed to this description of mental illness as well. [52] But experiences of a more personal nature also made their contribution. In the course of writing the novel, Strindberg became more and more prone to endow his hero with his own characteristics. The effeminate decadent presented in the first chapter is a variant of the type of personality that he considered ideal, but at the same time it differs in many respects from Strindberg's own personality. When the love episode begins, the inspector's character changes somewhat, and Strindberg lends him several of his own characteristics and past experiences; this change can be demonstrated in great detail.[53]

Nor can there be much doubt that Strindberg was thinking of himself when in the final chapters he described the inspector's "regression" or approaching insanity after he becomes totally isolated. The description is a projection of his own fears. Strindberg had long feared, at evenly spaced intervals, that he would lose his mind. During his fits of paranoia, he gained partial insight into the nature of his own sickness, as demonstrated by his continuous preoccupation with isolation and insanity. Finally, since his sojourn in Switzerland, he had been well aware of the fact that an isolated existence could lead to mental disorder.

The recluse was a type that Strindberg had already portrayed in some of the stories in *Life in the Archipelago* (1888). After returning to Sweden in 1889, he went out to the Stockholm archipelago, where he had the opportunity to study such isolated individuals in greater detail than before. The visit he made in 1889 to his old friend Ossian Ekbohrn, a chief customs surveyor at Sandhamn, provided him with psychological material that was particularly important for his portrayal of the inspector's breakdown. At the time of this visit, he had already begun to write *By the Open Sea*. In a letter from Sandhamn the same year, he informed his publisher, K. O. Bonnier, that he no longer had anything to do with Ekbohrn, who was "seriously neurotic." Shortly thereafter, he submitted the sixth chapter of the novel. Strindberg has discussed Ekbohrn's personality in both *Inferno* and an unpublished continuation of *Nemesis divina*. In the latter text he writes:

This man and his wife live together and see no other people. He is isolated as a result of his despotism and his persecution of the islanders, who hate him. He has not spoken for six months, and I was filled with pity when I found that my former enemy is now a shipwrecked man. He talks, talks—for five hours, ten hours, with froth on his lips and his brain afire. He has thought; he has philosophized; he has discovered many things that have already been discovered. I encourage him to trust me implicitly, and his outburst lasts for three days. His wife secretly confides in me that he is suffering from megalomania . . . You see! That's the trouble! He thinks he is Napoleon living in exile on St. Helena. He loves me, congratulates himself on having found an equal (hm!), honors me by confiding in me concerning his secret and sacred thoughts. I stand, humble and understanding, before his sweeping views of life and the universe.[54]

The winter of 1889–1890, after he had abandoned work on the novel, was a dismal time for Strindberg. He suffered because of his unproductiveness and was dogged by the economic worries that were to lead to the confiscation of his goods in March 1890. Whereas his tone had formerly been bitingly polemical in letters to Ola Hansson, a weaker, disillusioned—one is tempted to say "poetic"—accent begins to slip in here and there when he writes to him now. Just a few months after he completed *By the Open Sea,* he manifests the tired mood that was largely to dominate him during the first years of the 1890s: "Yes, dear friend, that's the way things are; and there is nothing I can do about it, because I am dead-tired and undone. I feel that the last stage of illusion has passed and that I have already entered upon *l'âge critique* of man that is supposed to begin around forty, when one sees through everything as if it were glass" (October 1, 1890).

At the same time, he thinks he can discern symptoms of mental illness in himself. He admits to Gustaf af Geijerstam that he is neurotic and adds an explanatory note: "agoraphobia, persecution complex, paralysis" (March 25, 1890). It is the same syndrome that one finds in the inspector, except for the fact that in the novel claustrophobia is substituted for agoraphobia.

Strindberg's feeling of emptiness probably stemmed primarily from the fact that he was on the point of losing his wife and children. His relations with Siri von Essen had been at the center of his enormously lively activity during the 1880s. His idealistic moods, as well as his paranoia, had been more or less directly inspired by the marriage. When the bond was broken, he was seized by a feeling of emptiness and desolation. During the period between his divorce from Siri and his marriage to Frida Uhl in 1893, he constantly sought new contacts, attempted to establish friendly or erotic relations with other women. It was not until the period during and after the Inferno crisis that he intermittently succeeded in replacing his need for human contact with an autistic relationship to God and with the ability to project himself into the lives of others by means of his imagination. The book entitled *Alone* (1903) gives ample evidence of the part that this sort of replacement was later to play in his life. Around 1890, isolation was still the most unbearable form of suffering he could imagine, because it produced a feeling of total emptiness.[55] Since a positive or negative relationship to his wife had been the most important cohesive bond in his entire intellectual and emotional existence, it seemed natural to him to let the inspector "be broken to pieces bit by bit" after Maria's departure has deprived him of all human contact.

This fear of isolation finds expression in a couple of the most powerful poetic themes in the novel. The inspector fertilizes an egg artificially in a watch glass and then observes its development under a microscope until "a movement of the adjustment mechanism caused the eggwhite to coagulate and the spark of life to go out." Later, when the inspector's mental degeneration is further advanced, he gathers up some dolls that have floated ashore from a wrecked steamer and fusses over them by the stove. According to Strindberg, the explanation for these peculiar actions lies in his "obsessive desire to have a child." The "reproductive instinct" has crept forth in the face of the desolation that accompanies the approach of death.

This emerges most clearly in a passage that Strindberg wrote a few weeks after he had finished the novel and which was inserted into the last chapter.[56] Borg is sick, and the preacher comes to visit him. The conversation that takes place between them seems to anticipate Strindberg's development during the Inferno crisis. The meaning of the passage can be gleaned from Strindberg's past experience, on which the scene is based. The kernel of the experience is something that happened to Strindberg himself in 1875 on the island of Dalarö, where he had gone in an attempt to flee from his love for Siri. At that time, religion presented itself as the alternative to love and friendship. As he wrote to C. G. Wrangel: "What is worst, but unavoidable—if I recover—we must part—I must be alone with

my God—You have been my idols—it is forbidden to have idols"
(Oct. 7, 1875).

Just before his divorce, Strindberg was tempted, as he had been
fifteen years before, to seek consolation in religion, that is, to find a
substitute for human relations (which for him were invariably accompanied by insoluble conflicts) by trying to establish relations
with God. Borg's first thought concerns the woman he has lost, for
"a woman is a man's roots in the earth." When he learns that she has
become engaged to his rival, he wants to hear the story about Tom
Thumb and the Lord. He does not believe in the Lord, he says, "but
the story will do him as much good as if he did. Anyway, when
death is approaching and one begins to regress, one loves old things
and becomes conservative." Since his separation from Maria, Borg
has become a powerless "mollusk" and has been possessed by a "horror vacui." He rejects Jesus, but feels that God would be able to restore his powers. God is a necessary scientific hypothesis, he says,
using a line of thought that is a variant of Spencer's ideas about "the
unknowable," but He is also a personal need:

The words, the old words, awaken memories and kindle powers, the
same powers that formerly strengthened the selfless person who sought
God outside himself. Do you know what God is? He is the fixed, external
point that Archimedes wished for and that would have enabled him to lift
the earth, if he could have used it for support. He is the imaginary magnet
inside the earth, without which the motion of the compass would remain
unexplained. He is the ether that must be invented in order to fill the vacu-
um. He is the molecule, without which the laws of chemistry would be mi-
raculous. Give me more hypotheses, especially the fixed point outside myself, for I am completely at sea.

In the novel about Fishery Inspector Borg, Strindberg reverts,
behind a mask of rationalistic worship of the superman, to thought
patterns that had been familiar to him in the 1870s. One glimpses
his religious problems in the background. But at the same time,
something new has appeared. Instead of seeking refuge primarily in
hysterical reactions, Strindberg now attempts to keep reality at a
distance by assuming an autistic posture. This is why one finds elements of dreamlike unreality in both the novel and "The Silver

Marsh." It also explains the visionary delusion that characterizes "The Romantic Sexton at Rånö," and finally, it enables one to understand why Strindberg frequently had the impression at the end of the 1880s that dream and reality coalesce.[57] This change can be regarded as a preparation for the Inferno crisis. Whereas dream and fantasy become increasingly real for Strindberg during these years, from now on he is almost constantly afraid of reality. The actual change occurred during his second marriage, before his paranoid and hysterical Inferno crises finally reactivated his underlying guilt complex and made him probe it once more.

T W O *The Inferno Psychoses*

The book *Inferno* opens shortly after Frida Uhl has left Paris to return to Austria and just at the moment that Strindberg thinks he has been restored to freedom. Although she does not appear as a character, Strindberg's relation to her, their correspondence, their separations, reconciliations, and divorce, all figure importantly in the book. Like the young Strindberg creating the heretical crisis religion, and like Borg in *By the Open Sea,* Strindberg finds himself torn between the woman he loves and his God.

The mother fixation that led to Strindberg's idealization of Siri and to his subsequent, guilt-laden disappointment provides a psychological explanation for the failure of his first marriage. But the pattern of events underlying the accusations in *A Madman's Defense* has no real counterpart in the second marriage. To be sure, Strindberg reveals in a letter to Frida in 1893 that he has "pretended—without knowing it—to be little, weak, so that you would be in a position to love me just as much in any case" (March 22, 1893). [1] But neither Strindberg's account of this marriage in "The Quarantine Master's Second Tale" (1902) nor Frida Strindberg's published letters give the impression that this attitude was dominant. Indeed, he

often played the older friend, the fatherly adviser, or the famous author in a way that was naturally out of the question when he met Siri
von Essen. Moreover, Frida Strindberg's presentation of the material
does not in any way suggest that Strindberg identified her with his
mother, much less that such an identification was a decisive factor in
their marriage. However, she does emphasize the role that a longing
for his mother played in Strindberg's relationship to his mother-in-
law whenever he stayed with her in Mondsee and Dornach. There he
relived the situation of his childhood home and subordinated himself like a child: "Mother has called!—What August Strindberg had
had to do without, what the child who lost his mother very early
had longed for during many painful years—he had found—a
mother had called him!" [2] This interpretation is quite in keeping
with the impression created by Strindberg's accounts of his encounters with Frida's family in such works as "The Quarantine Master's Second Tale," *Inferno* and *To Damascus,* where his alter ego ad-
justs easily to the strange family and he soon behaves like one of
their own children.

Like the tendency to identify his wife with his mother, jealousy
too was a less important factor in his second marriage. Karl Jaspers
has maintained that obsessive jealousy occurred only in the first marriage. Eklund has rightly objected to this argument, showing that
the letters to Frida Uhl and to his third wife, Harriet Bosse, prove
that Strindberg was capable of jealousy in his two later marriages. [3]
But the obsessive jealousy of his first marriage certainly seems to
have been a paranoid gesture of defense, a systematic attempt to cast
the blame on Siri. Energetic systematization was lacking in his relationship to Frida Uhl. Now and then his jealousy was aroused—
especially in a few accusing letters in the autumn of 1894—but these
statements impress one rather as routine admonitions than as obsessions and never acquired real weight. His accusations of wanton behavior were no less suitable now as arguments for his own liberation
than they had been in Siri's case, but this time liberation was much
easier to attain because the commitment had never been so deep. In
a letter to Richard Bergh, the painter, Strindberg writes: "I really do
not know very much about my marriage. We never took it very

seriously, as you may have noticed in Berlin, and it is probably heading toward dissolution—but I am not really certain" (Nov. 26, 1894).

From the very beginning, Strindberg was afraid of becoming dependent on Frida Uhl. In the early days of his marriage to Siri he had voluntarily isolated himself with her and curtailed all other social intercourse. Now, however, he deliberately endeavored to maintain contact with outsiders. He was tortured by isolation and sought to end it.[4] When this attempt failed, he took refuge in his work and shut himself up with his chemicals. The birth of their only child, Kerstin, served to dramatize this fear of dependency, for he purposely avoided becoming attached to the child in order not to be bound to Frida and her family. In a letter to his mother-in-law he writes: "So you expect me to become tied to the child by love first— in order to be torn to pieces later?"[5]

Quite early in his correspondence with Frida he expressed a determination to limit their relationship to an impersonal plane, and the skepticism that informed this determination was no doubt a result of the failure of his first marriage. In one of his first letters to her after their engagement in the Spring of 1893, he characterized love as "life's sweetest illusion, the divine lie that makes us happier than the most sublime truth can make us" (Feb. 26, 1893),[6] and a couple of months after the wedding when he had returned to Germany from their trip to England, leaving Frida behind to try to promote his works in London, he expressly warned against too great an intimacy: "I told you already in Gravesend: do not be too intimate! Do not go probing and poking about too much in the other person's soul; especially not when two souls as strong as ours have met" (July 23, 1893).[7] In August 1894, when he left Frida at her grandparents' estate in Dornach and went to Paris—the prelude to the final divorce— he was not fleeing so much from Frida personally as from the marital situation in general. According to "The Quarantine Master's Second Tale," it was a well-calculated maneuver designed to save his "independence": "Without any definite plan to abandon her, he persuaded her to remain. For a start he longed only to feel free."

Strindberg wished to keep his distance, and by and large he succeeded. Whereas in his first marriage he had discovered a method of "avenging" his own weakness on an innocent person, in his relations with Frida Uhl he first made extensive use of the technique of avoiding involvement, a sharper form of which was later to characterize his relations with humanity at large. On one page in "The Quarantine Master's Second Tale" Strindberg describes the vague, somehow unreal relationship that resulted from his new approach to married life. The important thing was never to dig into the past and never in the name of consistency to subject past statements to careful scrutiny: "Let it be new. All of life is still nothing more than a poem anyway, and it is much more pleasant to hover above the swamp than to stick one's feet down into it in an attempt to feel dry land, where there is none! " This explains all the sudden breaks and equally quick reconciliations that made the marriage seem somewhat desultory and elusive.

Consequently, Strindberg never really understood what sort of person Frida Uhl was. His portraits of Siri present a rather clear picture of her—be it true or false. But in Frida's case one gets no such picture, because Strindberg himself never had one—and never really wanted one. He constantly stressed her changeability, and in "The Quarantine Master's Second Tale" he writes: "For that reason they never found out about each other, so that at terribly serious moments they could both exclaim simultaneously: —Who are you? What are you, really? and both were unable to answer." In *Inferno* the divorce is correspondingly explained as the result of "an indefinable lack of agreement between our temperaments." [8]

Frida Uhl had the same impression. Strindberg's reactions often struck her as incomprehensible, as having no relation to reality. She also suspected the cause: she thought that Strindberg periodically identified her with his first wife and with his subjective image of woman in general. Theories and earlier experiences stood between them and served him as a shield against reality. "Sometimes Strindberg imagined us to be involved in situations that did not and could not obtain, but they existed for him—just as in his dramas. What would happen next is that he would say things to me that I had already read and was quite familiar with." [9] He thus suspected Frida of keeping his mail from him, just as he had believed of Siri or of "the league of women." [10] Frida Uhl was right when she spoke of the shadowy world "where memory, the present, and dream were fused into one." [11] In "The Quarantine Master's Second Tale" Strindberg places great weight on the fact that Frida Uhl read his book *A Madman's Defense.* Thereafter, he writes, "something fatal" entered their marriage. In the last analysis, perhaps the fatal element was not the fact that she had read the book, but the fact that he had written it and was constantly tempted to resort to an attitude similar to the one he had experimented with there.

Strindberg himself was aware of the power that the past held over his life. Time and again he expressed his disorientation in the present and referred to life as a dream. In June 1893 he wrote to his wife: "For me, everything, past and present, has been fused as in a dream, and life makes me seasick, even if the sea does not." [12] He also began to observe his nightly dreams in a different way and often related them in letters. Those dealing with Frida and their child are symbolic expressions of the same attitude that I have attempted to describe above. She is a stranger to him: appears with a black mask over her face, but also vaguely resembles Siri von Essen: "a tall lady, dressed in black." [13] Or, as he recounts in *The Occult Diary* (June 28, 1896), he sees her without teeth: a symbol of powerlessness that played a role in the first marriage. [14] When in another dream he sees the child "a year old, ugly, bloated with beer, and smoking cigarettes," [15] it is natural to think of the beer and tobacco orgies of which he accused Siri von Essen in *A Madman's Defense.*

Especially striking were Strindberg's neurotic tendency to repeat himself and the dreamlike arbitrariness that characterized the last stage of his second marriage. His leave-taking in October 1894 was cordial and was not regarded as final—at least not explicitly. Just after his departure they exchanged frequent letters. Those from Strindberg are filled with lyrical nostalgia and plans for reunion. But suddenly, about a month later, Strindberg wrote the letter full of bitter accusations that provided Frida Uhl with the grounds for divorce. Afterwards, he wrote that he felt "not pangs of conscience, only disgust and deep sorrow." [16] Then in December there were suggestions that Frida should come to Paris and that the marriage should continue, yet his tone was chilly: Strindberg dictated his "terms." In letters he wrote her after he was admitted to the Saint-Louis Hospital in January 1895 for a severe attack of psoriasis his tone softened once again, and he wanted to resume their former intimate contact: "Where are you living, where is little Kerstin (Lillan), what are you doing, and what do you hope for from this miserable life? " (Jan. 7, 1895) [17] But at the same time he explicitly rejected the thought of continuing their marriage; now, as "before," he had no right to be married. After a few renewed suggestions by letter that his wife come to Paris, he once again wrote a "farewell letter" in February 1895, milder than the first one: "Do not be my enemy! But just leave me in peace! Leave me in peace with my sorrows! " [18] In the spring of 1895 he often spoke of traveling to Dornach and once more seeing, if not his wife, at least his daughter. In May, Frida Uhl stopped writing, but for a long time Strindberg continued to send letters addressed to her mother and to their daughter, Kerstin.

Strindberg's correspondence with Frida Uhl was resumed on August 15, 1896, when he was invited to visit his daughter in Austria. According to *Inferno,* that letter "called him back to life." For a moment, Strindberg clearly believed in the possibility of resuming contact with Frida Uhl. These hopes were dashed during his stay in Austria, probably by the letter from Frida that he refers to in *The Occult Diary* on, September 28, 1896, with the single word "crash."

Not until this time, in other words, did Strindberg definitively surrender the idea of being reunited with his wife and child. During the greater part of the period treated in *Inferno* he counted upon reunion as a more or less distant possibility. He never took the divorce proceedings quite seriously; perhaps one can say that he regarded them as natural developments in the marital cold war. He could not imagine that he could ever completely lose the intimate relationship to a person with whom he had shared his life and his thoughts. The child unites the parents, he writes in a letter: "We shall never cease to be related! You and I! " [19] It appears from his letters that Strindberg hardly took notice of his wife's wishes and intentions. His ideas of what the future would be like are all based on his own plans, his own longing for—or revulsion from—marriage. That is why in the late summer of 1896, nearly a year and a half after they had stopped writing to each other, and despite all the bitter accusations and the divorce trial then going on, Strindberg could imagine that Frida Uhl was still waiting for him.

Strindberg's tendency toward autistic experience erected a wall between him and his wife while they were living together and made his second marriage in some ways less consequential than the first. It explains, moreover, why Frida Uhl's personality came to play such an important role for him during the Inferno period after their physical separation had become permanent. During his period of spiritual readjustment Strindberg was haunted by thoughts of his absent wife and child, by longings, self-reproach, and fear of marriage. Only from a distance could he really take possession of Frida and reshape her into a symbol for woman in general, transform her into the Lady in *To Damascus:* "It is peculiar, but I would also rather think of you as impersonal, nameless—indeed, I only half know what your name is now—I would like to name you myself—let me think what you should be called! Ah yes, you shall be called 'Eve.' "

During the time immediately preceding the crises Strindberg was in extremely straitened circumstances. Ever since the *Married* trial in 1884 he had been struggling against economic troubles. In 1892 in Berlin he was already being supported by friends and patrons, and when Frida Uhl's dowry ran out toward the end of 1893, the newly married couple was forced to depend on the charity of Frida's mother's parents and to stay with them at Dornach. A short time after they went to Paris in August 1894, their resources were totally exhausted. In January 1895, Strindberg finally gave up all attempts to extract money from his publishers or from theaters, as he wrote to Littmansson on Jan. 9, 1895: "To spare myself the mortification of disappointments I am setting myself up as a mendicant friar and am letting all remunerations and authorizations go to hell."

Through the efforts of the Swedish church in Paris, he was admitted to the Saint-Louis Hospital on January 11, where he remained until the beginning of February. In the beginning of March an appeal for support for Strindberg was sent out to "the poet's Scandinavian countrymen," signed by such well-known Norwegian writers as Jonas Lie and Knut Hamsun. In a letter to Lie (published in Frida Strindberg's book [20]) Hamsun explains how the appeal worked: one was to send money directly to Strindberg instead of letting it be conveyed to him by the committee. Strindberg is clearly thinking of these gifts in *Inferno* when he describes the summer and autumn of 1895 as one of "the happiest interludes" in his life: "Money comes to me of itself. I can buy books, natural history specimens, and best of all, a microscope that reveals the secrets of life to me." [21] But these sources eventually ran dry. In October 1895, Strindberg resumed his correspondence with Torsten Hedlund, the wealthy theosophist whom he had ceased writing to the previous year, and complained of lack of money. As a result, Hedlund sent him funds for the next two months and declared that he would later be willing to finance the publication of *Jardin des Plantes* (1896). Another break with Hedlund in December left him once more without resources, but in January they renewed their connections, and Hedlund promised to send him 150 crowns a month. [22] Strindberg probably received other contributions as well.

Thus, during the whole time that elapsed between Frida Uhl's departure in October 1894 and the great crises at the Hôtel Orfila in July 1896, Strindberg lived almost exclusively on gifts and benefactions. There can hardly be any doubt that during this period he was most obligated to the good will of others. There is much to suggest that he found the situation oppressive. For example, his jestingly arrogant tone in the letter to Littmansson (Jan. 9, 1895) openly conflicts with an episode in *Inferno* that bears witness to Strindberg's difficulty in accepting the role of "beggar" or "mendicant friar." While an out-patient at the hospital, he met a member of the Swedish colony on one of the boulevards: "And I feel in my bones that this man is one of my anonymous benefactors, that he has given me an alms and that I am a beggar, who has no right to go to cafés. A beggar! Yes, that is the word for it. It rings in my ears and sends a burning blush to my cheeks—the blush of shame, humiliation, and rage!" (*Inferno*). [23] From time to time he clearly feared total degradation. Shortly before his departure for Paris, the thought already haunted him: "I am looking for Lundin [a former officer who now lived as a beggar in Paris] and he will initiate me!—initiate me into the secrets of the trade. Down, down, down! Rest, rest, perturbed spirit. Rest!" (Aug. 13, 1894).[24] Such was his tone in 1894 when he was still able to sustain the gallows humor that generally characterized his correspondence with Littmansson. But later, as he came closer to suffering the same fate as his derelict friend Jean Lundin, such degradation began to lose its appeal as a subject for grim jesting. One day in May 1896 when he was about to take an absinth at the Brasserie des Lilas, a drunkard passed his table and fixed his gaze on Strindberg, who thereupon became disgusted with his drink and felt "glad that he did not look like this sot." [25] Behind this brief account one senses a secret anxiety, which shortly after the drunkard had passed, expressed itself openly when Strindberg threw out the contents of his glass.

This was only one of several mishaps that plagued Strindberg when he was about to take an apéritif. Another time flakes of soot fell into his glass; a third time he was tormented by the people sitting around him, one of whom laid a sou on his table in the belief that it was his. Strindberg's reaction was violent: "He gives me a sou, as if I were a beggar! A beggar! That is the dagger that I plunge into my breast. Beggar! Yes, because you earn nothing and you . . . ." (*Inferno*).[26] When he wrote *Inferno*, Strindberg interpreted this series of events as a providential warning, the work of "good spirits," intended to save him "from a vice that leads to the madhouse." [27] Psychologically, the drunken man, the soot, and the other disturbances appear to be projections of Strindberg's own fear of alcohol. As a matter of fact, this fear had become apparent even before the intervention of "spirits." In letters to Frida Uhl just after leaving Paris, he already speaks of "bad company, alcohol, *chat noir,* despair, and so forth—above all, paralysis, sleepless nights." "The tavern," he writes apologetically, saves him from suicide. (Nov. 4, 1894).[28] Later on, this theme comes up repeatedly, especially when he writes to "Mutter," his mother-in-law in Austria. "And without woman and home I am ruined! Doomed to drink!" (Feb. 16, 1897).[29]

The complex of notions connected with the "beggar-drinker" became particularly threatening to Strindberg at just this difficult moment because they coincided with his inability to support the children from his first marriage. According to his daughter, Karin Smirnoff, he owed them seventeen months' support in January 1895; by 1897 he was three years behind in the payments.[30] In other words, during the Inferno period he had only been able to pay a third at most of the amount required of him by the divorce settlement. Most of the people who knew him well bear witness to the fact that anxiety for his children played a great role in his life during these years. In her book, Frida Uhl repeatedly stresses the fact that the fate of his children weighed heavily on Strindberg's conscience.

Between 1894 and 1896 Strindberg experienced five distinct, acute psychotic states: July–August 1894, December–January 1894–1895, December–January 1895–1896, June–July 1896, and November 1896.[31] In large measure, they all followed the same pattern: an initial period of general anxiety, a feeling of sickness and fantasies of suicide and persecution; then a violent break with his surroundings and flight to a new abode, after which the crisis gradually subsided. In several cases, heightened productivity accompanied his psychotic outbursts, a concomitant feature of which was marked changes in Strindberg's outlook or interests. These five crises comprise the rhythmic pattern that underlay Strindberg's conversion.

On July 22, 1894, Strindberg wrote Leopold Littmansson an exultant letter from Dornach, where he and Frida were staying with her grandparents: "I do not know what fate now holds in store for me, but I feel that 'the Lord's hand' is poised above me. A change is in the offing—upward, or straight down to the center of the earth—who knows about such things?" he writes. Frida Uhl, describing "the dog days" that year, reports that Strindberg isolated himself with his chemical research in the upstairs of "das Häusel," a cottage on the Dornach estate to which Strindberg and Frida had moved early in 1894 after a quarrel with Judge Reischl, her grandfather. Strindberg complained of pains in his throat, and a doctor was summoned, who departed in terror after a tête-à-tête with

Strindberg.[32] Strindberg felt that he was being mistreated by his wife, whom he suspected of spying on him and intercepting his mail. He also prepared a solution of potassium cyanide with the determination to take his own life. "I shall probably either be murdered or be the victim of suicide! We'll see which!" he wrote to Littmansson on August 14, 1894. Shortly thereafter, he left for Paris, where the crisis gradually subsided.

Less is known about this crisis than any of the others because of the fragmentary nature of the source material, which does not provide sufficient information even to establish a precise chronology of the external events during his attack. The same is true of the interior, psychological context: one is partly dependent on guesswork. It is clear that Strindberg wanted to free himself from his situation in Dornach, which he regarded as "impure." No women, he proclaimed in an undated letter to Littmansson in 1894: "Suffering is sublime! Isolation is pure." However, it is apparent that by this time his psychosis had already transcended his actual situation and become attached to past experiences: "There are moments when memories of the unpleasantness I have experienced accumulate in me as in a storage battery and then the tension is so great that I think I will burst, but I do not," he wrote to Littmansson on August 14, 1894. Shortly before he made this statement, something had happened to revive Strindberg's memories of an earlier traumatic experience, the *Married* trial of 1884: this time he had been summoned to Berlin to face trial for *A Madman's Defense,* and he refused to go.[33]

The next psychotic state manifested itself in the beginning of December 1894. At this point Strindberg severed relations with two of his friends, the wealthy young publisher Albert Langen and his mysterious friend Willy Grétor, whom he suspected of being involved in a scandal concerning a forged painting that had aroused attention in Paris. On December 14, after the Paris première of *The Father,* Strindberg sent his apologies to Aurélien Lugné-Poe, the founder of the Théâtre l'Œuvre, who had invited him to attend: "I beg you to think of me as being sick, and—believe me—I have substantial reasons for seeking solitude." [34] Dating from the same time is the episode in *Inferno* in which he describes being "assailed" by coquettes and students on his way home from a party, who taunted him until he fled "scourged by the Eumenides." [35] In *Inferno* he describes his general condition as follows: "An incipient decrepitude gradually engulfs me. My black and bleeding hands prevent me from taking pains with my appearance when I dress myself. The fear of receiving my hotel bill robs me of all peace of mind, and I pace back and forth in my room like a wild animal in its cage." [36]

Now, as during the previous crisis, Strindberg entered a psychotic state characterized by premonitions of death and acute persecution feelings. On the day that he was admitted to the Saint-Louis Hospital in a state of nervous collapse with cracked and bleeding hands (Jan. 11, 1895), he sent a letter to Littmansson in which he described his premonitions of death: "I don't know, but lately things have been so ghastly for me that I have been living 'devant la mort' with a decided presentiment of the end, or is it the end?" The crisis seems to have reached its peak at Christmas time in 1894. In *Inferno* he reports only that he "slept badly": he felt a stream of cold air brushing across his face, and was awakened by the sound of a mouth organ. But a postcard sent to Littmansson suggests that he also thought someone had been trying to murder him: "—there was a devil here who wanted to murder me—so that the innkeeper and I had to barricade the door when the murderer tried to force his way in" (Dec. 25, 1894). Taken together, all the characteristics of this crisis in December–January 1894–1895 indicate that it was a prelude to his much more impressive attack in 1896. After Strindberg moved from his hotel to the Saint-Louis Hospital, his second crisis subsided.

The cause of this crisis is apparent. In the autumn of 1894 Siri Strindberg had commissioned her lawyer to appeal to Frida's father, Councilor Friedrich Uhl, to pay the 2100 crowns that Strindberg then owed her for the support of their children. [37] One can imagine Strindberg's anger, shame, and humiliation when he found out (sometime in November) what she had done. His first reaction was the "farewell letter" to Frida, in which the connection with Siri's appeal is especially evident when he writes: "I am being treated like a beggar, worse than rabble, and to such an extent that my children have cursed me." [38] The farewell letter is a typical Strindberg gesture of moral self-defense. His guilt feelings concerning the children from his first marriage occasion a series of accusations against his second wife. In the letter, Strindberg lays particular stress on the fact that he wants "to defend his honor and be avenged." In passing, he also accuses Frida of having ruined his business affairs. These accusations were obviously ridiculous; indeed, for some time while Strindberg himself was neglecting his business contacts, Frida Uhl had been doing her best to put their economy in order. Of course, his intention was to shift the burden of his own guilt onto her shoulders and thus to exculpate himself. Also, one is struck by the stereotyped and repetitious nature of these accusations. His indictment of Frida rests on roughly the same points as his case against Siri in *A Madman's Defense,* and Strindberg has not even bothered to adapt his accusations to the conditions of his second marriage. What frightened Frida Uhl above all else was his neurotic compulsiveness. "This time I cannot escape from his past; he has loosed it against me." [39] In several subsequent letters he assures her that he feels no compunctions about the way he has treated her. But in *Inferno* he speaks of "a frenzied desire to do myself harm," characterizes himself as a "suicide and an assassin," and talks of "pangs of conscience." [40] Consequently, it is extremely difficult to determine the extent to which Strindberg was consciously tormented by remorse during this crisis. The fact remains, however, that first through negligence, then through negative action, he had broken with both of his families. That this situation induced powerful guilt feelings is obvious.

The superficial cause that precipitated the crisis was an unpaid hotel bill. Naturally, one must take into account the possibility that when he approached a crisis, Strindberg more or less intentionally neglected to exploit possible sources of assistance. According to *Inferno,* his financial worries became acute just before Christmas. His persecution mania also manifested itself at Christmas time. Strindberg reacted hysterically to his situation: he shut himself up in his room, exaggerated the seriousness of the skin trouble that caused his hands to bleed, was finally taken in hand and sent to the Saint-Louis Hospital.

The Mother Superior at the hospital, whom Strindberg transformed into a surrogate for his mother, played a decisive role in his convalescence. "How wonderful it is to pronounce the word 'mother,' which has not crossed my lips in thirty years!" (*Inferno*). In a letter to Frida Uhl, he calls the nun "my mother" (Jan. 15, 1895).[41] Just as in childhood, the mother figure became the redeemer of his guilt: "Not a single word of reproach, no exhortations or sermons" (*Inferno*).[42]

His next attack occurred a year later, in December–January 1895–1896. The course of this crisis can best be charted by an analysis of his correspondence with Torsten Hedlund, who was by this time Strindberg's chief confidant. In the middle of November, Strindberg's letters are full of complaints about the proprietors of his hotel and "the evil ones," who are persecuting him; one letter ends with a cry for help: "Seek aid for me; otherwise I am lost" (undated). On November 22 he says that he feels someone is "tampering with" his destiny. At the beginning of December he breaks with Hedlund in an agitated letter, similar in tone to the violent indictments he was to hurl at him at the time of their final break six months later. Shortly thereafter, he gives instructions to Hedlund about dealing with his posthumous papers—"in case anything should happen to me" (undated). Their correspondence is discontinued for a month. During that time Strindberg believed, as reported in *Inferno*, that he was being purposely disturbed by noise and piano playing in the adjacent rooms at the hotel. "I think it probable that it is part of a plot, set in motion by those Scandinavian women from whose company I withdrew."[43] When the correspondence with Hedlund resumes on January 24, 1896, he expresses his agitation even more intensely; he speaks of "maenads" threatening Orpheus: "What is happening now is ghastly, but I suppose that is the way things have to be." Finally he fled, "abandoning his books and other personal effects" (*Inferno*),[44] and moved into the Hôtel Orfila on February 21, 1896. This move was followed by a calmer period that extended through the spring of 1896.

Strindberg had resumed his intimate correspondence with Hedlund on October 30, 1895, which in itself is a sign that his mental tension was already on the increase. In strongly affective language he speaks of "isolation," using the word primarily, as in *Inferno,* to mean not absolute isolation, but separation from his wife and child, a bachelor's solitude. His mode of expression recalls his "Buddhistic" letters to Littmansson in the previous year, but the tone is more agitated, and he singles out marriage as "the sin" that supersedes all others: "I have been bound with blonde ropes and black braids, with the rosy arms of children, but I have cut all the bonds until the blood ran. Only let my temptations cease! My isolation is dreadful and my suffering unspeakable, but I would rather burn up than return to sin, sanctified or not!"

In the following letter, written on November 10, sexuality is even more clearly identified as the actual source of "impurity." After some expository remarks about the "instinctive villainy" of women, he remarks:

They are sweet illusions, Lord, sweet—too sweet. But shall I never learn to stifle my flesh? It is still too young and burning, but then let it burn up! And it no doubt will! But my spirit! perhaps it too will be consumed!—

I shall never recover from this!—For me, a life of celibacy is partly filthy. Family life is the most beautiful thing—but!! but! even filthier, when one pokes into it! Outside it—absolute degradation and there one encounters the beast.

In these letters his sexual fear accompanies his hatred of women, leading to the conclusion: no more erotic relationships ever again, and no continuation of marital life. His treatment of the same material in *Inferno* gives another picture of the matter. Here, too, the theme of guilt occupies the foreground, but it takes an entirely different form. Sometime during the autumn of 1895 Strindberg is supposed to have perfomed certain magical operations on the portrait of his daughter Kerstin to make her fall ill. He hoped that her illness would provide him with the opportunity of being reunited with his family. According to *Inferno,* this was his "fall," and it gained him "the displeasures of the powers," which finally found expression in the terrible feelings of persecution to which he was subject while living on the Rue de la grande Chaumière in December and January 1895.

In view of the significant changes he made in the material, one might wonder if his account of the incident in *Inferno* adheres to the facts. One can tell from his mode of expression that at the time he wrote it, Strindberg was still extremely eager to prove that his "evil intention" was not fundamentally evil after all. His manipulations with the portrait were "an outburst of misguided love," an attempt to bring about a "catastrophe that could reunite two hearts, the way it happens in novels, where inimical hands meet over a sickbed." [45] If one bears in mind that Strindberg had always regarded Kerstin as the most important of the "bonds" from which he must free himself, and if one connects that attitude with his remarks to Hedlund about the "rosy arms of children" and the "bonds" he had cut so that "the blood ran," then his "magical" action seems all the more ambiguous. It is possible that Strindberg intended to do real harm to his daughter as a symbolic expression of his hatred of marriage.

During the course of 1895 Strindberg had also tried other means of liberating himself from his wife and child. Referring to the spring of 1895, he writes in *Inferno:* "Meanwhile—and in order to sever a fatal bond, I seek the opportunity to transfer my need for tenderness to another object, and my dishonorable wishes are immediately granted." [46] The woman he met at that time, an English sculptress known as Madame (or Mlle) Lecain, obviously made a powerful impression on him. He thought of her as a hetaera and Madonna combined in one person. In a subsequent entry in his diary he calls her "the beautiful sinner," but he also says that she made "a warmly maternal impression, so that at Mme. Charlotte's milk bar [his favorite restaurant] I often wished I were under her beautiful warm woolen coat, as in a mother's womb. But Gauguin says she is a demon and that she devours men." According to *Inferno,* Strindberg saw her several times; but external circumstances finally precipitated a break between them: "No more love! I have received a sign from the powers." [47] Actually, they did not part as abruptly as Strindberg's confessions lead one to believe. In May 1896 they met once again, and Strindberg noted in his diary: "She was *charmante.*"

Against this background, the statements in Strindberg's letters to Hedlund become completely comprehensible. The phrase "sin, sanctified or not" refers to Strindberg's situation poised between two potentially erotic relationships, one legitimate, the other illicit. He wished to solve the problem by renouncing both of them and "stifling his flesh." His guilt feelings kept watch on him from both directions: "Extremely poor, with unpaid debts to my wife and my child, I had wished to initiate a liaison that would dishonor a blameless girl of good family." [48] These motifs are easily recognizable. Behind the "unpaid debts" to Frida and Kerstin (which he need not have taken so seriously, since they were in no danger of suffering from lack of money) one glimpses his neglect of the children from his first marriage. Nor is it surprising that now "the beautiful sinner" suddenly appears as a "blameless" example of domestic virtue and filial piety, for here one witnesses the same oscillation between the "Madonna" and the "whore" that is a standard feature of Strindberg's erotic experience. Other observations he has recorded during this period point in the same direction: The woman's (or child's) hands that he thought he saw in the embryo of the walnut he was studying under his microscope made a very strong impression on him, because he took them to be a reminder of his guilt and an exhortation to be "pure" (*Inferno*). Similarly, the young woman whom he observed during the autumn of 1895 in the Montparnasse cemetery and whom he describes in the essay "In the Cemetery" led his thoughts to the sorrowing Frida Uhl, who he imagined was waiting for him, and thus became a palpable symbol for his own transgressions. [49]

This time, too, lack of money was the external factor that caused the crisis to break out into a persecution mania. On November 11, Strindberg sent Hedlund a plea for help, and in the beginning of December appeared the first signs that the crisis had entered an acute phase. The connection between his poverty and his anxiety is indicated in *Inferno*. Immediately before his brief account of the plots of "Scandinavian women," Strindberg mentions "the hotel bill and an accompanying letter." This unexpected blow caused him to "notice trifles that I had previously ignored." [50]

After he moved into the Hôtel Orfila, the crisis subsided. Besides the beneficial effects of a change of milieu—such changes nearly always served to relieve Strindberg's anxiety—another factor contributed to his recovery. At the Hôtel Orfila he met a German-American painter, "Hermann," [51] in whom he found an intimate friend whose unlucky fate seemed to him to resemble his own. For two months Strindberg "melted down" his own existence into this man's, read his own situation into the other's, and identified himself with his friend, so that his own misfortunes seemed easier to bear. Like Strindberg, the painter could not sit in a café without becoming the object of outrages, and his persecution too seemed to be edifying in a mysterious way, as Strindberg explained to Hedlund on May 15, 1896. Strindberg's attitude toward this young man was identical to the one he would later assume toward his young "adepts" in Lund in 1897. In both cases, Strindberg was able to alleviate the pressure on himself by fabricating destinies for other men, so that they appeared to be suffering from the same cruel fate as his. And in both cases he was able to project his own suffering into the lives of those whose situations did not materially correspond to his own.

The three crises dealt with so far are interrelated. They are comparatively poor in motifs and enacted primarily in the present, where the psychosis comprises a simple, direct answer to a situation that seemed unbearable to Strindberg. This is particularly true of the first and second crises. From this point of view, the third crisis is already "richer," for here a more extensive flora of symbols has begun to bloom around the fundamental mechanism, which is converting the pattern of guilt feelings into a persecution mania. This time, moreover, the crisis introduces some material that is more central to Strindberg's basic problem and which places greater emphasis on his guilt feelings. In other words, one can say that Strindberg began to come to terms with his "guilt" in December–January 1895–1896. In his correspondence with Hedlund it appears that he is attracted to a religious and moralistic interpretation of events after October 1895. But a really distinct change did not occur until sometime early in 1896 in connection with his move to the Hôtel Orfila, when the third crisis had begun to subside. As soon as Strindberg began to inquire into the "intentions" or the "purpose" of his "visitations," he began to take an active interest in his psychotic experiences. One indication of this interest is the famous "occult" diary that he began to keep after moving to the Hôtel Orfila and the simultaneous burgeoning of his confidential correspondence with Hedlund. From then on he paid close attention to his experiences for purposes that he reveals in a letter to Hedlund on May 15, 1896: "I observe, make notes, and wait! 'There is something behind it all'—that's all I know." Nor, one might add, did he simply keep an account of his dreams and observations; he also reworked them, treated them as a writer treats his material, went back to earlier experiences and fused them with new ones. In so doing, he brought to light the neurotic world of symbols that was to form the basis of his post-*Inferno* production. For that reason, the fourth and fifth crises are both thematically richer and decidedly more retrospective than the first three.

The central *Inferno* psychosis is the fourth crisis. The first unmistakable sign that Strindberg's anxieties had once again been aroused appeared on May 14, 1896, when he had a dream that he relates in *Inferno*: "A severed head had been attached to a man's body, and he looked like a drunken actor. The head began to speak; I was terrified and knocked over my folding screen in trying to push a Russian in front of me to protect myself against the furious man's attack." [52] The dream clearly expresses Strindberg's terror of "Popoffsky," his name in *Inferno* for Stanislas Przybyszewski, whom Edvard Munch had once painted with a severed head. At the end of the month, Strindberg drew strange conclusions about the letters arriving at the Hôtel Orfila. On May 26, he made peculiar observations in his diary concerning a "Dr. Bitter," and on June 9 he made similar notations about a "Schmulachowsky." In *Inferno* he says that the first of these mysterious letters to arrive at the hotel was one addressed to a certain "Student Uhl" and postmarked Dornach, where he knew there was no post office, but this episode actually belongs to the preceding period of anxiety. In a letter to Hedlund dated June 26, 1896, he uses the same expression he had used before: "Someone is tampering with my destiny." By July 13, his sense of premonition had grown sharper. Now he writes that he "is approaching the end with fatal consistency." On July 17, he informs Hedlund that he has stopped frequenting his usual eating place. The severe attack came on the 19th, when he at first felt as if he were paralyzed and believed himself to be the victim of "gas poisoning." That night he thought he was being subjected to an electric current, passing between the two rooms flanking his (*Inferno*).[53] After Strindberg left the Hôtel Orfila (on July 19, according to *The Occult Diary*) and moved to the Rue de la Clef, the attacks continued for the next few days, accompanied by sensations of suffocation, perceptions of noise, fear of paralysis, and fantasies that someone was trying to murder him with electrical currents. On the 24th he went to Dieppe and stayed with the Norwegian painter Fritz Thaulow, but according to *The Occult Diary,* his anxiety returned on the 25th. On the 27th he fled to Ystad in southern Sweden, where fresh though somewhat less virulent attacks awaited him. The most violent occurred on August 10. The crisis thus reached its peak between July 19 and August 10.

This psychosis was essentially concentrated around Strindberg's fear of the person referred to in *Inferno* as Popoffsky. According to Strindberg's description of his attacks in *Inferno,* his friend's favorite piano piece, Schumann's "Aufschwung," always serves as a sort of prelude to what is to come, and each bulletin about Popoffsky's desperate situation in Berlin further stimulates Strindberg's anxiety. Finally, the acute psychosis at the Hôtel Orfila, in the Rue de la Clef, and at Dieppe is dominated by fear of Popoffsky and "his friends." Strindberg's diary and his correspondence indicate that his presentation of this point in *Inferno* is quite true to the facts.

Popoffsky's counterpart in real life was the Polish writer Stanislas Przybyszewski. During the days when Strindberg frequented the Zum Schwarzen Ferkel café in Berlin in 1892–1893, Przybyszewski was a member of the triumvirate of gifted young men who were closest to him. Przybyszewski ran errands for Strindberg and respectfully listened to his pronouncements. The other two disciples were Bengt Lidforss and Adolf Paul. All three of these men broke with Strindberg. In the case of Lidforss and Przybyszewski, Strindberg took the initiative and precipitated the break. His psychological reason for doing so is not difficult to discern. The circle had been broken by the entrance of a young woman, Dagny Juel, who in Strindberg's correspondence is called Aspasia, and in "The Quarantine Master's Second Tale" is called Lais. It is difficult to determine the exact nature of her relations with Strindberg or even to say who took the initiative in their brief flirtation during March 1893, because the episode generated so much emotion in all the people involved in the intrigues that issued from the liaison that no one's account of it seems trustworthy.

One thing is clear: Strindberg withdrew from the game immediately and thereafter regarded "Aspasia" with hatred. If she did entice him into a sexual relationship, thereby causing him to be unfaithful to Frida Uhl, then according to the demands of his particular logic, Strindberg would have to be "avenged" for the injury. The opportunity for vengeance in fact came somewhat later, when Lidforss got into financial difficulties. Strindberg wrote to his friend and biographer, Birger Mörner, in Lund and asked him to arrange for Lidforss to be summoned back to Lund University for the commencement exercises and suggested that "Aspasia's" family should rescue her from a life of sin in the German capital. So much for Lidforss, who was naturally not pleased by that sort of benevolence. Instead of accompanying Lidforss back to Sweden, however, "Aspasia" remained in Berlin and married Przybyszewski. As a result of this marriage, Strindberg focused his hatred on the Pole, who had formerly been his favorite disciple.[54]

All of the evidence suggests that this erotic situation was the catalyst that precipitated Strindberg's violent emotional reaction. He began to hate Lidforss and Przybyszewski, mostly because of their connection with "Aspasia." Strindberg thought Przybyszewski hated him because, like Munch and Lidforss, he had been "Aspasia's" lover before her marriage. But when he remarks in the same breath that the Pole showed exaggerated tolerance for his wife's former friends (even allowing one of her admirers to be a regular visitor in their house), one is strongly tempted to conclude that this "enmity" was largely the product of Strindberg's own attempts to rationalize his situation. In other words, everything seems to indicate that his persecution feelings emanated not—as Strindberg believed—from

Przybyszewski's hatred, but from the guilt that had developed within Strindberg himself as a result of his sexual relations with "Aspasia" in March 1893.

In May 1896, Przybyszewski's common law wife committed suicide and, in a paroxysm of guilt, Przybyszewski turned himself over to the Berlin police, who released him after two weeks. In June, Munch showed up in Paris with reports of Przybyszweski's desperate situation in Berlin, and Strindberg apparently thought that Przybyszweski had murdered not only the woman he had abandoned for Dagny Juel but their children and might next come to Paris to settle their old "Aspasia" account. If one regards "Aspasia" as the prime factor and the reaction to Przybyszewski as secondary, one is better able to understand why Przybyszewski's expected arrival in Paris in 1896 awakened such violent anxiety in Strindberg. The similarities between his Berlin adventure and Przybyszewski's were all too striking. Just as Strindberg had momentarily deserted his fiancée to woo "Aspasia," Przybyszewski had permanently abandoned his first wife and their children to marry her. But another factor probably played an even greater role. Strindberg's recent Parisian escapade with Mme. Lecain was a repetition of his momentary infatuation in Berlin: he was awaited, on the one hand, by patient Frida in a serene domestic setting and, on the other, by the "beautiful sinner" in an emancipated, Bohemian milieu. Ever since meeting Mme. Lecain, Strindberg had been disposed to revert to the behavioral pattern he had followed in 1893. When he therefore heard someone playing "Aufschwung" in the distance and suspected that Przybyszewski had come to Paris, he was once more assailed by a guilty conscience and reacted in his habitual manner by falling prey to anxiety, to premonitions of unpleasant events, and to fear of his enemies.

The first stage of this crisis occurred between April 28 and May 26. His dream of the decapitated Przybyszewski belongs to this period, as do the "revelations" he describes in the sixth chapter of *Inferno* concerning the head of Zeus, the dragons, the demons, and the Madonna—all symbolic expressions of his erotic-moralistic dilemma. The dream he reports there about "Jonas Lie's clock," a clock belonging to his friend, the Norwegian novelist Jonas Lie, also belongs to this group of manifestations; even if one does not attempt to interpret the latter dream, one can hardly avoid noticing that the clock contained two female figures and that seeing them reminded him—as Strindberg himself observed in a letter to Hedlund—of both of his wives.[55] Furthermore, Strindberg was in the habit of admiring Carpeaux' statuary group, "The Four Corners of the Earth," in the garden of the Observatoire, because one of its female figures reminded him of his wife. There—as was also the case with "Jonas Lie's clock" in the dream—the ladies are holding up a globe. Finally, he was interested in tarot symbols and noted on May 29 that he had seen a nine of spades on the Rue Séguier: "Nine of spades means death! We shall see. 9 = the number for battle."

The reader of *Inferno* gets the impression that as soon as he heard "Aufschwung," Strindberg was firmly convinced that his life was in danger. However, his persecution mania did not reach the paranoid stage until May 26, when he records in his diary the name "Dr. Bitter," along with the other titles that appeared on letters addressed to him, which he had noticed on the letter rack in the lobby of his hotel. Strindberg also records his conclusions: "Consequently, a false name." On June 9, he made an entry in the diary concerning a mysterious person named "Schmulachowsky." During this period two things happened that might explain his increasing anxiety: on May 26 (the same day that he spied on Bitter) Strindberg met Mme. Lecain once more, and the next day—according to the diary—he was visited by a lawyer in connection with his divorce from Frida Uhl.

The situation finally came to a head on June 18, when Strindberg received a false report that Przybyszewski had been arrested for the murder of his common law wife and her children.[56] Strindberg's first reaction was relief; in a letter to Hedlund three days later he complacently remarks that something always happens to save him from his enemies. But he was only whistling in the dark, for this new state of affairs actually encouraged his tendency to identify himself with Przybyszewski. Needless to say, Strindberg's relation to his children was one of his most sensitive points. Hoping perhaps to undermine the health of Frida's child in order to effect a reconciliation, he felt himself sorely punished for such an evil design when he learned instead that Siri's children had fallen ill. Believing that Przybyszewski had actually murdered his unwanted children, Strindberg came to regard Przybyszewski as the personification of his own guilty conscience. On June 28, Strindberg dreamed that he too had been sent to prison. The mass poisoning that he attributed to the Pole was a "real-life" counterpart to the crime he imagined he had committed through evil intentions and neglect.

Gustaf Uddgren, a Swedish journalist who saw Strindberg in Paris at this time, was deeply impressed by his sick guilt feelings. On the day of their conversation, Strindberg was so anxious about Przybyszewski's fate that he seemed almost to regard himself as responsible for the arrest. According to Uddgren, if Strindberg had been able to carry out all of his plans to rescue his friend from prison, everyone would eventually "have gotten the idea that . . . Strindberg . . . was guilty of the murder in Berlin, and not the man who had been arrested." [57]

Strindberg's obsessive guilt feelings about Przybyszewski and about his attempt to make his daughter fall ill by "magic" re-awakened his belief that he was a sorcerer leaving a trail of misfortunes in his wake—a variant of the notions he had entertained about his "demonic" powers in youth. On June 25 he was invited to visit Dr. Papus, the notorious occultist and editor of *L'Initiation,* an important journal of the occult, at Marolles-en-Brie, and afterward he feared that everyone would regard him as a practitioner of black magic. On June 26, he repeats his familiar formula in a letter to Hedlund: "Someone is tampering with my destiny." According to *Inferno,* he also had premonitions of impending reverses—possibly of a journey. In letters to Hedlund he relates one story after another about previous "persecutions" to which he had been subjected. Finally, his discovery that Przybyszewski had been released from jail led to the acute phase of his crisis. He began to suffer sensations of discomfort and restiveness. By July 13, his morbid fears had reached their full strength, and he sent Hedlund a sort of last will and testament: "The end is approaching with fatal consistency." Five days later, on July 19, he suffered his first severe attack.

The crisis did not subside until the middle of August, when Strindberg was summoned to Austria to visit his daughter. In *Inferno* he eloquently describes the impression that Frida Uhl's letter made on him: "It is a resurrection to life!—I begin to be reborn, as if I were awakening from a long and evil dream, and I understand the benevolence of the severe Master, whose hard, punishing hand was guided by superior understanding." [58]

In what follows, he speaks of his trip to the Danube as a "penitential journey." The account of it given in *Inferno* is largely correct. Only in one point is there a clear error: his letters to Hedlund during the latter half of August show that Strindberg had hoped for a reunion with both wife and child, not just with his daughter. However, it is evident that he conceived of his reunion in moral categories. By now he regarded his tribulations as punishment sent by a higher power. Seeking the cause for this punishment, he found that his "crime" was the attempt to free himself from the obligation to support his family. All he had to do, therefore, was "resume the yoke, toil for his bread, and try to provide for all those he had brought into the world and who were now in need." August of 1896 brought Strindberg a good deal closer to the solution of his conflict, because he finally stopped projecting his guilt onto presumed "enemies" who were persecuting him and located it—for the first time— within himself. Relief was instantaneous. On the way to Austria, he passed through Berlin, where Przybyszewski lived. But now he was calm. His previous terror had evaporated, leaving only a residue of vague melancholy: "and at the same time I feel keenly that all of this is over, that it ought to stay buried in order to leave room for the new." [59] Finally, an entry in his diary at the beginning of his stay with Frida's family in Klam seems to serve as a symbolic expression of the fact that his conflict had really been resolved: "Threw Aspasia's picture into the sewer."

In the interim—before his general anxiety had quite managed to subside—a new series of attacks broke out during his stay in Austria. According to *Inferno,* he was forced to engage in another "nocturnal battle" on November 2, 1896, but "for some time" Strindberg had already been fending off "electrical attacks." In *The Occult Diary* he reports that he had "three attacks" on the night of Thursday, November 11, one more sign that persecution feelings had again taken possession of him. In a letter at the end of November he gave Hedlund to understand that he expected to be attacked by the theosophists. The handwriting of a letter he wrote on November 13 to Dr. Anders Eliasson, who had helped nurse him through his crisis in July and August, evidences his agitated state almost as effectively as one of the exclamations it contains: "Now you can erect the gallows!" Four days later he wrote the terrible letter to Hedlund that eventually led to a break between them; it ends: "Farewell, and dream about the fraternity of demons!" On November 27 Strindberg left Klam, and he arrived in Malmö on December 1. According to *The Occult Diary,* he settled in Lund on December 20.

From its very beginning, the fifth crisis had a conscious moral and religious dimension, which had been lacking in the four preceding crises. To admit his own guilt was an act of the greatest self-conquest for Strindberg. In return, he demanded that his sacrifice be accepted, that in other words, as a "penitent," he be allowed the possibility of building a harmonious life with his family. When reality hindered him from doing so, he rebelled and finally relapsed into his former state of mind.

This development is reflected in a thematic change that takes place in the motifs connected with the color "rose"—a change that is very important to notice because it directly anticipates the technique he was to use in his symbolic dramas. On his way through Berlin, Strindberg had observed a "rosy shimmer, but of a deep rosy hue," above the rooftops in the east. He had seen the same light in Malmö on the evening before his departure.[60] In *Inferno* the context allows no room for doubt that he associated this color with memories of "a springtime and a love that will never, never return."[61] One should bear in mind that Strindberg had always loved roses and that the first time he visited Frida Uhl she had decorated her room with roses, a detail he includes in "The Quarantine Master's Second

Tale." When he set out on his journey in August 1896, Strindberg was not quite so fully resigned to separation as *Inferno* would lead one to believe. He actually hoped for a reunion. Thus, he reacted very positively when he arrived in Klam and was shown into a rose-colored room. In *Inferno* he describes the mood of religious self-denial mingled with erotic reveries that seized him when once again he beheld the color rose. The chamber is "a vision," he relates, and "a poem created by a soul that only half inhabits the earth." The bed is "a young maiden's couch." [62] But when his hopes are disappointed, he begins to hate the color that had recently put him in such a tender mood. The rose room seems to him to have been transformed and now produces "a disharmonious impression that makes me sick." In the light of this psychic mechanism, one can readily understand an otherwise obscure passage in *Inferno:* "For lack of anything better, I have to make do with their ink, which is a bright red, rosy color! Anyway, it is very strange! A package of cigarette papers I bought contained, among a hundred white ones, one rose-colored paper! (Rose-colored!) This is hell with a low flame." [63] Now roses symbolize his thwarted erotic hopes, his "pure love." For that reason the rose room now strikes him as "a mockery."

All prospects of reconciliation were, from the outset, very dim. Shortly after Strindberg's arrival in Klam and his initial meeting with his daughter he was seized with terror, because the child had been afraid to touch his hand. His guilt feelings arose once more, this time in a configuration that was informed by his new, moral outlook. "That night I had the following dream: an eagle pecked at my hand to punish me for something I am unaware of." [64] He was not allowed to see his wife, and he soon relapsed into a state of dejection and bitterness. His wrath was directed against the grandmother, whose picture he cursed because he suspected her of intriguing against him and of preventing him from seeing Frida. But even his anger now had a metaphysical side, for it was at this time that Strindberg thought he noticed thunderstorms "taking aim at him" and that he began to observe other meteorological "signs" such as cloudbursts and cyclones. When Frida's grandmother, "Urgross-mutter" as he called her, suddenly fell ill, his guilt feelings became more intense than ever, leading him into the dilemma described in *Inferno:* "guilt feelings, on the one hand—fear on the other." [65]

Even though Strindberg had now acquired deeper moral and religious insight than ever before during this whole period of mounting anxiety, he was unable to escape his habitual pattern of behavior when the anxiety finally culminated in another acute crisis in October. It seems safe to assume that this crisis was provoked by a letter he received from Frida on September 28. She clearly intended it to be a final farewell. In *Inferno,* Strindberg's decisive change in mood occurs at the end of September—before he moves back into "the rose room." On September 22, he wrote to an acquaintance in Paris, F. U. Wrangel, that he was "always being accused of things, often without knowing why." In October, his persecution mania gradually increased, and his tendency to put a religious interpretation on events retreated into the background. Now he believed that he was being persecuted by people who were well-versed in occult practices and had the power to "destroy" people with magic. "Someone is tormenting me from a distance," he charges in a letter to Hedlund on October 25. In *Inferno* he describes repeated attacks of this sort during October. They reach their peak between the 2nd and the 21st of November and then gradually cease after his return to Sweden.

After the end of 1896, people and reality ceased to play any palpable role in Strindberg's process of conversion. In Lund he was surrounded by a circle of young "disciples," including Emil Kléen, a promising representative of the decadent strain in Swedish literature, and Bengt Lidforss, whom Strindberg had once heartily despised because of his connection with the "Aspasia" affair. But even though Kléen's illness and untimely death in 1898 clearly made a profound impression on Strindberg, he does not seem to have formed any really strong emotional attachment to this group. Instead, he used his young admirers as guinea pigs on whom to test the validity of his theories. Furthermore, Przybyszewski's brother-in-law, who lived in Lund and whom he had formerly regarded as one of the "murderers," seems hardly to have frightened him any longer. Nor does he seem to have been influenced by any women during the latter period of his conversion. After his most recent experiences in Austria, he abandoned all hope of reconciliation with Frida Uhl. He had broken off correspondence with Hedlund, who had no understudy to replace him in the role of confidant and father confessor. Strindberg's letters to Hedlund comprise his last great set of intimate letters to a friend.

At the same time, Strindberg's literary productivity was restored. In May and June of 1897 he wrote *Inferno,* then in September and October *Legends,* followed immediately by *Jacob Wrestles.* In January 1898 he sketched out the first part of *To Damascus,* thereby entering on one of his most fruitful periods of dramatic production, a period that lasted until 1903. As a result of his literary comeback, Strindberg's economic position gradually improved. His daughter, Karin Smirnoff, notes in her memoirs that Strindberg's abundant support at the end of 1897 brought "enormous relief" to the situation of Siri von Essen and her children.[66]

There was also another change at the beginning of 1897: after an absence of seven years, Strindberg moved back to Sweden. Although he had not originally intended to make a complete break with his cosmopolitan past, he gradually ceased to entertain the possibility of living abroad and decided to remain in his native country. He stayed in Scania—mainly in Lund—until August 1897, when he returned to Paris. Upon his arrival there he rightly suspected that the visit was to be his last. In the beginning of the following April he returned to Lund, which he did not leave—except for a short visit to Heyst-sur-Mer in Belgium—until 1899, when he moved to Stockholm.

Because he also resumed intercourse at that time with many former friends and acquaintances, the year 1897 initiated one of the most serene periods in Strindberg's life. As far as is known, he not only succeeded in keeping peace with the friends he saw daily, but he also cultivated old acquaintances whom he had previously neglected, or broken with altogether. Besides making up with Lidforss, he attempted to renew his contact with such men as Gustaf af Geijerstam, Leopold Littmansson, J. O. Strindberg, and Pehr Staaff—all friends of long standing. Sometimes he asked people to forgive him for the injustices he had done them; often his gestures conveyed a silent prayer for forgiveness, as when he sent a picture of himself to Hedlund in 1899.[67] In his books, he is very eager to set to rights what has been broken. Throughout *Inferno* he pays homage to Hedlund, and *Legends,* which was written with a relatively cautious hand, opens with an apology for the "sins of indiscretion" that Strindberg may have committed. Moreover, Karin Smirnoff's memoirs suggest that just at this time his attitude toward his children changed. "Strindberg showed an interest in their future. It made him happy when they wrote him long letters about their activities. He sent them his picture and wanted to have theirs. The tone in his letters to them becomes open and warm." [68]

One can trace this process of change from the beginning of 1897. According to Strindberg, it was the expression of his "atonement with the powers." At the same time, his persecution feelings diminished and finally disappeared altogether. After 1896, Strindberg was never again subject to concentrated attacks that led him to decamp. Nevertheless, at the beginning of his stay in Sweden he was still disturbed by noises and peculiar coincidences, haunted by "demons," and tormented "day and night" by "electric currents." A little later in the spring these sensations abated, and on March 2 the last entry about a "bad night" appears in the diary. Thereafter he was able to dispose of his physical symptoms—such as the "electric girdle" that he mentions in *Jacob Wrestles*—by regulating his mode of life according to moral and religious principles.

Strindberg himself attributed this result to Swedenborg. He states in *Legends* that Swedenborg saved him from insanity and restored his ability to sleep. In the same book he also speaks of his teacher's instructions in medical terms and refers to morality as the "prescription" by means of which he has regained his health and powers. That there is at least a chronological connection between Strindberg's reading in Swedenborg and his recovery is obvious: both occurred during the first half of 1897. The entry in his diary about "a bad night" on March 2 continues, "Went out, wandered about. Went into a second-hand book shop and got Swedenborg (Atterbom's paraphrase)." In *Legends* he places his decisive experience concerning Swedenborg in March 1897, while in *Inferno* he deals with the same material in the chapter entitled "The Redeemer." An entry in the diary for March 21 corroborates this dating. These facts indicate that when he associated his improvement with Swedenborg, Strindberg correctly understood the course that his "case" was taking. It only remains to examine the psychological implications of his "conversion."

Strindberg's whole series of dilemmas in 1896 revolved around his unwillingness to admit personal guilt. By means of a succession of different theories, he repulsed his increasingly violent pangs of conscience. Each of these theories was intended to prove that he had not personally done anything wrong. His ideas about undeserved suffering sent by God as a test of faith, about punishment for crimes committed in a previous existence, about original sin, about "unconscious" misdeeds, about earth as a hell, about his kinship with Napoleon, Robert le Diable, or the Devil himself—all these varying hypotheses, viewed psychologically, appear to be variants of Strindberg's crisis religion from the 1870s, and they clearly served the same function: to locate guilt outside and beyond himself, to free himself from personal responsibility.

Alongside these prevailing notions, however, there are indications that he was dimly aware of his own culpability. This deeper consciousness of guilt was particularly apparent just before the fourth crisis. On August 20, 1896, Strindberg confided in Hedlund that because he was not a righteous man himself, he could no longer find comfort in the Book of Job. He described himself as "a robber who had been crucified, because that is what his deeds deserved, and who should have been punished." The hope of reconciliation with the family in Austria had a great deal to do with this change of attitude. When his hopes were dashed, Strindberg reverted (during the fourth crisis) to his earlier demonic and Manichean ideas.

It was not until after his return to Sweden that Strindberg— under the influence of Swedenborg—first seriously attempted to make a moral interpretation of the course his life had taken. In Swedenborg's description of "devastation" and "the corrective spirits," he thought he recognized point for point the "afflictions" to which he himself had been subject during the preceding year. But Swedenborg depicts "devastation" and "the corrective spirits" as punishment for actual, personal crimes committed in this existence. This concept of punishment helped Strindberg to bring his guilt conflict into the light. He became aware of the connection between guilt and persecution—translated into psychological terms: between his guilt feelings and his persecution mania—and was cured of his psychoses as soon as this unconscious mechanism was revealed to him. A noteworthy passage in *Inferno* indicates that Strindberg himself was able to see the psychological consequences of his studies in Swedenborg and to evaluate their psychotherapeutic effect:

> Thus confined in this little city of the Muses [Lund], with no hope of escape, I join in dreadful battle against the enemy, myself.
>
> Each morning when I take my walk on the ramparts beneath the plane trees, the huge, red lunatic asylum reminds me of the danger I have evaded and of the future, should I have a relapse. By enlightening me concerning the true nature of the terrors that have beset me during the last year, Swedenborg has freed me from the electrical machines, the practitioners of the black arts, the wizards, the envious alchemists, and from the fear of insanity. He has shown me the only way to salvation: to seek the demons in their lair—within myself—and to kill them by means of . . . repentence. Balzac, as the prophet's adjutant, has taught me in his *Séraphita* that "remorse" is an impotent emotion leading only to fresh aberration. Repentence alone is strength. It alone brings everything to an end.[69]

When Strindberg transformed "remorse" into "repentence"—conscious, actively-refining remorse—he came into contact with the subconscious conflict that had dogged him all his life and that underlay many of his pathological reactions. Time and again in *Legends, Jacob Wrestles,* and *To Damascus* he describes how his whole life unfolds before him, how he is constantly forced to rehearse his transgressions, both great and small. By forcing himself to endure such tests, he transferred his conflict to a moral and religious plane. He was willing to admit his guilt, but how far he should carry contrition became a bone of contention between him and his God. One can pinpoint the nucleus of Strindberg's process of conversion in the events that occurred in the spring of 1897, when he underwent a decisive psychological change.

THREE *Jacob Wrestles*

Strindberg's actual religious development ran parallel both to his psychotic crises and to his speculations in natural philosphy. The gradual emergence of a sense of guilt led him from his initial, rather primitive mythology to moral questions in the Christian tradition. During the first phase of this development—from the summer of 1894 until the beginning of the year 1896—Strindberg's general mood was predominantly pessimistic and fatalistic. After the third crisis, this mood condensed into an esoteric and militant cult of Jehovah. Up to this point, he still showed no traces of a profound consciousness of guilt. But during the severe crises that he underwent in rapid succession during the latter half of 1896, he became dominated by the same concepts that had constituted his crisis religion, which served to repulse an ever more obtrusive guilt complex and its accompanying anxiety. After grappling with these crises, Strindberg finally arrived at a full consciousness of guilt in the spring of 1897, and this consciousness was a precondition for his coming to terms with himself and with reality. The entire development in turn provided much of the material both for his confessional works, like *Inferno* and *Legends,* and for his later plays, like *To Da-*

mascus. Although they became successively more intense, his fundamental attitudes during this whole period were identical with those that had informed his earlier religious outlook.

The new impulses that he received during his conversion were easily incorporated into his old frame of reference. The most important reason for calling this course of events a "conversion" is that Strindberg's struggle was essentially a moral one. The changing phases of the struggle determined the nature of his mythological concepts.

The first two crises did not yield any definite religious ideas, although they established a definable mood that largely dominated Strindberg until the beginning of 1896. It was a melancholy and lyrical state of mind, which entailed a certain fatalistic formality and a vague longing to escape the world.

These mental states were nourished by his reading. At Dornach in the library of Frida Uhl's grandfather, Cornelius Reischl, Strindberg found "Buddhist works," and during the course of 1895 he eagerly resumed his study of this subject. As early as the summer and autumn of 1894 his correspondence with Littmansson is filled with reminiscences of this reading. Strindberg calls himself "Buddha" or sometimes, referring to the exoteric side of his nature, "Buddha, the swine." He also expresses his longing for purity and for nirvana in melancholy, poetic outbursts, with constant repetitions that put one in mind of formulary Buddhist language: "I have also relapsed into superstition. I hear ravens in my garden, children crying on the other side of the Danube. I dream of the old days and long to fly in some tepid intermediary substance between air and water, dressed in white, to hear no human voices, to be free from the humiliating feeling of hunger, to have no enemies, not to hate, not to be hated . . . behold my weakness, my fatigue, my satiation" (July 22, 1894).

His ideal of the superman changed in accordance with this artistic mood. The Nietzschean will to rule over spirits remains with him, but now he also emphasizes the ruler's distance from the world and his apparent insignificance. The superman becomes a beggar who walks in the gutter and has *"Machtgefühl"* (a sense of power), a "Dominican" or a "Buddha." When individuality leaves the guardianship of the cosmos and goes its own way, it can become "something like Nietzsche's dimly perceived 'Superman' "—this was one of the theosophical ideas that Hedlund transmitted to Strindberg, whose correspondence with Littmansson shows that it fell on fertile soil. In a draft from the latter part of 1894, Strindberg indulges in a fantasy about the man of the future, whom he imagines as a refined type with weak muscles and a high forehead. "Everything reminiscent of the beast will disappear; superfluous organs will be reduced to a minimum." This superman is not distinguished, however, by any moral sensibility; in this respect, he has learned directly from Nietzsche and knows "the art of doing evil when the need arises." [1]

Naturally, Strindberg was eager to identify himself with this type of superman. But marriage and family held him in degrading bondage to material life. For that reason he wished to liberate himself and thought it was the threshold of a new period in his life. Of course, this psychological conflict lay at the heart of the entire crisis drama. But characteristically, Strindberg did not want to accept responsibility for the break; instead, he transferred it to something that was acting either within or outside him, so he could think that he himself remained inactive. "Therefore I put myself, as usual, into an unconscious state, let the forces do their work, and wait in a tense sort of quietism" (letter to Hedlund, August 11, 1894).

This attitude resulted in a vague fatalism, which he sometimes expressed in terms that have a religious ring: "What destiny now awaits me I do not know, but I sense 'the Lord's hand' poised above me. A change is in the offing, upward, or straight down to the center of the earth—who knows about such matters!" (letter to Littmanssson, July 22, 1894). The day after he wrote this letter, Strindberg himself accelerated the "change" by resuming his correspondence with Hedlund, after a lapse of three years. Hedlund's reply—the so-called "Danube letter"—confirmed his presentiments in equally lofty terms. He answered, in effect, that Strindberg was on the threshold of an extremely significant period in his "life cycle." Frida Uhl describes the powerful impression that this letter made on Strindberg.

In Paris, Strindberg was occupied for a time with literary and journalistic work, but after his second crisis and his stay in the Saint-Louis Hospital, he withdrew from "the world of vaniety and the living." During the course of 1895, an autistic, dreamy mood constantly overtook him. Because of the unfortunate lack of enlightening material from this period, however, it is difficult to analyze the mood in detail.

When he was a patient at Saint-Louis Hospital, Strindberg considered the possibility of seeking refuge in a monastery or of becoming a hermit, and on January 17, 1895, he wrote to Frida Uhl about these plans.[2] He wanted to enter a Dominican monastery during Whitesuntide in 1895, and with this in mind he paid a visit to Père Didon, the famous preacher.[3] Later he explained to Hedlund what had finally deterred him from his purpose: "I have considered entering a Catholic monastery, but that would entail confessions and a kind of obedience that I detest" (Nov. 10, 1895). His morning walks in the Montparnasse Cemetery, which to Strindberg represented the exact opposite of the bustling life of Paris, were a manifestation of the same desire for seclusion. He walked in solitude there, found a circle of acquaintances among the busts on funeral monuments, and pessimistically meditated upon the transitoriness of things. His essay "In the Cemetery," probably written in the autumn of 1895, contains a distillation of these experiences. Schopenhauerian-Buddhistic moods emerge from time to time, as when he speaks of the flowers, those "superior beings that have realized Buddha's dream of coveting nothing, of enduring all things, of descending into the self, even to the point of unconsciousness."

In *Inferno* Strindberg gives the following account of his religious state at this period:

Actually, a sort of religion has developed in me, although I would not be able to put it into words. A spiritual state rather than any opinion based on theories. A miscellaneous collection of impressions that have more or less condensed into ideas.

I read with devotion. I read an old Roman Catholic breviary that I came across. The Old Testament comforts and chastises me in a way that remains somewhat obscure, whereas the New Testament leaves me cold. But a Buddhist work makes a stronger impression on me than all the other sacred books, since it places positive suffering above continence.[4]

In the background here one catches a glimpse of the religious solution. This vague fatalism gradually "condenses" into more substantial notions, and at the end of October Strindberg is able to inform Hedlund that "someone" is directing his destiny and that "this someone is nearer than we think" (Oct. 30, 1895). This concept of God became fully articulate around the beginning of 1896. With this new concept, Strindberg had advanced beyond the groping stage, and his real religious development was underway.

In letters to Hedlund written during his stay at the Hôtel Orfila in the spring of 1896, Strindberg calls his severe but trustworthy God "the Eternal One from the Old Testament" or "an invisible hand." Strindberg feels very close to him; in fact, their acquaintance is "completely personal" (July 1, 1896). On the whole, Strindberg is on a good footing with this God. His intentions are sometimes difficult to divine, but in general He is benevolent, if also rather stern. The invisible hand "is poised above me, punishes me immediately when I succumb to temptation, but always helps me against my enemies, although at times they are used to chastise me." He is "great and reasonable" (undated, June 1896)—a God for individualists and anarchists, and when Strindberg, an isolated and exiled figure, is attacked by "the enemy," he can depend on being protected by the Eternal One.

Strindberg took the symbols for his relationship to this God from the Old Testament, especially from the Book of Job and the Psalms. The figure of Job suited him perfectly: by identifying himself with this unjustly punished man, who "was tested" by God in order to show how much a righteous man can endure, Strindberg acquired a symbol that expressed his need both to suffer and to feel innocent. Kierkegaard had used the same symbol in *Repetition* to express modern man's mixed feelings of confidence and revolt in relation to God. During the initial stage of the fourth crisis, when Strindberg was seeking help against the persecutions of his enemies, he recited the

Psalms of David. It appears that by combining these components, Strindberg had returned to his childhood concept of God: the often unjust chastiser, who was at the same time a protector.[5]

Strindberg's religion during this period is slightly esoteric. God wants to train him for something higher and does not allow him to mingle with the crowd. This "training" and this "chastisement" for a greater purpose, which he now saw as God's design, was a metaphysical periphrasis for his own conflict between a desire for solitude and a craving for human contact. The development of the self and self-glorification were still central for Strindberg. Part of his dispute with Hedlund concerned this very issue. In a letter from the Hôtel Orfila (May 17, 1896), Strindberg writes: "Why do you always exhort me to extirpate my self?—Indeed, it is my most sacred duty to nurse, cultivate, and observe this self, for otherwise it will be dragged down to the level of the horrid little selves that give nothing, only bleed one, cling to one, and smear one with filth."

Into this esoteric system Strindberg incorporated impressions received from Balzac's *Séraphita*. He remembered that the book deals with Swedenborg, and his reason for rereading it in March 1896 was that the person who had reviewed his own little book *Sylva Sylvarum* (1896) for *Initiation* hailed him as a countryman of the Swedish mystic. Of course, what Strindberg found in the novel was a philosophy of the superman that is closer to neoromantic spiritualism than to authentic views of Swedenborg. More important to Balzac than any other idea retained from his study of Swedenborg was the Platonic concept of the androgyne as the most perfect human type. But whereas Swedenborg incorporates this idea into his eschatological system, Balzac brings the ideal human down to earth and represents Swedenborg's disciples as living representatives of this superior form of humanity. Although the idea of the androgyne later assumed considerable significance for Strindberg, at this time he seems to have been captivated primarily by Balzac's exaltedly idealistic and somewhat haughty tone, by his contempt for the world, and by the cult of purity he describes. Strindberg reveals in *Inferno* that *Séraphita* caused him to "resume relations with heaven" and to despise the impure earth.

Strindberg's religion served simply to heighten his self-awareness. He had been chosen for a great mission in the service of God. God took particular care of him and had "plans" for him. When he wrote *Inferno,* Strindberg was moving toward a different frame of mind and a different concept of religion. For that reason, the book contains a sharp criticism of the posture he had assumed during the first period of his conversion, when conceiving himself as a superman supported by religion. He feels that he has committed the sin of *"hubris,* the only vice that the gods do not forgive" and defied "even the most elementary concepts of humility"; he speaks of his "pious vanity," "immeasurable arrogance," and so forth.[6] This self-exaltation was a direct continuation of youthful ideas about his vocation, of the programmatic egoism he had promoted in the middle of the 1880s, of the cult of the superman in *By the Open Sea,* and of the cult of the self expressed in his letters to Littmansson. Just as Jehovah encouraged Strindberg's autistic fear of the world, He also favored his paranoic self-exaltation.

Old Testament ideas came alive for Strindberg once again when his persecution mania reached its height between July and November 1896, but this time they were partly enveloped in a fantastic mythology of Strindberg's own devising. Clearly, this ideological system is a further development of ideas that Strindberg had entertained during previous periods of great anxiety.

During the crisis that took place at the end of 1895 and the beginning of 1896, he was already preoccupied with fantasies similar to the crisis religion of his youth. In an undated letter to Hedlund, he assumes the hypothesis that "this life is a sentence and earth a penal colony, where one serves time for unknown crimes committed in another existence," and he hopes that his "time of servitude will soon be up." He expresses the same idea in "In the Cemetery": "The earth is a penal colony, where we must pay for crimes committed in a previous existence and of which our consciences retain a vague memory. This memory drives us on toward improvement. Consequently, every one of us is a criminal, and the pessimist, who always thinks and speaks ill of his fellow man, is not so wrong after all." The first of these pronouncements can be assigned to December 1895; in all probability the latter was written just before or just after the beginning of 1896. In other words, both of them are chronologically allied to what is here called the third crisis.

The two subsequent crises vastly enriched the development of this myth; indeed, this idea inspired the title of *Inferno*. It turns up again in a letter to Hedlund on May 28: "We shall not be saved; we are in hell to be tormented according to our deserts." In August—that is, in the middle of the fourth crisis—the parallel between hell and life on earth becomes the center around which all Strindberg's other concepts revolve. On August 1 he had borrowed Viktor Rydberg's *Studies in Germanic Mythology* from Dr. Anders Eliasson, who was caring for him in Ystad. According to *Inferno,* reading this book convinced him that he was in hell. [7] In a letter written on the same day, he informed Hedlund that his study of the eschatological descriptions in Rydberg's book had carried him "a long way forward." In *The Occult Diary* (August 1, 1896) he states that he had read about Bhrigu, the legendary Indian figure whom Brahma punished for his pride by sending him to the realm of the unblessed dead, and "was liberated." Strindberg probably means that he was freed from his fear of persecution. The myth that he was in hell made further brooding about the origin of his persecutions superfluous.

Strindberg wanted to prove that certain people—maybe all people—have already been consigned to hell during this life. Nothing in Rydberg's *Germanic Mythology* supports his case. Quite disregarding the context, he had simply culled certain details from Rydberg's account of Old Norse eschatology and associated them with features from his own experience, so as to confirm his suspicion. His procedure was no less arbitrary a month later in Klam, when for the first time he studied the writings of Swedenborg.

Strindberg deals most extensively with the parallel between earthly life and hell in the central chapter of *Inferno,* which is entitled "Swedenborg." The justification for this title lies in the fact that the chapter treats his first direct contact with Swedenborg's works. Prior to the period described in the chapter, Strindberg had only read about Swedenborg in Balzac's *Séraphita,* where he got a general idea of Swedenborg's importance as a religious figure.[8] But the reader of *Inferno* certainly gets the impression that in the autumn of 1896 Strindberg had already become a disciple of Swedenborg's. Thus, at the end of the preceding chapter he speaks of "that time before I was acquainted with Swedenborg's teachings" and concludes with a formal tribute to the Swedish mystic.[9]

This impression is misleading. As Lamm has shown, Strindberg studied Swedenborg in Pernetty's French edition of *Heaven and Hell* and of *The Earths in Our Solar System.* Perhaps he did not even read the whole book at this time, for the latter portion contains passages, such as descriptions of conditions on the planet Jupiter, that were to acquire profound significance for him, but not until much later—in March 1897. What primarily occupied him now were the descriptions of hell. In Swedenborg's visions of hell he thought he recognized the landscape around Klam. When he also studied Dante's *Inferno* somewhat later, he found further confirmation for his belief that "we are already down there! The earth is hell, this prison built with superior ingenuity, where I cannot take a step without wounding the happiness of others, and where my fellow creatures cannot remain happy without adding to my pain."[10] Needless to say, this train of thought is related to Swedenborg only in the most superficial way: in short, Swedenborg supplied Strindberg with more material for his parallel between hell and earth.[11] The idea that engaged his attention at this time was the same one that had already been confirmed by *Germanic Mythology,* namely, that we are already living in hell. Strindberg read (or read in) the two works by Swedenborg at the beginning of September; two months later he summarized his own line of thought for Hedlund: "The world view that I have developed is closest to that of Pythagoras, which was later accepted by Origen: we are in Inferno for sins committed in a previous existence. Therefore: pray for nothing but resignation! and expect nothing, absolutely nothing, from life. Be happy, if possible, in your misfortunes, for with each misfortune an entry is expunged from your deficit column! Swedenborg's description of Inferno is so faithful an account of earthly life—though he did not intend it as such—so precisely correct that I am convinced" (Oct. 31, 1896).

This passage shows clearly that Strindberg's acquaintance with Swedenborg had not added anything new to his own line of reasoning. Swedenborg's naturalistic descriptions of hell had served only to strengthen an idea he already held. As Lamm points out, Strindberg's ideas about hell are extremely close to many comparisons in Schopenhauer's *The World As Will and Idea.* One thinks, for example, of the chapter entitled "On the Vanity and the Suffering of This Life," where the world is compared to a hell that surpasses Dante's in that "one man must be the devil of the other," and where human life is defined not as a gift but as a debt: "The calling in of this debt appears in the form of the pressing needs of existence, tormenting desires, and endless distress. As a rule, one's whole lifetime is spent paying off this debt; yet only the interest is thereby amortized. The capital is paid off by death." [12]

In other words, on reading Swedenborg's *Heaven and Hell,* Strindberg was not suddenly overwhelmed by the insight that earth is a hell. That was a view he had previously sought refuge in when he found himself in perplexing situations. All he did now was to work out the idea by making systematic excerpts from Swedenborg's descriptions of hell. He also looked for counterparts to his own experiences in other pictures of hell. Thus, in September he ordered Dante's *Inferno,* Hesiod, the *Eddas,* the *Rigveda,* and Grimm's *Fairy Tales.* He expected to find descriptions of hell in all these works. The result of his research appears in the epilogue to *Inferno,* where he reports that "the correspondences between Swedenborg's hell and Dante's and between those described in Graeco-Roman and Germanic mythology dispose me to believe that in order to realize their plans the powers have always made use of very similar means." [13]

During the third crisis, Strindberg had believed that people were persecuting him. He gradually abandoned this obsession and slipped into a "demonic" frame of reference, but so hesitantly and so obscurely that many times it is difficult to decide whether he is using expressions in a literal or a figurative sense. For example, the first time that he uses the word "elementals" (in a letter to Hedlund in May 1896), he remarks that the second part of *Jardin des Plantes* will never see light "if the elementals on the east coast are allowed to blow unchecked." From a previous letter it appears that "elementals" refers only to the critics who he feared would attack the book. But in letters that follow it is not certain whether Strindberg really believed in the existence of independent spirits or not. Mad people are not sick, he writes in one place, but are "possessed by demons"; women are "elementals," he states elsewhere. It is still possible that when he speaks in general terms about "being avenged on the demons" or about "the fraternity of demons," he is referring only to wicked people. However, he explicitly uses demonic notions when he writes to Hedlund on August 1, 1896, that "we are being persecuted—by what you and the occultists call 'elementals' or lower beings who envy us for our existence, drive us to suicide in order to assume what you call our 'astral bodies.' " And according to *Inferno,* he imagined in October that he was "being persecuted by elemental and elementary spirits, incubi, lamias, who are using their full powers in an attempt to prevent me from finishing the *Grand Oeuvre* of the alchemists. According to the instructions of the initiated, I buy myself a Dalmatian dagger and think myself well armed against the evil spirits." [14] In an article entitled "Le pain de l'avenir" (The Bread of the Future), written in the beginning of 1897 and published in *Hyperchimie,* there is the statement "the elementals are cunning,"—which he later canceled when he received the printed article. [15]

The only positive evidence that Strindberg entertained notions of demonism comes from the period between August and October 1896. To be sure, in *Inferno* there are accounts of exorcism and phrases like "demons at play" or "defy the demons" and the like, but they always refer to the latter half of 1896. In other words, this notion accompanied the crisis that grew directly out of Strindberg's fear of persecution.

The same is true of his references to "black magic." It too served to explain his delusions of persecution. It can be regarded as an intermediary stage between ideas about a "natural" human persecution that still dominated Strindberg during the greater part of the fourth crisis and the demonic notions that he occasionally uses later. He sometimes believed that he was the victim of "envoûtement," a murderous attempt made on him from afar by persons adept at black magic. This hypothesis alternated with the demonic one, but in general it seems to have captured his imagination more fully. These ideas had already begun to occupy him in June 1896—character-istically, he at first believed that he had unconsciously practiced witchcraft himself. Hence, after a visit to Dr. Papus, the well-known Parisian occultist, at Marolles-en-Brie on June 25, he feared that he would be suspected of instigating the supernatural manifes-tations in nearby Valence-en-Brie (*Inferno*). On July 11 he asked Hedlund if "attempts to murder people by means of black magic" were not "very common, without our knowing it." Thus far his in-terest had been mainly theoretical. But in October, during the fifth crisis, he was strongly tempted to believe that his enemies were tor-menting him from a distance. He also considered repaying them in kind, as he wrote to Hedlund on October 30, 1896:

> Assuming that *envoûtements* (magical assassinations) are possible, would it be a sin to 'envoûte' one's enemies? They are allowed to murder freely, but I am excluded from their ranks.
>
> I don't know if *envoûtement* is possible, but if it is, then witch trials and burnings will begin again. And above all: false accusations of witchcraft. Whoever is unlucky is lost. But that is certainly what all of this is leading to!
>
> I believe that someone is tormenting me from a distance. And others believe the same thing of me, but they are wrong.

Except for Strindberg's plans to avenge himself, all these ideas turn up in *Inferno*. Related to this body of ideas is his notion that cyclones are "streams of hatred" that may possibly be produced by "the wise Hindoos." Strindberg actually believed that he had been pursued by a cyclone when he fled from the Rue de la Clef.

Nor is it really surprising that Strindberg was afraid that the oc-cultists and the theosophists were using the black arts against him. Destruction by means of sympathetic magic (envoûtement) occupied a significant place in the minds of occultists and theosophists alike. Early in his correspondence with Strindberg, Hedlund indirectly warned him against practising black magic and thereby stimulated his speculations about the power of "the will to evil." In the spring of 1896, after Strindberg had published *Sylva Sylvarum,* he came into contact with the Paris Occultists; and in April he began to collaborate on their periodical, *Initiation,* where the theories of *envoûtement* were regular fare.[16] For a while, Strindberg styled himself an occultist. Writing to Hedlund about his first plans for *Inferno,* he proclaimed that he wanted to be "the Zola of occultism." According to *Inferno,* he became acquainted with the elements of black magic in May, and during the remainder of the year he made further studies of the writings of the Paris occultists. When he published *Inferno,* he added a selected bibliography of works by various members of this curious group.

Under the leadership of the energetic Dr. Papus,[17] the occultist school was one of the most striking features of *fin-de-siècle* intellectual and artistic life in Paris. Stimulated by the progress of spiritism and theosophy, Papus had attempted at the end of the 1880s to revive Rosecrucianism and Martinism in France. At the same time, he founded the Groupe Indépendant d'études ésoteriques, a "scientific" society devoted to research on occult phenomena. Theosophy, which is based on oriental mysticism, was the particular target of this group. The avowed intention of Papus and his followers was to oppose oriental mysticism with Western occultism, based on the hermetic tradition as it had been transmitted by thinkers like Paracelsus and Saint-Martin. The same antithesis appears in Strindberg's conflict with Hedlund: "I am moving toward the West, away from the sun, the way Culture has moved, and you are moving to the East, where decomposition begins" (Dec. 5, 1895). The French occultists succeeded in holding their own against theosophy. To the extent that it survives in France, the tradition stemming from Lévi, Guaita, and Papus still eclipses the theosophical orientation of Mme. Blavatsky. The rivalry very quickly broke out into open strife. As early as his "Danube letter" Hedlund had tried to alert Strindberg to the dangers of the Paris occultists. But his admonitions were unsuccessful. Whether or not he was justified in calling them "black magicians" is one of the leading themes of his subsequent exchanges with Strindberg.

Among other things, the Paris occultists succeeded in arousing the interest of various symbolist poets. Occultism was one element in the constellation of ideas that grew out of *fin de siècle* idealism. Huysmans' aestheticizing curiosity about Satanism in his novel *Là-bas* was regarded by the occultists as mere profanation, and their attitude gave rise to a vigorous polemic in *Initiation*. But other writers lived themselves into the occultist point of view in a more positive spirit. To this group belonged older men like Villiers de l'Isle-Adam and Ernest Hello and younger ones like Schuré, Barrès, and Mallarmé. Mysticism, esoteric contempt for the everyday wisdom of common sense, aspects of demonism—all such elements attracted the revolutionary poets. Indeed, for a time around 1890 it appeared that occultism might become the unifying outlook for the entire younger generation.[18]

Thus, it was not an obscure Parisian sect with which Strindberg became associated in 1896, but a trend that had been the focus of literary debate for several years. The sensation caused by the Guaita-Boullan affair in 1893 had even made it thoroughly familiar to the general public. Boullan was an heretical occultist who had provided Huysmans with material for *Là-bas*. Incited by Stanislas de Guaita, the school of Paris occultists took action against him, and mutual accusations of black magic followed. Then someone attempted to commit murder by means of witchcraft, and finally there was a proper duel. The affair caused as great a scandal as the news media were then equipped to create, and the Parisian newspaper-reader could certainly have received the same impression that Strindberg expresses in *A Blue Book II* (1908), namely, that "powerful spirits, especially in France, were attacking one another from a distance, sometimes with fatal consequences."

Like Mme. Blavatsky's theosophy, Paris occultism was broadly eclectic. Eliphas Lévi, the great teacher of the Paris occultists, was primarily responsible for transmitting the mystical and cabalistic traditions to them.[19] Among his predecessors were Böhme, Swedenborg, Görres, and Saint-Martin.[20] But the Paris group also responded to other elements in Lévi's works, where astrology, chiromancy, magnetism, and alchemy are all woven into a tissue of

cabalistic speculation and permeated by the heady incense of an esoteric temple cult. By forming a link with modern psychology, Papus
succeeded in opening a new approach to these speculations and gave
them a supposedly scientific character. Papus was primarily influenced in this undertaking by the findings of Bernheim and his followers in the so-called "School of Nancy." Their exaggerated notions about the power of suggestion—which Strindberg, of course,
shared—could rather easily become the opening to occultist speculation.

Torsten Hedlund was the man who pointed the way for Strindberg. In the summer of 1894, Strindberg stated that he believed
there were "neither white nor black magicians—no magicians at all
in fact" (Aug. 11, 1894). Hedlund replied by describing the experiments of Charcot and an occultist by the name of Albert de Rochas.
A work by the latter, *Les états profonds de l'hypnose,* had been published in Swedish translation the preceding year. There is, however,
no indication that Strindberg was directly acquainted with the
book. It was a later work by Rochas, *L'extériorisation de la sensibilité,*
which attracted his attention in the spring of 1896 and suggested
the article that he published in July of the same year in *Initiation*
under the title of "The Irradiation and Extensibility of the Soul."

Rochas was a mesmerist, and the idea for his research probably
came to him from a famous disciple of Mesmer, Baron von Reichenbach, who discovered a mysterious vital fluid he called "od." Rochas
attempted to show experimentally that suggestive and hypnotic
phenomena were brought about by currents, similar to electrical
currents. He thought that the sensibility could be "exteriorized," so
that people could enter into contact with one another from a distance. Under certain conditions, parts of this sensibility—the
aura—could be accumulated in a foreign medium. Thus, Rochas
could store up a person's sensibility in a water glass, and later—far
away and unseen by the subject—he could inflict pain on that subject by sticking a pin down into the glass. Here arises the possibility—at least in principle—of "tormenting someone from a distance,"
which played so great a role for Strindberg. Rochas was convinced
that his ideas provided a firm scientific foundation for occultist

theories about "destruction by sympathetic magic," and he attempted among other things to collect the sensibilities of various
people by taking photographs of them, in order to demonstrate the
possibility of magical torture via effigies.

Of course, Strindberg was already familiar with ideas of this sort
before he came across them in Rochas. In the 1880s, when studying
results of the psychology of hypnosis and suggestion, he had readily
interpreted them in accordance with Mesmer's views.[21] At the end
of the eighties, he had become acquainted with the works of Carl du
Prel, another successor to Baron von Reichenbach and Schopenhauer, who thought that during somnambulistic states man tran-
scends himself in time and space.

In his essay entitled "The Irradiation and Extensibility of the
Soul" (which he reprinted in *Legends*), Strindberg reports that on a
few occasions in Berlin and Brünn he thought that he had been mys-
teriously transported from one place to another. The experiences described appear to refer to absence states combined with a powerful
concentration of the imagination. From the essay, one gets the impression that when he had these experiences, he was completely unfamiliar with the occultist explanation of similar states. Such was
hardly the case, however. It is probable that he already had at least a
superficial knowledge of the occultists' theories of "astral bodies"
and "astral planes" and of their notions concerning the transmigration of souls. Various signs indicate, moreover, that du Prel's ideas
were very significant for him just at the beginning of the 1890s.[22]
Finally, at least one of the episodes he relates—how he was "transported" from Zum Schwarzen Ferkel to another Berlin restaurant—has all the earmarks of an intentional experiment.

When he read in Rochas about the "exteriorization of the sensibility," Strindberg found what seemed to him a likely explanation for
his own experiences. He stated that he was "certain that the soul is
capable of extending itself and that it extends itself very far during
ordinary sleep, finally to leave the body altogether at the time of
death and by no means to be extinguished." [23] Of course, these
conclusions far exceed the actual purport of Rochas' experiments.
According to him, it was not the entire soul that was exteriorized,

but only the sensibility (according to a theory he later advanced, "motricity" was also involved in this outward movement). But Rochas' results provided many tempting opportunities for further speculation. The Paris occultists used his data to support their theories, just as Schopenhauer and du Prel had taken mesmeric experiments as substantiation for their occult metaphysics. "Astral bodies" and "astral planes" are key concepts in all speculations of this nature.

The astral body, a notion that appears to have stemmed from Neo-Platonism and ultimately from primitive animism,[24] is the half-material substratum of the soul. Like the body, it can be located in time and space, but time and space do not bind it in the same way that they bind the body. The astral body can free itself from the person and migrate on the astral plane, where "traces" of everything past still remain and where distances do not exist. By applying this notion, one can find a common explanation for such diverse phenomena as migration of souls, magic, evocation of spirits, ghostly disturbances, premonitory signs, and "phantasms of the living."

Strindberg had always had a tendency to apprehend the spiritual as analogous with the physical, just as he often took the physical to be analogous with the spiritual. This inclination revealed itself in his panpsychism at the beginning of the 1890s. It was also evident a few years earlier in his interpretation of the phenomena related to suggestion. In the occultists he encountered the assertion that an "agent" mediates between the spiritual and the corporeal and combines the qualities of both. Moreover, this assertion appeared in the form of a scientific conclusion. It is not surprising that this animistic concept seemed to him to provide the key to a number of his own experiences. In his essay in *Initiation,* he lists all the conditions that can be explained if one assumes the irradiation of the soul: collective behavior, the power of actor over spectator, the erotic "bond" between lovers. Furthermore, this assumption lends a deeper significance to metaphoric expressions: I am not merely using an image when I say that my thoughts "wander" or that I am "absentminded," for these expressions literally refer to the migration of the soul. "The soul shrinks with fear and expands with joy, happiness, or success." [25]

Guaita is among the French *fin-de-siècle* occultists who acquired great significance for Strindberg. To be sure, his voluminous work *Essais de sciences maudites* is hardly more than a compilation, dealing largely with commonplaces of mystical speculation that Strindberg had also become acquainted with in other works. But correspondences between various details in works by both authors indicate that Strindberg studied Guaita with particular interest. Thus, *Essais de sciences maudites* is a suitable point of departure for studying the influence of theosophical-occultist speculation on Strindberg. In some respects this influence clearly occasioned a permanent change in his outlook.

Essais de sciences maudites appeared in three parts between 1890 and 1897, with a preface by Maurice Barrès. From a literary point of view, it is the most interesting of the numerous occultist works that first saw the light in Paris during the last decades of the nineteenth century. Guaita was also a symbolist poet, and he knew how to present his material in an aesthetically appealing form so that it could simultaneously describe a cavalcade of cultural history and function as an esoteric *jeu d'espirit.* Cabalistic speculation—the sort of abstract associations of thought that Strindberg abhorred when he encountered them in Wronski or the theosophists—occupy a subordinate place in Guaita's work. A large portion of the book is a fascinating account of the history of "black magic" with reports of notorious witch trials and the like. Even in the dogmatic sections Guaita sticks close to concrete reality, and thus, despite all the Paracelsian extravagances, he succeeds in preserving an air of modernity.

As a matter of fact, his metaphysics is nothing but the naturalistic psychology of the time, interpreted—with the help of the astral concept—along animistic lines. His point of departure was the same as Strindberg's: the criticism that Taine, Ribot, and the School of Nancy (which experimented widely with the psychology of suggestion) all leveled against the traditional concept of the unified personality. Ribot's study of the disintegration and doubling of the personality provided Guaita with evidence for the existence of demons, and his mesmeric interpretation of the findings of the School of Nancy turned the psychology of suggestion into evidence for the possibility

of black magic. It was not without reason that Strindberg spoke of a
"naturalistic" occultism. The critique that naturalistic psychology
made of older concepts of the personality is one of the assumptions
on which Guaita's demonology is based, and the naturalistic image
of man appears in his works in mythological disguise. On this point,
Paris occultism—and Guaita in particular—assumed a decisive and
enduring significance for Strindberg. Long after his notions about
"envoûtement" and "black magic" had been relegated to the background, Strindberg's psychological observations—those in *A Blue
Book I* (1907), for example—were still couched in mythological
terms that resembled Guaita's.

For the occultists, the ultimate explanation for all the phenomena
related to suggestion lay in the existence of an astral plane, which
they equated both with Schopenhauer's "will" and with the "unconscious" advocated by Hartmann, Richet, Janet, and Hericaut. Thus,
suggestion is capable of activating the real astral powers, which fall
somewhere between man's psychic and his physical powers. Indeed,
all movements of the human psyche are projected onto the astral
plane. If a man is contemplating murder, he sends an element of
murder out into the air—this example actually occurs in a book that
Strindberg read.[26] Guaita adopts the same line of reasoning in a passage that has counterparts in Strindberg: "Toute âme pense; et toute
pensée est elle-même une âme, à titre infinitésimal; et toute âme,
sur la terre, cherche à s'incarner; c'est encore une des formes de la
lutte pour l'existence . . . Que la pensée émise tache donc, par la
persuasion, de conquérir sa place dans les cerveaux étrangers, c'est
son rôle, et rien de plus juste" (Every soul thinks; and every thought
is itself an infinitesimal soul; and every soul seeks to become incar-
nate. This is one more form of the struggle for existence . . . But
after all, the prime role of thought is to try, by means of persuasion,
to win its place in the minds of others, and nothing could be more
natural).[27]

Not only does this hypothesis concerning psychic powers explain
the workings of suggestion, but it also clarifies the findings of collective psychology (which was then in its infancy): the astral bodies
of a certain number of persons combine to form a collective soul.

Such astral bodies can ultimately break loose from their human context and constitute independent entities. If, for example, many people believe in the same god, they direct their astral powers toward the same point and thereby create the god, who is finally brought to life through faith. One can see how Guaita glides from what one could call substantialization of the spiritual to hypostatization and personification, a path that leads him to a belief in spirits. The astral plane is filled with real beings, albeit they have different degrees of independence: sylphs, gnomes, dryads (in sum, elementals), elementaries (the astral bodies of dead humans), "shades," demons, and so forth. One need not dilate here on the distinctions that Guaita—like Papus and the theosophists—employs in an effort to separate all these animistic notions. In Guaita's case, however, one ought to emphasize the fact that he was very reluctant to relinquish the idea that spirits are of human origin. His demonism is anthropocentric. His spirits revolve around human beings and are more or less the projections of human desires, thoughts, and acts of the will. Naturally, man is also capable of consciously unleashing these astral powers. This is how he explains "les maisons hantées" (haunted houses) and destruction by sympathetic magic, two notions that exercised great power over Strindberg during his crisis.

For Guaita, the gods become a kind of projection of the psychic powers of believers—this is his exegesis of the words in Psalms, "Omnes dii gentium demonia" (For all the gods of the nations are idols) (Ps. 96:5). Since every thought has a soul, a power, the most important functions of the cult were "à créer, á nourrir, á entretenir les dieux" (to create, to nourish, to support the gods).[28] The real battle between two faiths is decided by the power injected into the strife by the faithful. This happens not directly but via the divine figures that they have created on the astral plane. Naturally, the morality of the gods is also dependent on the quality of the believers: just as a powerless community creates a powerless god, so evil people create evil gods. On this point, Guaita's mythology is nothing but the history of religion reinterpreted metaphysically. Strindberg was often attracted by this collective psychology of religion. In *Jacob Wrestles* he describes a Jesuit seminary as "a sort of terrible Vatican that emits measureless torrents of psychic power, the effects of which can be felt at a distance, if one is to believe the theosophists." [29] "Tout se décide entre les grands champions collectifs" (Everything is being fought out between great collective champions), Guaita writes [30] and tells how political and religious battles are decided in the "psychic heaven." A bit of contemporary history that Strindberg projected into a transcendental world for presentation in *Jacob Wrestles* is built on the same idea:

Woe be unto the children of mankind when the Principalities and Powers have fallen into dissention. Then one must listen sharply when the voices of the unseen command obedience, and one must know how to find the right path, for the victor is always right. Is it the world conflagration that is now at hand—or has already started? Are not all of the awakened divinities struggling above the sky for power? Of course, for a while Pan was on top and seemed to hold sway. Jehovah has, to be sure, protected his chosen people, and Christ has not abandoned his faithful. Allah recently showed that he could still defeat the Olympians at Thermopylae, and Buddha is pushing himself forward with a violence that seriously threatened the Nazarene for a moment! [31]

Lamm seems to take such fantasies a bit too seriously when he asserts that Strindberg's concept of "the gods" and "the powers" is modeled on these occultist ideas.[32] For the God and the demons that Strindberg struggled with sprang from his own inner conflicts in quite another way and took their character from those conflicts. From Guaita he borrowed the tendency to project sense experience into a postulated supersensible medium, and in his works it usually has all the earmarks of being a dramatic or poetic *jeu d'esprit,* as the above passage shows. It was "more fun" to conceive of things in this way, just as it was poetically more satisfying to imagine that the world is alive or was created by hand. Moreover, even Guaita is conscious of the lyrical character of his demonology: "Fais-nous sourire et pleurer encore—nous et ceux-là même dont le spleen a pâli les lèvres et bistré les yeux—fais nous pleurer et sourire encore, naive légende qui nous vient du passé obscur, sur le riche langage banalement fleuri, sur le langage héréditaire des vieilles inintelligentes!" (Make us smile and weep again—us and even those whose spleen has paled their lips and put dark circles around their eyes—make us weep and smile again, naive legend, which comes to us out of the dark past along the rich, banally, flowery language, along the hereditary language of chattering old crones).[33]

The idea of the migration of souls is more germane to Strindberg's own conflict. As a matter of fact, it seemed so applicable to his own situation that he regarded it more as an insight than as a theory. The idea as such was not new to him. In a letter to Ola Hansson, in 1889, he was already toying with the thought that he might have inherited the soul of Edgar Allan Poe: "Is it possible that he, who died in 1849—the year I was born—could have smouldered right down through hosts of mediums to me!" (Jan. 3, 1889). Since that time, he had become acquainted with several variants of this belief among the Buddhists, theosophists, and occultists. It flashed up as a possibility around the beginning of 1896 (see "In the Cemetery") and became a matter of personal concern for Strindberg during the two subsequent crises. The idea that earth is a penal colony obviously takes preexistence for granted, and Strindberg began to brood over whose guilt he had inherited. As revealed in *Inferno,* his interest in Napoleon, "the greatest homicide of the century," arose from just such a configuration. He also reports that "the populace" believed him to be Robert, Duke of Normandy. This identification was a very real one in Strindberg's own mind as well, and the working title for *To Damascus* was "Robert le Diable."

Strindberg was even more interested in the Doppelgänger phenomenon than in transmigration. According to the theosophists and the occultists, these spiritual doubles represent a sort of migration of souls in space. In *Inferno* Strindberg gives a minute account of his theory that his friend "Hermann" was actually the Doppelgänger of the well-known American faith healer Francis Schlatter. In April he wrote to Hedlund: "Just between us: I think I have noticed that our bodies are only petals and that one soul can be transferred into another. —Where are our souls at night? Do we lead double lives so that we live one life here by day and another when it is day on the other side of the earth?" (undated). Later, one encounters this thought several times in his letters to Hedlund during the latter half of 1896.

Strindberg himself has explained why he attached so much importance to the Doppelgänger theory during his studies of the occult. In
an interesting passage in his article on the irradiation of the soul, he
writes:

For the past several years, I have made notes on all my dreams and they
convince me that man leads a double life, that one's imaginings, fancies,
and dreams possess a sort of reality. Consequently, all of us are spiritual
somnambulists and in our dreams we commit acts that—according to their
nature—either fill us with a feeling of satisfaction or torment us with pangs
of conscience, fear of the consequences. And for reasons that I reserve the
right to comment on at another time, I think the so-called "persecution
mania" often has a solid foundation in remorse for bad deeds one has committed "in his sleep" and in the hazy memories of those deeds which haunt
us. [34]

This survey of Strindberg's favorite ideas during his occultist
period—that is, the period coinciding with his two most severe
crises—indicates that his guilt conflict was struggling ever closer to
consciousness. Concepts like "crime," "punishment," "atonement,"
"chastisement," and several others with a moral and religious over-
tone occur more and more frequently. Such is the case if one confines
the investigation largely to primary sources—as has been done here.
In Strindberg's subsequent handling of the material in *Inferno*, these
concepts are even more predominant. During this whole time
Strindberg had the feeling that he was being "punished." He was, as
he writes in a letter to his friend and benefactor F. U. Wrangel,
"always being accused of things, often without knowing why"
(Sept. 22, 1896). Sometimes he could even correctly identify the
source of his persecution feelings as "remorse for bad deeds," as in
the passage above.

But he was still not willing to admit that his unspecified remorse
was justified. In psychological terms, the "other life" that he talks
about in his essay on the irradiation of the soul would be called "the
unconscious"—the world of dreams, fancies, remorse, and suppressed desires. By resorting to the Doppelgänger theory, he indicated an unwillingness to admit the objective justification of his
guilt feelings. If his Doppelgänger commits a crime, Strindberg's

conscious self is obviously not responsible. Similarly, his theory about the transmigration of souls and his self-identification with great criminals functioned to suppress guilt feelings. Strindberg felt that he was being punished on someone else's account. The same thing is true of his idea about the earth as a penal colony: he was being punished for offenses of which he had no memory—"impersonal offenses" one might say. In short, Strindberg accepted the punishment and the suffering, but refused to confess his personal guilt. In order to hold this line of defense, he made use of occultism and demonology. After the last crisis, when he maneuvered his guilt conflict into a new position by means of the study of Swedenborg, these ideas became superfluous and were discarded. To the extent that they occur at all after *Inferno*, "occult" ideas play a less central role in his outlook.

During his "demonic" period, Strindberg relegated the idea of God to the background. During his initial period of anxiety, he sometimes felt that he was on familiar terms with his God; at other times he thought he was being subjected to trials intended for his own edification. Taken together, these two attitudes reflect the image of a benevolent but severe Jehovah, and the symbol for Strindberg's relation to him was Job, the innocent man who was punished. During the period when he suffered from delusions of persecution, the thought of his own guilt pressed its way to the surface, only to be energetically and instantly suppressed. His relation to God was thereby altered. In the initial stages of the fourth crisis, Strindberg still defended himself against his enemies by reciting selections from Psalms. Then he mobilized a battery of predominantly occult ideas in order to defend himself against his own awakening sense of guilt. Thereafter the persecutions to which he was subjected became either the work of wicked people or else a punishment that was justified in principle but remained impersonal because it did not apply to offenses committed by Strindberg's conscious self. At this juncture, his image of God—like the rest of his conflict—was transferred to an impersonal plane. Obviously, his hypothesis concerning edifying tribulations was incompatible with his theory of punishment, which involved a more conscious sense of guilt. For if Strindberg had wanted to maintain an intimate relation to the father-God figure he acknowledged, it would have been absolutely necessary for him to confess his own guilt. To the same degree that he put the blame on the universe, impersonality and abstraction also became characteristic of its supreme ruler.

According to *Inferno,* Strindberg's friend Dr. Anders Eliasson had impressed on him in the beginning of August that the Almighty was no longer interested in human faith, an idea that made a powerful impression on Strindberg: "Now there is no longer any groveling before God, and I agree with the basic tenet of Mohammedanism— that one should pray for nothing except the ability to bear the burden of existence with resignation." [35]

During this period, the symbol for Strindberg's relation to his God is no longer Job, but Jacob, who struggled with God. This symbol appears for the first time in an undated letter, written immediately before his trip to Dieppe, and it recurs a few days later in an undated letter to Hedlund in connection with a description of the attacks that Strindberg ascribed to his enemies:

> Who would believe it? And will I be tempting God, if I remain? Indeed! Then I want to tempt him, force him to reveal Himself to me so clearly that I shall never again lose faith in Him.
> Jacob struggles with God and God asks, "What is thy name?" And he answers, "Jacob." And God says, "Thy name shall be called no more Jacob, but Israel: for as a prince hast thou power with God and with men, and hast prevailed."
> This is incomprehensible to me, but it is my own fault.

As he admits in *Inferno,* Strindberg was still dominated by the spirit of the Old Testament, but his change of symbols evidences a shift of emphasis. Job is the passive, Jacob the active seeker of God. Strindberg's choice of a new symbol is obviously related to the increased sense of distance and diminished confidence between him and God that prevailed during the acute stages of his crisis. During the initial stages of this crisis, Strindberg had "been sought" by God—he uses these very words in correspondence with Hedlund— and according to *Inferno,* he had even imagined that he could treat God like a "familiar spirit." When his guilt conflict reappears and relative harmony is broken, God retreats and his intentions seem unclear. Then Strindberg has to seek him and "struggle with him." The reason he now preferred Jacob to Job as a symbol for himself resides in a mere nuance, but this nuance nonetheless mirrors the whole shift in his emotional attitude.

From an intellectual and theological point of view, however, the difference is small. Strindberg's God is still the Old Testament God, an individualistic God for an essentially innocent believer. By the time he wrote *Inferno,* Strindberg equated both these attitudes with arrogance: "Of all conceivable humiliations there is not a single one that I have not tasted, and yet my arrogance still increases in direct proportion to my abasement. What does this mean? Jacob, who struggles with the Eternal One and emerges from the strife a trifle maimed, yet honored by the marks of war? Job, put to the test and persevering in order to justify himself in the face of such undeserved punishment?" [36]

After November 1896 no source is available to fill the same function as Strindberg's invaluable correspondence with Hedlund, in which he makes almost daily reports on his state of mind. The material in *The Occult Diary* is mainly important in helping to establish the chronology of events, for as a rule Strindberg records in it only the naked facts—coincidences, trips, titles of books he had read. Finally, his published accounts of his conversion are unreliable, for on closer scrutiny it appears that his description of the later phases of his crisis (in the latter part of *Inferno,* in *Legends,* and in *Jacob Wrestles*) is misleading from certain points of view.

This kind of subtle distortion is particularly noticeable in Strindberg's references to his study of Swedenborg, which occupied him time and again up to the autumn of 1897 and which had such decisive significance for him. In *Inferno* and *Legends* he speaks repeatedly of his research in Swedenborg's works, and he does so in a manner that suggests progressive discoveries, an "order of penitence." Actually, he was dealing the whole time with the same experience of Swedenborg, which he twisted and reshaped in the spring of 1897 until he was finally able to come to terms with it.

In December 1896 he borrowed the master's magnum opus, *Ar-*

cana coelestia (Heavenly Arcana) from Lidforss. On December 17, he reported his first impressions to his mother-in-law in Austria: "Am now reading Swedenborg's *Arcana coelestia* and am terrified. The whole thing seems to me to be true, but too cruel of a loving God." [37] According to *Inferno,* he was still searching through Swedenborg for confirmation of his old belief that earth is hell: "In *Arcana coelestia,* the riddles of these past two years were explained, and the explanation was so faithful right down to the last detail that I—a child of the latter half of the famous nineteenth century—derived from it an unshakable conviction that hell exists, but here on earth, and that I have just gone through it," [38] When he wrote *Legends,* Strindberg still had the impression that *Arcana coelestia* was full of severity and devoid of compassion: it "only speaks of hell and of punishment instituted by evil spirits, that is to say, by devils." [39] Later in the same work, he states that it is "unending hell, with no hope of an end and no word of comfort." [40]

Later—the date is difficult to establish—he came across Swedenborg's *Book of Dreams,* where he discovered that in 1744 the master had undergone "the same nightly torture as I have lately suffered myself." This, he reports in *Legends,* "enlightens me concerning the benevolent intentions of the Invisible One—without comforting me, however. Not until I had read *Heaven and Hell* did I begin to feel edified." [41] Thus, the order in which Swedenborg's works fell into Strindberg's hands must have been: (1) *Arcana coelestia,* (2) *The Book of Dreams,* and (3) *Heaven and Hell.* It is not clear just when he read *Apocalypse Explained.* According to the information given in *Legends,* he was also acquainted with this work before March 1897, when he ran across first *The Marvels of Heaven and Hell* and then *On Conjugal Love* "in a secondhand bookshop." He did not finally study *True Christian Religion* until much later.

Most striking are Strindberg's statements about *Heaven and Hell,* which he claims to have stumbled onto in one of Lund's antiquarian bookshops in March 1897. Strindberg maintains that discovering this book inspired his decisive conversion from religious doubt to full confidence. But *Heaven and Hell* was one of the two works that he had already studied in Pernetty's French translation in September of the preceding year. In Lund, he doubtless had in his possession the French translation of the book, which he had read in Austria. On March 19 and 21 he quotes two passages from Swedenborg in his diary, one from *Heaven and Hell,* the other from *The Earths in Our Solar System* in French and in phrasing that is at least partly identical with Pernetty's. [42]

Thus, what happened in March 1897 was not that Strindberg got hold of a new work by Swedenborg that opened fresh perspectives for him, as implied in *Legends.* Instead, he reread a work that he already knew and which had once made a deep impression on him—but he reread it in a new spirit. He may merely have retouched a few details here at this point in *Legends* to heighten the dramatic effect of these events, but probably the real explanation for this new spirit lies deeper.

Strindberg did not become interested in Swedenborg until being hailed as his countryman in *Initiation.* Later, in Balzac's *Séraphita* he found Swedenborg described as a great prophet whose philosophy had emerged from the mists of Scandinavia and from the deep soul of the Nordic people. One notices that in presenting this information in *Inferno,* Strindberg is at pains to represent himself as the heir of Swedenborg. "The sanctuary is ready, draped in white and rose, and the saint will soon take up residence with his disciple, who was summoned here from their common homeland in order to rekindle the memory of the man who was endowed with greater gifts of grace than any other man born of woman in modern times." [43] Through these clouds of incense one glimpses a Strindberg who imagined that it was his mission to revive Swedenborgianism in France. One must bear in mind that *Inferno* and *Legends* were written in French, with a French public in mind, and that Swedenborg was one of the mystics whose names had created a stir in *fin de siècle* circles. As Strindberg explained in a letter to Hedlund, "Swedenborg is very much in the ascendant here and is thought of as the first theosopher in modern times before Allan Kardec; and I frequently read that I am from Swedenborg's homeland and so forth" (May 15, 1896). Under such conditions, it was tempting for Strindberg to dramatize and exaggerate Swedenborg's significance for himself. It is also clear that he had this end in view when retouching the picture for inclusion in *Legends*.

This line of investigation can be carried even further. At this juncture, Strindberg was more inclined to identify himself with Swedenborg (or attempt to do so) than to be his disciple. Whereas he combed the theosophists or occultists for doctrines that suited his purposes, he read Swedenborg mainly to find experiences analogous to his own. In September 1896 he believed he had proof that Swedenborg had seen and described the same hell in which he was living himself. This parallel became essential for him, and he paid no heed to the fact that Swedenborg did not intend to describe earthly life as a hell. The identification became even more striking when he resumed the study of Swedenborg in the spring of 1897. He discovered his own experiences in *The Book of Dreams,* in *Heaven and Hell,* and above all, in *The Earths in Our Solar System;* and because of these parallels he attributed importance to Swedenborg in connection with his own development.

The trait of Swedenborg's that most attracted Strindberg must have been his concrete, everyday relation to the divine—the rationalistic matter-of-factness that permitted him to describe heaven and hell as if he were writing a travel book about foreign countries. As in *Inferno,* concrete experiences—some of them very bizarre—play a significant role both in Swedenborg's story of his conversion and in his subsequent hallucinations. Both his conversion and Strindberg's took place in broad daylight, so to speak. But their differences are greater than their similarities. Swedenborg's hallucinations served to confirm a mighty theological system built on rational principles deriving from the Neo-Platonic doctrine of emanation. Strindberg was neither a visionary nor a rationalistic systematist. He never made contact with Swedenborg's Neo-Platonism. On the whole, it must be admitted that Strindberg's insight into "the doctrines of Swedenborg" always remained inadequate. He read Swedenborg's works in a spirit partly alien to that in which they had been written, and much that was central to Swedenborg's system escaped him. During this time, Swedenborg was important to Strindberg as a "teacher" and a "leader" because he supplied his imagination with much new material, and as a "guide" because he provided Strindberg with current Christian moralism.

If one scrutinizes the passages that Strindberg quotes from Swedenborg in order to demonstrate the identity of his own fate with that of the master, one discovers that *Arcana coelestia, Apocalypse Explained,* and *True Christian Religion*—the three great theological works—played a subordinate role during the Inferno crisis. One can scarcely doubt the significance of *The Book of Dreams.* In addition to this curious book, the two works he had cited in Pernetty's edition still exercised the greatest power over Strindberg's outlook when he wrote *Inferno* and *Legends.* He gave no less than three accounts of his decisive experience with Swedenborg in March 1897. The first occurs in the chapter entitled "The Redeemer" in *Inferno;* the other two appear as chapters in *Legends,* called "Education" and "Studies in Swedenborg." The quotations from Swedenborg that occur in these chapters are practically all taken either from *Heaven and Hell* or from *The Earths in Our Solar System.* Just as Strindberg had previously compared the appearance of hell with the landscape in the vicinity of Klam, he now compares his own experiences with Swedenborg's accounts of the ways in which man is "trained" by "corrective spirits." The correspondences between the two lead Strindberg to conclude that he has been subjected to the same sort of severe treatment as Swedenborg.

Even if Strindberg's assimilation of Swedenborg's theories appears to be much slighter than supposed, his renewed study of the texts unquestionably brought him a step closer to the master. The prerequisite for this change was the psychological process that caused him to become fully conscious of his guilt in March 1897. After that, he could read Swedenborg's descriptions of hell and of the activities of the spirits on Jupiter in the same spirit as they had been written—that is to say, in a moralistic spirit. The punishments and the hells in Swedenborg are just retribution for personal offenses. By laying aside his arsenal of demonic notions and using instead Swedenborg's word "destruction" as the full explanation for his sufferings, Strindberg calls attention to the change that has taken place in him. "Destruction," an idea that Swedenborg borrowed from St. Paul, is exhaustively described in *Arcana coelestia.* It is also mentioned in *Heaven and Hell.* According to Strindberg's account, "destruction" is abandonment of oneself "to Satan for the mortification of the flesh" [44] and in "preparation for a spiritual life." [45] Evil for its own sake does not exist. Acceptance of this idea enabled Strindberg to write: "my hope of finding peace of mind through contrition and strict observance in thought and deed was reborn." [46]

It was not until he himself had accepted this essentially moral interpretation of his sufferings that Strindberg could assimilate Swedenborg's optimistic concept of the problem of theodicy. "Not until then am I freed from the nightmare that had haunted me ever since the first revelation of the invisible powers." [47] These words seem to imply that not before Strindberg had read *Heaven and Hell* for the second time did he grasp the real meaning of Swedenborg's presentation of the afterlife. When constructing his theology, Swedenborg endeavored as much as possible to limit God's personal responsibility for evil. The origin of evil lies in the free will of mankind, and instead of being imposed from without, punishments inhere in the sinner's own character. Sin literally punishes itself in Swedenborg's hell, when the people follow the promptings of their own hearts and wallow in vices and filth.

This theodicy made a powerful impression on Strindberg when he discovered it in March 1897, principally through a rereading of *Heaven and Hell.* In all three accounts of his Swedenborgian experience, he expresses this new insight in almost identical terms. For example, in the chapter entitled "Studies in Swedenborg" he writes: "God is love. He does not reign over slaves, and therefore He has permitted mortals to enjoy free will. There are no powers of evil; instead there is a servant of the good who functions as a corrective spirit. Punishments are not eternal; every man is perfectly free patiently to atone for the wrongs he has done." [48] This somewhat unorthodox concept of the nature of evil, which Strindberg took from Swedenborg, introduces an evangelical tone into his religious frame of reference, [49] and with it an echo of the optimistic mood that dom-

inated him prior to the two great crises: "These inexplicable sufferings do have a purpose: the improvement of my self and its development into something greater—the ideal that Nietzsche dreamed of,
although differently conceived." [50]

He now conceives of "improvement" and "development" of the
self not in an aesthetic and esoteric sense, as he had before the crises,
but in ethical terms. In each of his accounts of his Swedenborgian
experience, he emphasizes his consciousness of personal guilt, his
remorse, and the demands of morality. "Then the problem of evil
rears its head once more, and Taine's moral indifferentism falls to
the ground when faced with the new demands," he states in *Inferno,* [51] just before he speaks of killing demons by means of remorse.
Finally, in the chapter entitled "Studies in Swedenborg," where
Strindberg advises the man who is suffering punishment "patiently
to atone for the wrongs he has done," [52] he intimates what this
moral attitude has meant for him personally: "Likewise, there are
unwholesome temptations. Malevolent spirits evoke in the depths of
the soul all the evil that he has committed since he was a child and
in such a way that it is distorted and magnified in the direction of
immorality. But the angels reveal what is good and true in the person who is being tormented. This is the strife that appears under the
name of remorse." [53]

A few pages later in *Legends,* Strindberg writes: "[I] long ago instituted a meticulous test of my conscience, and faithful to my new
program of assuming the burden of guilt, instead of blaming my
neighbor, I find my past life detestable and feel disgusted by my
own personality." [54] But he had already dealt with these experiences
in *Inferno,* shortly after describing his great Swedenborg experience:

Have you noticed in the stillness of the night or even in broad daylight
how memories, revived from your past, stir you—singly or in packs. All
the mistakes you have made, all the offenses, all the follies you have committed—they send the blood tingling to your ear lobes, the cold sweat to
your hair, the chills to your spine. You relive your life from the day of your
birth to the present moment. You suffer once again through all your past
sufferings. You empty all the cups that you have already drained to the

dregs so often. When there is no longer any flesh to crucify, you crucify your skeleton. When your heart is laid in ashes, you burn your soul on the pyre.[55]

I have quoted at length from the passages in which Strindberg, referring to the spring of 1897, speaks of his newly aroused remorse, because these feelings effected a decisive change in his outlook. The inextirpable guilt feelings, which he had still rejected during the great crises, now emerged into his conscious mind. Such accents never occur in anything Strindberg wrote during his atheistic period, and they are still unknown during the initial stages of the Inferno crisis. Of course, even during this period he was much given to examining his past life, but never for the purpose of finding and confessing his own guilt. In "Sensations détraquées" (Deranged Sensations), an essay written in 1894, he concludes a description similar to the one quoted above by remarking: "Indeed, it is not the evil we have done, not our crimes that we are ashamed of—it is our follies!" [56] After 1897, it was chiefly his crimes that concerned him. With this concern a new dimension, the moral dimension—as significant from a psychological as from a religious view point— became a part of Strindberg's outlook. Thereafter, his discussion was essentially moralistic. In *Inferno, Legends, Jacob Wrestles,* and *To Damascus* the basic problem concerns such questions as: What shall I regret? How much remorse should I feel? What is the relation between the crimes I have committed and the punishment I have been subjected to? How should I live my life in order to satisfy God? The obstinate attitude toward God that was so characteristic of the latter part of Strindberg's life—his bookkeeping system for guilt and punishment, his revolt against his God at moments when he thought the punishment too hard—all these reactions were determined by his new moralistic outlook.

Inferno was written after Strindberg's decisive experience of Swedenborg. Strictly speaking, the actual idea of *Inferno* was no longer central to his new situation. He had replaced the pessimistic idea that earth is a hell with the concept of "destruction." Moreover, active remorse had replaced the obscure guilt feelings that he had thought were derived from a "previous existence." But his position was ambiguous. Writing *Inferno* (which he began in a spirit of self-criticism and self-assessment inspired by the study of Swedenborg) involved reconstructing—almost reliving—all the horrible ordeals to which he felt he had been subjected. As a result of this creative effort, he found it increasingly difficult to accept the burden of guilt, so that when he finished the book, he was on the point of resuming all the attitudes he had just managed to overcome. When he later renewed the attempt to assess himself in *Jacob Wrestles* and *To Damascus,* he was able to view the issues much more clearly.

When writing *Inferno,* Strindberg was bent on determining which of his offenses had provoked the punishment that befell him. In the first five chapters he constantly hints that his tribulations were especially designed to punish him for the lack of consideration he had shown to his dependent wives and children, (of which he was now aware), and the title of the last of these chapters elucidates this purpose: "The Fall and Paradise Lost." At one point in the beginning of the book, he admits frankly: "But no sooner had I sinned than I was caught in the act, and the punishment appears with such exactitude and such refinement that it allows no room for doubt that some power is intervening to chastise me in order to reform me." [57] Thus, Strindberg feels that his break with Frida Uhl occasioned both the persecution he suffered around the beginning of 1895 and his sojourn in "the purgatory of Saint-Louis." Also, he regards the humiliations of his affair with Mme. Lecain as a just, though "insufficient" punishment for his criminal desire. Later on, he implies that the dreadful events which caused him to move into the Hôtel Orfila stemmed from his manipulations of his daughter's picture. This crime-punishment formula was the guideline Strindberg used in reconstructing the events that took place before 1896, when he began to keep a diary.

At the same time, one notices in these first five chapters how difficult it was for Strindberg to adhere to a program of blaming himself for everything. Sometimes he assumes guilt and attempts to transfer it to someone else, all in the same breath. What results is a curious vacillation, which manifests itself in a peculiar stylistic effect. One finds examples of this effect in the opening pages of the book, where Strindberg discusses his wife. He first refers to her as "my dear wife," but in the next paragraph calls her "my beautiful prison-keeper, who spied on my soul day and night . . . jealously observed my spirit's struggle toward the unknown." [58] When Strindberg treats his farewell letter, he writes: "In an attack of righteous pride, seized by a raging desire to do myself some harm, to commit suicide, I send an infamous, unforgivable letter." This act, he reports, makes him both "a suicide and an assassin," [59] and he later refers to the action as "crime." Underlying this accumulation of contradictory moral and psychological characteristics is his own vacillation between different concepts and tendencies, between self-blame and self-exculpation.

When he wrote *Inferno,* Strindberg was still in doubt about the prudence of his actions. On the one hand, he had a moral obligation to provide for his family; on the other hand, he was still haunted by the notion that had been uppermost in his mind when he broke with Frida Uhl, namely, that the "cultivation" or "refinement" of his own self demanded that he sacrifice his family's happiness. He still suspected that his "crime" ought strictly to be regarded as a case of justifiable self-conquest. One finds support for this interpretation of the obscure opening passages of *Inferno* in a letter that Strindberg sent to the Uhl family on February 23, 1897—that is, before his crucial Swedenborgian experience. He writes: "Am now reading Bulwer's *Zanoni!* With terror! It's all right there! I, Frida—all because he had drunk the elixir of life! He is always looking for his Viola, and she flees, even though she loves him! Read the book! Fillide (Aspasia) is in it too!" [60]

Shortly thereafter, on March 1, 1897, he writes his mother-in-law that his *"Inferno* is planned; I have found the form and now I want to write it." [61] Actually, he did not begin composing the book until two months later, but it is not unreasonable to suppose that the finished *Inferno* retains some elements of the plan he had worked out in March.

Love occupies a peculiar place in Bulwer-Lytton's book about the magician Zanoni. Sensual love is unconditionally forbidden for the magician. When the other main character in the book, Glyndon, undertakes to be initiated into the arcana of Rosecrucianism, he fails because of his love for Fillida and is then subjected to terrifying, punitive experiences. Zanoni goes through a similar ordeal. Even though his love for Viola is of a higher sort, it nonetheless brings him into the power of "the Guardian," the infernal monster that frightens away all adepts seeking wisdom. Not until he sacrifices his immortality for the life of the woman he loves is he reconciled with the higher powers.

Thus, throughout the book love is for Bulwer-Lytton an alternative to wisdom. The magical superman must choose between the two, and there can be no compromise. This thought was not new to Strindberg. During his Buddhist period in 1894 he had already come to regard family life as degrading to a sublime spirit. But it is not unlikely that his reading of Bulwer-Lytton's novel helped revive the idea for him.

In addition to this occultist morality with its roots in Neo-Platonism and oriental mysticism, Strindberg drew nourishment from the sturdier Lutheran moralism that he had come into contact with through Swedenborg. It is chiefly his vacillation between these two moral concepts that casts such a hesitant, inconsistent light on the material in the first chapter of *Inferno*.

Strindberg's attempt to put a moral interpretation on his tribulations met with other, more particular difficulties. He sometimes finds that the punishment is too severe; thus, at the beginning of the second chapter he interrupts the flow of the narrative to interpolate a reflection that is clearly the fruit of retrospective observation: "If I had avoided these people because of unjustified arrogance, the punishment would have been logical. But in this case, where my reserve was the result of an effort to purify my individuality, to refine my personality in the self-imposed trials of a life of isolation, I do not understand the course of action that Providence has chosen." [62] At other times he is astonished at the mildness of the punishment: "Although the punishment was harsh and instantaneous, meted out by a practiced hand that I could not fail to recognize, it struck me as being insufficient." [63]

In subsequent discussions of moral problems, Strindberg depends less and less on these ideas. In their place one finds him accusing himself of arrogance, hubris, conceit—"the only vice that the gods do not forgive." [64] When Torsten Hedlund had accused him of similar faults in 1896, Strindberg counterattacked bitterly. Now, however, he never tires of asserting that vanity and spiritual pride had infected his religious ideas during the crisis. But even when he is accusing himself, Strindberg also takes the offensive. Immediately after making the above confession, he enters upon a polemic directed against Torsten Hedlund and labels "the denial and annihilation of the self" as "madness": "Before whom then shall I bow? The theosophists? Never! Before the Eternal, the Powers, Providence I still attempt to curb my wicked impulses every day, insofar as it is possible. To strive for the preservation of my ego against all the influences that a domineering sect or party may try to impose on me, that is my duty, dictated by the conscience I have acquired through the grace of my divine protectors." [65]

But later in the book he characterizes a similar state of mind as "pious vanity." It is clear from many passages that this inconsistency in fact represents a dialogue mirroring the struggle that was going on inside Strindberg while writing *Inferno*. When describing his attacks while living on the Rue de la Clef, he mentions having read the penitential Psalms and then inserts some paragraphs that have a direct bearing on his new moral outlook.

But should I read the penitential Psalms? No, I have no right to repent, for I am not the one who has guided my destiny. I have never done evil for its own sake, but only to defend myself. To repent is to criticize Providence, who imposes sin on us as a form of suffering intended to purify us through the disgust that our bad deeds engender in us.

My account with life ended thus: Let us say we are even. If I have sinned, I have surely been punished enough for it. That is certain! Should I fear hell? But indeed, I have gone through a thousand hells in this life without faltering—more than enough to awaken a burning desire to leave the vanities and deceptive pleasures in this world, which I have always abhorred. Born homesick for heaven, as a child I wept over the filthiness of existence, felt like a stranger among my relatives and in society. Ever since childhood

I have sought my God, but found the Devil. I have borne Christ's cross in my youth, and I have repudiated a God who is content to rule over slaves that cringe before their tormentors.[66]

These indictments of Providence are Strindberg's answers to his own moral self-criticism, which he had developed in loose adherence to the teachings of Swedenborg. The same arguments recur later in *Inferno,* when he describes his state of mind in the spring of 1897. Further variants of these arguments turn up in *Jacob Wrestles.*

It would appear that Strindberg's tendency to self-exculpation grew more intense while he was working on *Inferno.* Even if it required a degree of self-conquest, he could finally induce himself to regard his admitted injustices to wife and child as real sins demanding punishment. As soon as "pride" entered the foreground, his problem came into sharp focus. Using a common religious mode of thought, Strindberg was eager, on the one hand, to regard pride as the root of all the evil in his life. On the other hand, he could not accept the new view of himself that would result from submitting to the demands of "humility."

One reason that this dilemma emerges with such clarity at this point is that Strindberg is about to embark on an account of his two most severe crises. When he wrote *Inferno,* of course, he regarded them as some sort of "punishment" for crimes he had committed— at least, he intended to regard them as such. But when recalling the dreadful experiences he had been through, he found it difficult to admit that his punishment was really just. One notices that at times during the composition of *Inferno* he feels hesitant about the background of these events and is once again tempted by theories he had entertained six months earlier—theories that located the cause of his persecutions either in evil demons or in vindictive human beings: "At this moment, as I write, I do not know what happened on that July night when death rushed in at me." [67]

While he was writing *Inferno,* his old ideas about "unjustly imposed sufferings" and its demonic and Manichean antecedents constantly crowded in on Strindberg's mind. The conflict between these earlier notions and his new religious moralism becomes so intense in the last three chapters that arguments and counterarguments follow one another thick and fast like speeches in a heated discussion. The chapter entitled "The Redeemer" concludes with the explanation that demons are "corrective spirits" whose goal is good, and that the Devil has no independent existence—such was his interpretation of the teachings of Swedenborg. But in the very next chapter one finds attitudes that Strindberg himself had equated with "self-exculpation and pride." The appearance of such attitudes threatens his conviction that the intentions of "the Powers" are basically good. To repent is to indict Providence, and Strindberg makes Providence responsible for the whole muddle of his life. Perhaps the gods are demons, Christ himself an "avenging spirit," and life nothing but a huge joke: "Are we not tempted to believe that the gods are jesting with us mortals and that this is why the conscious banterers among us can laugh at the most painful moments of our lives!" [68]

Not until he made a retrospective analysis of his experiences of 1896 did Strindberg explicitly revert to the Manichean religion that he had advocated around 1877, when he wrote the *Epilogue to Master Olof.* When suffering from delusions of persecution, he had sometimes toyed with the idea that there is a lower order of gods, the demons, or else that he had been placed in a hell for unknown sins. But somewhere in the background had always been a just God—or at least, a God who was benevolent in principle. Now that this God had emerged far enough from the clouds to impose strict morality and to demand remorse and purification, Strindberg responded with open defiance and reversed the formula: he is the one who is just; God or the gods are unjust—God himself is a demon. All the misfortunes that befell him in 1896 clearly developed in Strindberg a more radical kind of doubt about the good intentions of "the Powers" than he had entertained at earlier stages of the crisis. But behind this doubt still loomed the moral question: Have I deserved my punishment? Should I be contrite? Now, however, Strindberg's whole discussion of this question was conscious in a way that it had not been before, when he had occasionally resorted to Manichean notions without first instituting an ethical inquiry into himself. And naturally, defiance did not have the last word. Later in his description of this internal battle he writes:

The sun is shining; daily life continues on an even keel; the noise the workmen make puts one in a happy frame of mind. It is at such moments that one gets up enough courage to revolt and then flings his challenge, his doubts at the heavens.

But at night, silence and solitude engulf one; his insolence is dispersed; his heart pounds audibly and he feels constrictions in his chest. Then, fall on your knees in the brier patch outside your window; go fetch a doctor or find a friend who will sleep in the same room with you! [69]

Strindberg tells about a very similar series of events in "The Spirit of Contradiction," a chapter in *Legends* which, as a matter of fact, deals with more or less the same period as the final chapters of *Inferno*. In an occultist periodical, Strindberg had read about some ancient mythological ideas to the effect that the gods were originally human beings who had risen to power and now held other beings in check. [70] Thus, the gods are the natural enemies of mankind. In this context, Strindberg remembers Prometheus, the rebel who was "taken up into the realm of the Olympians without making *amende honorable.*" [71] These Manichean and occultist ideas have made a powerful impression on him because they give metaphysical expression to his own unwillingness to repent and to put the blame on himself; but at night he is punished for his rebellious thoughts: "Hurl your arrows, proud Gaul, against heaven; heaven never rests." [72]

The vacillation evident in *Inferno* is inherent even in the thought that gave the book its title—the thought that earth is a hell. During the actual crisis, Strindberg conceived of this idea solely in pessimistic terms, with the result that he viewed earth as a penal colony, whose entire population was doing penance for crimes committed in a previous existence. He chose "Inferno" as the title of his projected book just at the time when he was most deeply concerned with this idea in its original form. Even though other experiences intervened and the plan of the book probably changed during the months preceding its composition, he retained the title. The fact that his original idea of "Inferno" was incompatible with the more moralistic interpretation he began to make of his experiences after March 1897 is the reason for the obscurity surrounding this essential point in the book itself. After having explained in the chapter entitled "The Redeemer," that evil does not exist as an independent power—an idea borrowed from Swedenborg—Strindberg raises the question once more in the epilogue. This time he can find no solution:

> This Prince of the World, who condemns mortals to sins and punishes virtue with the cross, the stake, insomnia, nightmares—who is he? The chastiser, to whom we are consigned because of unknown or forgotten crimes that we have committed elsewhere? And Swedenborg's corrective spirits? Guardian angels that protect us against spiritual evil!
> What a Babylonian confusion! [73]

Here, as everywhere in *Inferno,* his former Manichean, pessimistic attitude is at variance with his newer moral and religious mood. An intermediate form of these concepts is the idea that "certain individuals have already found their hell during this life," for which Strindberg found confirmation in Luther. Strindberg himself hesitated to feature the idea of hell in the title of his book. Not until he had made a collection of excerpts from Viktor Rydberg's *Medieval Magic* did he finally find the confidence to proclaim that his first choice had been the best title after all: "Do you think I did not know what I was doing when I named my book *Inferno?*" [74]

Strindberg was torn between two kinds of metaphysics, the occultist-Manichean and the religious. Nor was he alone in this dilemma. The whole occultist movement in France held an ambiguous attitude toward the Catholic Church. Some of the occultists doubtless considered themselves good Catholics, but many others preferred to explore and develop heretical doctrines, like those that Strindberg discovered in the occultist periodical. Like Strindberg, Paris occultism had inherited many ideas from romantic Manicheism. Though they seldom expounded these dangerous thoughts dogmatically, the occultists often treacherously smuggled them into their doctrines along with other more innocuous precepts. Eliphas Lévi in particular was fond of Promethean ideas. Moreover, a Catholic writer, Fernand Divoire, wrote a brochure criticizing Sar Péladan and Lévi for their "pride" and claiming that Lévi's self-assertion had gone so far as to abolish God and invest man with his prerogatives.

That Catholicism should have been Strindberg's alternative to oc-

cultism when he finished *Inferno* is quite in keeping with the manner
in which the question had been set forth by French writers. For him,
it was not really a question of accepting Catholic instead of Protestant dogma. His "homesickness for the bosom of the mother
Church" was an expression of his effort to "humble and sully" himself [75] and, at the same time, to seek protection against the world
and his own evil inclinations. This is why Strindberg petitioned in
May 1897 for a "retreat" in the Abbey of Solesmes. [76] For a Catholic,
of course, a "retreat" implies a temporary sequestration from the
world. The actual story of his "journey to a monastery" typifies the
vacillation manifested by Strindberg at the time of completing *Inferno*. He states on the last page that while finishing the book, he
was awaiting an answer from the monastery, and he subsequently
added the famous closing lines: "Quelle blague, quelle lugubre
blague que la vie!" (What a jest, what a lugubrious jest this life is),
which were later changed to: "By the time this book is in print, I
should have received an answer. And then? Afterwards? Yet another
jest by the gods, who roar with laughter when we shed hot
tears?" [77]

Strindberg describes the outcome of this episode in *Legends*. According to this version of the story, on arriving in Paris, he is supposed to have decided to seek a ' retreat" in the monastery. [78] This
decision, he reports, was "not absolute, I must confess," and he
postponed taking action on it. While still pondering a withdrawal,
he read in *La Presse* that the abbot of the monastery had been re-
moved from office for indecent assault. He thereupon exclaimed:
"Am I still a plaything of the invisible powers!" [79] a paraphrase of
the closing lines of *Inferno*. Actually, the case was not quite the same
as presented here. On September 2, Strindberg noted in his diary
that he had read about the scandal at Solesmes and added, "where I
once thought of going." In other words, he had already abandoned
the plan, and the scandal served only to corroborate his suspicions
that "the Powers" wanted to turn him to ridicule.

This event suggests that on completing *Inferno* Strindberg was no
more certain than ever which way his path was tending. The liberating insight he had gained in March 1897, when he discovered a

moral meaning in his tribulations, had given way to a mood of agitation, which gradually grew more intense as Strindberg noted the apparent absurdity of his moral obligations. Then his demonic and Manichean notions cropped up once more as tempting alternatives to religious moralism. These notions predominate in the Epilogue, where Strindberg, referring to sources he had found in Rydberg's *Medieval Magic,* speaks of the independent existence of demons, of destruction by means of sympathetic magic (envoûtement), of the earth as a hell. Strindberg once again adopts the outlook he had maintained during the latter part of 1896 and exclaims: "A man's life can appear to be a melancholy jest!" [80] The last three chapters of *Inferno* and the Epilogue constitute a network of contradictions. Their tone is one of self-criticism and passionate doubt.

The peculiar religious terminology in the book must also be seen against the background of this battle between arrogance and humility, of this dialogue between moral contrition and self-justification that Strindberg was engaged in when writing *Inferno.* In his correspondence with Hedlund he had generally spoken about "God." Axel Herrlin reports that when Strindberg first arrived in Lund, he used to divert his friends with stories about the interference of "the invisible ones," but as the spring wore on he began to speak instead of "the powers." [81] Herrlin also opines that Strindberg's use of the word must have been inspired by the example of the contemporary press, which had begun to refer to "the powers" instead of "the world powers." Lamm, who dismisses this hypothesis as unsatisfactory, believes instead that "the origin of the term as well as of the concept" stems from occultist notions about beings inhabiting the astral plane, sometimes called "les puissances invisibles" (the invisible powers). [82] Finally, Eklund has pointed out that the expression "the powers" occurs in works Strindberg wrote prior to his sojourn in Lund and that it may also be found in some of his contemporaries, like Brandes and Maupassant. [83]

Eklund's examples of the use of the word "powers" to mean "metaphysical powers"—not to mention the other examples of this usage that can be found in the early Strindberg, or in works written before or during his time—show quite clearly that the expression was current.[84] One can hardly maintain that it "came from" the newspapers, from the Paris occultists, or from any other such source, since Strindberg had long been familiar with it and might even have encountered it first in the works of St. Paul. The problem remains: why did Strindberg in the spring of 1897, just when he was about to write *Inferno,* abandon "the invisible ones" and begin to speak of "the powers"? Herrlin's reference to journalistic usage would not seem to provide an adequate explanation. But neither does Lamm's reference to the Paris occultists, for Strindberg's outlook was only partly informed by occultist ideas when he wrote *Inferno.*

Lamm has pointed out that the phrase "the invisible ones" corresponds directly to the "puissances invisibles" of the Paris occultists. When Strindberg arrived in Sweden around the end of 1896, he was still full of his experiences of the last crisis, in which occultist notions had played an important role; it is therefore quite probable that he used the term "the invisible ones" at this time to designate beings comparable to the "elementals" of the occultists.

Strindberg, however, began to use the term "the powers" at the same time as he was seriously attempting a moral interpretation of his experiences, that is, in the spring of 1897. The connection seems to be significant. When Strindberg devised the terminology used in *Inferno,* his delusions of persecution had faded and his metaphysical notions had been elevated from the purely demonic stage they had reached during his fifth crisis to a higher plane. The nucleus of his outlook at this time was a conviction that someone (or some beings) were "guiding his destiny," and when he began to write the book, he felt that this guidance aimed at his moral edification. However, he was not completely convinced that the universe was essentially moral, and during dark intervals he suspected that it was basically evil, or at least ironical. "The powers" was a conception well suited to cover his vacillation on this question. As opposed to the "puissances invisibles" of the occultists, the banal expression "the powers" could describe any attitude at all—from simple fatalism to a religiosity inspired either by Manichean ideas or by Swedenborg. Precisely because of the uncertainty of his attitude, Strindberg chose concepts that were as vague as possible. Instead of "God"—a word

that would tend to bind him to a more orthodox form of religion—
he speaks of "the invisible hand," of "the gods," or of "the eternal."
But in general, these expressions are used in conjunction with definite predicates—"the invisible hand" punishes or crushes, "the eternal" sends tribulations or avenges wrongs, "the gods" rejoice at the
sufferings of mankind, and so forth—and thus, each of these terms
expresses one phase of Strindberg's metaphysical system. "The
powers," in contrast, is a generic term, which can accommodate
practically all the functions of his metaphysics. "The powers" are
neither clearly good nor evil. They guide his destiny as does "the invisible hand," protect him as does "the eternal," deny him advantages, withdraw their favor from him, and pardon him again. They
are not so cruel as humans, but they are sometimes angered. The
very ambiguity of these terms and their lack of sectarian precision
made them appropriate for Strindberg when he wrote *Inferno.*

Another factor may have contributed to his choice of "the powers"
as a favorite term. Just as Strindberg chose his companions from
among the "freethinkers" in Lund, so he directed his book not to
religious people but to those whose thinking had been formed, as
had his own, in the light of naturalistic and positivistic critiques of
religion. To gain such an audience, the obvious course was to play
down religious factors and to emphasize quasi-scientific mysticism
instead. As he himself points out in *Legends,* this was the position he
took during discussions with friends at the cafés in Lund: "I cut my
personality in two and show the world the naturalistic occultist, but
inside I preserve and tend the seeds of a confessionless belief." [85] He
is more frank in *Inferno,* but such considerations may nonetheless
have had significance for him when choosing the words "the powers"
to convey his new experiences. "The powers" was a concept used by
men who were skeptics or atheists on principle—Schopenhauer,
Maupassant, Hamsun—when they occasionally were tempted to
consider a higher ruling principle in the world. Many times when
Strindberg referred to "the powers," he could just as well have used
"God," as he does in his letters to Hedlund. He chose the former
term because it was less defiant, less definite, and because it permitted him to retreat to a skeptical fatalism.

Jacob Wrestles deals with the continuation of Strindberg's conversion and describes his situation in the autumn and winter of 1897. But in approaching this work, one must obviously take into consideration the fact that it was intended as a literary account of Strindberg's experience and that the method of composition differed greatly from that employed in writing *Inferno* and *Legends*. In *Jacob Wrestles*, the religious struggle is stylized and concentrated on the essential moments of the action. Moreover, the work is a fragment. One can hardly assume that the tired mood into which he lapses at the end of the book was originally intended as the terminus of conversion. Perhaps Strindberg wanted to let himself be led gradually to the doors of the Catholic Church, as he is later in *To Damascus*.

In an attempt to simplify the religious equation in *Jacob Wrestles*, Strindberg emphasizes the moral aspects of his situation. The factual, more or less "supernatural" happenings that stand in the center of *Inferno* and *Legends* here occupy a subordinate place: the real drama is staged within Strindberg's own mind and consists of a dialogue between him and his conscience. He is still at pains to interpret the signs and warnings sent by a higher power, but moral dicussion is the nucleus of the drama. *Jacob Wrestles* represents Strindberg's most systematic attempt to come to terms with the problems of theodicy and guilt.

In the central section of *Jacob Wrestles* there are no fewer than four long monologues—all of them more or less elaborate apologies, even though the third one contains violent self-accusations. But self-defense presupposes self-reproach. In the dialogue, Strindberg transfers the accusations to a power outside himself, while he takes charge of his defense. Actually, of course, the dialogue is between two parts of his own self—between his ego and his superego, to use psychoanalytical terminology.

In the first monologue, Strindberg revolts against four distinct points in the prevailing religious moralism of his time. A secluded and ascetic life does not lead to improvement of the character, he remarks, because self-denial, poverty, and loneliness engender a desire for the world and its pleasures—at this point one recalls that Strindberg had recently read Flaubert's *The Temptation of Saint An-*

thony, which depicts this psychological process. Nor can he accept in categorical form the Christian commandment to love one's neighbor, because he does not want to love "criminals, suicides, those perjurers who poison and falsify the truth." [86] In support of this attitude, he cites the songs of vengeance from Psalms. Furthermore—and at this point the problem of theodicy appears—he makes the classical objection to the tenets of Christianity, namely, that the world is far too unjust a place to allow one to imagine that a thoroughly benevolent God is its sole ruler. Among his examples he includes only those cases in which he has been unjustly treated himself. A draft of *Jacob Wrestles* shows, however, that he was familiar with the broader aspects of the problem: "The Blindness of the Powers; the lack of attention shown to Subordinates; The Beggars in Lund, in Paris—Injustices. The innocent man punished: Fr. Lundgren." [87] Finally, he cannot bow to the Christian demand for absolute humility before God, and he cites Moses and Job as exemplifying the ideal relationship between man and God, for at some point in their lives both men became outspoken opponents of God's designs.

In this apology one glimpses certain heresies that Strindberg seems to be on the point of suggesting as possible explanations for the problem of evil: that Providence has "satraps" (he may simply mean women) who rule the human world, that the Son, "the idealist," or Satan himself has taken command—but these ideas are simply metaphysical projections of his objections to the Christian moral commandments. The exclamation, "Where is he, the Heavenly Father, who should smile indulgently at the follies of his children and then having punished them, could forgive them?" [88] is not intended as a bold theological or philosophical analysis. Strindberg does not brood theoretically upon the nature of God. His metaphysical notions are simply symbolic expressions of his moral dilemma. Although he revolts against the strict demands of Christian morality, one side of his nature nonetheless accepts them. His revolt expresses itself in his search for an everyday God, who is more understandable and more human, "the master who maintained good order in his house and kept an eye on the overseer to prevent injustices." [89]

In the second apology Strindberg continues his critique of Christian moral doctrines. He had just read *The Imitation of Christ* and was full of objections. Is it proper to despise "the world," which is the creation of the eternal? And the ascetic life? Not only does it generate an unwholesome life of the imagination, but it also disrupts his affairs so that he cannot fulfill the obligations to his children. He feels no vocation to become a "prophet," partly because all prophets have been "half charlatan, half madman," partly because his own character has never been free "from all the destructive passions that are degrading for a preacher." [90] To imitate Jesus Christ is a manifestation of pride. It makes one "a hypocrite." "No, it is blasphemous to imitate the eternal, and woe be unto him who believes he is capable of doing so." [91] In passing, Strindberg also attempts to defend himself against the accusation of ingratitude. He is not really guilty but is "condemned to ingratitude," he states, because he has been forced to "remain under an obligation to the first person who came along," and when that person demanded too much of him— thus forcing a break between them—Strindberg suffered "the mental anguish and pangs of conscience of a thief when he makes off with property that does not belong to him." [92]

This opposition to the moral demands of Christianity culminates in Strindberg's suspicion that "all misfortune, all injustices, the whole mechanism of salvation is only a huge ordeal that one must resist." [93] Despite the apparently moral overtones in his phraseology here, this suspicion indicates that he has relapsed into his premoral interpretation of the events in his life—the idea of Job and of unjust suffering returns: "If the misfortunes and afflictions that befall me are not punishment, then they are entrance examinations. I want to interpret them in this way and let Christ be my model, since He has suffered much, although I do not understand what so much suffering can do, unless it be to provide a foreground to heighten the effect of the bliss to come." [94]

The central issue in the fourth monologue is the question of pride. At various times Strindberg had opined quite justifiably that the real obstacle to his acceptance of Christian morality was his desire to assert himself. As a consequence of this insight, he had come to regard pride as the gravest of all sins, the deadly sin that the gods cannot forgive. Now he remarks that it is degrading to humble one-self in comparison with others. Such behavior, moreover, implies criticism of the force that has guided one's destiny. Besides, Strind-berg has not criticized everyone; he has also been capable of admira-tion. He has spoken out against tyrants on behalf of the downtrod-den, and because he has continually fallen into the hands of the incompetent and the arrogant, he has been forced to rise up in pro-test against them. Furthermore—and here the problem of justice in the world recurs—existence is not ordered according to the Chris-tian principle that all men are of equal worth. "And still I should be forced, contrary to human as well as to divine order, to recognize a fact that is disproved every minute of the day, a fact that for that matter does not even exist." [95] But Strindberg has a still more pro-found concept of the problem of humility. "If I speak on my own behalf, then I am guilty of pride; if I say that everything I possess comes from God, then I am guilty of blasphemy." [96] Thus, the Christian demand for humility seems to him to lead to sheer absur-dity, and faced with all these notable inconsistencies, Strindberg once again takes refuge in a polytheistic line of reasoning, which he tentatively propounds in the form of a question: "Is God divided against himself or have his satraps fallen into dissension?" [97]

This entire critique is expressed in metaphysical terms that have religious overtones. In conformity with his old deep-seated belief that higher powers were guiding his destiny, Strindberg has pro-jected the argument into the metaphysical plane. But despite this disguise, the basic ideas are in full agreement with many well-known criticisms of Christianity, belonging to the tradition that stretches from Enlightenment figures like Voltaire to Strindberg's contemporaries like Nietzsche. For that matter, since the necessity for love and humility and the notion of God's omnipotence and be-nevolence are so central to the whole Christian tradition, one can regard Strindberg's apology as simply one more critique of Chris-tianity. Like Voltaire, Strindberg feels that the presence of evil in the world militates against the idea of a thoroughly benevolent and omnipotent God. Like Diderot, he thinks that asceticism leads to pharisaism and to debauchery. Like Nietzsche, he believes that "the essence of the battle of life is to resist the temptation to bow to others."

It is worth noting that during the period preceding the composition of *Legends* and *Jacob Wrestles,* Strindberg's studies were not wholly—or even predominantly—devoted to religious literature. Indeed, his selection of reading matter reflects his ambivalent attitude toward religion. According to *The Occult Diary,* on August 10 he read Saint-Martin's *Des erreurs et de la vérité.* Five days after reading this work of occult speculation, he chose a purely anticlerical book, J. H. Michon's *La religieuse.* Shortly thereafter, he studied Diderot's novel of the same title. At the same time that he bought Rodolphe Töpffer's *Le presbytère* in the Odéon arcades, he also picked up Flaubert's *The Temptation of Saint Anthony*—in other words, Flaubert's book did not quite fall into his hands "by chance," as he claims in *Legends.*

Naturally, this critique of Christianity and these attempts at self-justification are answers to Strindberg's self-reproaches and the demands he made on himself. If he had not already—at least partly—accepted the Christian doctrine of penance, he would not have felt such a strong need to defend himself against the moral teachings of Christianity, which he had studied mainly in Thomas à Kempis. The third long monologue gives some idea of the counterweight on the other side of the scale.

Instead of meeting the Stranger he encounters in the Luxembourg Gardens according to *Jacob Wrestles,* this time Strindberg dreams himself back to a museum in Stockholm, where he pauses to scrutinize a medal that was cast to commemorate his *"Married* trial" in 1884. It bears the device: "The truth is always bold." Actually, despite his reputation for probity, Strindberg had not always told the truth. Observing the medal, he recalls a definite lie he had told and reflects on the catastrophic consequences of this suppression of the truth: in his treatment of masturbation in *The Son of a Servant,* he had concealed his subsequent feelings of remorse. This is the "mea culpa that makes me blush when faced with the inscription of the medal, which I, of course, had nothing to do with." [98] But he im-

mediately begins to defend himself. He has not been a corrupter of
youth, for he had good intentions: to liberate them from fear. Ignorant of the consequences of his action, he had simply tried to follow
"the example of the Redeemer, who acquitted the adultress and the
thief." [99] The grounds for this self-accusation may well seem somewhat inadequate. Indeed, they indicate that Strindberg was still not
capable of revealing the true source of his guilt feelings openly and
unambiguously. His guilt obviously stemmed not solely from the
half-truth in *The Son of a Servant,* but from his sexual life in general,
as is clearly shown in an eloquent passage in *Legends,* where sexuality
becomes the fountainhead of sin, the most treacherous and insidious
sin of all:

> Guiltless in his own eyes and yet tormented by misgivings and pangs of
> conscience that drive the wretch toward religion, which neither forgives
> nor comforts, inasmuch as it condemns him to madness and hell—the poor
> innocent creature, the victim, who lacks the strength to resist the superior
> forces of omnipotent nature. But the infernal embers are aglow and will
> light his way to the grave, whether they blaze in solitude beneath the ashes
> or spring from the fuel supplied by a woman. If one attempts to extinguish
> this flame by continence, he will see his passion diverted into perverse
> paths and his virtue punished in an unexpected manner. Try pouring oil on
> a lighted pyre and you will get some idea of licit love! [100]

One can hardly doubt that guilt feelings of this sort occupy a significant place in Strindberg's review of his own past offenses a few
pages later, which he concludes, as if he wished to suggest that he
had not really told all: "Everything is there! All the horrors, the
most secret sins, the most repulsive scenes in which I play the leading role." [101] Torsten Eklund has asserted that Strindberg's self-accusations appear feeble in comparison to the indictments he hurls at
others. This is not quite true. In *To Damascus,* for example, there is
a list of self-accusations oppressive enough to burden even a rather
insensitive conscience. Still, one often has the feeling that Strindberg's public self-inquiries lack candor, that he frequently fails to
advance motifs which arouse real guilt feelings in him. In the last
analysis, it would appear that Strindberg did not really take such
things as his literary and ideological mistakes very seriously. The

most essential causes of his guilt lie on a plane that he did not dare talk about in public. In both *Inferno* and *Legends* he gives mysterious advice to young men who suffer from insomnia. In the first case, he only urges his young friend to guess at his meaning. "The young man guesses what I mean and lowers his eyes.—You have guessed it! Then go in peace and sleep well." [102] In *Legends* he writes: "Below I shall write four words that contradict all the doctors' orders: 'Never do it again!' Everyone is free to interpret the little word 'it' as best suits him." [103] Something of the same secretive, insinuating tone occurs in the monologue in *Jacob Wrestles,* and there the ordeal ends with complete submission: "Mercy! Have mercy! And I shall refrain from justifying myself before the eternal, and I shall refrain from accusing my neighbor." [104]

Balancing Strindberg's overwhelming consciousness of guilt is his desire to assert himself. In *Jacob Wrestles* this opposition informs the dialogue in which his religious position emerges. As long as the problem remains unresolved, Strindberg's religious preference at any given moment is governed largely by external circumstances, and he rejects all forms of religion with equal alacrity whenever feelings of rebellion and pessimism provoke his familiar criticism of Christianity. In this connection, Strindberg's uncertainty is as great as ever. Referring to the period treated in *Jacob Wrestles,* he signs himself on one occasion as a "spiritist." Another time he acknowledges his debt to Swedenborg, and finally, he repeatedly insists upon his Catholic sympathies.

Spiritism plays the least important role in this religious dialogue. Strindberg had come across Allan Kardec's *Le livre des esprits* (The Book of Spirits), and he notes (both in his diary and in *Legends*) what a powerful impression that work made on him: "I pick it up and read. Why, it is Swedenborg and, more especially, Blavatsky; and when I find my own 'case' everywhere, I cannot conceal from myself that I am a spiritist." [105] "Spiritist," as it is used here, obviously does not mean someone who attempts to communicate with the spirits of the departed. These experiments never interested Strindberg, even though he occasionally admitted the possibility of this kind of communication. Allan Kardec's book is a sort of catechism, arranged in the form of questions and answers, and it was dictated, according to the author's claim, by "esprits supérieurs." Its doctrines concerning the spirit world have several points in common with the doctrines of Swedenborg: both writers share the same notions about a hierarchy of spirits, as well as those concerning the educative function of these spirits. A sober tone and a somewhat "knowing" tendency to moralize form another link between them. [106] Thus, it was only natural that Strindberg should recognize the spiritual milieu in Allan Kardec's book.

It is impossible, however, to demonstrate any very specific influence from Kardec. Because of his rationalism and his heretical views of the dogmas of the church, Kardec clearly occupied a place that is rather far toward the "rebellious" left in Strindberg's own religious dialectic. Moreover, Strindberg laid Kardec's book aside when he noticed that it was "forbidden to probe into the secrets of the powers."

His most important change was that from Swedenborg to Catholicism. In *Jacob Wrestles,* Strindberg is really defending himself more against Catholicism as represented by *The Imitation of Christ* than against Swedenborg. Around 1890 Strindberg began to feel attracted to the cultural sphere of Catholicism. *Inferno* ends with the explanation that "for me personally it looks as if the way of the cross might bring me back to the *faith of my forefathers.*" [107] As late as June 20, 1898, he explained in a letter to his children in Finland that he did not know if he would become attached to any form of organized religion—"but if I do, it will be the Roman Catholic." These frequently recurring moods are connected with his plans to seek refuge in a Catholic monastery. Finally, *Jacob Wrestles* is full of very suggestive stage props of Catholic tradition: images of Christ in the shops selling Catholic religious objects on the Rue du Four and the Rue Bonaparte; the crosses on the Panthéon, Saint-Sulpice and Saint-Germain-l'Auxerrois.

This interest in Catholicism has strong aesthetic overtones. Strindberg was attracted by the outward forms of Catholicism because they were so rich in cultural associations, and in this connection he was following a current in contemporary cultural life. Nor

was he unaware of his affinity with a modish interest. In *Jacob
Wrestles* he gives an eloquent description of the *fin-de-siècle* mood in
Paris:

The Middle Ages, the age of faith and piety, is approaching in France.
This new period was introduced by the overthrow of an empire and of a
miniature Augustus, just as during the decline of the Roman Empire and
the barbarian invasions. And we have seen Paris-Rome in flames and the
Goths let themselves be crowned in the Capitolium-Versailles. The great
pagans, Taine and Renan, have descended into oblivion and taken their
skepticism with them, but Jeanne d'Arc has been restored to life again.

Indeed, it is the Middle Ages—the costume and hair style of primitive
woman. The young men wear monks' robes and tonsures and dream of a
monastic life. They write legends and perform miracle plays, paint ma-
donnas and carve statues of Christ, drawing their inspiration from the mysticism of the magician who enchants them with Tristan and Isolde, Parsifal
and the Grail.

The beautiful Middle Ages, when people knew how to enjoy life and to
suffer, when power and love were revealed for the last time, when beauty
last appeared in color, line, and harmonies—before it was drowned and
massacred by the renaissance of heathendom called Protestantism.[108]

Besides dealing with a wealth of material from the first decades of
the Third Republic and capturing so successfully the *fin-de-sièle*
mood in various literary circles, this compressed description is
thoroughly and consciously based on themes that were "modern" at
the time it was written. The parallel between Roman decline and
modern European decadence had been a commonplace ever since
"decadence" became a slogan. Verlaine had already hinted at the
comparison, which was later taken up by Huysmans in the chapter
of *Against the Grain* that describes des Esseintes' studies in late Latin
literature. The comparison is even more elaborate in Sar Péladan's
roman à clef, La décadence latine, which Strindberg also studied. The
closing lines about "the beautiful Middle Ages" reflect the aesthetic
enthusiasm for the Middle Ages that was nourished by such groups
as the Pre-Raphaelites.

The connection between Strindberg's Catholic sympathies and
these modish ideas is very obvious here. To be sure, he had flirted

with Catholicism before. But as soon as he became aware of the wave of conversions that was sweeping through the intellectual world, he began to approach Catholicism much more directly. Sar Péladan, whose works he studied for the first time in May 1897, inspired him to proclaim in *Inferno:* "Catholicism now makes its ceremonious and triumphant entry into my life." [109] Later—on May 17—he read one of the religious works by the converted Dane, Johannes Jørgensen. In the following September he recorded in *The Occult Diary* an impression he had just gained from first reading Huysmans' *En route:* "It is noteworthy how his development follows the same course as mine. From magic and Satanism to Catholicism." From this time on, the Catholic Church loomed more clearly as his imaginary goal. His enthusiasm for Catholicism reached its apex in the winter of 1897–1898, when Strindberg wrote *Jacob Wrestles* and the first two parts of *To Damascus.* But even after this interest had begun to wane, Catholicism and the colorful Middle Ages still represented the world of religion to Strindberg, as one can see quite clearly in two later plays, *Advent* (1898) and *The Saga of the Folkways* (1899).

Careful scrutiny of Strindberg's statements about Catholicism reveals that dogmatic considerations played no part in bringing him to the threshold of the church. Once in *Legends* he noted that Swedenborg "preached faith *and* works, just as the Roman Church does," which implies that he was more sympathetic to the Catholic than to the Protestant doctrine of salvation. Other dogmatic issues—such as the sacraments, the papacy, absolution, and the role of the saints— he passes over in silence. Strindberg was still so dubious about Christianity in general that he was certainly not ready to concern himself with the subtleties of Catholic dogma. Moreover, even though the atmosphere he evokes in *Jacob Wrestles* creates an aura of Roman Catholicism, the doctrines he opposes himself to in that work are not exclusively Catholic, but belong to the general Christian morality of renunciation.

What was the reason, then, that Strindberg "locked up" the Protestant Swedenborg in the autumn of 1897, found his way to Catholic churches, and even tried crossing himself? He himself gives the following motive: "I have abandoned Swedenborg's Christianity be-

cause it was vindictive, petty, servile, and full of hate, but I retain
The Imitation with certain reservations; and a quiet religion of compromise has succeeded the state of perplexity and anguish that accompanies the search for Jesus." [110] As Strindberg had explained
shortly before, it was Swedenborg the free-thinking theologian, the
rationalist, and the dogmatist who repelled him when he read
Apocalypse Explained and *True Christian Religion.* "I want religion
to be a quiet accompaniment to the monotonous melody of everyday
life, but in these works one encounters the professional religious
man, pulpit disputation, and thus the struggle for power."

These statements may seem surprising. Earlier in *Jacob Wrestles*
Strindberg had given an account of his own theological disputation
with the Stranger who appears in that work, which bore all the earmarks of a struggle for power. Although he reserved the right to oppose God, he was unpleasantly affected by the fact that Swedenborg
took issue with Calvin, Luther, and Melanchton. Against the background of the subjective nature of Strindberg's religion and its function in his life as a substitute for experience, this reaction is easy to
understand. For Strindberg, religion was not a matter of conviction.
It was a mood, an attitude, and a system of reactions, but not a
theory or a dogma. It expressed both his desire to submit to God and
his need to use dialectic and rational arguments to oppose Him—not
as a means of finding truth, but solely for the sake of opposition. His
study of Swedenborg had always been characterized by this sort of
subjectivity, so that he identified himself with Swedenborg more
often than he learned from him. When he now stumbles across Swedenborg the theorist and theologian, he reacts quite consistently by
resisting. He "locks him up," not because he considers him wrong,
but because he is not interested in speculating about the truth. He
had accepted Swedenborg the moralist, though not without grum-
bling, but he rejects the speculative theologian.

Thomas à Kempis' book was simpler, more ingenuous, and quite
unspeculative—it suited him better. But it would be wrong to let
Strindberg's presentation of this material fool one into believing that
he was facing a choice simply between Protestantism and Catholicism. Behind this opposition can be glimpsed a deeper one: whereas

Swedenborg represents Strindberg's "father-religion," Thomas à Kempis and Catholicism are very close to his "mother-religion." Although he was led to Protestant moralism by the virile Swedenborg, he approached a gentler and more emotional Catholic religion under the guidance of female and maternal figures—"Ma Mère" in the Saint-Louis Hospital and "Mutter" in Austria. When he complained to his mother-in-law about Swedenborg's cruelty, he was appealing to maternal sympathy just as he had during childhood; and when he "locked up" Swedenborg and took out Thomas à Kempis, he was manifesting the same sort of hope for redemption and forgiveness that he had shown during his youthful outburst of pietistic fervor. A statement about Catholicism at the end of *Legends* delineates in a profound and beautiful manner the deepest impelling forces behind Strindberg's religious strivings and conflicts. He has dreamed, he writes, a dream about redemption: "Ever since that night I feel more homeless than ever here in the world, and like a tired and sleepy child at evening, I want to be allowed to go home, to rest my heavy head on a mother's breast, to sleep on the lap of a woman and a mother, the chaste wife of an inconceivably vast God, who calls himself my father and whom I dare not approach." [111]

It was no accident that Strindberg turned to Thomas à Kempis just when his youthful hope for salvation revived and his contempt for the world returned. During his pietistic period, *The Imitation of Christ* had been one of his sacred texts. When he reread the book during the 1880s, he still found it "a wonderful book." He describes the impression it made on him: "although it is just as pessimistic as Schopenhauer, it is not lacking in comfort, for it at least wants to persuade the unhappy reader that things are better in another world." And in 1897 he read the book again in a spirit that is much more reminiscent of his youthful pietism than of Catholicism: "Living to die from the world, the contemptible, stupid, filthy world— that is the theme." [112]

But in 1897 Strindberg was no better prepared to accept the idea of Christ's vicarious suffering than he had been thirty years earlier. Certainty of salvation remained a dream for him. Once again, however, one must be careful not to reduce this opposition to intellectual terms. Strindberg would certainly not have found the idea of atonement through death unreasonable or improbable in itself—indeed, it is no more eccentric than many of the mythological ideas he cherished. His opposition to it lay on the subjective and moral plane. "I prefer to pay my debts with my own suffering," he writes in *Legends*. Later in the same book he gives a more elaborate statement of the same position: "For more than a year I have been pursued by the Savior, whom I do not understand and whose help I have wanted to make superfluous by bearing my own cross, if possible, because of a remnant of manly pride in me that finds something repugnant in the cowardice that heaps its faults onto the shoulders of an innocent person." [113] On this point, he remains closer to the providential viewpoint of Swedenborg, who held that man was provided with free will so that he could assume the burden of responsibility for his own salvation. Applying this sort of "providentialism" to the idea of man's responsibility for his own salvation, Strindberg moves to the question: "Has Christ's function been abolished?" [114] When men tire of hearing about Christ, His vicarious satisfaction ceases, and "we have to begin bearing our misery and our guilt feelings alone." The only Christ he understands is the child-god whose mission is not atonement, but who has descended to earth "in order to see how difficult it is to be encumbered with human life."

On November 24, 1897 (that is, while he was writing *Jacob Wrestles*), Strindberg drew up a declaration of his religious position.[115] In it he claims to have "no definite point of view" on Catholicism. His relation to occultism is "impersonal." Buddhism he considers unsuitable for occidentals, and he only accepts theosophy with the important objection that "Karma" ought to be understood as a personal power outside the human being. Finally, it appears from *Jacob Wrestles* that he no longer considered himself a Swedenborgian either. In other words, he made use of ideas and moods from all these faiths, but remained an eclectic and an individualist.

Actually, Strindberg was not interested in embracing a doctrinal system. What he wanted was "to go home." That he finally did return to Sweden, become reconciled to Protestantism, and restore Swedenborg to his place of honor shows once again the extent to which the father figure dominated his religious life.

The nascent conflict between self-effacement and self-assertion—

between Christian morality and a profane demand for justice—
which one could already sense in *Inferno,* comes to a head in *Jacob
Wrestles.* These incompatible antitheses are juxtaposed in this fragmentary work, which does not, however, provide any solution for
the problem of guilt underlying Strindberg's Inferno crisis and determining its course. Despite his failure to find a solution to his
problem, Strindberg decided after writing *Jacob Wrestles* to "cut
short this brooding over religion," as he explains in a letter to Gustaf af Geijerstam. "With that," he adds, "my religious struggles
are over, and the whole myth of Inferno is at an end (Mar. 2,
1898).[116] When Strindberg wrote these words, he had already been
hard at work on *To Damascus* for two months—the first and second
parts of the play were finished in July 1898. The following December 1898 he finished *Advent.* In 1899 he wrote *Crimes and Crimes*
and *The Saga of the Folkways.* To a certain extent, this change seems
to confirm his notion that "the myth of Inferno" had come to an end
around the beginning of 1898, when he stopped working on *Jacob
Wrestles.*

In the afterword to *Jacob Wrestles,* Strindberg gazes back down the
pathway he has taken and observes that, "like all religious crises,"
his attempt to reach religion "has resulted in chaos." Religion is an
axiom that cannot be demonstrated, and "every attempt to approach
religion by means of argument leads to absurdities." Religion is
"forming ties with the beyond." It is the straw that lifts the drown-
ing man out of the waves, a "credo quia absurdum" (I believe it
because it is absurd). These are, to a great extent, the same defini-
tions that Strindberg had already used in the earliest draft of *Inferno*—from the spring of 1896: "Religion = renewal of ties =
Anschluss with what has gone before, a preexistence. God became
both a scientific discovery and a need. Life is hopeless, lacking in interest, inexplicable without some sort of religion = *Anschluss* with
another existence." [117] Thus it may appear that two years of extraordinary experience, pangs of conscience, and religious brooding had
merely led Strindberg around the periphery of a circle right back to
the attitude he had held before the central crisis.

The afterword to *Legends,* however, deals with metaphysical theories, notions about the nature of the universe. Here, too, Strindberg's ideas remain at least as vague and obscure in 1898 as they were in 1896. There is only one idea that he really clings to: that human destiny—and above all his own destiny—is guided into moral channels by one or several personal powers. For that reason, he sees a deeper meaning in everything that happens. But what this meaning is, what the intentions of the powers may be, what they demand, what sins he is being punished for, what awaits man after death—his answers to all these questions vacillate in response to his changing notions about the nature of "the power" or "the powers." Although he remained a monotheist in principle during his later years, he sometimes seemed to revive certain polytheistic notions to help him around metaphysical dilemmas. The whole circle of theories from the Inferno period—occultism, Buddhism, the Swedenborgian doctrine of spirits, Byron's Manicheism, Schopenhauer's pessimism—all these approaches were still viable for Strindberg in 1906–1907 when he wrote *A Blue Book*. His religion, in other words, lacked theoretical consistency.

What was essential to his development lies on the moral plane. Concepts like "guilt," "crime," "punishment," and "grace" are the flesh and bones of his post-*Inferno* works, especially those he wrote during the years around the turn of the century. The most important factor in this development is his own sense of guilt, which at first overwhelmed him and then finally entered his consciousness during the last phase of the Inferno crisis. But when it comes to deciding the exact relationship between crime and punishment, his discussion always becomes obscure and uncertain.

From the Hôtel Orfila, Strindberg wrote to Hedlund of the Old Testament God, who can "hate and strike, but also forgive" (undated). He expresses a similar idea in the draft of *Jacob Wrestles:* "Can God forgive? Yes, if He can punish first." This idea—rather than some abstract notion of justice—characterizes Strindberg's concept of religion after *Inferno*. Punishment first, then mercy. One needs only to examine the endings of some of his dramas to find variations of this idea. Maurice in *Crimes and Crimes* is punished for his evil thoughts and for two days suffers "as intensively as if it had been eternities." After that, he receives "absolution" from Providence. *Advent* has a similar ending. "But my misdeed is greater, greater than can ever be forgiven," says the Lawman, the villain in the play, and the answer is: "There you go overestimating yourself again!" The text suggests that he too receives "forgiveness" when his "punishment" is over. Sometimes the "punishment" seems to be nothing more than a good-natured warning—more like an admonishing finger than a chastizing hand. Such is the case in *Gustav Vasa* (1899), where the king is forgiven without having encountered any serious misfortunes and without even feeling really contrite.

The Old Testament maxim "an eye for an eye and a tooth for a tooth," which Linnaeus has recourse to in his notes about Nemesis, covers only one aspect of Strindberg's religious experience. Nor did the doctrine of Karma, with its mathematical principles of justice, exercise a really decisive influence on Strindberg. The image of a blindly acting Ananke occasionally arose in his mind when he felt inclined toward pessimism or Buddhism, but his primary religious experience was the experience of a personal God—possibly of several personal gods. A statement made in a letter to Hedlund expresses his most essential religious experience: "No, I experience God as a completely personal acquaintance" (July 1, 1896). Strindberg's God was a person with a completely human essence or character: He could become angry, punish, forgive; He could sometimes be just and sometimes manifestly unjust; He could turn away from Strindberg, and He could approach him as a friend. For Strindberg, He always remained something of an enigma—in the way that an intimate friend can—and Strindberg never ceased to ask himself these questions: Is God good or evil? Is He fundamentally just or unjust? Can He—does He want to—forgive me? Has He rejected me? Or does He look upon me with favor?

Egocentricity and anthropomorphism are the most characteristic features of Strindberg's religion. They, in turn, give rise to his lack of theoretical consistency. God's relation to Strindberg can be characterized in a single word—"father." The heavenly father shared Carl Oskar Strindberg's severity and moral puritanism, but unlike his earthly counterpart, He could be appeased and could content

himself with a reprimand, when a sound whipping would really
have been in order. That the guilt-punishment formula assumed
such a central place in Strindberg's outlook is in fact not surprising.
After all, the idea of a chastizing God is a part of the Christian heritage. Whatever specific explanation one feels called on to provide for
Strindberg's outlook will be found not primarily in the books that
he read but in his childhood milieu. It was in that milieu that life
first appeared to him as a penal colony; it was there that his sense of
guilt was established. Guilt feelings, remorse, dogmatism, defiance
and idealization of the father figure—all these are elements in the
same complex of experiences. The Inferno crisis gave a metaphysical
dimension to all these elements.

From this point of view, one can also understand how Strindberg
could suddenly cut short his discussion of religion, despite the fact
that the conclusions he reached were so meager and uncertain. Psychologically speaking, he had already attained what was essential to
him: a God-father who watched over him, to whom he could confess
his guilt, by whom he could be punished and forgiven, whom he
could criticize, defy, cast suspicion on, humble himself before—in
short, a suitable correlative for all his aggressive and masochistic
needs. Whether or not this change of attitude consititutes a "conversion" may be debated. One might conceive of it as a "regression,"
but one cannot deny that it provides the immediate basis for a series
of literary works sustained by a new and higher tone than anything
Strindberg had previously achieved and resulting in one of the most
significant innovations in the history of modern literature.

FOUR *A New Cosmos*

In the first draft of *Inferno,* composed in the spring of 1896, Strindberg declared that "God had become both a scientific discovery and a need." [1] In this statement he isolates the two separate paths that had led to his religious conversion in the 1890s: mythological speculation and natural philosophy. His preoccupation with mythology grew directly out of his crises and expressed a psychic need; his sallies into the realm of natural philosophy were primarily confined to the periods between his crises and appeared rather more like free *jeux d'esprit.*

Needless to say, these two lines of development were related. One is immediately struck by the chronological connection between them. The psychotic outbursts that punctuated Strindberg's central religious development also separated the different periods of his speculation in natural philosophy—this is especially true of the first and the third crises. In general, one must assume that the psychological forces that gave rise to Strindberg's typical Inferno ideas also determined the orientation of his scientific studies.

His development in the area of natural philosophy was characterized, however, by a certain independence. Thus, instead of slavishly following the development of the crises, some of his themes cut right through the Inferno periods. When he was busy over his crucibles, Strindberg was freer—was further from psychotic experience—than when he was studying primitive mythologies. Besides, certain features of his development during the Inferno crisis, especially the notions about a crisis religion, have no parallels in his thought about natural philosophy. There the course of his development was both simpler and more complicated than in his central, religious development: simpler because the changes occurred less abruptly, more complicated because his natural philosophy contained a great many ideas borrowed from different sources.

The men who participated in what is called "the modern breakthrough" in Scandinavia (from about 1870 until about 1890) believed that advances in the natural sciences had provided a firm base on which to build the future. Their deterministic conviction that all life conforms to the laws of nature found an optimistic correlative in their doctrine that life was mechanically advancing toward improvement. When it suited him to do so, Strindberg, too, freely strewed his pages with references to scientific authorities. But, as Lamm and Eklund have both maintained, the concept of law and the idea of development were essentially alien to his way of thinking. When he borrowed ideas from the leading exponents of natural philosophy among his contemporaries, he changed their meaning according to his own extrascientific purposes. This was true even during his naturalistic period, when he thought he was applying a strictly scientific viewpoint to existence. In addition to all the technical details that Strindberg gleaned from zoological, botanical, and geological handbooks for inclusion in *By the Open Sea,* that novel is full of Darwinian and Haecklerian borrowings. Yet the most essential questions that it raises in natural philosophy really lie outside the realm of science.

Because Strindberg did not readily think in scientific categories, concepts of law, purpose, and causality were largely foreign to him. His fundamental concern was not with rational ways of explaining existence, but with competing visions of the world. To find a coherent pattern in the larger chaos was, as Strindberg saw it, the basic

problem in natural philosophy, and the character of his own quest
for this pattern was clearly prescientific. Either the world is nothing
but chaos in constant flux, or else there is a secret order behind the
course of events—this was Strindberg's point of departure, to which
he stubbornly adhered.

Karl Groos finds that all talk about the primacy of natural forces
is basically abstract—indeed, that it is tinged with mythology. If
the study of natural philosophy is limited to direct, concrete experience, its basic problem must be apprehended in one of two ways: either as an "empirische oder positivistiche Radikalismus [empirical
or positivistic form of radicalism]," which only admits of change,
multiplicity, relativity—or as an "Einheit der Substanz, unverän-
derliches, ewiges, absolutes, vollkommenes Sein [a unity of substance, an immutable, eternal, absolute, complete being]." [2]
Groos' distinction is relevant here because it also describes Strindberg's way of apprehending the problems of natural philosophy.

Besides being what Groos considers the empirical and basic way
of posing the question, however, this view of the matter can be
linked with a particular period in the history of ideas. Strindberg
was already employing the very same formula—"the coherent pattern in the great chaos"—as early as the 1880s, and he probably borrowed it from Victor Hugo.[3] It points beyond the positivistic, deterministic outlook in his works of that period and harks back to the
romantic ideas that had made such a profound impression on him in
youth. A specialized study of this aspect of the subject would doubtless show that the impulses Strindberg later received from thinkers
like Moleschott, Darwin, and Spencer tended—even during the
1880s—to lead him right back to this romantic antithesis. Therefore, when he began to make scientific experiments around 1890 in
an effort to compete with the scientists of his day, he did so in a
spirit decidedly different from that of modern science.

Strindberg himself sometimes traces his interest in the study of
the natural sciences, especially chemistry, back to his school days.[4]
The year 1883, however, is the date he usually mentions. In "Pangs
of Conscience" (1884) he lets the hero of the story indulge in fan-

tasies about methods of utilizing the nitrogen in the air. It is
known, of course, that Strindberg entertained similar fantasies
himself in the 1890s, but his correspondence with Hjalmar Öhrwall, a prominent physiologist in Uppsala, shows that by 1884 he
already took these ideas seriously. In a letter to Geijerstam the following year, he discusses the holly's thorns, and the same problem
was later the object of long discussions with the botanist Bengt Lidforss. In 1887 he even wrote an essay entitled "Attempts to Explain
Polar Light as a Halo Phenomenon," which is preserved among his
unpublished manuscripts.[5] He also treated a number of scientific
problems in popular style in his series of essays entitled *Flower Paintings and Animal Pieces* (1888).

After 1889 Strindberg's scientific interests acquired increased significance for him. In 1890, when he was writing *By the Open Sea,*
which in certain respects can be regarded as a treatise on the philosophy of nature, he sent for a great deal of scientific literature and
began to study chemistry. In correspondence with Ola Hansson he
mentions the "future *Antibarbarus*" [6] as early as July 6, 1889, and in
the same letter he states: "Literature makes me sick and I am gradually moving over to science, which it is a matchless joy to practice." At the beginning of that year he had already sent Ola Hansson
a "scientific sketch" for the inspection of the chemistry teacher at the
folk high school, which Hansson's brother had opened in Skurup
(Denmark); and in their correspondence he repeatedly proposes
chemical hypotheses, of which Hansson claimed not to understand a
single word. After publishing *By the Open Sea* in the autumn of
1890, Strindberg began to make systematic experiments in order to
determine the composition of air. On February 22, 1891 he wrote
the first laboratory report to which a date can be assigned.[7] After
that time, natural science—especially chemistry and botany—
became his dominant interest. The periods of his most intensive experimentation occurred between the autumn of 1893 and the summer of 1894, and then again in the spring of 1895; but he did not
abandon scientific work completely until 1898, that is, until after
having passed through the crisis that led to his conversion.

Strindberg's chemical and botanical experiments issued directly from his broodings over the problems he encountered in natural philosophy. *By the Open Sea* suggests the kind of speculation that preoccupied him at this time. Therefore, both his published and his unpublished laboratory protocols should be regarded not as the results of what is now defined as scientific research, but as expressions of a particular attitude toward natural philosophy. Strindberg's method of presenting his "discoveries" and his affectation of the entire apparatus of the professional research scientist misled his contemporaries—as it often does today—to such an extent that nearly everyone has concentrated on his individual experiments and discussed their validity. Actually, as a scientist, he assumed the same philosophical, poetic, and groping attitude as did Inspector Borg when peering through his waterglass to study the fantastic world under the sea in *By the Open Sea*. [8]

Was Strindberg himself aware that his approach to experimentation was more philosophical and lyric than scientific? He was certainly not wholly unconscious of the true nature of his interest in science, even though he also believed—especially during his alchemic period—that his experiments had led to epoch-making discoveries. From the very beginning his research was aimed at revolutionizing the understanding of nature. When he made his first experiments, he declared to Lidforss: "What awakened my disgust for modern science was the way in which many 'small minds' have elevated the gathering of data to a position above that of the philosophy of natural science" (Mar. 15, 1891). While making his first experiments with sulphur on the island of Rügen, he told his wife he intended to give lectures in Berlin about the "philosophy of chemistry" (July 2, 1893). In the period after 1894, his scientific hypotheses represented integral steps in a vast effort to create a new cosmos, as he indicates in the Preface to *Jardin des Plantes*. It is not unlikely that Strindberg was originally inspired to this effort by Ernst Haeckel, who was his mentor in the beginning of the 1890s and who spoke in similar tones of the need for a renaissance of natural philosophy.

That there were also elements of playfulness and historical masquerade in Strindberg's scientific activity is apparent from the titles of his larger scientific works: *Antibarbarus* (1894), *Sylva Sylvarum* (1896), and *Hortus Merlini* (1896–1897). Not only does he frequently use Latin quotations, which lend a learned and mysterious air to these works, but among his cartons of notes there is even one draft in which he took the trouble to translate his chemical principles into Latin. Moreover, instead of turning to contemporary scientists, he preferred to study the classical authorities.

The classic natural philosopher who had most significance for him was Francis Bacon. He is already mentioned in Strindberg's correspondence with Ola Hansson on Jan. 19, 1889; two years later, in a letter to Lidforss on April 1, 1891, Strindberg quoted him exhaustively as an authority on natural philosophy. One page of a manuscript dating from Strindberg's days in Germany (1892–1893) contains excerpts from Bacon's *Sylva Sylvarum,* which also lent its title to one of Strindberg's works.[9]

Bacon was one of the writers who transmitted Aristotelianism and the alchemic tradition to Strindberg, but in this context his greatest significance lay on another plane. Strindberg imitated Bacon's attitude, his style of research. Bacon is full of the Renaissance sense of power and hope for the future, when the principles of reason will have been applied to scientific research. He feels that he stands at the beginning of an epoch. For him, everything that has been accomplished by earlier scientists is only material for his *Instauratio magna*. Once his method has been universally accepted, everything will emerge in a new pattern with a new meaning. Strindberg likewise feels that he is breaking new ground. "I have wandered in the dark," he writes in *Antibarbarus,* "groped my way forward, stumbled on contradictions, and knocked over new probabilities." He is hesitant about the exactness of his discoveries, but suspects that he is touching on great secrets that will be fully revealed in the future: "I am so far into the mountain that I cannot turn back, for no Ariadne has given me the thread to fasten by the entrance. Thus, I rest for a moment and then proceed in the hope that farther on someone will find me, living or dead."

As the founder of the new science, Bacon does not allow himself time to verify his hypotheses in detail—a task he leaves to posterity.

In *Sylva Sylvarum* he constantly throws out sudden conceits and hypotheses of uncertain value, but because they might be true, he does not want to waste them. It is the same with Strindberg: "I know that I am on the right path; I do not know if I have reached the goal." He impatiently sets forth his ideas helter-skelter, afraid that someone else may anticipate his findings. At the end of his life he still imagined that it might be possible to publish his laboratory protocols in their entirety. What he was unable to execute himself would be carried out by disciples. To fill this function, he hoped to appoint men like Lidforss and The Svedberg, the celebrated Swedish chemist.

Bacon also became his stylistic model. Writing to Hedlund about the essays that were later included in *Sylva Sylvarum* and *Jardin des Plantes,* he maintains: "They retain the sparse, slipshod, arrogant style that one acquires when one makes discoveries" (Nov. 10, 1895). This description also applies perfectly to Bacon's aphoristic mode of presentation, especially as it appears in *Sylva Sylvarum*. Strindberg's scientific style, which is frenetic and packed with information, probably owes a good deal to that work. A striking mannerism shared by both Bacon and Strindberg is their tendency to list observations and experiments without commentary, sometimes with a hasty recommendation to posterity to subject the matter to more thorough testing.

In this context, one is reminded that at the end of *By the Open Sea* Strindberg praises Latin as the language of European cultural unity, and in a letter to Karl Otto Bonnier he describes that novel as "a thunderous book in a great, new Renaissance style" (June 7, 1890). In the autumn of 1889—about the same time that he published his famous literary manifesto entitled "Renaissance"—the famous Swedish poet and novelist Verner von Heidenstam sent Strindberg a letter in which he argued for the "Renaissance features" in the Swedish temperament. The Nietzschean cult of the Renaissance was a common denominator for both these poets. But Strindberg, who was alien to Heidenstam's nationalism, was skeptical about his friend's literary program. The great extent to which Strindberg had actually been influenced by the modern enthusiasm for the Renaissance did not become apparent until he took up scientific studies. His scientific attitude was formed in competition with Heidenstam, whose books—according to the above letter to Bonnier—he considered "apocryphal." Hoping to beat Heidenstam at his own game by indulging in genuine Renaissance thoughts and displaying genuine Renaissance learning, Strindberg took Bacon as his model.

Two basic features of Strindberg's scientific technique—his suspicion of textbooks and his dependence on intuition—also served to link him with Bacon. According to Bacon, the scientist ought to work without any presuppositions and should eradicate from his mind all current ideas about natural phenomena. This principle, which Bacon had directed against the reigning Aristotelianism of his day, Strindberg applied to nineteenth century science. His favorite targets were the most widely held, firmly established truths, of the sort that are expounded in every schoolbook. For example, he attacked the idea that the earth is round.

This method was for Strindberg the key to new discoveries. If he could only forget what he had learned, the real truth would emerge through an act of intuition. In a letter to Lidforss on April 1, 1891, he describes the procedure: "I place myself in a state of unconsciousness," he reports, "and then I let my brain work freely, without regard for results or approval, and then something that I believe in emerges." Afterward, he undertook experiments in order to prove the correctness of the whims produced in this fashion. It is the same method he used in creative writing. During this period Strindberg placed great emphasis on the intuitive and unconscious elements in his poetic work. Indeed, in *Causeries on Mysticism* (1897) Ola Hansson portrayed him as the very prototype of the inspired poet.[10]

Obviously, this theory of intuition is less suitable for science than for poetry. Also, on closer inspection Strindberg's supposedly original scientific intuitions dissolve into a multitude of reminiscences from his previous reading, which, besides scientific literature, included a great many philosophic and poetical works. Nor does any coherent system emerge from this multiplicity of fanciful ideas; one can only discern certain tendencies. Precisely because Strindberg worked in this intuitive and groping manner, however, his scientific whims are of great interest to the student of his literary works. For one thing, he reproduced ideas that had impressed him strongly on first acquaintance. Moreover, his scientific writings reveal that he preferred to view the world independent of authorities and of current views.

In his first scientific work, *Antibarbarus,* Strindberg labeled himself a "monist." He thereby wished to call attention to his doubts about the stability of the basic elements and to his belief that they could all be reduced to a single "ur-element." He would often reinforce this position by referring to the leading exponents of the doctrine of evolution: "No, sir, I am a transformist like Darwin and a monist like Spencer and Haeckel."

At that time "monism" was the favorite slogan of popular philosophy—particularly in Germany, where Haeckel's influence had reached its apex. This designation became a portmanteau word for all attempts to arrive at a doctrine of immanence. Haeckel himself, Eduard von Hartmann, and Carl du Prel all called themselves monists, despite the fact that the former placed more emphasis on the mechanical and material, the two latter on the final and spiritual sides of the unity that they posited in nature. Moreover, all these German thinkers were influenced by the pantheism of Goethe and Schopenhauer. The reason that Haeckel's influence was so great was that he collated the latest results of biological research with a basically romantic system of natural philosophy. The concept of monism, then, is sufficiently vague that Strindberg, who had been strongly influenced by all these men, doubtless had as much right as they to call his natural philosophy "monistic."

The nucleus of Haeckel's monism was a theory of evolution in the regenerated form it had assumed following the achievement of Darwin. After the mechanism of evolution had been expounded, one had only to follow out all its consequences in order to reach a unified world picture, in which everything—organic and inorganic—could ultimately be understood as the product of a single primordial material. In his *Morphology,* Haeckel carried out the system for the organic world, which he traced back to the protozoa and to the self-generating, primordial, organic material, which was once thought to have been isolated in *Bathybius Haeckelii*—in other words, Oken's "protoplasm" returned as an established truth.

"In my capacity as a monist, I have committed myself for the time being to the assumption that all elements and all forces are related. And *if* they derive from one source, then they sprang into existence by means of condensation and attenuation, of copulation and crossbreeding, of heredity and transformation, of selection and struggle, addition and substitution—and whatever else one wants to suggest." This is how Strindberg expresses his chemical principles at the beginning of *Antibarbarus*. Using this point of departure, he begins to apply such concepts as "genealogical table" and "ontogeny" to matter. Thus, sulphur has "at different temperatures gone through its regular pattern of individual development, or its ontogeny," as he states later in the book, applying Haeckel's ontogenetic law to inorganic matter. His obvious next step was to apply the theory of evolution to chemistry as well. Ever since Mendelieff had proposed a periodic system, people had become accustomed to speaking of "natural families" among the elements. From this habit of speech it was but a short step to the point at which one could view these families in a genetic light corresponding to the one that had illuminated so many biological or botanical problems.

Nor was Strindberg the only person attracted by this idea. He admits that the impulse came to him from C. W. Blomstrand, the Swedish chemist.[11] In all probability, however, he also got it at first hand from a hint dropped by Haeckel himself. In October 1892— shortly after Strindberg had moved to Berlin—Haeckel held a sensational lecture at a congress of scientists. Shortly thereafter the lecture was published under the title "Monism as a Link between Religion and Science." In it Haeckel sanctions an attempt made the preceding year by a German scientist to look at chemistry from a "biogenetic" point of view, and he surmises that the elements "nur historische Entwickelungsproducte sind, entstanden durch verschiedenartige Lagerung und Verbindung einer wechselnden Zahl von Uratomen" (are only historical products of a process of development and that they have come into being through heterogeneous stratification and combination of a varying number of ur-atoms).[12] In this connection, he also suggests that the alchemist's dream of transforming the elements might very well come true. In any case, these statements gave Strindberg the impression that his own speculations in *Antibarbarus* were in complete accord with the findings of modern science.

But Strindberg went much further than Haeckel, who had not, after all, abandoned the atomic theory. In contrast, Strindberg's "monism" not only presupposes a theory of complexity to describe the nature of the elements but also involves a peripatetic concept of matter. He regards the elements as infinitely changing and adopts the idea of a formless primordial matter than can assume all sorts of shapes. Indeed, this hypothesis becomes one of the points of departure for his research. Among his earliest scientific notations appears a page [13] on which he arrived at a formulation that he was to trace back to Aristotle when he wrote *Antibarbarus:* "For an element, to be is only to be at a certain given moment and under certain conditions." Observing sulphur, he finds it is a "Proteus that is not the same from one moment to the next," and he draws up entire catalogues of all its metamorphoses.

By returning to the Aristotelian view of matter, which was also the view held by medieval alchemists, Strindberg placed himself outside the science of his own time. With a single blow he abolished the boundaries between concepts like "mixture" and "chemical compound," between the superficial and the fundamental properties of an element. When he saw materials change color, form, and odor in his crucible, he thought he was witnessing a radical transformation of matter. His theory that sulphur is a resin was arrived at by comparing some of the properties of sulphur with analogous properties of the resins.

Strindberg criticized prevailing chemical methods from the same point of view. Thus, in 1892 at the very beginning of his chemical research he turned against qualitative analysis, and shortly after his trip to Germany he jotted down a three-page "Kritik der Qualitativen Elementar-Analyse" (Critique of the Qualitative Analysis of the Elements), a procedure that he calls "completely worthless." [14] These ideas recur in an essay that he published in *Hyperchimie* in

1897, in which he hoped to prove that the analysis of elements is actually synonymous with their transformation. At the very outset he guards himself against all possible objections on the part of analytical chemists by explaining that "Precipitation means reconstitution. Dissolution means decomposition." [15] Naturally, the case of spectral analysis was no better. In an essay in *Initiation* he presents a series of observations concerning the spectroscope that are designed to demonstrate "the worthlessness of all spectral analysis." [16] In neither of these cases, however, did Strindberg really question the method of analysis. What he actually doubted was the presupposition upon which analytical chemistry was based—the existence of stable elements that can enter into chemical compounds. Compounds, mixtures, properties that change when external conditions change—for Strindberg, all these phenomena were only stages in the great process of transformation through which matter was constantly passing.

Schopenhauer was the last important thinker to make the Aristotelian, scholastic concept of matter an essential point in his philosophy. With his Kantian background, Schopenhauer certainly did not regard matter as having immediate existence; he deduced its nature from man's a priori categories of thought and defined it as an "objectification of the will." After having reached this result, however, he made use of the classical distinction between essence and accident. He referred to the scholastic formula *forma dat esse rei* (form gives being to the thing) and established the fact that whereas "form" shapes individual objects, "die Materie als in allen gleichartig gedacht werden muss" (matter must be thought as homogeneous in all things). In other words, there is only one kind of matter. The elements are the different states of this matter, and they differ from each other not through substance but through "accidents." Matter is "bleibende Substrat aller vorübergehenden Erscheinungen, also aller Aeusserungen der Naturkräfte und aller lebenden Wesen" (the permanent foundation of all transitory phenomena, hence of all expressions of natural forces and of all living beings). Consequently, Schopenhauer claims, one cannot give up the idea that everything can be transformed into everything else—lead into gold, for example. [17]

Of course, Schopenhauer zealously resisted the atomic and

mechanistic outlook of modern science. Nature, as the materialists see it, is not the empirical nature found in reality, but "ein blosses Abstraktum jener wirklichen Materie" (a pure abstraction of that real matter). They have abstracted all the mechanical properties from nature and constructed their world picture wholly of that paltry stuff. Analogous to this argument is his critique of the atomic theory, of which he is archly contemptuous: "nicht bloss die *festen* Körper sollen aus Atomen bestehen, sondern auch die flüssigen, das Wasser, sogar die Luft, die Gase, ja, das Licht, als welches die Un-dulation eines völlig hypothetischen und durchaus unbewiesenen, aus Atomen bestehenden Aethers seyn soll, deren verschiedene Schnelligkeit die Farben verursache" (Not only are the *solid* sub-stances supposed to consist of atoms, but also liquid ones, water, even air, gases, indeed, even light, which is supposed to be the un-dulation of a fully hypothetical and completely unproven ether, con-sisting of atoms whose various speed gives rise to the colors). The trouble with science is that it reads into nature certain properties that it has already determined to find there and ignores the rest. If science had started instead with "die wirkliche und *empirisch* gege-bene Materie" (real and *empirically* proven matter) with all its chang-ing properties, it could have accomplished something useful. Thus, it is really philosophy that produces the most profound reading of nature, because philosophy regards matter as nothing more than "das *Vehikel* der Qualitäten und Naturkräfte, welche als ihre Ac-cidenzien auftreten" (the *vehicle* of the qualities and natural forces, which appear as their accidents),[18] and consequently, science should once again look to philosophy for guidance.

This same criticism of the scientific approach turns up in Strind-berg. Time and again he points out that the presiding scientific ideas are nothing but powerless abstractions, against which he wishes to propose his own positive, empirical observation of nature. He maintains that by means of his interpretation of the nature of sulphur he is returning to reality, and he proposes his "positive anal-ogy between sulphur and a resin in opposition to the poetic or meta-physical simile that would label sulphur with the interim concept 'element.'" He summarizes his criticisms of science in a similar manner in his essay on atomic weights: "In short, subsidized chemistry works with conventions, with approximations, with licenses that one is tempted to call 'poetic,' and the presiding atomic theory is based on a hypothesis—the existence of an indivisible particle, a weightless atom (that nonetheless has an atomic weight)." [19]

That one element ought to be capable of being transformed into another is the obvious consequence of this approach. Strindberg was particularly preoccupied with "transmutations," especially transmutations of metals. But producing gold (or any other element) was not his most important goal at first; not until 1896, in fact, did he become desirous of achieving such results. What he lists in his notes under the rubric of "transmutations" are common chemical reactions or changes of properties in elements, which his chemical principles led him to regard as transmutations. Strictly speaking, therefore, "The Transmutations of Zinc" means "The Chemical Changes of Zinc." Under the heading of "transmutations" Strindberg includes remarks upon the "fatness" of sulphur or lead and comments that tin "smells of fish," that lead oxide is like silver or tin, and so forth. Only a man with the eyes of an Aristotelian alchemist could find evidence of transmutation in these banal observations. "On Chemical Reactions as Transmutations," the title of an uncompleted essay dating from his stay in Germany, supplies the key to all this "experimentation." [20] What Strindberg wanted to introduce was a new way of looking at things. Given such a point of departure, "the discoveries" made themselves.

Strindberg's concept of matter, like Aristotle's, precludes any possibility of determining the nature of the elements. Indeed, if the elements changed as rapidly as Strindberg thought and were now one thing, now another, then of course one would have to abandon the whole concept of "elements" and replace it with a notion of "substance" and "accident"—thus equating substance with indeterminate matter. But like the alchemists, Strindberg insisted on finding at least one thing in the material flux that was relatively stable—something corresponding to Aristotle's "element" or to Albertus Magnus' basic elements, arsenic, sulphur, and water.

Like a consistent monist, he at first thought that there had originally been only one element, and he sought this primordial element chiefly in hydrogen, the lightest of the basic chemical elements. He formulated his hypothesis in a rough draft, which appears from the handwriting to be very early:

> There must be only one basic element = *Hydrogen,* just as there is but a single protoplasm, one cell, from which everything else develops by means of differentiation.—All the other so-called "basic" elements must be combinations, concentrates of hydrogen or of its concentrates.—That the "basic elements" cannot decompose must result from the fact that they are good species (= fixed).—But if one finds Casium and Rubidium in wood ash, one can assume that these are degenerate species of Calium—regressive, diluted (as opposed to concentrated).[21]

In this hypothesis he allows Darwinist terminology ("differentiation," "good species," "degenerate") to represent a concept that has a rich tradition dating back to the alchemists and to Ionic natural philosophy ("concentration," "dilution," "fixing"). The same is true of the sketch that Strindberg made on January 24, 1892, for a work to be entitled "The Pedigree of Matter"; in this work, too, he makes hydrogen the primordial element.[22]

It is not surprising that he settled on hydrogen as the putative ur-element. William Prout, the most celebrated modern champion of the idea of the unity of matter, had arrived at the same conclusion. Moreover, the very fact that it had been possible to set the atomic weight of hydrogen at one is likely to suggest the same idea. But one other factor contributed to the acceptance of hydrogen as the primordial element. Because of the theory of evolution—and especially because of Haeckel's research—it was generally believed that water was the origin of life. This idea underlay the famous words in *By the Open Sea* about the sea as "the universal mother, from whose womb the first spark of life was lighted, the inexhaustible well of fertility, of love, life's origin and life's enemy." It seemed plausible, therefore, to believe, as the Neptunists had, that water was also the origin of the inorganic world.

Strindberg formulated several variants of this doctrine. On a page of a rough draft having the title "The Basic Elements of Matter, or Monist Chemistry," he argues, using Aristotelian terminology:

Just as there is only one kind of electricity, which can differentiate itself into positive and negative electricity, so there is only one element, the positive (active or aggressive) manifestation of which is called oxygen, the negative (passive or additive) hydrogen. (Cf. heat and cold.)

Thus, oxygen and hydrogen are not contrary elements, but only manifestations of the same force, aspects of the same matter.

Water, which appears to be the primordial element, does not consist of oxygen and hydrogen, but from water one can derive oxygen and hydrogen—along with all other elements, which are concentrations that either approach the negative (or hydrogen) pole or the positive (or oxygen) pole.[23]

Later, Strindberg became less interested in speculations of this sort, and by the time that he was seeking the unity of the cosmos in numerical regularity, the number of his primordial elements had increased (as many of his notations show) to four: C, H, O, and N.[24] But he never completely abandoned his initial idea, and after the turn of the century he made excerpts from the work of a certain Hungarian scientist named Winterl, who advanced a theory about an ur-element called "andronia."[25]

Before Strindberg went to Germany, he was preoccupied with air and water; after arriving in Germany, he focused attention on sulphur. But his speculations about water and air (which are partly reported in *Antibarbarus*) are important because they are characteristic of his whole approach to chemical problems. The idea that perhaps there was no nitrogen at all in the air had occurred to him as early as 1883, and in the 1890s it gave rise to many of his speculations and experiments. These "cruel doubts concerning the composition of air or water," as he describes them in a letter to Lidforss (Apr. 1, 1891), appear in Strindberg's laboratory protocols dating as far back as the beginning of 1891, when he confined small animals and plants in an air-tight bell jar in order to get to the bottom of this secret. A sketch he made for a work on the composition of air, which may be his earliest extant scientific draft, seems to indicate that an analogy between air and water was his point of departure:

Hypothesis I: The composition of air cannot differ from that of water, of which air seems to be an aggregate form. The Book of Genesis Hypothesis. *Natura non facit saltus: ergo* the two milieus of the amphibians cannot be so different as water and air are assumed to be.

Hypothesis II: Either water must contain nitrogen too, or air must be without it. According to current theories (Pasteur), all organic life must have ceased when the earth was in a molten state with water gas. But if one imagines that there is nitrogen in water and makes protozoa into crystallized albumen (coagulating at 100° C. = cf. ice crystals), then the organic world can also be deduced from water. Then clouds and rain would not be vaporized water, but another aggregate state of "air."

If air consists of oxygen and hydrogen, then lightning becomes the ignition of an oxyhydrogen gas mixture, oxygen and hydrogen *mixed* (or air and hydrogen), and a thunder shower is the chemical combination of oxygen and hydrogen (= water). (Seen as a hypothesis, this point is pretty damned good.) [26]

The same comparison between air and water occurs in a section of the poem entitled "Haze," which describes how Strindberg dives down into the sea and sees "another world, where the trees were as red as seaweed and the air was emerald green, like sea water." What had formerly been no more than a poetic image he now takes seriously and uses as a battering ram against current scientific theories. Air and water seem so similar that their chemical composition cannot be very different. According to the letter he wrote to Lidforss on April 1, 1891, Strindberg did not become acquainted until later with Pliny's thesis that water is "condensed air." Actually, this is a well-known Aristotelian idea that he could also have found in Bacon.

In the sketch quoted above, one already glimpses the idea of "concentration and dilution" that he was later to use as the explanation for changes occurring in matter. The phrase "The Book of Genesis Hypothesis" shows that Strindberg was aware that he was returning to a very primitive sort of natural philosophy. The Book of Genesis, of course, asserts that water existed before Creation, but it does not

mention air. To reinforce the idea that water is the origin of everything, Strindberg used another poetic analogy that had preoccupied
him ever since 1889. In a draft he writes: "Water is the transition
between the colloids (organic) and the crystalloids (inorganic), for
when the bottom of the sea freezes, it gelatinates and ejects plantlike
forms in the patterns of the frozen crystals (ice ferns)." [27]

His observation of frost patterns ("ice ferns") led Strindberg to a
hypothesis that was in perfect harmony with his "monism": the idea
of the fundamental unity of organic and inorganic matter. In a letter
to Ola Hansson on January 28, 1889, he refers to Haeckel's morphology, where Haeckel "had made the 'discovery' that the lower
animals only obey developed laws of crystallization." Strindberg
turned the argument around, however, and asserted that inorganic
nature can produce formations which are just as complicated as those
made by organic nature. His notes are filled with observations of
frosty window panes or of crystallizations in the laboratory. The conclusion he draws from all this is that one ought "to imagine that
plant life originated from the increasing concentration of water on
the surface of the earth—hence also on the window pane." One ought
to mention that Schopenhauer, too, paused to brood over the frost
patterns on window panes. Of course, both his and Haeckel's "mor-
phological" speculations ultimately derive from Goethe's natural
philosophy. In the organic world, matter is primary and form is secondary; in the inorganic world, the opposite is true. Because of this
division in nature, Schopenhauer believes that it is impossible to
cross the boundary between organic and inorganic matter. But even
inorganic life shows traces of a will, and it also seems to have made
some effort to achieve form. Thus, he concludes that crystals form a
bridge between the two worlds: "Im Anschiessen des Krystalls sehen
wir gleichsam noch einen Ansatz, einen Versuch zum Leben, zu wel-
chem es jedoch nicht kommt" (In crystallization we see, as it were, a
beginning, an effort at living, which is, however, not successful). [28]
In the same connection Strindberg spoke of a "formation instinct
that causes inorganic nature to strive toward the forms assumed by
plants," a concept he had already used in an exegesis of the alchemic
point of view: "These ancients still had a certain respect for matter,

ascribed some measure of soul to it—soul or formation instinct; they
paid more attention to the properties of bodies and derived their
concept of nature from the activity of these bodies." In Strindberg's
"formation instinct" appears a new version of Aristotle's "entelechy"
and Schopenhauer's "form." [29]

Obviously, concepts like these can be defined in different ways. It
is quite clear, however, that they readily lead to a pantheistic or
hylozoic concept of nature. And indeed, until he moved to Paris,
Strindberg's speculations did move in this direction. Hylozoic
anthropomorphism has affected the language of chemistry, and
traces of its influence can still be found in the chemical literature of
Strindberg's day. To speak of one element's "desire" to combine
with another is to use an expression with hylozoic overtones. Fairly
early in his career, Strindberg used this analogy between inorganic
matter and psychic life for poetic purposes; in a fable entitled "Natural Selection" (1885), for example, he describes the chemical elements metaphorically: "To deny that a chemical compound is like a
marriage would be to do nature an injustice." This sort of erotic
chemistry returns in his works written in the 1890s. In addition to
Strindberg's theory of "active" and "passive" elements, concepts like
"crossbreeding" and "copulation" between elements reappear constantly. Indeed, he even wants to rank the elements on the basis of
their behavior. In a rough draft, he states that platinum "is the most
perfect (from our point of view!) because it protects its individuality
better than any other element = does not readily copulate." [30] Thus,
to Strindberg's way of thinking, platinum was a mineral counterpart
to the inspector in *By the Open Sea,* whose "strong ego had revolted
against becoming a woman's means of reproducing her race."

Whenever he spoke of "psychology" in connection with chemical
phenomena, Strindberg had in mind observations of this sort. An
outline of a work on sulphur prepared on June 8, 1893, bore the
German title "Zur Psychologie des Schwefels." [31] Perhaps he had acquired this usage from Schopenhauer, who speaks of "Suchen, oder
Verfolgen, und ein Meiden, oder Fliehen" (Seeking or pursuit, and
an avoidance or flight) as the basis of inorganic life, who refers to
Goethe's *Elective Affinities,* and who notes with satisfaction that J.

de Liebig has also spoken of affinities between the elements. Hydraulics, he writes, can "als eine Charakterschilderung des Wassers aufgefasst werden, indem sie uns die Willensäusserungen angiebt, zu welchen dasselbe durch die Schwere bewogen wird" (be understood as a description of the character of water, inasmuch as it indicates to us the manifestation of will, to which the water is moved by gravity).[32]

"But you do not know Strindberg's Law of Ancestral Energies, with which one can explain the universe!" Strindberg wrote to Littmansson on August 6, 1894. Of course, it is inconsistent for Strindberg, who did not believe that nature conformed to any laws at all, to use the word "law" in this context. But the fact that his idea was supposed to be an application and expansion of Haeckel's biogenetic law suggests that he may have borrowed the usage from Haeckel. According to Haeckel's law, each individual recapitulates the development of the race in summary fashion; according to Strindberg's theory, the chemical elements possess inherited tendencies that can be ascertained from their behavior. Thus, in a Swedish sketch entitled "Toward a Psychology of Sulphur"—probably written on the island of Rügen at the same time as the German essay on that subject—he uses the phrase "ancestral desire for combination." In *Antibarbarus* he presents the following formulation of the law: "Bodies that have once been components in a compound still retain the energy of the compound after they are separated from the compound." If one peels away the pseudoscientific language, the remaining idea is rather simple. Strindberg posits some sort of memory in matter, consisting of the traces left by a compound on an element that has been liberated from the compound by chemical change. Thus, in this point too his Darwinist language appears to have the function of enabling him to reformulate his romantic ideas so that they look both original and scientific. About a year later—when Strindberg had come closer to metaphysical ideas and was consequently less concerned with maintaining a scientific façade—his theory of ancestral energies emerges directly as a variant of his basic hylozoic position. In an article about sulphur in *Le Figaro* on February 12, 1895, he states explicitly: "There is some sort of memory in matter, which you call crude, whereas I consider it to be living. And because it is living, it is subject to heredity, and its tendencies are inherited." [33] In "The Sighing of Stones" (1896), he reports that every drop of wine repeats "its recollections of the metempsychosis that it has gone through, from the body of the animal in the barn, from the human body, from the grapevine, from other plants."

In those days, when people believed that acquired characteristics could be transmitted to succeeding generations, heredity was regarded as the expression of some sort of memory on the part of the cells. Th. Ribot, for example, used the word "heredity" in this sense. Back in 1870, Ewald Hering had formulated the "mneme theory" more systematically, and it later emerged as a serious competitor to the genetic theory established by August Weismann. Haeckel's theory of "Perigenesis of the Plastidule" (1876)—according to which memory and the ability to reproduce itself were fundamental characteristics of organic matter—shows that he too was an adherent of Hering's idea. It is impossible to determine whether or not Strindberg was acquainted with these theories of Hering and Haeckel. In any case—true to his habit of going the authorities one step further—he has expanded the basic idea by letting it apply to inorganic as well as organic matter.

Considering his hylozoic principles, it is quite natural that Strindberg should be inclined to ascribe psychic activity to plants. In this case, as in others, he retreats from scientific theories to an earlier, more primitive way of grasping phenomena. Back in the early 1880s, when he was interested in forcing cucumbers at his summer place on the island of Kymmendö, he thought he had discovered "some sort of intention, unconscious perhaps," in the movements of the tendrils. In 1888, when he communicated these observations in an article entitled "The Intelligence of Animals and Plants," he came close to attributing "judgment," "deduction," "free thought," and "reflection" to plants. During his summer visits on the island of Runmarö in 1890 and 1891, his studies of the behavior of the insectivorous sundew (*Drosera*) served to corroborate this earlier impression. Strindberg's point of departure was the analogy between plants and animals. He gave eloquent expression to this analogy in "Sensations détraquées" (Deranged Sensations), where he writes that the pine "is a living being, a large animal that eats, digests, grows, and loves." [34]

Whether or not plants had some sort of psychic activity ("soul") was one of the most debated questions in scientific circles in the nineteenth century. Primitive natural philosophy, both in Greece and in India, took it for granted that plants have "souls," but this idea was discredited by Aristotle and his followers. Linnaeus assumed a hesitant attitude toward the question, but finally rejected the idea. Romantic natural philosophy reactivated the whole question, however, and in 1848, Gustav Theodor Fechner promoted it with great forcefulness in his book *Nanna, oder über das Seelenleben der Pflanzen* (Nanna, or on the Psychic Life of Plants), which gave rise to a sensational polemic between him and contemporary plant anatomists. The argument from analogy—to the effect that some plants are like animals, some animals like plants—was very important to the spokesmen for the vegetable soul, and the romanticist Lorenz Oken even went so far as to assert that the plant is an animal, since it possesses the same "irritability" as animals. [35]

Schopenhauer elaborates these ideas with great energy. In sharp contrast to Aristotle, he sees desire (or "the will") as being characteristic of plant life, and he regards the irritability of the plant as a manifestation of this life force. But he denies them imagination and consciousness. [36]

One thing that these writers avoided, however, was any talk of a nervous system in plants. They clearly did so in order to avoid a hazardous conflict with the findings of contemporary plant physiology. Plant physiologists considered themselves capable of demonstrating that plants, like animals, could respond to stimuli or were mobile. As far as nerves were concerned, these physiologists attempted to bridge the gap by explaining that certain animals could also live and move without sensory organs. At this point, Strindberg took a different road and—from the similarity he observed between plants and animals—drew the opposite conclusion: he opined that there must be some sort of nerves in plants as well. In this instance, he was following Eduard von Hartmann, who rejected the idea that

nerves are necessary for consciousness and perception, while suggesting at the same time that the "spiral vessels" in the stems of plants
might serve the same purpose as nerves in animals.[37] The summer of
1894 seems to have been the time when Strindberg was most enthu-
siastically engaged in experiments of this sort. He attempted to
"chloroform" plants, as Claude Bernard had done, and he dissected
roots and stems in order to find the nerve substance. He suspected
that the apex of the root might be the center of the plant's nervous
activity—Darwin had also studied the root cap—or it might be the
so-called *Siebröhre* (sieve tubes) in the stem. Relatively-speaking,
this supposition is perhaps the most successful of Strindberg's scientific hypotheses. As a matter of fact, recent research has demonstrated the existence of sensory apparatus and organs that conduct
stimuli in plants, especially in the stems and root caps.

Strindberg's scientific research during the first years of the decade
did not lead him to any clear, conclusive results. Moreover, it was
contrary to his nature to create a system. "It is very modern of
Nietzsche not to make a system," he wrote to Littmansson in 1894.
For him, nature was too disorganized, too self-contradictory and
complicated, to be forced into abstract theories. His outlook was
still skeptical. Whenever he heard about a logical, speculative philosophy—like that of the Polish occultist Hoene Wronski—he bris-
tled at once: "You still seem to want to arrange, to systematize and
trilogize, the great confusion that simply is, and is marvellous in
its disorder = freedom" (letter to Littmansson, July 22, 1894). His
speculation is basically a revolt against the checkered, schematic,
and deterministic outlook of modern science. He valued any argument that upset recognized theses and scientific truths. Thus, he
writes of "panspermy" (Arrhenius' theory that life might have appeared on earth by means of "life-sperms" traveling through space
from the stars): "I do not believe in the zoösperms from the stars,
but admit them provisionally, since they advance disorder" (to Littmansson, July 29, 1894). And in the introduction to *Jardin des
Plantes* he invited pilgrims to follow him and breathe more freely,
"for disorder reigns in my universe, and that is freedom."

From logic and abstraction, Strindberg turned to direct observation, which he considered unbiased. When he observed the chemical elements unimpeded by theory, he found that they were constantly changing and that they were similar to each other. On these observations he founded his monistic chemistry. The elements were attracted to each other and repelled by each other—hence they were alive. Plants made premeditated movements—thus they had souls and perhaps nerves as well. His direct observation has an anthropomorphic tendency, from which science had been at great pains to free itself. With the aid of this anthropomorphism Strindberg developed his hylozoic outlook.

Thus, through the philosophy of revolt and chaos in Strindberg's scientific drafts from 1890 to 1894, one glimpses the contours of a romantic world picture. At first glance, his dry laboratory protocols seem only to contain isolated observations and passing fancies; but if one scrutinizes them more carefully, one sees that all his experiments have a common tendency. Despite their inconsistency, hesitancy, and groping, they do point toward a spiritualistic conception. His connection with Spencer and Darwin was something of a camouflage, which Strindberg soon discarded. In Haeckel, it was the strains of romantic natural philosophy to which he clung. Moreover, in Schopenhauer and Hartmann, his philosophical masters when he was young, he had become acquainted with ideas that stemmed from the prescientific tradition of natural philosophy. Through them he found the road back to Aristotle and to Ionian natural philosophy.

However, one cannot deny that Strindberg had a certain connection with contemporary currents of thought. In fact, he was fully aware of what was going on in genuinely scientific circles. Toward the end of the nineteenth century one can discern a rather widespread reorientation, a movement toward a more romantic conception of nature. Bergson's philosophy is the most striking expression of this shift in intellectual climate, but similar ideas also penetrated to the public through the so-called "vitalistic" biology, of which Hans Driesch was the leading exponent. At the same time that Strindberg began to experiment with plants, Gottlieb Haberlandt undertook his studies of the sensory organs of plants that were to rehabilitate Gustav Theodor Fechner's ideas. The so-called "Mneme theory," which was advanced by Richard Semon at the beginning of the twentieth century, even provided a sort of counterpart to Strindberg's risky idea of "ancestral energies." Although this tenuous rapport with contemporary trends in natural philosophy hardly provides reasonable grounds for claiming that Strindberg was a scientific pioneer, he nonetheless sensed what direction certain aspects of scientific development would take, for late nineteenth-century scientific research was subject to some of the same romantic and idealistic tendencies that helped form the character of *fin-de-siècle* literature. One must also take into consideration the fact that when his ideas matured, he was in close contact with a plant physiologist like Bengt Lidforss and a biologist like C. L. Schleich—the latter a full-blown scientific romanticist himself.[38] Through these men he found out what was going on in laboratories; then his racing imagination took over, and he spun out his speculations to the point where they became risky or even irrational.

Although it is proper to conclude that during his first period of scientific activity Strindberg was striving toward a romantic natural philosophy involving a fusion of elements taken mainly from Schopenhauer, Hartmann, and Haeckel, one must qualify this conclusion by injecting a few reservations. Whereas Schopenhauer and Hartmann assumed a finalistic point of view, Haeckel was a mechanist. Strindberg did not wish to be counted in either of these camps. He agreed with Haeckel's criticism of teleological speculations and in one place even uses the same term, "dysteleology"—or in Strindberg's translation, "the stupidity of nature." On the same page he writes: "No purpose, but a certain order nonetheless." [39] But this order was not constituted by the "laws of nature," resulting from the mechanistic approach. "The idea of law always led me to think of the legislator, and I do not believe in laws of nature—except in a restricted sense," he explains on March 15, 1891, in a letter to Bengt Lidforss. And in his correspondence with Littmansson he speaks on July 22, 1894, of "the dangerous word that begins with 'a' and ends—in Greek—with 'a' and that is the secret of creation" (Strindberg is thinking of the Greek word *anarkhia*, "anarchy"). Until

1894 this awareness of the "great disorder" dominates Strindberg's world picture. He was still using similar expressions at the beginning of 1895, but starting in the summer of 1894 new elements gradually emerged and reshaped his outlook.

There is no sharp line of demarcation between these two periods. Hence, his hylozoic tendencies survive his discovery that the world is a work of art, fresh from the hand of the artist-creator. But the shift of accent is obvious. A shaping hand begins to appear more and more clearly above the cosmos, and the secret connection between the creator and his work shines forth like a pattern in the chaos.

Before he published *Antibarbarus,* Strindberg wished to reshape chemistry or plant physiology. In his works written after 1895 he had a greater purpose in mind: to create a new cosmos. Like Aristotle—to use his own analogy—he moves from physics to metaphysics. In an undated letter to Littmansson in 1894 he exclaims, "Behold, a new world opens before me! Es ist eine Lust zu leben (It is a joy to be alive)!" His preface to the catalogue for Gauguin's first exhibition, dated February 1, 1895, ends with a confession that he too is "beginning to feel an enormous need to become a savage and to create a new world." This was exactly what he was later trying to do when he wrote *Sylva Sylvarum* and *Jardin des Plantes;* and in 1895 when Brunetière proclaimed "la faillite de la science" (the bankruptcy of Science), Strindberg was quite prepared to agree with him.

The change can be dated to the summer of 1894. Strindberg has given an account of it himself in the introduction to *Sylva Sylvarum,* which was written at the end of 1895 or the beginning of 1896. There he recounts that in the middle of life's journey he had sat down to rest and reflect. "Everything was repeated with killing monotony; everything was the same as always; everything happened all over again. The older generation had said, 'The universe has no secrets; we have solved all the riddles; we have solved all the problems.' " Faced with this perspective of hopelessness, Strindberg decided to "disappear" and lit the spirit lamp beneath his retort in order to produce potassium cyanide. But just as he bent over the fumes and began to feel stifled, he saw an almond tree in bloom and heard an old woman's voice: "No, child, do not believe in it!" Since this experience, Strindberg had thought about the great disorder, in which he "finally discovered an infinite coherence," and in *Sylva Sylvarum* he held out a new world: "Look, here is my universe, as I have shaped it, as it has been revealed to me."

The change certainly did not occur as quickly as Strindberg's account would indicate. Even before 1894 he had believed that there were riddles still to be solved and that these riddles were being neglected by official science. Moreover, romantic and subjective strains had been part of his concept of nature from the start. But one must bear in mind that Strindberg himself stressed the connection between his philosophical liberation and the crisis that occurred in July 1894. Another aspect of the crisis was a "longing for purity," tinged with Buddhism, which Strindberg revealed in letters to Littmansson. In this longing for purity one can locate the psychological connection between the growth of his new world picture, on the one hand, and his religious and moral development, on the other.

External circumstances also played a part. When Strindberg published *Antibarbarus,* he believed that he "had expressed the most secret thoughts of contemporary thinkers." Consequently, he was disappointed when the book was coldly received—or greeted with open criticism—by the experts.[40] As was so often the case, he reacted to this reception with defiance. If the scientists did not want to recognize him as a guide, he would in the future take no notice whatever of them. The frank subjectivity of his later writings is connected with this reaction. In a letter to Hedlund on November 10, 1895, he contends, "now I have the courage to be myself, the courage not to shield myself behind a sneer—against the sneerers." This opposition to professional scientists also helps explain why Strindberg tried again and again during the course of 1895 and 1896 to perform verifiable miracles, to decompose basic elements like sulphur, or to produce them synthetically—as in the case of iodine and gold. He no longer appealed to the experts; from now on he wanted to force them to acknowledge his ideas.

In July 1894, when Strindberg was in Ardagger at the house of

Frida Uhl's grandparents, Littmansson sent him two newly-published French books, *La vie et l'âme de la matière* (*The Life and Soul of Matter*) by Fr. Jollivet-Castelot and *Les métamorphoses de la matière* (*The Metamorphoses of Matter*) by Claude Hemel. There are many testimonies to the strong impression made on him by these two works. He speaks of them in letters to Littmansson and to Hedlund, and he sent several pages of excerpts to his friend and biographer Birger Mörner, who was then supposed to write an article about them and, by so doing, to create greater respect for Strindberg's *Antibarbarus*. In these two works Strindberg encountered a hylozoic mysticism strongly reminiscent of the concept of nature that he himself had advanced in *Antibarbarus*. (He also suspected that both Frenchmen had plagiarized his results.) The books were even more important to him from another point of view: they directed him to the Paris occultists. Here was a chance for Strindberg to find a new public, new connections. He no longer felt "alone in the desert," as he put it in an article in February 1895.[41] No longer would he turn to an audience of experts, as he had done when publishing *Antibarbarus;* from then on he had in mind the occultists and the news-hungry, *fin-de-siècle* Parisian public when announcing his scientific findings.

The most important difference between Strindberg and these two French occultists lay in the fact that whereas they could fall back on a solid tradition of natural philosophy, he had groped his way forward completely on his own. Interest in magic and the occult had never completely died out in France, and even before Paris occultism emerged as a "movement," the problem of transmutation had preoccupied hermits like Louis Lucas and Henri Tiffereau. Besides, in the historian Michelet, France had an intermediary for the romantic enthusiasm for nature, who had also won great popularity as a scientific author. His lyrical presentation inspired Claude Hemel to write tirades such as the following one: "Nous savons aujourd'hui interroger la nature. Nous avons découvert son perpétuel enfantement et le sens de l'allégorie paienne nous est devoilé. Le vieux Pan ressuscite. Il ne conduit plus dans les prairies humides, le long des frais ruisseaux, son cortège de Faunes et de Dryades. L'idée seule du grand Tout subsiste, mais elle a repris sa haute portée philosophique" (Today we know how to interrogate nature. We have discovered her perpetual proliferation, and the meaning of the pagan allegory is unveiled to us. Old Pan is resuscitated. No longer does he lead his train of fauns and dryads through damp meadows, along fresh brooks. Only the idea of the great All subsists, but it has regained its high philosophical scope). [42] The words resound in their turn in Strindberg's fantasies about Orpheus in *Jardin des Plantes.*

This kind of enthusiasm for nature became suffused with the impressions that Strindberg had formed of the "Buddhist works" which he had found in the library at Dornach. Buddhist subjectivity and the doctrine that all of existence is illusory fitted in well with thoughts that Strindberg had previously developed. Now he began once again to favor ideas that he had long ago found in Schopenhauer—the inevitability of subjectivity, the isolation of the self. "The only thing that exists is the self (le culte du moi), and I know nothing about the world and 'other people' except through my self," Strindberg wrote to Littmansson on July 22, 1894, at the same time that he was expounding this idea in the uncompleted essay entitled "Moi."

The phrase *"le culte du moi"* shows that besides realizing that the roots of his position lay in the past, Strindberg was also aware that he had an affinity with the brand of subjective idealism cherished by the younger generation of Frenchmen. Other statements made by him around this time point in the same direction.

It is improbable that Strindberg had any intimate knowledge of symbolist ideas at this time. But the mood that fostered those ideas he certainly understood, and he therefore sensed that there was a good chance of his winning a hearing in Paris, particularly for his revolutionary scientific ideas. In the essay "Deranged Sensations," which was written shortly after his arrival in Paris, and published in installments in *Le Figaro littéraire* on November 11, 1894, January 26 and February 9, 1895, he presented many of his scientific ideas in a literary, conversational form intended to catch the fancy of the *fin-de-siècle* Parisian public.

Because it apparently documents psychotic experiences like those from the latter half of 1896 described in *Inferno,* "Deranged Sensations" has hitherto been regarded almost exclusively from a psychological point of view.[43] This, as far as I can see, is the wrong way to approach this curious text. The Swedish title of the essay, "Förvirrade sinnesintryck" (Confused Sense Impressions), gives only an imperfect approximation of the French title, "Sensations détraquées." "Detraquée" is much stronger than "förvirrad" or "confused"; it means "distracted," "half-mad." But at the same time, one must be aware that "détraquée," like the word "décadent," was used by *fin-de-siècle* Parisian *littérateurs* as an accolade. People wanted to be "détraqué," mad in a brilliant and sensitive way. Behind this fashion lay the idea that the higher, more refined intellectual life was closely allied to madness, or that in any case, it must appear so to the uninitiated masses. Psychiatric discoveries concerning the connection between genius and mental illness, as well as the examples of Poe, Baudelaire, and Verlaine, helped to foster this idea. Related to this new respect for madness was a notion that the use of alcohol and narcotics could contribute to the creation of a higher human type. In his essay entitled "Charles Baudelaire," Verlaine speaks of "l'homme moderne, avec ses sens aiguisés et vibrants, son ésprit douloureusement subtil, son cerveau saturé de tabac, son sang brulé d'alcool" (modern man, with his senses sharpened and vibrant, his mind grievously subtle, his brain saturated with tobacco, his blood burned by alcohol.)[44] One hears an echo of the same idea in Strindberg when he asks himself, "Have not insomnia and dissipation sharpened my senses and my nerves?"[45]

In "Deranged Sensations" Strindberg tried to assume an attitude that is best described by a line from the *Anacreontea* quoted in his last letter to Nietzsche in December 1888, "I do, I do want to be insane!" To be insane and hypersensitive was at the same time to be "a modern man"—in the sense in which the Décadents used this term. Describing the first installment of the essay, he wrote to Littmansson on October 15, 1894, that it was a "symbolistic, détraquistic compromise between science, poetry, and frenzy. I believe it is mad enough to be modern, and shrewd enough not to be." His experimental purpose appears even more clearly in a letter written on November 26, 1894, to the painter Richard Bergh: "Sent you some time ago an article from *Le Figaro,* 'Deranged Sensations' where in a good disposition that I had worked up I tried to anticipate the capacities of a future, more highly developed psychic life, which we still lack and which I can only sustain for an instant before falling back, exhausted by the effort, into my old frame of mind.''

At the beginning of the first article he describes an actual pathological experience. He is about to cross the Place d'Armes to the palace of Versailles, but the building seems to be retreating into the distance, and he is frightened by the open space in front of him. It is well known that he often suffered attacks of agoraphobia, but this fear was not particularly characteristic of the Inferno period. Frida Uhl has described a similar attack that he had in Hamburg in May 1893; [46] and in a letter to Geijerstam, Strindberg speaks of his agoraphobia as early as March 25, 1890. One can establish the fact that after arriving in Paris in the autumn of 1894, he went through a period of depression, which was clearly identical with the one described in the first installment of "Deranged Sensations." While he was living on the Boulevard Lesseps, he reported to Frida Uhl that his nerves were "ultra-sick." [47]

Thus, although one cannot deny that this description of agoraphobia is based on Strindberg's own experience, such does not seem to be the case with some of the other sensations he describes. For example, he sees mysterious forces above the arch of the Orangerie, radiating above the arcades like the aurora borealis. One finds no evidence to indicate that Strindberg was subject to this sort of visual hallucination, either before the time he is dealing with or afterward. In the works of du Prel, however, he had become acquainted with the idea that under certain circumstances a person's "aura" can become visible as a magnetic field. Carl du Prel was a mystic, who attempted to elucidate the structure of the future human type by studying the achievements of mediums and hypnotists. Possibly Strindberg was inspired by such theories when imagining the sight of a magnetic field above the arcades. Something similar probably also underlies his auditory hallucination in the formal garden, where he thinks he can hear the voices of Paris. Of course, auditory sensations played a role for Strindberg during the Inferno crisis, but almost without exception they were given a rational explanation. Before the crisis they did not occur. As Strindberg explains himself, this experience was inspired by the idea that "the formal garden resembles the auditory canal of a huge ear, the auricle of which is formed by the wings of the building." [48] Later, when he tries to explain the murmur he thinks he hears when pressing his ear against the wall, a "vague memory from his youth" occurs to him. It concerns a sailor who could hear the bells of Lisbon ringing two days out to sea, because the sail served as a burning mirror for the sound waves. Actually, a vague memory from his youth had also inspired his first fantasy of hearing the voices of Paris. The original idea of focusing sound in this way comes from the ancient story about the system for spying on prisoners installed by Dionysius the Elder in the prison at Syracuse. Nor was Strindberg the first writer to pick up the idea. E. Erckmann and A. Chatrian, whose *Fantastic Tales* he had borrowed from the Royal Library in 1879, describe in a story a building that is constructed like an ear and thus traps sound. [49]

Elsewhere in "Deranged Sensations" Strindberg describes an experience in which he glances out of the window only to see emptiness. Seeking to free himself from vertigo, he finally finds support by watching a balloon rising from Meudon. In this instance he is reproducing an experience that had long been familiar to him and which he had already used in a piece written at the beginning of the 1880s. In an early draft of the poem "Haze," he is looking for a fixed point above the horizon of the sea and makes a landfall by watching a butterfly that flutters past. [50] Likewise, the experience of heightened sensibility was a theme he frequently used: it is found in *A Madman's Defense,* "The Romantic Sexton," and *By the Open Sea.*

Strindberg's hypernervous state following the crisis of July 1894 was unquestionably the basis for these experiences. But "Deranged Sensations" does not deal with the sort of experience that is typical of the Inferno crisis. The essay is clearly literary in character and chiefly foretokens *Inferno* and *Legends,* not because it deals with the same kind of experience, but because it marks Strindberg's first attempt to fuse "science, poetry, and frenzy" into a literary whole. In the second article, Strindberg presents a number of his scientific ideas—regarding, for example, the motion of the earth, the way in which plants emit carbonic acid, and the reason that plants must have nervous systems—not as scientific hypotheses, but as half-poetic fancies. "I discard the mask of the citizen, who has never recognized the so-called social contract; I let my rebellious thoughts roam freely, and I think, think . . . unafraid—with no reservations. Then I see with the penetrating vision of the savage. I listen and I sniff the air like a redskin!" [51]

The change that took place in Strindberg manifested itself in his chemical studies. He ceased to regard matter as being in a constant state of flux and began instead to speculate about the relations between the numbers corresponding to each element. In the fourth fascicle of *Antibarbarus* he had already begun to compare the tables of atomic weights in order to track down the relations between elements. The Svedberg is wrong, however, in assuming that *Antibarbarus* marks the end of Strindberg's interest in chemistry and the beginning of "his period of numerical speculation." [52] On the contrary, one might say that by adopting this form of numerical speculation, Strindberg came closer to an approach that was at least less foreign to contemporary chemistry than his Aristotelian principles had been. As early as 1816 the English chemist William Prout had proposed the hypothesis that hydrogen is the basic element and that its atomic weight ought to be fixed at one. He wished to regard the other elements as concentrates of hydrogen. Time and again during the nineteenth century this idea tempted chemists; and it gained currency once again after 1869, when Mendelieff proposed his periodic system for the elements, which was based on the relation between the atomic weights of elements and their properties. Using this point of departure in 1887, William Crookes believed that he had been able to isolate the primordial element, which he called "protyl." [53]

Thus, the idea that a numerical comparison of atomic weights could account for the relations between elements was nothing sensational, and up to this point there was nothing remarkable about the fact that Strindberg's chemical meditations took this direction. But

it is striking from another point of view. By attributing vital significance to atomic or molecular weights, he made a concession to the
prevailing chemistry of his day and abandoned his Aristotelian principles. Strindberg himself was aware of the difficulty. In one draft,
for example, he criticized the valence theory, and this point of view
probably represents his original position: "The sheer weight of authority alone has given rise to an artificial system similar to Linnaeus', where unrelated plants were grouped together." [54] When he
later became interested in the relations between atomic weights, he
attempted to redeem himself by the hypothesis that the atomic
weight only expresses the relative concentration of an element. Despite this suggestion, it is obvious that he had made a concession to
the sort of chemistry that in the first fascicle of *Antibarbarus* he called
"weighing-scale chemistry" or "cipher book chemistry."

What had only been hinted at in *Antibarbarus* became the predominant method of Strindberg's chemical research after 1894. The
two large chemical works that he later wrote, *Introduction à une chimie unitaire (Introduction to a Unitary Chemistry;* 1895) and *Types and
Prototypes* (1898), are filled with numerical speculations, which gradually become more and more fantastic. The latter work ends with
the assertion that "Pythagoras' idea" seems to have been corroborated. In a draft Strindberg had written "Aristotle's idea." [55] The
correction indicates the path he had taken: from Aristotle's precept
of formless primordial matter to Pythagoras' belief that things are
really numbers and that numbers give form.

But when Strindberg makes a grand declaration of his program in
Introduction to a Unitary Chemistry, he takes only the first step down
this path. By applying Prout's idea, he attempts to reduce all elements to hydrogen. He keeps the atomic weight of hydrogen at one
and reduces those of the other elements to whole numbers. He places
an equal sign between elements or compounds that have the same
atomic weight, although he clearly does not mean that these elements or compounds are completely identical with each other. Since
he counts on the fact that the carbon atom is 12, he considers it
proper for him to designate carbon by writing "H_{12}." Oxygen he
designates as "H_{16}" or "CH_4," both of which give approximately

the atomic weight of oxygen: 16. From this hypothesis he later draws far-reaching conclusions, but his method is always the same: he starts with the numerical relation between atomic weights.

The very fact that these relations play such a vital role here presages his later interest in numerology. Very seldom—and only if it suits him—does he make any attempt to check his results. Already at this stage the effort bears all the earmarks of a loose *jeu d'esprit.* Indeed, although it simplifies his task, his radical method of eliminating decimals in the atomic weights once and for all bespeaks increased nonchalance and greater impetuosity.

In any case, as early as 1894 Strindberg had devised the alchemic methods that he was later to propound,[56] but 1895 and 1896 seem to have been the years during which he was most actively interested in making gold. There is nothing either in *Antibarbarus* or in *Introduction to a Unitary Chemistry* to indicate that during the earlier stages of his chemical research Strindberg's real goal had been to make gold. But after the unfavorable reception of *Antibarbarus,* he was spurred to seek real and forcible evidence for the validity of his unitarian chemistry, and he settled on gold as the most sensational element. He was convinced that the discoveries he had made would change the future development of science; but he was impatient: "Let us make hay while the sun shines; otherwise we shall have to wait for ten more years," he writes in a letter to Jollivet-Castelot on March 1, 1895.[57] Perhaps this haste is the most important reason that Strindberg's chemistry was involved with gold to such a great extent in 1896. That was also the year in which he published his first essays on alchemy.

His eagerness to publish his results (with each essay dated exactly) seems to be connected with the fact that at the time there was discussion in the newspapers of an American alchemist whose efforts had been crowned with success. Strindberg states in a letter to Hedlund on September 7, 1896, that if "Stephens" patents his method of making gold, Strindberg will publish his results; and on September 18 he sent Hedlund the essay entitled "The Synthesis of Gold." The fear that he might be anticipated must have been the impelling force. But deeper motives were probably also at work. It can hardly be an accident that Strindberg mentions gold-making for the first time in the summer of 1894, at the same time that he declares to Littmansson that the supreme value in life is to "walk in the gutter and have *Machtgefühl* (a sense of power)" and begins to speak of himself as a "beggar" or "mendicant friar." Gold was the symbol for the vain world that he turned away from during the period 1894 to 1896. He wanted to produce the gold that he himself so bitterly lacked and to demonstrate in his laboratory that this precious element was worthless. He explained in a letter to Hedlund on July 20, 1896, "But as to my search for gold, I pursued it because I believed it was my duty to overthrow the golden calf by unmasking its symbol, gold."

Strindberg's attempts to make gold do not represent any change in his approach to natural philosophy. As usual, he proceeded from atomic weights, thus splitting the problem of transmutation into two phases. The first was to find a chemical compound that had the same atomic weight as gold—Strindberg usually favored compounds containing iron—the second was to "fix" this element at the stage where it had become gold. In addition, he applied an idea that he seems to have taken from Henri Tiffereau, namely, that the occurrence of gold in nature can tell something about the elements that have contributed to its formation. There is nothing here that exceeds the program he had outlined in *Antibarbarus;* it is simply the romantic character of the problem that has led people to regard it as a typical expression of Strindberg's "occultism."

At this time Strindberg had come into contact with the Parisian group centered around *Hyperchimie.* Although he began to correspond with the editor of that periodical, Jollivet-Castelot, in July 1894, they did not engage in a lively exchange of ideas until 1896. Strindberg collaborated in the periodical, and Jollivet-Castelot's work *Comment on devient alchimiste* (*How to Become an Alchemist*) contains many respectful statements about Strindberg the alchemist. Yet the rapport between Strindberg and these modern alchemists was ambiguous. Jollivet-Castelot was eager to call attention to Strindberg's greatness as a dramatist and to his successes on the Paris stage. It is thus apparent that Strindberg's fame greatly enhanced the promotional value of his connection with the group—a thought that also seems to have occurred to the Paris occultists. As a matter of fact, however, the views expressed by Strindberg and Jollivet-Castelot in their dogmatic works differ rather widely. In his book, Jollivet-Castelot distinguishes between esoteric and exoteric monism. Whereas the former is cabalistic, the latter appears to him—as also to Strindberg—to be a natural consequence of the teachings of Darwin. Nor does he attempt to conceal his opinion that exoteric monism is valuable only because it can lead the adept to esoteric monism. He is extremely polite to Strindberg, but when he comes to Tiffereau, he writes, "M. Tiffereau, like M. Strindberg, has not passed the boundaries of *routine experimentation,* that is, only what is carried out with the tools of the ordinary laboratory." [58] In contrast, when Strindberg presents modern alchemy to the Swedish public in his "Present-Day Alchemy" (1896), he does not bother even to mention either Jollivet-Castelot or his cabalistic authorities, but refers only to certain classical chemists and to modern chemists and metallurgists, like Tiffereau, L. E. Vial, and Le Brun de Virloy. He explicitly states that Tiffereau "is unacquainted with the alchemists and is the naturalist among gold-makers." Thus, like Jollivet-Castelot, Strindberg was aware of this dissention within the ranks of the contributors to *Hyperchimie,* and there can hardly be any doubt that he also counted himself as "a naturalist among alchemists."

The differences between these two men emerge even more clearly when one examines Jollivet-Castelot's position. For him, alchemy is only a part of occultism. Like Strindberg, he can speak of the unity of matter and refer to the discoveries of scientific chemistry, but this he regards as merely the outworks. Indeed, he feels that laboratory work is only one of the alchemist's many occupations. For Jollivet-Castelot, becoming an alchemist is practically the same thing as becoming a magician. Will is the alchemist's most essential instrument. Prayer is also important, for the adept is comparable to a messiah. Jollivet-Castelot therefore prescribes chastity during periods when engaged in "the great work." It is clear from both his own exegeses and his quotations from cabalistic writings that "le grand oeuvre" involves not just the production of gold, but also the acquisition of absolute magical power over the forces of nature. To the *lapis philosophorum* he expressly attributes the property of curing sickness. He also identifies it with the astral light that the occultists often spoke of, describes it as a "condensation of life," and the like.[59] Finally, his entire presentation of "hermetism and the spagyric art" rests on the Tarot cards, as they had been interpreted by Eliphas Lévi and Papus. This sort of reasoning differs widely from Strindberg's.

At a somewhat later date, however—at the beginning of 1897— Strindberg, too, began to exploit mystical ideas within the framework of his chemical research. Then numerical correspondences freed themselves from their fixed foundations, and he soon began to see secret correspondences between widely different phenomena. In January 1897 he published "La synthèse de l'iode" (The Synthesis of Iodine) in *Hyperchimie*. His chemical method in this article is based on the familiar procedure of finding numerical correspondences between atomic weights (he even mentions Prout in the essay). But between algae, iodine, and manganese he also finds a correspondence in color, which he chooses to call "occult." His speculations about numbers become increasingly rash. Thus, in his essay entitled "Notes et observations sur la chimie actuelle," (Notes and Observations on Present-Day Chemistry), numerical correspondence is no longer a sign of any ordinary sort of resemblance, such as chemical affinity or the like; for when he compares the normal temperature of blood, 37°C., with its double, 74°C., which is the temperature at which albumen coagulates, or with the freezing point of mercury, which is −37°C, neither Strindberg nor anyone else can divine the connections between them. Nor does he pretend to do so. He closes a section filled with similar comparisons concerning the sun by asking, "What does this mean?" [60] From now on, a characteristic feature of Strindberg's chemical reflections is that he completely loses contact with reality. No longer does he attempt to find a rational explanation for an "affinity." The very fact that it exists is enough and has become for Strindberg the sign of an unknown link in the cosmos, a coherence that he sometimes suspects ought to remain a mystery.

By the time that he wrote *Types and Prototypes* (the first part of which is dated March 1898), this development was complete. Here it is not his hypothesis concerning the unity of matter that he finds most important to assert. In fact, that hypothesis only serves to support a greater cause, that is, it helps to prove the existence of God. This purpose is already apparent from the epigraphs that introduce the book. An idea from "Les minerais paraissent . . ." (The Ores Seem . . .) concerning the relation between the percentages of metals in alloys and their atomic weights recurs throughout this book. Moreover, he supplements the idea with a method that allows him to rearrange the numbers in an atomic weight or in a percentage which he calls "commutation." Now the main point is that he finds numbers in similar combinations. Behind this phenomenon he senses a hidden connection between all created things. "It is apparent from all this that nature only works with numbers and with one element." When he finds the numbers 15 and 85 in both the composition of air (15 percent nitrogen and 85 percent oxygen) and the atomic weights of oxygen and nitrogen (15.85 and 15), he supposes that he is face to face with "one of nature's axioms, the unity of matter, which because it is an axiom *cannot* be proved."

In *Types and Prototypes* Strindberg adduces the relations between numbers as proof of the existence of a cosmic master builder who works according to mathematical principles. In the conclusion he openly expresses his basic Pythagorean view at the same time that he provides—at the chemical level—a solution to the problem of chaos versus coherence:

> In a word, Pythagoras' idea that the world is really constructed on numbers seems to be confirmed, and behind these numbers one can discern the master builder, conscious, calculating, measuring, writing his record of creation. Sometimes his record is right side up, easily legible; sometimes he conceals his purposes in cipher-writing that runs backwards or is disguised, so that through their arduous searching men will learn to appreciate the infinitude of his wisdom and their own ignorance.
>
> This is the endless coherence in the great, apparent chaos!

The development of Strindberg's chemical theories indicates that he turned away from the superficies of things and that beyond the level of the directly observable he found a mystical connection between phenomena. Quite consistent with this development is the fact that after 1894 he became increasingly inclined toward subjectivity. A number of observations he made in 1895 and 1896 are intended to show how illusory our world picture really is.

In May 1894 he attempted to photograph the moon, the sun, and the stars without a lens and sent his results to the Astronomical Society in Paris. This action was prompted by the idea that the lens of the camera distorts reality, just as the lens of the eye may do. A curved surface gathers light rays into a point and gives "a little round image, similar to the one we call the moon and see with our eyes." In "A Glance into Space" (1896) Strindberg recreates the fantasies that underlay his experiment:

> Then it was that the thought struck me: is the sun round because it looks round to us? And what is light? Something outside me or within—subjective perceptions?
>
> Light is a force, not an element. Of course, it should not be visible, since forces are not otherwise visible.
>
> Might the sun be the omnipresent primeval light, which my faulty eye can apprehend only as that round, yellow spot on the retina?

In "Deranged Sensations" he had already observed that the overly tired eye produces subjective spots and interpreted this phenomenon as a projection of the corneus tunic. "Do you suppose that my eye is developing into an extraordinarily powerful solar microscope?" [61] Strindberg elaborates on this idea. He points out that by pressing on the eye, one can produce images of suns and stars. He had also compared ophthalmoscopic plates with astronomic plates and been struck by their similarity. "Where does the self begin and where does it end? Has the eye adapted itself to the sun? Or does the eye create the phenomenon called the sun?" The same idea recurs in "La distance du soleil de la terre" (The Distance Between the Sun and the Earth) of May 1896, where he states that "the sun itself is a virtual image. But an image of what? According to some, it is the omnipresent, universal light, which is reflected by the sphere of heaven." [62] The horizon is not round, he asserts elsewhere; it seems round because the eye wants to apprehend everything spherically. His conclusion is that the earth is not round either. All these speculations point to the conclusion that he arrives at in "La terre, sa forme, ses mouvements" (The Earth: Its Form, Its Movements) of 1896: "So it would seem, but it is not certain, since our entire world appears to be illusory." [63]

Schopenhauer's physiologically motivated idealism and Buddhist subjectivism are the most obvious sources for these ideas. On other points, of course, Strindberg was profoundly impressed by these two positions; and in "A Glance into Space" he supports his view by quoting a pronouncement of Schopenhauer's to the effect that all objects are "cerebral phenomena." Moreover, a statement like "our entire world appears to be illusory" has the unmistakable ring of Buddhist or Schopenhauerian subjectivism.

Yet Strindberg's way of posing the problems is ostensibly scientific, concrete, and based on the experimental method. His point of departure is neither mystical, as in Buddhism, nor primarily theoretical, as in Schopenhauer. One can probably locate the origin of these favorite ideas of his somewhat more precisely, however, for although they do not dominate his thought until sometime during the course of 1895 and 1896, one can trace strains of subjectivism far back in his career. The first time that a similar notion appears is in *Flower Paintings and Animal Pieces* (1888), in the essay entitled "The Intelligence of Animals and Plants," where he remarks of bees:

> Physiologists also believe that insects see their world in a mosaic pattern, and I have once made a freehand hypothesis that when bees and wasps are going to build their combs, they proceed subjectively *aus der Tiefe seines Bewusstseins* (out of the depths of their consciousnesses) and build their cells according to the form of their eyes. Thus, a honeycomb would be an image of the facets or ommatidia of the compound eye—and all the talk about the maximum suitability of the honeycomb to its purpose would thereby disappear. Now let the learned ascertain the validity of this hypothesis.

This was written in Denmark in the autumn of 1888. In the preceding year, Prel published his *Doctrine of the Soul Presented from the Viewpoint of the Unity of the Human Being,* a work that Strindberg had almost certainly read. Citing another occultist, Prel introduces the theory of "the projection of organs." [64] He uses this term to designate the tendency of humans to base their inventions—particularly their technical devices—on an analogy to their own organs. Thus, the pump is an imitation of the heart; the camera obscura is a large eye; and the grand piano has the shape of an ear. Strindberg's "free-hand hypothesis" about honeycombs is clearly copied from this doctrine.

It is an easy step from the idea that bees see the world in a mosaic pattern because their eyes are composed of facets to the assumption that man perceives all things as round because his eye is round. One glimpses this thought in *By the Open Sea,* and it must have been fully developed by December 26, 1893, when Strindberg wrote to Lidforss that he was going to compose a "letter" entitled "The World As It Is and the World As It Seems, Wherein the Author Reveals the Secret of the Sea's Horizon and Explains Why We See Everything As Round." [65] It is also probable that Strindberg's discovery of "the personal field of observation" contributed to his skepticism concerning the reliability of human sensory organs. In the 1880s Strindberg was vitally interested in the fact that differences in human reaction times lead to a disparity in evaluating scientific data—as in astronomy, for example. In Bacon, he found statements that grew out of a similar, if even more pervading skepticism about the human capacity for knowledge. Bacon claims, for example, that the human intellect "is like an unequal Mirror to the Rays of Things; which mixing its own Nature with the Natures of things, distorts and perverts them." [66] It may have been this very simile that inspired Strindberg to let the celestial bodies delineate themselves on a plane mirror rather than through the lens of the eye or the camera.

Starting from this idea, which exposes the Copernican world view as a subjective hallucination, Strindberg wanted to reshape current celestography. He had entertained doubts about the global form of the earth ever since the 1880s, when he came across Max Nordau's bold suggestion that the earth was perhaps not round. There is plenty of testimony by those who knew Strindberg during his residence in Berlin—Carl Ludwig Schleich, Adolf Paul, and Frida Uhl—to show that the idea was still important to him at that time.

At first his thought was hardly more than a criticism, which appeared to be inspired by nothing more serious than the pure enjoyment of contrariness. But during the period between 1894 and 1896—while extending his interests to other celestial bodies besides earth—he attempted to give this idea a more positive shape as well as to give intimations of his own concept of the cosmos. He was aided in this attempt by a Catholic engineer and writer, P. F. P. Delestre, to whose work *Exploration du ciel théocentrique* (*Exploration of the Theocentric Heaven*) he often refers. In fact, it appears that this work provided Strindberg with the quotation from Tyndall that he uses at the conclusion of *Jardin des Plantes*. [67] Delestre's basic idea is that the earth and the sun both gravitate around a common center; in other words, his conception is neither geocentric nor heliocentric, but "theocentric." [68]

Strindberg writes in one place that the geocentric world picture is at least as good as the Copernican, since it enabled the Assyrians and Chaldeans to anticipate eclipses as accurately as our system does; Columbus, moreover, discovered America before Kepler's laws were propounded. He adopts the theory of a "primeval light" that may stream down to earth through holes in the sky—the stars. This latter idea he borrowed directly from Delestre, who accepts the ancient doctrine of an empyrean filled with light, which streams down to earth through the nebulae. [69] It is also clear that Strindberg was thinking of the famous phrase about "the world egg" by E. J. Stagnelius, a Swedish Romantic poet, when he asked, "Are the stars then holes in the egg shell called heaven?"

Concerning the shape of the earth, Strindberg was especially interested in the curious idea that it might be shaped like a hollow rolling pin. He expresses this idea in an undated letter in the autumn of 1894 to Birger Mörner: "I have just read that Nordenskjöld has discovered the Saturn's ring of Earth. I described it four months ago in *Antibarbarus, II,* but took Earth to be the ring and its inner splendor = the polar regions, so I say that Nansen, if he succeeds, may come out at the South Pole." This notion, like the one about the stellar pores in the sky, bears the obvious stamp of pure, lyrical fantasy. And it may well derive from a writer whose suggestive powers of narration fascinated Strindberg. In Poe's *Narrative of A. Gordon Pym* there is an account of a voyage to the South Pole. When the voyagers have passed the barrier of ice at 70° latitude, the temperature begins to rise again, and after having been stranded on a hellish island with people who hate everything white, they continue through a shower of ashes toward a pillar of clouds in the south, out of which "the white giant" finally emerges.

During the course of 1895, Strindberg's scientific meditations tend to be conflated with his religious speculations. While his science becomes more and more bizarre from a factual point of view, it acquires an increasingly dreamy, poetic quality. In the sketch entitled "In the Cemetery," which was probably written at the end of 1895, he describes very beautifully the mood in which he now makes experiments: an absorption in melancholy fancies with literary ties both to Romantic graveyard philosophers and to Hamlet.

But unlike Shakespeare's famous grave scene, the closing cadence here does not suggest an awareness of the transitoriness of things. After Strindberg has poured a drop of acid on the dead matter he has found in the Montparnasse cemetery, it begins to swell and proves to be something more than a piece of clay that "might stop a hole to keep the wind away." Ever since Strindberg had studied ice crystals on window panes, he suspected that the difference between organic and inorganic matter was not great. He now replaces these terms with the concepts "life" and "death." In "The Sighing of the Stones," an essay written a few months later, he returns to the question of the life-giving effect of acid and writes:

Diluted sulphuric acid is called a fermentative, since it causes certain elements to ferment.

Of course, fermenting is rather analogous to rotting, that is, to dissolution, but out of putrefaction comes life, from which it appears that the difference between life and death is not so great.

Seen in conjunction with his scientific discussion, this view implies that Strindberg agreed with those who felt that the simplest living organisms are capable of spontaneous generation, and he applied this argument to mold. But he went further. Because he found silicon and carbon everywhere—in the organic world as well as in the inorganic world—he suspected that dead matter—including metals and even mountains—is endowed with life and can "give birth to" organisms: "Great Pan is certainly not dead, though he has been sick; but an Orpheus must descend once again into the underworld to sing life into the stones, which are not dead, but only asleep!"

Strindberg hereby accepted the consequences of the vitalism that had colored his thought ever since the beginning of the 1890s. He made everything in existence into something living, but this view still does not guarantee personal survival after death. Vitalism is not his sole approach to the problem, however. In "In the Cemetery" one glimpses other possible solutions. At the end of that essay, for example, Strindberg recounts that he has found a pupa on an iron fence. It is dead; it contains "nothing but animal slime, formless, totally lacking in structure, and emitting the odor of fresh corpse." Yet it will be resurrected. Will not all the dead, who are now being transformed in their pupae, also arise someday as butterflies? This is still not a conviction, only a presentiment; but as such it clearly breaks away from the framework of Strindberg's pantheistic viewpoint and introduces a supernatural strain of thought. The thought recurs in a letter to Hedlund on January 24, 1896, and this time Strindberg draws a decided conclusion: "I consider the immortality of the soul to be entirely self-evident. I feel that I am immortal; thus I am immortal. That the body decomposes—and it is not certain that it does—proves nothing to the contrary!"

What Strindberg has actually done here is to disguise a poetic and religious idea as a "scientific" observation: the butterfly had already occurred in Greek funereal art as a symbol of the liberation of the soul from the body through death. Strindberg was doubtless aware of this fact. The pupa is a work of art, he claims: "Like any artist, the great Artist-Creator has enjoyed creating forms without thinking of practical ends. This is art for its own sake—perhaps a symbol."

Strindberg had begun his scientific speculations as a convinced adherent of the theory of evolution, one of the most important tenets of which is the opinion that man is descended from apelike ancestors. A concomitant feature of his change of attitude in 1894, however, was the fact that he began to resist even this firmly established scientific truth. He observed that the child represents a more ideal type of human than the adult and that old people resemble apes more closely than young people do. Next, Haeckel's biogenetic law provided the silent premise for his conclusion in "D'où nous sommes venus" (Whence We Are Come), one of his essays written in Dornach and Paris in the autumn of 1894: "Then we come from heaven, and we continue our descent toward anthropoid apes. Is life a development backwards?" [70] In the same essay he prophesies a renaissance of interest in Rousseau, whom Darwinism had made obsolete. One can well imagine, Strindberg writes, that earth has witnessed a golden age, a sort of paradise that was followed by some catastrophe like the Flood: "Therefore there must have been at least two creations, and the child between three and six years old would represent a reminiscence of paradisal man. And we would once more have the right to use the term antediluvian, but in a more beautiful sense." [71]

Perhaps this thought was no more than a passing fancy when Strindberg wrote his *Vivisections II* (probably written between July and October 1894), because other essays in the same collection reveal a more orthodox Darwinian point of view. But this concept of evolution in reverse gradually became one of his favorite ideas. It turns up again a year and a half later in "In the Cemetery" and provides the basis for Strindberg's sentimental portrayal of children in *Advent* and for his anti-Darwinian polemic in *A Blue Book* (1907) and its three sequels (1908, 1908, 1912).

As in the case of the butterfly and the pupa, Strindberg's effort here is to rehabilitate ancient myths by presenting them in seemingly modern form. From this point, he slipped over into purely occultist or theosophical speculations concerning prehistoric giants. His preoccupation with these ideas seems to have begun in the spring of 1896. He remarks in "The Sighing of the Stones" that Fingal's Cave may be man-made, "because the basalt blocks are doweled together and the joints show traces of cement, and also because one can see where the stone has been broken." Somewhat later, on May 17, 1896, he informs Hedlund that he has just completed a study of the great pyramid. It is unlikely, he feels, that the pastoral Egyptians could have built them. Therefore, he guesses that they must have been made by "the same race that built the famous grotto on the island of Staffa (Fingal's Cave), the megalithic grave barrows (dolmens), the Cyclopean walls—in a word, the giants." From now on these fantasies become a regular feature of his world picture. During excursions to Scania in the spring of 1897, he discovered what he believed to be examples of primitive stone sculpture. Whereas in *The Scanian Countryside* (written around the beginning of the year 1897) he cautiously attributes these works to Bronze or Iron Age people, in *Legends* (written between September 22 and October 17, 1897) he asserts that they are "relics of preadamite sculpture." In *A Blue Book* (1907), Strindberg attempts to prove that a great many natural formations are actually the remains of "prehistoric architecture."

Strindberg's interest in "prehistoric giants" may have been aroused by almost any of the occult or theosophical works he had begun to study at this time, for giants recur constantly in occult speculation. Madame Blavatsky in particular lavishes a good deal of attention on them. According to her, many races resembling man have preceded him—among them a race of giants who, she suggests, have chiseled out many monuments, including the stone blocks on the Salisbury Plain.[72] In the same letter to Hedlund, Strindberg cites Genesis and Ovid's *Metamorphoses* to show that giants are well attested in mythology.

Strindberg's natural philosophy became clearly religious around the end of 1895 or the beginning of 1896. At that time he abandoned pantheism and postulated God as the ultimate explanation for everything. He had been preparing himself to take this step for a long time. In a loose memorandum, which appears from the handwriting to date from the beginning of the 1890s, he reflects on "the dangerous consequences of Darwinism": "Development is the word.

But from what? Why stop with the primordial element? If one returns to the primordial element, then one also wants to know how it
was set in motion. And then about the 'Mover' (Aristotle's)." [73] Just
as in *Sleepwalking Nights* (1884), a collection of poems where Strindberg ridicules those who "believe in the shoe, but deny the shoe-
maker," he still believed that the idea of development carried with it
the idea of God. "With law I always associated the legislator." During the course of 1895, "coherence" or the presentiment of coherence became more and more prominent in Strindberg's observations
about nature. That he accepted the final consequences of this position and rejected a monistic and pantheistic concept of nature in
favor of a dualistic and theistic one was consistent with his habitual
attitude toward this question. He also suspected that it would eventually come to that. In his correspondence, he often uses the word
"God"—followed by a question mark. In the undated letter to Hedlund in the autumn of 1895 outlining the plan for *Jardin des Plantes,*
he comments: "If I finally meet God, perhaps you—as a pantheist—
will wish to have nothing further to do with me, but we shall see
about that when the time comes."

At the same time, Strindberg began to suffer from the delusions
of persecution that finally occasioned his flight to the Hôtel Orfila.
This was the third of his five crises. As a result of this crisis, he
begins to speak explicitly of "God" in his correspondence—God as a
personal acquaintance whose chief function is to protect him from
his enemies. At this juncture, the central body of his religious concept lies so close to his ideas about natural philosophy that a great
deal of reorientation takes place in both areas. Strindberg's study of
nature is now directly aimed at proving the existence of a personal
creator, thereby satisfying his need for religion.

Strindberg wrote *Sylva Sylvarum* at the end of 1895. This work
contains no concept of God. But shortly thereafter he wrote "In the
Cemetery," in which he speaks for the first time of the "artist-creator" in connection with his observations of the pupa, which seemed
to hold out to him the promise of immortality. And in "The Sighing
of the Stones," written in March 1896, he criticizes the mechanistic
geology introduced by Charles Lyell: "No revolutions, no outbursts

of unbridled forces, no whims on the part of the creator, or artistic fantasies on the part of nature, or—to use a more picturesque word for the same thing—on the part of the Creator!" At the same time in a letter to Hedlund on March 28, 1896, he expresses his desire to have done with "physics in order to move on, as Aristotle did, to metaphysics, to man and God, and to the secrets of creation. You say 'Karma'! Why not speak in plain terms: God. It takes courage to do so, for it is not modern." In another letter to Hedlund on July 20, 1896, this concept of God appears in fully developed form:

Since I have access to the Jardin des Plantes [in Paris] at all times of the day and see the animals arise from their night's sleep and go to sleep at night, see them in all possible situations—even when they believe they are unobserved—I now see their existence in a completely new light. My latest opinions—namely, that they have been created by the hand of a great Artist, who has made sketches, rejected them, begun again, and developed both Himself and His skill in the process—are fully confirmed here. But He reveals Himself as so completely free that He surpasses all laws, all conformity to law. And like a great artist, He shows Himself to be "capricious," which is an expression of the highest independence, of freedom.

The Creator appears to Strindberg to be an artist who sometimes succeeds, sometimes fails. The introduction of this concept of God into his world picture shows that Strindberg has moved very far from his point of departure in evolution. However, since he still assumes that creation is a continuous process, he has not quite returned to the Biblical account of Creation. The development and mutation that one finds in nature is attributed not to natural causes, but to the Creator himself. It is He who is developing and improving his work little by little.

At first glance this notion of God appears to be reasonably curious. Scholars have readily seen in it some sort of projection of Strindberg's own personality. Lamm speaks of "this great Artist, who—like Strindberg—so often failed in His experiments and whose creations give such a strong impression of being chaotic." [74] Naturally, the parallel between Strindberg's own character and his concept of God is not entirely unjustified—the notion of an artist-God was personally satisfying to Strindberg. At the same time, however, the idea is not so bizarre that one cannot also find it in the scientific literature of the period.

Because of its criticism of the Biblical account of Creation, Darwinism met with a good deal of resistance, even among conservative biologists. But these men were placed in a difficult position. It was no longer possible to adhere explicitly to the concept of Creation as presented in Genesis. One could no longer deny paleontological evidence for the existence of extinct animal species. Thus, if God is the originator of Creation, He must have formed the world gradually and have made new inventions at the beginning of each new period in the history of the earth. Such was the opinion of Louis Agassiz, one of the most influential opponents of Darwinism. Instead of postulating extinct, intermediate forms linking the species, as the evolutionists did, he felt that each species really had been created at its appointed time, and he defended this view with great energy and talent.

It is impossible to determine whether or not Strindberg became directly acquainted with the works of Agassiz. However, he was undoubtedly familiar with the exhaustive critique of Agassiz' system that Haeckel provides in his *Natürliche Schöpfungsgeschichte* (*History of Creation*). Haeckel has a great deal of fun with Agassiz' "artist-God," who continually makes designs for creation and then rejects them:

Sie sehen, der Schöpfer verfährt nach Agassiz' Vorstellung beim Hervorbringen der organischen Formen genau ebenso wie ein menschlicher Baukünstler, der sich die Aufgabe gestellt hat, möglichst viel verschiedene Bauwerke, zu möglichst mannichfaltigen Zwecken, in möglichst abweichendem Style, in möglichst verschiedenen Graden der Einfachheit, Pracht, Grösse und Vollkommenheit auszudenken und auszuführen . . . In dieser ganzen Vorstellungsreihe ist der Schöpfer weiter nichts als ein allmächtiger Mensch, der von Langerweile geplagt, sich mit dem Ausdenken und Aufbauen möglichst mannichfaltiger Spielzeuge, der organischen Arten, belustigt. Nachdem er sich mit denselben eine Reihe von Jahrtausenden hindurch unterhalten hat, werden sie ihm langweilig; er vernichtet sie durch eine allgemeine Revolution der Erdoberfläche, indem er das ganze unnütze Spielzeug in Haufen zusammenwirft; dann ruft er, um sich an etwas Neuem und Besserem die Zeit zu vertreiben, eine neue und vollkommnere Thier- und Pflanzenwelt ins Leben.

(You see, in the production of organic forms the Creator proceeds, according to Agassiz' idea, exactly like a human architect, who has set himself the task of conceiving and executing as many different edifices as possible for as many different purposes as possible in as divergent a style as possible in the most varied degrees of simplicity, splendor, size, and perfection. In this whole chain of ideas the Creator is nothing more than an omnipotent man, who, plagued by boredom, diverts himself with the contriving and erection of the most diverse possible toys, of organic species. After he has entertained himself with them for a series of millennia, they become boring to him; he destroys them with a general revolution of the earth's surface, in the course of which he throws the whole vain plaything into a heap. Then he calls to life a new and more perfect animal and plant world, in order to while away the time with something new and better.) [75]

It appears likely that Strindberg accepted Haeckel's caricature as a suitable formulation of the concept of God toward which he himself was groping. There is probably an element of conscious defiance in his phrase "handmade." The point that the Darwinists found most paradoxical in the theistic concept of creation was the very one which Strindberg adopted in his own view. Strindberg's account in *Inferno* of how he "discovered" the Creator in the Paris zoo, the Jardin des Plantes, not only underlines his attack on Darwinism, but also demonstrates his relation to contemporary scientific discussion of the matter: "The Creator—that great artist who develops himself as He creates by making rough drafts that He rejects, by taking up abortive ideas once again—perfects, multiplies primitive forms. Most assuredly, these are handmade. By inventing species, He often makes prodigious advances. And then science comes along and asserts the existence of lacunae, missing links, and imagines that there have been intermediate forms that have now disappeared." [76]

As an alternative to Darwinism, Agassiz' system was considerably out of date. By means of his polemical skill, he succeeded in keeping alive a concept of nature that really belongs to the theism of the late eighteenth century. He is usually called a disciple of Cuvier's, and his entire attitude toward nature—which he considered both a product of God's creative powers and a testimony to them—puts one in mind of the period immediately preceding the pantheistic mysticism of Goethe, Schelling, or Schopenhauer, that is, the time in which theistic rationalism and enthusiasm for nature were fused in masters like Buffon and Linnaeus. Strindberg was also moving toward this tradition. Despite all the ties he formed with Renaissance and Medieval concepts during his period of panvitalism at the beginning of the 1890s, he nonetheless remained well within the intellectual milieu of the nineteenth century. He simply retreated from modern mechanistic views to romantic pantheism (animation of nature). Now he takes another backward step. In the library of Frida Uhl's grandfather at Dornach he had read Buffon. He also studied Alexander von Humboldt and Cuvier.

Nor was this field completely novel to Strindberg. In his youth he had written essays about "the Creator in nature." The Linnaean tradition was still alive in Uppsala when Strindberg was a student there, incarnated in the elderly Elias Fries, whose *Botanical Excursions* (1852) was a popular and much appreciated work in its day. Strindberg studied it early in life. Fries still retained something of Linnaeus' caution in the presence of nature—as well as his reverential feeling that he was "prying into God's secret designs." In an essay on the sunflower, which was probably written in the autumn of 1896, Strindberg refers to Fries and summarizes a description of the sunflower from *Botanical Excursions*. The summary reads:

At one point the author speaks of the relative superiority of various flowers, and he awards the prize to the sunflower for the following reasons: the sun, the omnipotent, the source of life, light, and power, makes its influence directly felt throughout the plant kingdom. Plants, the daughters of the sun, adapt themselves to their mother and strive to imitate her. None has succeeded so well in this effort as the sunflower, whose floral leaves form the image of the sun—the sunflower, which follows the movements of the sun and completes its growth within a year, the time it takes the sun to traverse the twelve houses in the zodiac.

This account appears to have been written from memory and is not quite exact. Fries does discuss the advantages of various species and asks which plants ought to be considered superior: the most complicated or the simplest, those that protect their organs or those that expose them, and the like. On the basis of such considerations—and not, in other words, for the reasons given by Strindberg—he finally settles on the sunflower. The passage that Strindberg had in mind is but a rhetorical peroration: "Like a favorite son, it (the sunflower) bears its father's name, nurtured in his purest tropical light; but it easily spreads to all zones, because the annual species completes its rich development within a few months. Throughout the day it lifts its rich, curly head toward the source of light and bows it at night, only to greet the rising sun the following morning." [77]

The difference here is not merely stylistic. The "affinities" between the sunflower and the sun to which Strindberg refers do not exist for Fries, who only gives poetic expression to the general connection between vegetable growth and the sun. Whereas Fries confines his lyrical divagation to general terms, Strindberg's is filled with concrete analogies. Although it is undoubtedly correct to locate one source of Strindberg's theistic natural philosophy in the Linnean tradition transmitted by Fries, this difference must be borne in mind. What they share is a concentration on formal similarities, a view of creation as one and indivisible, and a fundamental belief in God. But Fries's definition of "the oneness of the infinite multiplicity" is much more abstract than Strindberg's. Whereas he believes that "nature reflects in infinite gradations a common basic type," Strindberg contents himself with collecting resemblances in details.

A writer whose cast of mind was considerably closer to Strindberg's was Bernardin de Saint-Pierre, whose *Harmonies de la Nature* (*Harmonies of Nature*) he unquestionably had at hand when writing his essay about the sunflower. He reports that in Saint-Pierre's book he found "Fries's idea, but more fully developed and more palpable." It was Saint-Pierre who "opened the world of harmonies" to Strindberg. Also, he impelled Strindberg to study the sunflower. This plant is mentioned by Saint-Pierre, and in his works there are intimations of the method that Strindberg used and which led him to the results he attributes to Fries. In his essay, Strindberg cites a passage on the harmonies that exist between plants and the moon, but he excludes the lines that may have been the direct source of his idea. Under the rubric of "Harmonies végétales du soleil et de la lune," Saint-Pierre writes:

Il est possible qu'il y ait des fleurs entièrement patronnées sur le soleil. Nous en trouvons dans les orchis, qui imitent la forme d'une abeille, d'autres des figures humaines, et sont, pour cet effet, appelées personnées. Pourquoi n'y en aurait-il pas qui, dans leur intérieur, contiendraient une topographie de l'astre du jour, qui a sur elles tant d'influence? Les asters sont rayonnant comme des astres, dont ils portent le nom. La marguerite, comme nous l'avons vu, imite dans son disque entouré de pétales et couvert de fleurons, un des hémisphères de la terre avec son équateur et ses genres de végétaux disposés en spirale. Il est possible qu'une fleur renferme dans son sein le plan même du soleil, que nous refusent nos télescopes. Pourquoi n'y en aurait-il pas où seraient figurés les premiers linéaments de cet astre, lorsqu'il y en a tant qui nous représentent des figures d'insectes, d'oiseaux, et de têtes d'animaux et d'hommes?

(Perhaps there are some flowers patterned entirely after the sun. Flowers of this sort we find in the orchids, which imitate the shape of the bee; because others suggest human faces, we call them "personate." By the same token, might there not be some that house the topography of that day-star, the sun, which has had such a strong influence on them? Asters are radiant like stars, whose Latin name they bear. The daisy, with its petals surrounding a disk covered with miniature flowers, imitates—as we have seen—one of the hemispheres of the earth with its equator and its vegetal species arranged in a spiral. Perhaps in its breast one flower conceals the very structure of the sun that our telescopes refuse to give us. Since there are so many flowers that represent the shapes of insects and birds and the faces of animals and men, why should there not be some that bear the first lineaments of this star?) [78]

In addition to analogizing the sun with the sunflower, Strindberg suggests that the sun may have something in common with gold. He constructs his essay on what he calls a "trimurti" or trinity: "the sun, gold, the sunflower!" This analogy also played a significant role for Bernardin de Saint-Pierre. According to him, gold is clearly in "rapport" with the sun "par son poids, son incorruptibilité, sa couleur jaune, son éclat, sa ductilité, qui approche de celle de la lumière, et parce qu'il est le premier mobile des sociétés humaines, comme le soleil l'est du système planétaire" (by its weight, its incorruptibility, its yellow color, its brilliance, its ductility, which resembles that of light, and because it is the prime mover of human society, as the sun is of the planetary system).[79] Strindberg plays imaginatively with these elements, looking for similarities between the sun, the sunflower, Peru (the land of the cult of sun-worship), the pith of the sunflower, and ancient Greek and Peruvian coins. "The sun is gold," he states quite simply. And on a draft sheet, which probably dates from the same time, he notes: "Gold is the light of the sun, photographed and fixed." [80] Not without reason does Strindberg claim in this essay to have been led by his "teacher and master" Saint-Pierre.

What appealed to Strindberg in Saint-Pierre's *Harmonies of Nature* was precisely the feature that had repelled all fairly critical judges of the book when it first appeared: the process of free association which informs the method, the capacity of "seeing similarities everywhere"—to use Strindberg's phrase—without bothering to determine either final or casual connections. In his earlier work *Etudes de la nature* (*Studies of Nature*), Saint-Pierre had remained within the boundaries of a more normally teleological view of nature, and inspired by Fénelon, he had attempted to demonstrate that everything in the world has been created with an eye to its usefulness to man. In *Harmonies of Nature,* a work written late in his life, teleology has more or less retreated into the background. Although "harmony" may serve a functional purpose, as often as not the correspondence between natural phenomena is quite meaningless, as in the passage above. A single example will suffice to show how Saint-Pierre amasses detailed observations, on which he subsequently bases his pious hymn to the perfection of creation. Discussing palm trees, he points out that the single fruit of the palm resembles a negro's head, and the double fruit reveals an even more striking similarity to "les parties antérieure et postérieure du corps d'une négresse à sa bifurcation" (the anterior and posterior parts of the body of a negress at its place of bifurcation). But this observation does not exhaust all the "harmonies" between the palm and man. The proportions of the palm, whose height is one and one-half times its girth, are the same as those for man—" car ses bras étendus ont une longeur égale à sa hauteur, et sa tête ombragée d'une chevelure flottante imite en quelque sorte la cime ondoyante de ce bel arbre" (for his extended arms are as long as he is tall, and his head, shaded by flowing hair, in a way imitates the waving fronds of this beautiful tree). Finally, the palm is similar to a Grecian column and has served as a model for it.[81]

Saint-Pierre also regards as "harmonies" those characteristics of the palm that are useful to man. Strindberg ignored such combinations. What awakened his enthusiasm was simply the eccentric process of association. Saint-Pierre did not teach him to see similarities everywhere, for from the very beginning, the association of similarities had been the essence of his scientific method. But finding this method in the works of another writer did in some measure legitimate his own use of it and encouraged him to remain on the level of mere observation, without seeking rational connections.

Strindberg became acquainted with Bernardin de Saint-Pierre's work no later than the end of 1895. At that time, he was engaged in writing the essay entitled "The Death's-Head Moth," one of the sections of *Sylva Sylvarum*. He calls it an "experiment in rational mysticism" and poses the problem of how to explain the death's-head on the *Acherontia atropos*. Strindberg refers to a number of other animals whose markings may have resulted from environmental conditions. He argues that protective camouflage derives from the ability of the skin to "photograph" the environment. The fact that the death's-head moth turns up during plagues gives him the occasion to create a fable, in which he tries to show that the death's-head was projected onto the moth's back as it flew about in cemeteries, "where there was nothing to light its way except bleached skulls." This much Strindberg had written before he became acquainted with Saint-Pierre. Though these speculations are exceedingly fantastic, he gives them the appearance of rationality with his hypothesis about "photography," which he supports by suggesting various possible chemical reactions that may have induced the change. In any case, this still represents an attempt to "explain" a mysterious phenomenon.

He then began to read Saint-Pierre, after which he added a passage of an entirely different character:

> Since the preceding portion of this essay was written, I have read in Bernardin de Saint-Pierre that the death's-head moth is called the *Haïe* in French because it makes this sound.
> What sound? "Ai!" The cry of pain among all peoples!
> The scream with which the tree sloth laments the pain of existence. Apollo's expression of bereavement after the death of his friend Hyacinthus, which marks the flower bearing his name.
> But another flower bears this lament in the bottom of its house. We have all read about it when we were children and could hardly read. It is the cyanic blue larkspur, which Ovid, a consistent transformist, says sprang from the earth on the spot where the blood of Ajax flowed.
> Blood and Cyanogen! Battlefields, cemeteries, cadaverous poison and death's-heads! Ai!

Under the influence of Saint-Pierre, the "similarities" that Strindberg had at first taken to be signs of a more profound, more inaccessible, but rationally comprehensible, coherent pattern become both independent and self-sufficient. Indeed, the correspondences themselves constitute the coherent pattern. The mode of apprehension that most closely resembles this is the ancient doctrine of *signatura rerum,* which Saint-Pierre had become familiar with through writers like Virgil and which he then transmitted to Strindberg.

One can trace the same shift in other essays that Strindberg wrote around the end of 1895 and the beginning of 1896. In "Holly" (written about the same time as "The Death's-Head Moth") he interprets the similarities between the leaves of different plants in accordance with his idea that creation is a continuous process. Moreover, he wants to apply this idea to an observation he had borrowed from Bacon, who records that tree stumps give rise to leaves of completely different plants. But in the next essay, "Paralipomena and Repetitions," the "similarities" are everything. He draws up a list containing many parallels. The last item on the list calls the reader's attention to the fact that in the shell of the tortoise one can see the forms of the pine, the pineapple, and the cypress—an observation that is irrelevant to any possible form of the theory of evolution.

In a letter to Hedlund on October 12, 1896 Strindberg not only speaks of Saint-Pierre's "marvelous book in *Oeuvres posthumes*" but also reveals that Swedenborg's word *correspondence* "gave me the key to my method: to see similarities everywhere." According to another letter to Hedlund, he had first become acquainted with Swedenborg during the preceding month. At that time he read Pernetty's French edition of *Heaven and Hell* and *The Planets in Our Solar System*. *Arcana coelestia,* the work in which the doctrine of correspondences is most fully presented, did not fall into his hands until December 1896, when he was in Lund. Under the influence of Saint-Pierre at the beginning of the year he had pushed his method of "seeing similarities everywhere" about as far as it could go. It is clear that Strindberg—who had been deeply affected by Swedenborg's message for other, quite different reasons—wished to believe that his method was consistent with Swedenborg's. Such, however, was hardly the case; and even in the four *Blue Books,* which were written after he had formed a much deeper impression of Swedenborg, Strindberg does not follow Swedenborg's procedure, where the doctrine of correspondences is—as Lamm has demonstrated—a variant of Neo-Platonic thought.[82] By "correspondence" Swedenborg means an agreement between two phenomena, one of which has a higher degree of intelligibility than the other. This much is clear from passages in the work on heaven and hell, where Strindberg stumbled onto the concept. "Correspondence" means that "il n'existe rien dans l'Univers corporel, qui n'aît son correspondant spirituel; elle [la science des correspondances] donne même la connaissance des objets qui se correspondent en particulier" (there is nothing in the corporal universe that does not have its spiritual counterpart; it [the science of correspondences] even tells which objects correspond in particular).[83] Swedenborg's presentation of celestial objects is marked by the notion that there is a correspondence between the microcosm and the macrocosm, so that he defines the different localities in heaven by referring to various parts of the body. One can occasionally find similar collocations in Strindberg's collections of excerpts, but they never assumed any real power over his thought. His principle was to look for the secrets to be found in concrete correspondences between concrete objects. He lacked the Neo-Platonic inclination to indulge in abstract speculation and continued instead to follow the road that Saint-Pierre had indicated to him: "Les détails, dans ceux [les ouvrages] de la nature, présentent toujours des idées neuves. C'est en descendant dans les plus petits, qu'on entrevoit son immensité. La nature, dit Pline, est grande dans les grandes choses, mais elle est trèsgrande dans les plus petites" (The details in these [works] of nature always present new ideas. It is in descending to the most minute details that one realizes its immensity. Nature, says Pliny, is great in large things, but magnificent in the most minute things). [84]

In Strindberg's notes and in his letters to Hedlund during the course of 1896 he records a great many such concrete correspondences: between the crab and a sleepy person, between pansies and the human face, and the like. They play an important part in *Inferno* as well. This method appears in fully developed form in the essay entitled "Some of the Flowers' Secrets," which was probably written in the spring of 1899. Here Strindberg expresses the wish to "call attention to a number of *similarities* that show the traces of an interrupted but coherent pattern in the universal chaos." He now regards nature "macroscopically," for with approaching age his eye has lost its sharpness for details. Instead, he bears in mind the coherent pattern seen "with the eye of an artist" and believes that he perceives similarities between wintergreen (*Pyrola*) and the pear tree, between the cucumber and the cactus, between the chestnut and the horse chestnut, and between innumerable other plants. "So infinite is the coherent pattern in the great, apparent chaos."

Strindberg stops here. He does not dare draw any conclusions from all these parallels. "What does this mean?—I do not know! Is it a conscious practical joke or only the expression of an immanent energy with a clear, but unconscious purpose?" Here the Schopenhauer—Hartmann theory of an unconscious will underlying form appears once more as an alternative to the idea of a God of creation. What is characteristically Strindberg's about this reaction is his skepticism concerning all abstract formulations. The observations become an end in themselves; they are no longer links in a soritical chain. It is difficult to understand clearly the importance of these observations for Strindberg. At first, his enumerations of correspondences appear to be quite dull and lifeless. Only by concentrated effort does one begin to get an idea of the fear and trembling with which Strindberg studied them. Beyond the superficies of things there were a thousand incomprehensible secrets. He listened to the language of objects as one listens to a human discourse that is near enough to be heard and too distant to be understood.

Strindberg's natural philosophy culminated in a search for the correspondences and harmonies in existence. This search implies that he had reached a point where it was impossible not only to conduct scientific research, but even to speculate about natural philosophy. His observations now produced only a single result: that two objects are similar to each other. For example, Strindberg was eagerly engaged in observing the walnut. At the end of 1895 he already knew that its cotyledons resemble a human brain and its embryo a heart. Finally, on June 25, 1896, he records in his diary, "Finished 'Le Noyer.' " His extant notations and his letters to Hedlund show that in the meantime he was constantly brooding over his observation that the brain is like a walnut and vice versa. In *A Blue Book* (1907) he finally presents his results: the same analogy carried to somewhat greater lengths, but no more profitable from an intellectual point of view.

Consistency was not Strindberg's desired goal in his natural philosophy. Indeed, his intuitive method prevented him from systematizing results or from assuming a definite point of view. His career as a scientist represented constant experimentation with points of view. For a long time he accepted the vague designation of "monist," and he gave his friends in Berlin to understand that he was also a "mechanist." Thus, Carl Ludwig Schleich calls him "ein Mechanist des Lebens von reinstem Wasser" (a mechanist of the first water in his view of life).[85] But one can hardly be a mechanist without assuming the existence of indivisible particles upon which the mechanism builds, and Strindberg rejected atomism. From the start he showed a tendency to apprehend material as living, indeed, to see it in terms of analogies to the human. This tendency drew him away from the framework of a mechanistic world view. Later—after his change of attitude in 1894—vitalism became the most striking feature in his thought. But at the same time, a tendency toward dualism began to emerge, and he was more and more prone to abandon reason in favor of the purely associative method of research. At the end of 1895 and the beginning of 1896 he began to acquire a theistic mode of apprehending nature, which certainly appears to have been his predominant outlook during the entire period between 1896 and 1898. In 1898 Strindberg entered into a personal and moral relationship with a supernal world. When the crisis came to an end, he returned to a more cautious point of view; but ever afterward his reverential associative experience remained dominant in his attitude to nature.

By means of his scientific work Strindberg had found the way back to poetry tinged with religion. "If this is but a poetic image, then what is poetry worth?" he writes in "The Death's-Head Moth." At the same time, he had achieved something "new," for which he had consciously striven since at least 1894. His new cosmos was a lyric cosmos, and Strindberg frequently demonstrated its literary fruitfulness in the works that followed his Inferno crisis.

Thereafter, his own opinion was that "the powers" forbade him to engage further in science. In a letter to Jollivet-Castelot on December 9, 1898, he writes: "Forgive my silence because my thoughts are elsewhere, far from chemistry and even further from occultism. As a matter of fact, I have seriously taken up the art of the theater once again. That is my profession and I *must not* dabble in magic any longer—my religion forbids it." [86] He had expressed this idea much earlier. In an article entitled "A Recollection from the Sorbonne," written in the spring of 1896, he maintains that Berzelius "feared to probe too deeply into nature's secrets." On August 18, 1896, he sent a letter to Hedlund in which he asks himself if he has been punished because he "inquired into hidden things." Thus, ever since the beginning of 1896, when the concept of God had become essential to him, he was plagued with doubt as to whether or not his scientific work was really permissible.

One must view these statements against the background of the opposition between "scientific" and religious occultism, which was particularly lively in Paris. To use the word "magic" to refer to chemistry in the letter to Jollivet-Castelot was a serious reproach in a language that the recipient understood. Occultists of the school of Jollivet-Castelot, Papus, and Guaita were often manifestly upbraided by champions of the Catholic Church for working with "black magic." In this letter, Strindberg takes the Catholic position.

One must also assume that these ideas meant a great deal to him. In his research, of course, he had stopped short of the great mystery in nature, and he did not wish anyone else to approach the secret too closely. The loosely conceived, the vague, and the groping were all fundamental tenets of his poetic-religious experience, and a respect for these qualities typifies the position that he held ever afterward. "I no longer wish to know what it is," he had written (in another context) at the time that his autistic tendencies became fully evident in 1894.[87] He no longer wished to know the facts. He wanted to be free to indulge in fantasies. Above all, he wanted no careful articulation in these matters!

With his new, autistic view of life Strindberg had salvaged both his skepticism and his veneration for God in nature, and he had found a kind of solution to the question of "the coherent pattern in the great chaos." Scientific research had served its turn, and beginning in 1898 it assumed a subordinate role in Strindberg's thought.

FIVE *Toward a New Poetics*

When Strindberg emerged from the Inferno crisis in 1898 and resumed his career as a writer, his style was transformed. This stylistic change bespeaks not so much a new attitude toward aesthetics as a new outlook on life. In this respect, his development contrasts sharply with the direction taken by the writers who dominated the literary scene in Sweden during the 1890s. Their initial rallying point was a literary program centered largely around aesthetic problems, and they did not take a stand on other matters until a later stage in their careers. From this point of view, Strindberg is closer to the French symbolists. According to Guy Michaud, one of the most penetrating critics of this movement, the primary impact of symbolism on modern literature was not in its revolutionary implications for aesthetics, but in its "message," a new mystical and romantic vision of the world. One must qualify this evaluation, however, by adding that the message of the symbolists was often obscured by their interest in purely technical innovations, like verbal music or free verse.

Aesthetic questions clearly played a subordinate role for Strindberg. His chief interests during most of the 1890s were "scientific" and religious, and not until these paths had led him to a new world picture did he seriously begin to look for a poetic form corresponding to his new experiences. Before 1898, however, one can find him discussing artistic questions and making certain formal experiments which indicate that the thought of returning to literary creation had never completely left him, even though it had been relegated to the background for several years. His literary pronouncements during this period of his life, while he was tending to suppress or disregard aesthetic problems, are characteristically hesitant and obscure. But it should be pointed out that although Strindberg was generally too individualistic to imitate other writers, in this case decadent and symbolist aesthetics were fairly important sources of stimulation and inspiration for him. The symbolists can therefore be said to have contributed indirectly to the new form of drama created by Strindberg with the first part of *To Damascus.*

When Verner von Heidenstam and Oscar Levertin emerged as the reformers of Swedish literature early in the 1890s, Strindberg's negative reaction to them had little to do with their neoromantic ideas and their antirealist literary principles. His position was dictated primarily by personal antipathies and by a concern for his own literary standing. Indeed, he was rather inattentive to the aesthetic debate. Although he disliked Heidenstam's tendencies toward "idealism" and patriotism, he had no objections to his demand for aesthetic freedom. Nor did Strindberg consider "social significance" or realistic documentation indispensable to poetry, and in various connections he too had defended the rights of the individual artistic temperament. Rather, he chose to regard Heidenstam's "Renaissance program" as an act of aggression against his own literary territory, and this attitude is the real basis for his gradually increasing detestation of the new directions in Swedish literature.[1]

Although the issues in this debate were never fully clarified, the changes in the literary climate of Sweden at the beginning of the 1890s corroborated the sense of isolation that Strindberg had long felt in his ungrateful homeland. Convinced that Sweden was prepared to repudiate "the Realistic breakthrough" of the 1880s, in which he himself had played the leading part, he now looked outward, toward the larger scene on the Continent, and found in Ola Hansson a zealous guide to the newest examples of late naturalistic and decadent literature in foreign countries. His reaction was mixed, and his attitude was not free from a certain condescending nonchalance. But in Bourget, Huysmans, and Maupassant at least he found interesting features, especially in the new depths to which they were able to penetrate with psychological analysis.

Strindberg's real literary ideal around the 1890s, however, was Edgar Allan Poe and his fantastic stories. Strindberg's intense one-acter *Simoom* (1889) shows that Poe taught him how to generate violent tension in short, apparently realistic scenes. His preference for bizarre and atmospheric stage props in his post-*Inferno* works is another, even more important legacy from Poe. "Thus when I read *The Goldbug,* I was overwhelmed and yet driven to read on. Your [story] Pariah is not there, but the butterfly net—everything that enticed and attracted me (is there)," was Strindberg's report to Ola Hansson on January 3, 1889, of his first impression of Poe. *The Goldbug* is not a mystical but a mystery story, describing the clever solution of a cipher. Most of its romantic luminosity emanates from the props, which Strindberg exclaims over with such enthusiasm: the butterfly net, the death's-head, and above all the golden scarab, which figures in the treasure hunt as nothing more than a weight on a line. One finds similarly unmotivated but suggestive details in *By the Open Sea.* Here the "infinitely small detail" does not always serve to "reinforce the illusion of reality"—as it should according to the literary principles of Georg Brandes and the realists. Instead, it at times opens a window onto something beyond the real—although one often has difficulty in stating clearly just what illusion is reinforced. For example, Inspector Borg, the hero of *By the Open Sea,* wore a bracelet representing a serpent biting its own tail, a well-known mystical symbol. When he cured Maria of hysterics, the bracelet slipped down below his cuff, "fascinated her and awakened her fear of something unknown." Such details serve to mystify the reader, and this enigmatic manner is most characteristic of the romantic tale. Indeed, in the letter mentioned above, the discussion of

Poe leads Strindberg to advert to an earlier favorite of his, E. T. A. Hoffmann.

Subjectivism was basically incompatible with the naturalists' positivist approach to literature, and Strindberg's subjectivism did more to alienate him from orthodox naturalism at the beginning of the 1890s than any other single factor. His subjective ideas, which were primarily inspired by Schopenhauer, later became an essential factor in the development that led him away from the positivist world view. Notions like "naturalistic mysticism," "late naturalism," and "decadence" are difficult to define; but however one defines them, one must recognize that all the forces of incipient opposition to the literary programs of Zola and the Goncourt brothers shared a strong tendency toward subjectivism and individualism—or various other manifestations of the "cult of the self." In 1890 Ola Hansson, Strindberg's closest literary friend at that time, wrote an article entitled "Skandinavische Litteratur" (Scandinavian Literature), in which he coined the happy phrase "subjective naturalism." With its *contradictio in adjecto,* this phrase aptly describes the transitional state of European writing at this period.[2] It is also perfectly applicable to the Strindberg who wrote *By the Open Sea* (1890) and *The Keys of Heaven* (1892) and who planned the Poesque story "The Silver Marsh (1892–1898)."

Writers like Villiers de l'Isle-Adam, Bourget, Huysmans, and the symbolists frequently asserted that the external world is only a continuous, dreamlike apparition created by the thinking subject and that nothing but the self is real.[3] Such thoughts were also current in the German-Scandinavian circle of writers in Berlin to which Strindberg, Hansson, and Przybyszewski belonged. In "Scandinavian Literature" Ola Hansson wrote: "And the fixed center around which all of these dreams hover, like the dust rings about a nascent planet, is the sovereign personality, which uses all of external reality only as an instrument on which it can play all of the proud melodies that slumber within its own soul."[4] According to Maxime Herman, Przybyszewski's position around this period was "a sort of absolute literary idealism."[5] He supports this statement by quoting the following passage from Przybyszewski's lyrical rhapsody *Totenmesse*

(*Requiem*) of 1893: "Mein Subjekt sitzt einfach auf dem Isolirsche-mel. Es ist das Gravitationscentrum, um das das illusorisch Seiende oscillirt; es guckt durchs Mikroskop oder, je nachdem, durchs Fernrohr; und in der Souveränität Meines Subjektes erlaube Ich Mir zu denken, dass alles nur ein Traum ist und das 'Wirkliche' nur eine besondere Form des Traumes und Ich mir selbst so fremd wie Euch" (My subject simply sits in the isolation booth. He is the gravita-tional center around which that which is illusory oscillates; he looks through the microscope or, according to circumstances, through the telescope; and in the sovereignty of my subject I allow myself to think that everything is only a dream and that what is real is only a special form of the dream, and I am as alien to myself as to you).[6]

This kind of unrestrained subjectivism became a guiding aes-thetic principle for Przybyszewski. Reality has no independent place in *Requiem,* where the separate fragments taken from reality only provide material for the errant moods produced by the author's brain under the influence of sex and alcohol. It is difficult to determine who really provided the stimulus in this case—Ola Hansson and Przybyszewski learned from Strindberg, just as he learned from them. But ideas like these were current in the Berlin coterie, and they undoubtedly served as the matrix for Strindberg's later, subjec-tive poetry.[7]

Just as Przybyszewski, contrary to the German habit, wrote "Ich" with a capital letter, Strindberg later wrote an essay in French that he provocatively entitled "Moi" (July 1894). People have reproached Strindberg, he writes, for being too subjective. But all people fight to make their subjective ideas valid; everyone lives in his own uni-verse and imposes his own point of view on phenomena. To symbol-ize this subjectivity Strindberg presents the image of a man sitting on a bench and writing in the sand with his cane—just like the Stranger at the beginning and end of the first part of *To Damascus.* This image, he explains, expresses "the self's impulse to expand, the tendency to make oneself the world's axle, the inclination to encircle a patch of earth, acting through the cane to describe a horizon around the self—this radiation of a circle that each of us carries with him and cannot get rid of."[8] Strindberg is more practical about this matter than Przybyszewski—at least he does not deny existence to other people. In him, moreover, one notices a strain of Nietzschean activism. But whereas he had formerly been capable of finding ways to transcend subjectivity, he now regards it as inescapable.

His subjectivity soon encouraged him to favor a new idea of literary creation based on the notion of intuitive inspiration. Not only did he apply this idea to scientific investigation but in the beginning of the 1890s he also regarded his literary production as the result of an unconscious formative process. Discussing the origins of the poetic work in his essay "Methods of Spiritual Production," Ola Hansson dubbed Strindberg a representative of the poetic type he found most sympathetic: "The Chosen Children of Inspiration," as he awkwardly put it.[9] A suggestive statement in one of Strindberg's letters to Hansson on October 1, 1890, certainly lends support to this evaluation: "[Strindberg] knows nothing about his writing and its goals, for his poetry grows freely in his head like grapes or like mold."

Symbolist idealism grew out of the favorite moods of late naturalistic and decadent writers. Hansson and the Bohemian circle that gathered in the famous Berlin café that Strindberg called Zum Schwarzen Ferkel cultivated the very same moods. Belief in inspiration and intuition prepared the way for their romantic re-evaluation of the artist's vocation. Their subjectivism became idealism tinged with religion. Their study of the movements of the unconscious mind eventually led them to transcendental mysticism. According to Michaud, decadence and symbolism are "two successive phases of the same movement."[10] One can study this development in several of Strindberg's friends during his Berlin period: Ola Hansson, Richard Dehmel, Przybyszewski, and Edvard Munch.[11] Although his development took place a bit later, Strindberg followed approximately the same pattern. At the beginning of the 1890s he was still unable to decide which camp he belonged in. For the most part he supported naturalism, but his attitude contained elements that pointed beyond it. His vacillation in literary matters corresponds exactly to the mood that governed his scientific activities, where behind a façade of Darwinist monism his propensity for romantic speculation gradually gained the upper hand. And just as his first great crisis (late in the summer of 1894) occasioned a change in his scientific orientation, it also affected his literary tactics: at that juncture symbolism proper also became a factor in Strindberg's development.

In the autumn of 1894, Strindberg was preparing his entry into Paris, the literary capital of the world. Here they were more advanced than they were in Berlin. Besides, the situation had changed during the years that Strindberg had been buried in chemical research. The day of decadent, subjective naturalism was already over, and many writers were now in open revolt against Zolaism. Emerging from the obscurity of the café coteries half a decade earlier, the symbolist school now dominated the scene. Current literary and artistic discussion was preoccupied with the verse theories of Mallarmé, the medieval masquerades of Péladan, Gauguin's paintings, and Wagner's music. If he wished to carve a place for himself in Paris, it was imperative that Strindberg clarify his own attitude toward the new movement.

In a letter to his old friend Littmansson on August 15, 1894, Strindberg sketched his plan of attack. Probably referring to the conservative position of Anatole France, he writes: "The best way is to begin in France's camp and then immediately afterward to write prefaces for the symbolists (without slashing at the others—at least not at Zola, who publishes with Charpentier). It is certainly good to have a party behind you, but it is hell to have one against you the very next moment." [12] Strindberg tried to remain good friends with both the symbolists and their conservative opponents. He harbored a great veneration for Zola, partly spontaneous no doubt, but also partly dependent on his own literary pretentions and aspirations. Strindberg compared Zola's achievement in France to his own accomplishments in Sweden and thought that the younger generation in both countries had broken faith with their former masters. In an unpublished essay, "Les Barrabas," which he wrote in the early autumn of 1894, he enumerated the injuries inflicted on Zola and used the opposition between "the great" and "the small" to explain them: "The great man's existence is a permanent insult to the small man." [13]

At the same time Strindberg took a stand regarding Maeterlinck, the symbolist poet who was most in vogue at the moment.
He later wished to promote the idea that when he first became acquainted with them, Maeterlinck's plays were for him "a closed
book," because he was still so deeply "immersed in materialism." At
the beginning of his stay in Paris, on October 8, 1894, Strindberg
wrote a letter to his friend Birger Mörner that serves to verify this
utterance, for he unquestionably sides with what survives of naturalism against symbolism and Maeterlinck: "Naturalism is not dead: it
is thriving here: Zola, Goncourt, Hervieu, Prévost, Huysmans,
Becque, etc. Naturalism or the poetic portrayal of nature can never
die before nature dies. But Maeterlinck, a caprice, a bibelot that en-
tertains me in a tired moment, is stillborn. And to revert to fairy
tales and folk tales is sometimes amusing, but cannot be the necessary consequence of the development we have experienced up to
now. And it will not become a "school"; for it has not made a single
discovery about human nature, and to write folk poetry nowadays is
eclecticism and amateurism."

This, however, was neither the first position that Strindberg took
in the question of Maeterlinck's symbolism, nor the last. His opinion was less categorical in his "tired" moments, as he himself admits
in the letter to Mörner. His essay "L'origine d'un style" (The Origin
of a Style), which was probably written about the same time as the
letter, evidences something besides lack of understanding: it shows
active interest or at least curiosity. Even here Strindberg does not by
any means want to be regarded as an admirer of the Flemish poet.
But nevertheless he calls Maeterlinck "an interesting phenomenon:
to study, not to imitate." [14] By some whim of nature he has never
been able to leave the rudimentary stages of childhood, and he has
thus succeeded in creating a new style, marked by the "charm" and
the "lack of coherence" that one finds in children. However, Strindberg continues, he is more captivating as a "naively unconscious"
writer than as a "consciously naive" one. Since the critics have
praised him, he comes close to being coquettish.

It is also apparent from this essay that the new symbolist ideas
about style had interested Strindberg; they had become a problem
and perhaps even a temptation for him. To shed light on the prob-

lem of Maeterlinck's style, Strindberg compares his work with the literary and artistic attempts of his own children and shows that their departures from reality have nothing to do with lack of skill; they simply think that it is "more fun" to create monsters on their own than to imitate reality. Strindberg considers that they have thereby created a new "style." Thus, though he does accept the antinaturalistic principle underlying the symbolist style, he degrades it by putting it in a Darwinist frame of reference and implying that it represents an outgrown stage.

A few months later—after the second crisis—he wrote a preface to the catalogue for Gauguin's exhibition. Here it becomes apparent how short the road was for Strindberg between the negative and the positive aspects of problems like these. Just as he had identified Maeterlinck with a child, he now identifies Gauguin with a savage. And even though Strindberg says he cannot love Gauguin's paintings, near the end of the preface he shows a clear understanding of the principle that underlies expressionistic creation: not in harmony with reality, but in defiance of it:

He is Gauguin, the savage who hates a bothersome civilization, something of a Titan, who, jealous of the Creator, makes his own little creation in his free moments, the child who takes his toys to pieces in order to make other toys from them. One who denies and defies, who would rather see the heaven red than, like ordinary people, blue.

A contemporary writer has been reproached for not depicting real people: he has, they say, *quite simply* constructed his figures. *Quite Simply!*

Strindberg's opposition to naturalism's demand for observation comes out clearly in the last words here, which probably refer to the criticisms of *The Father* that had appeared in the French press.[15] Strindberg often hinted that already in the 1880s his work was based on principles similar to those of the new school. On the whole, this maneuver is characteristic of his attitude toward symbolism. It was beneath his dignity to be apprenticed to the young writers; however, he was glad to be thought of as having anticipated them. He did not let himself be influenced directly by symbolism. But he adapted himself to it, by emphasizing certain features in his early works that were compatible with symbolist ideas. He also restored to a place of honor certain romantic ideas that he had cherished in his youth, but had scrapped during his realistic and naturalistic period. In this manner, he succeeded in accommodating himself to the new literary situation without sacrificing either his integrity or the continuity of his development.

The essay "Deranged Sensations" must be regarded as an attempt to beat the modernists at their own game. In the letters he wrote to Littmansson at the time he was preparing to come to Paris, Strindberg often evidences intentions of this sort. For example, when *By the Open Sea* was published in France, Strindberg wanted it to bear the subtitle "conte symboliste" (a symbolist tale) because, as he wrote in an undated letter, "that would make me into a modernist and the young Swedes wanted *By the Open Sea* to be considered old-fashioned." Strindberg also wanted to be thought of as having anticipated the symbolists in the matter of free verse, one of their most talked-about innovations. In a letter written on August 13, 1894, he refers to *Sleepwalking Nights* (1884), where he claims he "did away with metrical feet and the cesura to great effect." One attempt to assert this priority was probably the dinner he describes in the letter of October 18, 1894; the dinner was to take place in the editorial offices of the symbolist periodical *La Plume,* and Strindberg was to "recite verses." Also, he now describes an earlier novella of his, "The Romantic Sexton," as that "symbolist-fantasist-story," and he complacently asserts on August 7, 1894, that he was the first ever to depict "symbolic nature."

The best evidence of Strindberg's new aesthetic orientation during the latter half of 1894, however, is his essay entitled "Des arts nouveaux! ou Le hasard dans la production artistique" (On the New Arts! or the Role of Chance in Artistic Production).[16] The very title rings like a *fin-de-siècle* fanfare. In the letters he wrote to Littmansson in 1894, Strindberg frequently shows a taste for what is new, original and preferably bizarre. He wants to reform music, the mode of dress, the way of life, and naturally, literature and science: "New! It's got to be new!" he wrote on August 3, 1894. This rejoicing in the new, which led Martino to speak of the "neologism" of the decadents, had already found cogent expression in the works of Baude-laire, Verlaine, and Rimbaud. The *fin-de-siècle* poets, who were so eager to experiment, inherited it from them.[17] By offering his Parisian audience recipes for "new art forms," Strindberg purposely entered into competition with the inventors of "free verse," "pure poetry, " and "le drame intérieur."

The "random art" that he recommends in this essay is chiefly his own invention. *A Madman's Defense* contains a description of a party given by a group of bachelors who try some peculiar musical exercises. The piano, "which had been purposely untuned and then retuned in an unknown key, wrings out a groaning rendition of a Beethoven march in so distorted a condition that it was impossible to recognize anything but the rhythm." When Strindberg describes more or less the same incident in "On the New Arts!" he explains that it was unbelievably pleasant to hear an old piece rejuvenated.[18]

Music, however, was the only art in which Strindberg was willing to leave creative activity entirely to chance. Perhaps this was because it was the art about which he knew least. In the case of painting and poetry, he recommends that the artist be on the lookout for fortunate accidents which may occur while he is creating, and that he follow the suggestions of his artifacts as they take shape in his hands, instead of sticking to his own predetermined plans. Just as the exigencies of rhyme can inspire the poet to find new and more expressive phrases—all poets are basically "echolalists," like Maeterlinck [19]—the painter can bring out "that charming confusion of the conscious and the unconscious" [20] by letting his palette knife work at random. Here Strindberg is describing his own work habits as a painter and a versifier and using examples from his own practice as illustrations. Because it never becomes more than half-comprehensible, the "automatic art" he is talking about is all the more suggestive. Clarity, Strindberg explains, is actually incompatible with aesthetic pleasure. In an illuminating passage he describes the artistic, dreamlike moods and vacillating associations which also characterize his scientific thought during the Inferno period: "At one moment it was a cow; next it was two peasants embracing one another; then a tree trunk, then . . . I like these changing impres-

sions . . . an act of the will; then I no longer want to know what it
is . . . I feel that the curtain of my consciousness is rising . . . but
I do not want it to . . . now it is a *déjeuner sur l'herbe,* with food
. . . but the figures are motionless as in a panopticon . . . aha
. . . now I see it . . . it is an abandoned cart on which the farmer
has flung his coat and hung his sack. That is all there is to it!
Nothing else to see. Pleasure has fled." [21]

This kind of mood was not new to Strindberg. One finds similar
fantasies described in *Utopias,* (1884–1885), "The Romantic Sexton" (1888), and *By the Open Sea* (1890), but by adding circum-
stantial reservations in each of these cases, he had refused to be identified with his visionary characters. By elevating suggestive
obscurity and the deformation of nature into an artistic principle, as
he now does, Strindberg is adapting himself to symbolist ideas.
Concepts like the unconscious and the indefinite— "l'indécis"—certainly played an important role in symbolist aesthetics, and by coun-
tering accusations that they were obscure with a demand for obscurity, the young poets did exactly the same thing that Strindberg
was doing. Mallarmé, for example, in his famous answer to Jules
Huret's *Enquête* (*Inquiry*), expanded the same idea that had informed
Strindberg's essay:

> Je pense qu'il faut, au contraire, qu'il n'y ait qu'allusion. La contempla-
> tion des objets, l'image s'envolant des rêveries suscitées par eux, sont le
> chant; les Parnassiens, eux, prennent la chose entièrement et la montrent;
> par là ils manquent de mystère; ils retirent aux esprits cette joie délicieuse de
> croire qu'ils créent. *Nommer* un objet, c'est supprimer les trois-quarts de la
> jouissance du poème qui est faite du bonheur de deviner, peu à peu; le
> suggérer, voilà le rêve. C'est le parfait usage de ce mystère qui constitue le
> symbole: évoquer petit à petit un objet pour montrer un état d'âme, ou, in-
> versement, choisir un objet et en dégager un état d'âme, par une série de
> déchiffrements.

On the contrary, I think there should be nothing but allusion. Poetry is
the contemplation of objects, images taking wings from the reveries born
of this contemplation. Those Parnassian poets fix entirely upon the object
and describe it; therefore they lack mystery. They withdraw from the spirit
that delicious joy of believing it is creating something. *To name* an object is

234 Strindberg in Inferno

to supress three-quarters of the enjoyment of the poem, which derives from the happiness of guessing, little by little; to suggest the object—that is real poetry. The perfect use of this mystery constitutes the symbol: to evoke an object gradually in order to exhibit the interior of a soul, or inversely, to choose an object and by a series of decipherings to elicit from it a poetic mood.[22]

In his utterances about Maeterlinck and Gauguin, Strindberg only hints at the idea that each work of art is a "neologism," but in the essay entitled "On the New Arts" he uses this idea as the basis for a literary program. Here he says that the artist works "like nature, capriciously, and with no definite goal." He imitates "nature's creative method." [23] Strindberg had formerly rejected this theory of art, which he had found in the Romantics. In *The Red Room* (1879), for example, he let Olle Montanus explain that "in art man wants to play God; it is not as if he were capable of producing anything new (he cannot do that!); he merely remakes, improves, arranges." Now, however, Strindberg becomes the prophet of belief in the creative function of the imagination, inspired no doubt by the example of the symbolist school, whose leaders found similar ideas in the works of their favorite writers, especially Baudelaire.[24]

Strindberg's new scientific orientation, when he discovered God in nature, came less than a year after he had begun experimenting with these ideas. In fact, these are two phases of the same development. First, man as artist becomes creator, then the Creator becomes an artist. One cannot say that these ideas are complementary; indeed, they rather seem to be mutually exclusive, for if the universe itself is God's artifact, then the artist's activity appears to be what Olle Montanus thought it was: an unmotivated attempt to usurp the functions of the Creator. Still, both these ideas appear to be variants of his effort to make existence poetic. Along with his moral self-searching, this effort is the most important feature of the Inferno crisis.

At first, Strindberg made no direct attempts to apply these aesthetic ideas by producing literary works of his own. However, he did give a symbolist interpretation to paintings he made in the autumn of 1894, and he regarded them as exemplifying the role played by chance in the creative process.[25] But even though his aesthetic thought tended to be characterized by momentary whims and was motivated by a desire to play literary politics, his essays on Maeterlinck, Gauguin, and the "new arts" evidence a change in taste. He now regards naive, romantic, and suggestive art with greater understanding. As early as 1895—that is, before his central religious and moral crisis took place—this new orientation in aesthetics had already given rise to certain features that one can observe in his works written after the Inferno crisis.

The most important of these new features is his fondness for the naive, for the rigmarole of children's games, for lullabies, and for fairy tales. Of course, the fairy tale element was nothing new in Strindberg's writing, but in his earlier fairytale plays and fables he had used this naive invention to frame a moralistic or satirical content. Beginning in 1895, when he once more deals with elements of this sort, he unambiguously emphasizes irrational and childish elements. In 1894, Strindberg still spoke half-condescendingly of Maeterlinck's "childishness." Talking about similar matters a year later, however, he assumed a different tone. In the essay entitled "In the Cemetery" (written in fall 1895, published in *La Revue des Revues,* July 1896), he quotes "an old Swedish folksong," which he states is "as meaningless and as charming as a fairy tale." It runs:

> Spelar min lind?
> Sjunger min näktergal?
>
> Is my linden playing?
> Is my nightingale singing?

From now on the suggestive simplicity of the folksong became a standard feature of Strindberg's lyrical ideal, and one can hardly overlook the fact that this element corresponds to the sort of symbolist naiveté that is best exemplified in some of the works of Maeterlinck and Francis Jammes. In *Wordplay and Small Art,* a verse collection that he wrote between 1902 and 1905, Strindberg still shows a fondness for onomatopoeia and the musical jingle; and reading a poem like "Villemo" in this collection, one is reminded that several years earlier he had defended "echolalia."

Strindberg also defends the fairy tale in his essay "In the Cemetery." Why, he asks there, does one tell children stories about giants, elves, and pixies as if they were really true? The reason is that these stories may indeed be true: before birth the child has experienced things that can only be assigned to the world of make-believe. Here Strindberg forms a link with another symbolist interest: authors like Maeterlinck and Mallarmé eagerly adopted themes from the fairy tale (or *conte de f ée*). Of course, Strindberg made his own later fairy tales more realistic and added moral and scientific elements to suit his didactic purposes. Nevertheless, the fact that he had already turned his hand to this genre as early as 1895 must bear some relation to the literary climate he knew in Paris at the time. The little fable he wrote in that year concerns the death's-head moth, and in it his characteristic "folk" style is already fully developed:

Once upon a time there was a diurnal moth that lived on privet leaves, which are very innocent. The privet leaves gave out in the winter, and when the pupae hatched in the spring, there was nothing to eat. But since all moths are mighty botanists and know the natural phyla like the soles of their feet, they sought out lilacs, which are closely related to privet. But one day a moth flew astray into a region where no lilacs were to be found, and she laid her eggs on a plant that resembled the lilac in color, but did not smell so sweet. And then she died. When spring came, the little larvae crept out and ate of the little tree of knowledge, of which they were ignorant. They spun their chrysalises and the moths came swarming out and around the belladonna, where they were born. But look, they could no longer bear the light of the sun, for the atropine had dilated their eyes so that they could not close them. And therefore they slept by day and only went out after sundown. This might be the way nocturnal moths originated.

But when the privet moth began to eat of the hawthorn berry, he grew sleepy and overslept through the day, went out at night, but only before midnight. These habits made him fat and he began to grow—just as one fattens pigs in France by feeding them the soporific leaves of the hawthorn bush. But when he left the delicious pink juice of the privet berries, he lost the pink stripes on his abdomen and grew as ugly as a dormant creature.

When intoxicated by love and delirious from the poison, he did not always find the right poisonous plant, despite the fact that its flowers do not emit a fragrance until after seven o'clock in the evening—while the leaves stink throughout the day. And in the dark he was led to carrion—perhaps to cemeteries, where there was nothing to light his way but whitened skulls. And there he laid his eggs. The larvae ate carrion and solanine (nightshade) alternately, and when they were ready to enter the cocoon stage, they shunned the light and dug graves for themselves—for, of course, they had no inkling that they would be resurrected.

Scientific material has here been arranged into a prose poem with peculiar powers of illumination. Moreover, Strindberg has replaced the argumentative form of *Sylva Sylvarum* with a narrative presentation, and he has all but abandoned his scientific pretentions. What interested him—and what fascinates the reader—is the arabesque that results from the interlacing of chains of association. In this connection one is reminded that several months later Strindberg read André Chevrillon's description of the fantastically intricate pattern on an Indian vase and thought of entitling *Inferno* (the work he was then planning) "Le vase de Bénarès" (The Benares Vase). Of course, his obvious pleasure in imaginative arabesquerie is yet one more expression of his autistic flight from reality, but it is also one more point where he approached the taste of the symbolists. Indeed, according to his own theories in "On the New Arts," one's experience of a work of art is supposed to consist in gliding from one image to another. In the original French text of "In the Cemetery" Strindberg included a passage in which he let associations dance around in a modernistic muddle that is even less restrained than the style in the tale about the death's-head moth. Chauveau-Lagarde, the name of a French lawyer during the revolution, is his point of departure:

Accustomed as I am to observing everything that happens in my soul, I remember that I was seized with unaccustomed terror while the images crowded one another helter-skelter like the imaginings of a madman. I saw Louis XVI's defense attorney with the guillotine behind him. I saw a great river lined with green hills. A young mother leads a little girl along the water: then a monastery with an altarpiece by Velasquez. I am in Sarzeau, at the Hotel Lesage, where there is a Polish edition of *Diable boiteux:* I am behind the Madeleine, on the rue Chauveau-Lagarde: I am at the Hotel

Bristol in Berlin, where I am sending a telegram to Lavoyer at the Hotel London: I am in Saint-Cloud, where a woman in a Rembrandt hat is writhing in the agonies of childbirth: I am sitting at the Café de la Régence, where the Cologne cathedral in unrefined sugar is on display . . . and the wine waiter maintains that it was constructed by M. Ranelagh and Marshal Berthier.[26]

As a whole, "In the Cemetery" is the prime evidence for Strindberg's adaptation to the wave of neoromanticism (or symbolism) in Paris around the middle of the 1890s. In this essay—as in a poem by Musset or Nerval—one finds talk of wisteria, roses, cypresses, and turtledoves. Indeed, a famous strophe by Victor Hugo might well serve as the epigraph to this piece:

> Là je rêve! et, rôdant dans le champ léthargique,
> Je vois, avec des yeux dans ma pensée ouverts,
> Se transformer mon âme en un monde magique,
> Miroir mystérieux du visible univers.
>
> (There I dream! and, wandering in the lethargic field,
> My eyes turned inward on my open thoughts,
> I see my soul transformed into a magical world,
> The mysterious mirror of the visible universe.)[27]

A gloomy and melodious melancholy fuses the meditations of the lonely wanderer in the cemetery into a unity that is neither epic nor argumentative, but purely lyric. This tone is new in Strindberg's writing, and it is perfectly consonant with the *fin-de-siècle* poetic reveries found in Verlaine or Maeterlinck—which does not, of course, exclude a literary connection with Hamlet and with the lyricism elicited from many a romantic soul by thoughts of transitoriness. One can hardly mistake the aesthetic purpose behind Strindberg's cult of atmosphere in the Montparnasse Cemetery, nor be surprised to encounter an unmistakably symbolist arrangement like the grieving woman before the mortuary cross: "The contours of her emaciated body etched themselves against a cross behind her, as if she had been crucified, and then that inscription above: *O Crux, ave spes unica.*"

But despite these changes in style, Strindberg never became a moody symbolist poet. In the works he wrote after *Inferno,* one sometimes encounters resonances and techniques that are reminiscent of symbolism, but on the whole he created a personal brand of symbolism—particularly in his dramas—which has no counterpart in French *fin-de-siècle* literature. Therefore, in order to evaluate his independence and originality, one must balance this investigation of the similarities between Strindberg and the symbolists with a discussion of the differences between them. It is at this point that the Inferno crisis plays an important role in Strindberg's artistic development.

Like Strindberg, the symbolists were fond of speaking both of internal parallels (or "correspondences") between natural phenomena and of the "correspondences" between natural phenomena and man. But for the symbolists this sort of speculation usually led to little more than an abstract manner of speaking with a broadly mystical ring. Strindberg, in contrast, filled his new picture of the world with a multitude of concrete analogies from many different spheres of activity. Scholars like Guy Michaud have described the "poetic universe" that the symbolists wanted to create. Strindberg too created a poetic universe, and he was conscious of the role played by the creative imagination in that connection. But even though his aesthetic position was conscious and playfully poetic (like that of the symbolists), he ventured much further than they in search of secret connections and correspondences, and his philosophy of nature thereby acquired a character that is completely different from their abstract analogies between tones, colors, and forms. Ultimately, Strindberg was much closer to the occultists than to symbolism proper. But even the occultists frightened him away with their generalizations and abstractions.

The same is more or less true of the actual Inferno experiences that provided Strindberg with the immediate point of departure for his new literary style. Here too one finds a general similarity with symbolism. *Inferno* and *To Damascus* can be regarded as evidencing an exploration of the poet's subconscious mind. Strindberg himself was not alien to this point of view. Influenced by Schopenhauer, Hartmann, and the new psychology, he had already begun to be interested in the subterranean world of the psyche back in the 1880s. The possibility that his peculiar experiences during the crisis were actually projections of his own mental state presented itself as a viable alternative to his other hypotheses, and he could speak of Swedenborg and religion in terms that are almost psychotherapeutic. In an undated letter to Hedlund in July 1896, Strindberg wrote: "Hallucinations, fantasies, dreams—seem to me to possess a high degree of reality. If I see my pillow assume human forms, then the forms are there; and if anyone says that they have only (!) been fashioned by my imagination, I answer: '*Only,* you say?' What my inner eye sees means more to me!" This sentiment is completely in the spirit of Schopenhauer, Carl du Prel, and the symbolists. The generation of Mallarmé and Laforgue also wanted to find a path through the imagination to something more real than everyday life: to the transcendental world of the subconscious.[28] Like Strindberg, they too went from pure subjectivism to a supposed new objectivity under the sign of mysticism.

There is a work that can be regarded as a symbolist rejoinder to Strindberg's *Inferno:* Rimbaud's *A Season in Hell,* which (though published back in 1873) remained unknown until 1895, when Verlaine brought it out in a new edition. Since Strindberg was in Paris at that time, it is certainly not impossible that he knew something about Rimbaud's work. Indeed, the thought behind Rimbaud's title is common to both authors. As Rimbaud expressed it: "I believe I am in Hell, therefore I am there." [29] Moreover, the two works share many characteristics: evocation of religious moods from childhood, satanic elements, defiant discussion of moral problems, and self-criticism. The narrative line is almost equally chaotic in both works, and ultimately neither work is fully intelligible without the assistance of modern psychology. Still, these books are quite different in style and in mode of presentation. Rimbaud's writing is lyrical and exalted, visionary or hallucinatory—"dematerialized," to use a word with which Strindberg characterized another symbolist work.[30] By comparison, Strindberg's book appears almost pedestrian in its realism. Actual experiences also provided the background for Rimbaud's soul-searching, but they merely flit past behind a curtain of suggestive word combinations. Reading *A Season in Hell,* one comes to realize that despite all the fanciful schemes it contains, Strindberg's *Inferno* is a relatively sober account of actual experiences. Strindberg places the emphasis on objective past experience, whereas Rimbaud gives precedence to the creative and reshaping power of the imagination.

Nothing separates Strindberg from the symbolists so decisively as his stronger dependence on concrete reality and actual experience. The symbolists either created their symbols by an act of the imagination or else appropriated them from the fairy tale world of romanticism. Strindberg found most of his symbols in exactly observed reality. Whereas the symbolists directly reproduce a mental state with the vagueness and elusiveness that accompanies their kind of mood painting, Strindberg's mental state in *Inferno* is revealed only indirectly, through details seized from the world around him. Strindberg did not close his eyes in order to evoke a fantastic world in his consciousness. His "inner eye" saw faces in his pillow, as he described in the letter to Hedlund, and this formulation is typical: even his "inner vision" turned outward, toward his surroundings. He externalized his subconscious conflict and let it be symbolized by the faces of the pansies and the convolutions of the walnut. A symbol is always something concrete that entails something abstract, but whereas the symbolists emphasize the abstract element, Strindberg stresses the concrete.

Neither the musical nor the speculative ever became Strindberg's real domain, because his writing depends to such a high degree on visual memories. For that reason, literary critics have found it rewarding to compare his descriptions from the '70s and '80s with paintings from the same period. Still, it is scarcely credible that he allowed himself to be inspired by, say, the impressionists. Therefore, a similar juxtaposition of his new style after *Inferno* with expressionist painting should not be interpreted as a hypothesis about direct indebtedness. But if one turns from Verlaine's verse music and Rimbaud's word magic to the later work of Gauguin, one will—despite the differences in subject matter—recognize something that is reminiscent of Strindberg's dreamplay technique. Of Gauguin's paintings, which are simultaneously enigmatic and crystal clear, Mallarmé wrote, "Il est extraordinaire qu'on puisse mettre tant de mystère dans tant d'éclat" (It is extraordinary that one can put so much mystery into such dazzle).[31] One could say the same thing about Strindberg's "symbolist" plays.

Although he was often counted among the symbolists, Gauguin himself would never accept such a label. His symbols were not allegories—like those of Puvis de Chavannes—and if his own statement is to be trusted, he did not generally start out to express an "idea" in a work of art. He himself did not "understand," in an intellectual sense, the content of his paintings, and he thought that the value of his symbols resided precisely in the element of "vagueness" and "incomprehensibility" they contain. The large canvas entitled "D'où venons-nous? Que sommes-nous? Où allons-nous?" (Where do we come from? What are we? Where are we going?) was the picture of a waking dream and was not named until after it had been finished. The name, moreover, is not a title but a signature.[32] The same is true of Strindberg's relation to the symbolic material in *To Damascus* (1898) or *A Dreamplay* (1902). He was only half-conscious of what it expresses. And like Gauguin's symbols, Strindberg's are "vague" and "incomprehensible" because rather than confining himself to a definite idea that he wished to express, he too began with what he had seen and experienced.

Strindberg's closest association with the symbolist movement occurred in the latter part of 1894 and during the course of 1895. After the beginning of his crisis in 1896, his development led him away from the tender mood-painting that one finds in "In the Cemetery." Strindberg found his own form and developed the kind of dramatically charged symbolism that characterizes *Inferno* and—especially—*To Damascus*. In the extant drafts of the work that was eventually entitled *Inferno,* one can follow, at least roughly, this process of development.

Strindberg took the first step toward writing *Inferno* on February 21, 1896, when he began to keep the so-called *Occult Diary.* Eventually, this diary contained a great many rather trivial notations, but as the name implies, his original intention was to record only such occurrences as appeared to be peculiar or significant. Since this diary later became Strindberg's prime source when writing *Inferno*, it is apparent that he had no desire to render a complete account of what happened to him during his years of crisis. The material was already sifted and winnowed by the time the diary was written.[33] In the diary, Strindberg recorded dreams, found objects, unexpected letters. Without yet understanding its deeper significance, he recorded everything that seemed mysterious. Not until the great crises does the diary acquire a more dramatic nature, only to change by degrees after the Inferno crisis into the sort of record that the word "diary" commonly denotes.

According to the earliest extant draft—probably from the spring of 1896—*Inferno* was also supposed to have been a "Diary of Peculiar Coincidences." [34] The principal title of the draft, "Le Vase de Bénarès: Le grand désordre," gives some indication of the spirit in which Strindberg wishes to treat his "coincidences" and observations. The expression "the Benares vase" refers to descriptions of an Indian milieu that Strindberg had found in a travelogue by André Chevrillon, an author who was very close to the symbolists:

Regardez ce vase de cuivre de Bénarès. Vous admirez le brillant du métal, le fini des ciselures; mais ce sont là des caractères particuliers qui n'appartiennent qu'aux vases de cuivre. En voici un autre, plus intéressant parce qu'il est très général. Ces ciselures de notre vase: que représentent-elles? Tout d'abord, on n'en sait rien: on n'aperçoit qu'un fouillis de lignes contournées, enlacées, confondues au hasard. Peu à peu, un enchevêtrement de formes vagues apparaît: des dieux, des génies, des poissons, des chiens, des gazelles, des fleurs, des herbes, non pas groupées autour d'un motif, mais jetées là, entassées pêlemêle, en masse confuse et vivante, semblables à ces paquets informes de boue sous-marine que le filet ramène et dans lesquels, parmi les amas d'algues embrouillées, on voit grouiller des pinces, luire des écailles, frétiller et se tordre des corps mous. De même, chacune de ces ciselures est d'une complication infinie: ces dieux ont six bras, ces plantes traînent de tous cotés en lames et en feuilles, ces fleurs s'enroulent et se confondent. Bref, rien n'est simple, tout est multiple, touffu, et cette compléxité, faute de lignes directrices, reste irrégulière.

(Look at this copper vase from Benares. You admire the brilliancy of the metal, the delicate detail of the chiseling, but those are characteristics that only copper vases possess. Here is another, more interesting because it is so common. What does the chiseling on our vase represent? At first, one has no idea. One sees nothing but a jumble of twisted lines, intertwining, merging at random. Little by little, a network of vague forms appears: gods, genies, fish, dogs, gazelles, flowers, herbs, not grouped around a design, but tossed there, heaped pell-mell in a chaotic, living mass, like one of those shapeless lumps of submarine mud brought up by a fishing line and in which, among the clusters of algae, one glimpses spots alive with claws, glistening with shells, squirming and wriggling with soft bodies. Likewise, each of these chiselings is infinitely complicated: its gods have six arms, its plants trail down on every side in blades and leaves, its flowers twine and merge. In short, nothing is simple; everything is multiple, confused, and, lacking lines of direction, this complexity remains irregular.) [35]

One learns from a letter to Hedlund on March 28, 1896, that the vase described here by Chevrillon had come to symbolize for Strindberg the suggestive chaos that he thought he experienced when putting himself in a receptive mood. The human brain that resembled a walnut, the lumps of carbon that looked like elves—to judge from the title, this kind of associational rapprochement of objects was to have constituted the content of the book that Strindberg was planning before his great crisis; and a religious and pessimistic world picture was to emerge from observations of this nature. If that had been the case, the book would have resembled the works that Strindberg had just written, *Jardin des Plantes* with its esoteric speculation and "In the Cemetery" with its meditative symbolism. In the finished version of *Inferno,* this sort of material remains only as scattered entries and digressions, interpolated into a narrative framework.

In the autumn of 1896, Strindberg resumed his plans for *Inferno,* for which he had then selected the final title. He wishes to become "the Zola of occultism," as he explained in a letter to Hedlund on August 28, 1896: "But with great, exalted tone. A poem in prose: called *Inferno.* Same theme as in *By the Open Sea.* The downfall of the

individual when he isolates himself. Salvation through: work without honor or gold, duty, the family, consequently—woman—mother
and child! " Later, on September 12, Strindberg wrote to Hedlund
that he was going to illustrate *Inferno* in his own "occult" fashion.
Here it is clearly a question not only of collecting occult observations, but also of providing a form much closer to the novel, having
a line of development and a moral. "Call it a novel, if you like,"
Strindberg wrote Hedlund on August 18, and added that the book
was to describe his great crisis of that summer. His change of plans
was probably the direct result of the dramatic nature of the crisis itself. His talk of illustrations and of a "prose poem," however, may
suggest that he still envisaged the work as being interspersed with
occult and poetic observations. The headings in a draft which probably dates from this period seem to mark it as an intermediate stage
between the original idea and the one later executed: "Inferno: Le
vase de Bénarès." [36]

When *Inferno* was finally written in the spring of 1897 the intended line of development had changed, and Strindberg's moral
conclusions had altered, both because of the disappointment of his
marriage and because of his reading of Swedenborg. His chief concern, however, was still to give a narrative account of the course of
events and to try to determine their meaning. In the finished book,
the lyrical and meditative elements are sharply reduced, and the
book's chief aim is no longer to present an occult world picture.
Strindberg has rejected elements like "the Benares vase" in favor of
descriptions of his moral and religious struggle. For that reason, the
bibliography of occult works that he placed at the head of the book
is relevant only to certain parts of the framework of *Inferno,* not to
the actual narrative. Inasmuch as Strindberg included parts of *Jardin
des Plantes* and "In the Cemetery" in the original French edition of
Inferno, he reverted to his original idea. By doing so, he emphasized
the connection between occultism and symbolism, and he probably
did so because he expected the *fin-de-siècle* French public to have a
finer ear for such things. The greater unity of the Swedish edition
doubtless results largely from the fact that these excerpts were omit-
ted.

The change reflects Strindberg's own development throughout the year 1896 and the beginning of 1897. At first he actively sought out peculiar and "symbolist" experiences, but during the great crises he received so many suggestive impressions that he began to fear for his sanity. In 1894, Strindberg writes in the epilogue to *Legends,* he abandoned skepticism "on principle." That was when he entered into competition with the young symbolist poets by intentionally cultivating a heightened sensibility. But this psychological experiment did not produce the expected results: "In the course of it, when the author had suspended all resistance, he found himself attacked by influences, powers that threatened to tear him to bits." [37] Strindberg is referring here to the crises. Increased impressionability made him the helpless victim of his own psychotic persecution feelings.

At this point, his symbols also changed character. Instead of the speculative and aesthetically appealing series of associations from the "Benares vase" period, Strindberg now became involved in a system of symbols that tended to terrify him because they represented a projection of his own neurotic conflict. An example will clarify this distinction. In the autumn of 1894 Strindberg received a golden pen and silver writing set from an anonymous donor. He was heartened by the occurrence and interpreted it as symbolic encouragment: "A chance happening, but one that makes an impression. And now I shall write golden words and white, like silver and egg white," as he wrote to Hedlund on October 30, 1895. Shortly thereafter, he observed a walnut kernel in his microscope and saw two hands, clasped as if in prayer. According to *Inferno,* this sight filled him with "horror," because it was a symbolic reminder of his neglect of his children. In both cases his psychic disposition was the same: receptivity to the kind of associational connections that he had praised in "On the New Arts." In both cases these associations resulted in the creation of a symbol, but the symbols relating to his unsolved neurotic conflicts activated anxiety.

Critics usually emphasize the fact that *Inferno* is a "poem," in which Strindberg has reshaped his real experiences poetically. [38] Strindberg, on the contrary, claimed that it is only an "expanded and ordered excerpt" from his diary. It is possible to resolve this contradiction without making any attempt to calculate the measure of Strindberg's veracity. Although *Inferno* can be regarded as a poetic work, it was essentially created not when he wrote the book in 1897, but earlier, during the very moments of his experience.

Strindberg did, to be sure, arrange the material to a certain extent when composing the work, and he tried to reshape it according to his current concept of the causal connections behind or between his experiences.[39] But it is not these interpretations and emendations that make *Inferno* into a poem. The book's fascinating power is connected above all with its peculiar world of symbols, which indirectly reveal his neurotic states of anxiety. And in this matter one cannot prove that Strindberg made any essential changes in the material provided by his diary and his memory.

Therefore, *Inferno* is perhaps best classified among the "documents humains." Such more or less truthful reports from an author's own life were not uncommon during the late naturalistic period, when there was great interest in psychological curiosities. And these works certainly did not slight the pathological aspects of psychic life. Several people very close to Strindberg had written such accounts. Przybyszewski's *Requiem* describes the changing moods of an alcoholic sex maniac, and Hamsun's *Hunger* shows the distortion of reality that results from prolonged starvation. Even closer to *Inferno*—so close, in fact, that one can perhaps regard it as a model—is Maupassant's "The Horla" with its gruesome description of pathological experiences.[40] All of these works are written in the first person. Also writing in the first person, Strindberg described the experiences of a neurotic in a style that aspires to naturalistic exactitude. In principle, Strindberg's ambition is the same as that of the other late naturalists, even though he also attempted to provide his work with a moral interpretation and wished to present himself to the reader now as model, now as a horrible example.

The edifying tendency is even stronger in *Legends,* but on the whole that less important work represents a continuation of *Inferno:* symbolist and religious content in a naturalistic form. Not until *Jacob Wrestles,* which was written toward the end of 1897 and was intended as a third part of the Inferno cycle, did Strindberg attempt "to delineate the author's religious struggle in figurative terms."

His Swedish expression, "figurerad," is a gallicism based on the French word *figurer,* meaning "to represent allegorically." Although *Jacob Wrestles* begins and ends like an autobiographical report of the same type as *Inferno* and *Legends,* Strindberg himself singles out the allegorical part as the heart of the work. Within this framework he apparently intended to review those phases of his conversion that belonged to the time before or during the period described in *Inferno.* On a page of notes entitled "Mea culpa" [41] he has listed a series of "sets" that he had considered using in the third part of *Inferno.* Besides the ones that he actually did use in *Jacob Wrestles*— Paul Hermann's stairway, Luxembourg, the café La Frégate, the Tuileries, Les Halles, the Swedenborg chapel on the Rue Thouin— there are a number of localities that Strindberg had frequented much earlier: Gauguin's studio, the house of William Molard, the Rue de la Clef, Passy, and Versailles. All of the places he listed are in Paris. Thus, one can conjecture that along with the synthetic review of his conversion, Strindberg also planned to present a more literary description of Paris than he had in *Inferno,* and that the section about the Luxembourg Gardens and his morning walk in the *Latin Quarter* was intended as the opening.

In this case, Strindberg reverted to a technique similar to one he had tried in "In the Cemetery." To use his own words, he began "to write pleasantly" again. The first and most important section of *Jacob Wrestles* is framed by a romantic description of the Luxembourg Gardens. According to Strindberg, they are like the holy city of Revelations. The custodian's cottage on the Rue de Luxembourg recalls an "unpublished idyll" with its pond and roses; the alleys and lawns become "Elysian fields" and a "paradisal landscape." The butterflies and turtledoves are like "illustrations for fairy tales." The Louvre becomes a mountain chain, which leads one's thoughts first to the days of Atlantis, then to medieval France: "Its magical power made me think that the Barbarossa of France had awakened, that Saint Louis was celebrating his coronation with a gala feast, to which all the monarchs of the earth had been invited in penitential homespun and, kneeling, were allowed to serve at the table." [42] These and similar learned associations with Biblical, legendary, and pastoral worlds cloak his direct observations in a shimmer of lyricism.

Within this framework of symbolist mood-painting Strindberg has placed a passage that he himself described as "figurative." One evening when Strindberg is strolling down the Rue Bonaparte, he sees before him a stranger who reminds him of someone he knows. Although there is no breeze at all, the stranger's cape is briskly flapping; and after both men have been miraculously transported into the Luxembourg Gardens, the stranger is encircled by a bright light that revives summer in the midst of chilly autumn: salvia blooms, bees swarm, and doves coo. At last the stranger stops at the other end of the garden, and Strindberg approaches him by the longest path—"the way of the Cross, and perhaps the fourteen stations, if I am not mistaken" [43]—perceiving at the time a "balsamic odor" that reassures him. After hearing Strindberg make a plea on his own behalf, the stranger disappears, and Strindberg is once again standing in the street outside the park.

In examining this passage, one would do well to bear in mind the fact that Strindberg was never subject to hallucinations, only to illusionary experiences. "I am not a spiritseer, for I do not believe that spirits can be seen," he wrote to Hedlund in April 1896. And everything known about Strindberg would seem to indicate that this statement is literally true. In contrast to the "miracles" reported in *Inferno* and *Legends,* the magical apparatus surrounding his meeting with the stranger has no anchor in Strindberg's actual experience. Instead, it is a poetic construction in an allegorical, "symbolist" manner. Nor is there difficulty in finding literary counterparts for it. Balzac's Séraphita, in the first chapter of the novel bearing her name, is similarly encircled by a magical bit of summer in the midst of a severe Nordic winter.

It is impossible to determine the identity of "the stranger" who appears in *Jacob Wrestles.* He bears a certain resemblance both to Christ and to Strindberg himself, but in his long monologues he sounds very like the God to whom Strindberg is directing his complaints. Here once again one finds the element of vagueness and uncertainty that Strindberg had recommended for the new art back in

1894. But instead of allowing nature to follow its own course and thereby to achieve a degree of suggestive uncertainty, Strindberg has manufactured uncertainty in the figure of the stranger, who for that very reason becomes more mystifying than suggestive.

Martin Lamm was of the opinion that this poetic costume fits the content of *Jacob Wrestles* perfectly.[44] Strindberg himself, however, was of another opinion. In the epilogue he calls his allegorical presentation "a failure." In any case, it is apparent that the fiction he had begun to develop simply proved unsuitable in the long run. The mysterious figure, who listens with a smile to Strindberg's recitation without uttering a single word, has dwindled to a lifeless image by the time he makes his second appearance. In short, he becomes the least appropriate kind of figure imaginable to be presented in the Strindberg style. Moreover, inserting the visions into a story frame that is subject to the ordinary logic of everyday life clearly presented Strindberg with difficult artistic problems. Should the apparition disappear without a trace? One notices how Strindberg's sense of reality reacts against the unnatural elements in this fiction. He has the stranger leave an odor behind him, first of phenol, then of carbonic oxide. Though this information is entirely devoid of poetic value, its crass naturalism serves to re-establish the equilibrium after the foregoing pastel tones.

Moreover, the stranger serves no purpose when Strindberg is accusing himself, only when he is defending himself. This may be the reason that Strindberg employs another device in the third of the great monologues representing an imaginary journey back to Sweden—more or less the same device that he had used in *Sleepwalking Nights* (1883)—which he ends with the following illustration of his pangs of conscience: "Utterly depressed, I stop a moment before the vast trail of tears, when beneath the barren trees a ball of light approaches borne upon a pair of buzzard's wings. It stops in front of me at eye level, and in the clear glow emanating from the ball I see a piece of white paper decorated like a menu. At the top I read in smoke-colored letters: 'Eat!' "[45]

It is not surprising that Strindberg found this allegorical game unpromising. In the last big monologue he abandons all artifice, and toward the end of the fragment he assumes a simpler narrative style.

When he wrote the first part of *To Damascus*, Strindberg grappled once again with the problem of dealing with his conversion in a synthetic form, and this time he solved it. On January 19, 1898, a short time after he had stopped working on the third part of *Inferno*, he set about dealing with the same material in dramatic form. "Got the theater craze once more and planned Robert le Diable," he writes in his diary. This drama subsequently became *To Damascus*. Lamm is probably correct in his supposition that the experiment of *Jacob Wrestles* led Strindberg onward to drama.[46] The monologues in that work possess great dramatic vigor, quite reminiscent, in fact, of one of his naturalistic one-acters, *The Stronger* (1889). Like that play, *Jacob Wrestles* represents a tug-of-war between two opponents, one of whom is silent.

When Strindberg wrote the first part of *To Damascus* in the spring of 1898, his point of departure was his own experience of reality—with all the synthesis and symbolization that these experiences had already entailed. He created the remarkable dramatic form of the play by pushing these experiences further in the same direction, by intensifying them, by rearranging his material for greater dramatic effect, by simplifying, conflating, and accentuating—all for the purpose of illumination. Therefore, despite the fact that Strindberg took his material directly from his own life, *To Damascus* became a synthetic and symbolic drama. Close inspection of the play will illuminate this process. In this connection, one must first examine the thematic material.

The elements of the plot in the first part of *To Damascus* are very simple. The Stranger meets the Lady and abducts her from her first husband. They marry, and economic need drives them to seek refuge with her family in the country, where they find a mixed reception. The Mother coaxes the Lady to read the Stranger's latest book. Despite her promise not to do so, the Lady does read the book. The Stranger leaves her and later finds himself in an asylum. After the

moral crisis that he undergoes there, he retraces his steps—part of
the time accompanied by the Lady—and discovers that he has
treated people unjustly. When he returns to his point of departure,
he finds a money order that had been awaiting him all the time at
the post office. The play ends with a bit of moralistic wisdom: "It
was my own stupidity, or my wickedness . . . I did not want to be
life's dupe, and therefore that is exactly what I did become!"

One recognizes most of the external details in this plot as being
drawn from Strindberg's second marriage. Certainly there can be no
doubt that Strindberg was thinking of Frida Uhl when he had the
Stranger meet the Lady in a literary salon, where they "talked
together for four hours." Their own bewildering game of hide-and-
seek and the subsequent economic worries that characterized their
marriage also turn up in the play, just as the scene at the mountain
home of the Lady's family directly reflects the Austrian milieu in
which Frida's family lived in Dornach and Klam. But even though
the skeleton plot can be related to Strindberg's experiences during
the years between 1892 and 1894, his intention was hardly to portray either this or any other segment of his life.[47] Interwoven with
the material from his second marriage are reminiscences from before
and after that brief episode.

The Lady in *To Damascus,* in contrast to Frida Uhl when she met
Strindberg, is already married, and the Stranger "liberates" her from
her husband the Doctor (or "the Werewolf," as he is called). Of
course, this situation makes one think of Strindberg's first marriage,
but this marriage triangle has still older roots in Strindberg's life. In
an early letter to Siri von Essen on March 12, 1876, Strindberg
revealed that he had previously "protected a woman against her own
husband." He was referring to a love affair that preceded his meeting with Siri von Essen and which was to weigh on his conscience
long afterward. By thus conflating his second marriage with previous erotic experiences, Strindberg attained a dramatically palpable
expression for the guilt incurred by the Stranger. He also calculated
a fitting punishment for the crime, although he did not permit it to
be carried out in the play. The Stranger indulges in fantasies about
marriage between "the Werewolf" and his own first wife, which

would turn his rival into the guardian of his own children. The source of this theme is obvious. Strindberg's long-standing fear that Carl Gustav Wrangel would seek revenge has been fused with his terror that the children from his marriage to Siri would come under the influence of a stepfather.

The Stranger, however, has an older debt to pay to the Doctor. Once when they were schoolboys together, the Stranger played a prank, for which the Doctor was held responsible. This is another theme that recurs frequently in Strindberg works, and it very likely derives from an actual experience of Strindberg's. The hero of *By the Open Sea* unexpectedly meets an old school friend when he encounters Olsson, the preacher. At school, he had once made fun of Olsson, whose life consequently took another direction. Similarly, the Stranger imagines that the Doctor has "become a werewolf because as a child he lost faith in divine justice when he suffered innocently for a trick that someone else had played." Naturally, it is also possible that literary reminiscences—such as Rousseau's famous anecdote about the theft of a hair ribbon—may have contributed to the development of this theme. [48]

With the aid of *Inferno*, one can easily see that the scenes involving the Doctor were suggested by Dr. Anders Eliasson's residence in Ystad, where Strindberg stayed as a sort of "patient" for short periods of time in 1895 and 1896. It is not unlikely that something of the Doctor's character and his slightly condescending but amiable relation to the Stranger is based on Strindberg's memories of experiences in Ystad. In *Inferno*, Eliasson is described in terms that apply rather well to the Doctor's skeptical resignation to fate: "A widower, a recluse, a self-contained individual, he has gone through the hard school of life and looks down on people with the strong and lofty contempt that derives from a profound knowledge of the relative lack of value of everything—including one's own self." [49] In the first part of *To Damascus* the Doctor appears as a superior spirit, who toward the end of the play achieves true nobility of soul.

For this reason, it is difficult for the spectator to gain a proper perspective on the Doctor's other side, the one suggested by his nickname, "the Werewolf." Here, too, Strindberg's memories of his

visits in Ystad come into play: for a moment he had suspected Eliasson of plotting against his life, and the episode in *Inferno* where the
doctor exhibits a stillborn child is echoed in *To Damascus,* where the
Doctor displays severed limbs from his icebox.[50] Here again, however, is another fusion of motifs. When Strindberg spent a few days
in Weimar at the end of 1892, he met the Finnish writer Karl
August Tavaststjerna and fell in love with his wife. In a communication to Adolf Paul on December 7, 1892, he wrote: "A two-
day novel in reality. Incredibly pleasant, interesting. Battle of the
brains and of the males! Neue Liebe! Full declaration of love in the
presence of the male. Jalousie. Alles." [51] This situation, depending
as it did on Tavaststjerna's deafness, occurs in *To Damascus,* in the
scene where the Doctor turns his back while the other two discuss
him in his presence: "You don't have to whisper, because my husband is hard of hearing but reads lips."

Strindberg's stories about his visit to Ossian Ekbohrn at Sandhamn in 1889 provide the most apposite psychological background
for the Caesar motif in *To Damascus.* He had already used these experiences when writing *By the Open Sea* in 1890.[52] Strindberg accused
his friend Ekbohrn of being subject to both persecution feelings and
megalomania or (as it was often called in those days) "Caesar-mad-
ness," but between the lines of his fervent attack one can easily read
the anxious question: "But what about me?" Toward the end of the
1880s, Strindberg was extremely fearful that he would go insane,
and he was familiar with the idea that both suspiciousness and a tendency to overestimate oneself might be symptoms of mental illness.
From this perspective, Ekbohrn became his mirror image, a sort of
Doppelgänger for Strindberg himself. The situation is brilliantly
foreshortened in *To Damascus* during the first meeting between the
Stranger and Caesar. The madman "boards" at the Doctor's house—
Eliasson is said to have had a "feeble-minded" patient in the
house.[53] He wanders about brooding over "the lack of plan and purpose in nature" and "rearranges creation," Strindberg writes, using
terms that make one think of the superman Borg in *By the Open Sea.*
When he sees the Stranger, who is presented as a great writer, he
immediately says: "He may be Caesar, but he is not great," that is,

he suffers from megalomania but he is not really great.[54] The identity of the Stranger's former nickname with the madman's present name heightens the Stranger's anxiety, and the name "Caesar" reappears throughout the play, partly as a reminder of the painful events in his youth, partly as a sign of the insanity that threatens to engulf him.

When Strindberg wrote the second part of *To Damascus*, he was captivated by the scenic possibilities of the Doppelgänger motif, which he exploited rather cavalierly. But in the first part, the motif is psychologically motivated and constitutes an organic part of the drama. Strindberg's interest in this occult concept during the Inferno period has suggested to some critics that Caesar and the Beggar in the first part of *To Damascus* were intended as counterparts to Poe's William Wilson or to Hoffmann's Brother Medardus.[55] Of course, when Strindberg uses the Doppelgänger motif in a literary work, he naturally established ties with romanticism and with occultism. But here—just as everywhere else in his works— one should avoid overemphasizing his interest in the purely speculative. When faced with some of the interpretations to which *To Damascus* has given rise, one is tempted to quote Strindberg's own injunction on September 10, 1902, to Emil Schering, the director of another post-*Inferno* play, *Crimes and Crimes:* "And then: do not hint at depths where they do not exist! or at profundities that were never intended!" Even when he was creating his best and most "mystically" resonant work, reality and actual experiences served as Strindberg's point of departure.

Just as the Caesar figure is based on Strindberg's experiences in Sandhamn, the other Doppelgänger motif in the play—the one associated with the figure of the Beggar—is based on the fears and imaginings that haunted him in Dornach and Paris. The background for this figure was Strindberg's critical financial situation and his fear of being overwhelmed by poverty and drink. As so often happened, his attitude fluctuated, so that he sometimes idealized the beggar figure, sometimes feared it. He could speak of "walking in the gutter and experiencing *Machtgefühl*" as a desirable condition, but he could also react with abhorrence at the thought that he could detect a corresponding thought about himself in the eyes of other people.

The figure of the Beggar in the first part of *To Damascus* represents a projection of Strindberg's speculations about a way of life that preoccupied him. Real people may also have influenced his use of the theme, but instead of portraying them directly, Strindberg presented them indirectly, tentatively identifying himself with them and thinking himself into their situations. In this connection, one thinks above all of Strindberg's old friend Jean Lundin, who lived in poverty in Paris and in whom Strindberg saw a likely instructor in "the secrets of the trade"—that is, in the craft of begging. But there was also another "beggar" in Paris whose existence captured Strindberg's imagination. In an undated letter to Littmansson in July 1894, he expressed a longing to go to the French capital, "where Verlaine, an ex-convict who has never been able to stay out of debt, is a famous man because he has talent." Verlaine's name occurs here and there in Strindberg's notations. It is interesting to note that the name also turns up on a flyleaf of *The Occult Diary,* next to a motif that found its way into *To Damascus.*[56]

"Begging" both frightened and fascinated Strindberg. For that reason, the appearance of the Beggar terrifies the Stranger at the same time that it fills him with a feeling of inferiority. The Beggar is bitter and satirical. He quotes Latin. According to his own statement, he is not even a real beggar. Thus, he is the incarnation of the pauper with "Machtgefühl" that Strindberg himself once feared he would become—and sometimes wished he could become. Strindberg lets the Stranger ask the Lady (just as he might have asked Frida Uhl about, say, Verlaine), "Is he really like me?" But the Lady does not answer the question. Using one of the ingenious transpositions that often occur in Strindberg's dialogue, she departs from the real question, the one that motivates the Stranger's anxiety: "Am I really like him?" She wisely answers: "Yes, if you keep on drinking, you will be like him." Simple as it may sound, this is the essence of the figure of the Beggar, his *raison d'être.* Even though Strindberg underscores the theme by providing the Stranger and the Beggar with certain striking external similarities—like the scar each bears on his forehead—he avoids emphasizing the mystical aspects of the Doppelgänger phenomenon. The double must function as the incarnation of one of the possible directions in which the Stranger could develop. This function prevents the technique of doubling from dwindling into a series of occult mystifications in the tradition of the gothic novel. In the later parts of the play the Beggar frees himself from this connection and appears as an independent character, but at that point he also ceases to function as a double and the motif retreats into the background.

In the first part of *To Damascus* there is one other person who can be considered a Doppelgänger for the Stranger, just like Caesar or the Beggar. That person is the corpse which is buried by a group of mourners who enter dressed in brown in the first scene. After the funeral, the mourners sit down in a café, and a conversation develops:

THE STRANGER: It was a happy corpse, I take it, since the mourners are getting drunk right after the religious ceremony.

FIRST GUEST: Yes, a worthless person who couldn't take life seriously.

THE STRANGER: And who probably drank too much, too?

SECOND GUEST: That's right.

THIRD GUEST: Besides, he let others provide for his wife and children.

THE STRANGER: That was very wicked. But that is certainly why his friends are giving him such a fine eulogy now. —Please don't bump against my table while I am drinking.

FIRST GUEST: When I am drinking it is all right . . .

THE STRANGER: When I do, yes; for there is a great difference between me and the others.

The Stranger feels piqued when the guests begin to speak ill of their dead friend and immediately takes the "eulogy" to be a critique of himself. In this case, one can unequivocally trace the motif to Strindberg's earlier literary output: he has fastened upon a completely natural occurrence that made a great impression on him, and in developing it later, he has sharpened its contours slightly, creating in the process a mysterious atmosphere. On May 12, 1891, when Strindberg was living on the island of Runmarö, he wrote to Ola Hansson: "I am staying in a cottage where a childhood friend of mine lived two years ago, at which time he drowned himself in a nearby marsh—because his wife had left him and taken his children with her." Strindberg was much affected by this tragedy, which happened to occur at the very moment when he had lost his own children. Perhaps he expected the same fate to overtake him. In the short story "The Silver Marsh" he lets the principal character view the corpse of a drowned man and he briefly draws the parallel:

> When their terror of death had subsided, the villagers gathered, and now the eulogy began:
> —"He was mean to his wife."
> —"And think how much he drank."
> —"She really must be a fine woman."
> —"How awful!"
> —"There's no doubt that it was suicide."
Deeply upset, the inspector left the group; it was almost as if they had been scourging him.

Though the café scene in *To Damascus* is more ingenious and much more dramatic, the material Strindberg uses there actually contains nothing that is not already present here. Whereas he could simply inform the reader of "The Silver Marsh" that the hero feels guilty because of his impression that the remarks apply to him, he could not make the same point directly in a play. For this reason he had to make the allusions more explicit. Accompanying the dramatic events in *To Damascus* is a series of symbolic details that tend to recur and form a kind of leitmotif. When the play is staged, these details contribute considerably to its effectiveness. Of course, the same symbolic technique occurs frequently in drama. But Strindberg's symbolism in the first part of *To Damascus* is strongly individual. Maeterlinck uses a high degree of stylization to imbue his scenes with a strange, suggestive atmosphere. And one might find traces of the same technique in *To Damascus,* especially in stage directions like the following: "From inside the church one hears women's voices singing—almost shrieking a high polyphonous chord. The lighted rosette window quickly grows dark; the tree above the bench trembles; the funeral guests rise from their seats and look up to the sky as if they saw something unusual and terrifying."

But this kind of effect is not characteristic of Strindberg. His symbols—in contrast to Maeterlinck's—also have intellectual content, and for that very reason they acquire an element of mystery which is lacking in Maeterlinck's massive effects. In Ibsen, one finds fully developed intellectual symbolism; but whether they are transparent or not, his symbolical vignettes readily acquire an element of conscious calculation, of rebus. Strindberg's symbols flash forth from the structure of the drama much more capriciously; they are therefore extremely difficult to pin down and interpret.

Strindberg's kind of symbolism can only be understood against the background of his creative practice. The symbolic structure of this play is no more the product of lucubration and literary imitation than are its concentrated action or its use of the Doppelgänger motif. For these symbols had deep roots in Strindberg's experience and in many cases were already saturated with a powerful but obscure symbolic value for him even before he included them in the play.

The attendant symbols emerge as projections of the Stranger's subconscious fears and desires. To all outward appearances—especially in the first half of the play—Strindberg's hero is a skeptical "gentleman" with a defiant and superior attitude toward existence. The symbols indicate—in a way that is quite obvious to the spectator—what is going on inside the protagonist. Therefore, the drama takes place on two levels—one conscious, the other subconscious—and these symbols concretize an "esoteric" world that the Stranger's conscious self only gradually accepts.

A canceled speech in *To Damascus* shows that Strindberg actually intended to effect a scenic representation of the borderline between the conscious and the subconscious minds. When the Stranger meets the Mother, he learns from her what motivated him to name the Lady Eve: like a sorcerer, he wants to destroy the whole race of women in "the Eve of his own making." The Stranger is astonished at the Mother's discernment and asks her how she arrived at such a conclusion. In the printed version of the play, she answers simply: "They [the conclusions] are yours." One is apt to imagine that she found them in the Stranger's book that is mentioned so frequently in the play—that is, in *A Madman's Defense*. But judging from the remainder of the speech, which Strindberg canceled, such was not his intention: ". . . But you do not have the power to bring them forth into the light yourself . . . or else you do not have the courage." The Mother's intuition discovers thoughts in the Stranger's subconscious mind that he is not willing to recognize himself. Something similar obtains for the whole symbolic world in the first part of *To Damascus.*

In the first scene, the Stranger tells the Lady that he does not fear death. "Not death, but loneliness" is what frightens him, and the awareness that he holds the power of death in his own hands gives him "an incredible feeling of power." Nevertheless, he is noticeably irritated by Mendelssohn's "Funeral March," which is heard repeatedly in the background. In Paris, Strindberg had been similarly terrified by Schumann's "Aufschwung," because it reminded him of Przybyszewski and his putative plans to murder Strindberg. (Originally the Schumann piece figured in the manuscript of *To Damascus.*) The peculiar contrast between thoughts of suicide and a gripping fear of death that is so strikingly demonstrated in the first scene of *To Damascus* is also present in *Inferno.* The ambivalence of the Stranger's attitude becomes even more apparent in his involvement with the pallbearers, when they speak to him about a *timmerman,* the Swedish word for "carpenter," which is also the popular name for the *Lamia aedilis* or "deathwatch beetle." According to folk superstition, the characteristic sound of the deathwatch beetle forbodes death. As Lamm points out, Strindberg himself had imagined that he heard a mysterious ticking sound like that of the deathwatch beetle inside his own vest.[57] The Stranger, however, retains his insolence. "If that's the case, let me say that I am not frightened and that I do not believe in miracles." Nonetheless he experiences a feeling of anxiety, which the subsequent discussion of the drinking habits of the deceased does nothing to allay. In *Legends* one finds an account of the real experience that underlies this bizarre scene. Strindberg recounts there that one day he heard the continuous tolling of death knells from the church and in the afternoon encountered two funeral processions. "How everything smells of death today!"[58] That evening he saw an intoxicated man by the wall of the café and later learned that the man had died. Taking all this to be an "admonition to drinkers," he ordered milk for his supper. In *To Damascus* this "secret dread" is made dramatically expressive by means of the *timmerman* symbol and the "eulogy."

During his Inferno period, whenever Strindberg received impressions like these that activated his anxiety feeling, he was obsessed by the notion that they were not fully real. He called them "half-visions." The beggar he saw at the Brasserie des Lilas and describes in *Inferno* struck him as just such a half-real figure, as did the people who appeared on the Boulevard Saint-Germain while Strindberg was sitting before a glass of absinth. Perhaps his fear of delirium tremens had something to do with this reaction, but still his description of the different levels of reality that he perceived is quite exact. For example, the element of "warning" which he read into the scenes he witnessed was "unreal" in the sense that it stemmed from his own guilt feelings. In order to present this tenuous quality of reality to a theater audience, Strindberg let the mourners appear dressed in brown instead of black, provided them with an scythe wreathed with spruce twigs (symbolic of death), and gave to the dialogue the color of a conversation in a folktale by filling it with jests and letting the characters talk at cross-purposes:

THE STRANGER: Excuse me, but who was the deceased?

FIRST MOURNER: A carpenter. (*Makes a noise like a clock.*)

THE STRANGER: A real carpenter, or the kind that sits in the walls and ticks?

SECOND MOURNER: Both, but mostly one that sits in the walls and ticks—what is it they are called?

THE STRANGER (*to himself*): That joker! Now he wants to trick me into saying "deathwatch," but I shall say something else in order to irritate him. Ah, you must mean "goldsmith."

Although Strindberg projected his fear of insanity and poverty mainly into the figures of the Beggar and Caesar, he also expressed it it other ways. According to the stage directions, outside the door to the Rose Room there is "a dark, dismal building with black, curtainless windows," a poorhouse. The Stranger tries not to look in that direction. The poorhouse, he says, seems to have been built entirely for his sake: "And besides, a woman is always standing there waving in this direction." In *Inferno* Strindberg remarks that he saw both the madwoman and the poorhouse in Austria.

Throughout the play there is also a mysterious connection between insanity and the frequently-recurring mandrake plant ("Christmas rose"). This plant is the object of Caesar's particular attention. He considers it "stupid to let the Helleborus stand out in the snow and freeze," and he therefore brings the flowers into the cellar for the winter, so that they bloom in the summer instead of at Christmas time; this is his way of "rearranging nature." The Lady wears a Christmas rose on her breast and gives it to the Stranger as a "medicine," which "has cured insanity in the past." During his odyssey, the Stranger and his companion are tormented by the "eternally withering Christmas rose." Summer becomes autumn then winter; winter gives way to spring; but the Christmas rose remains there withering. In Strindberg's symbolism the Helleborus acquires an affinity with insanity because it blooms irregularly and withers just when other plants are awakening from their period of winter dormancy. A fresh series of associations arises from the fact that Caesar finds the peculiar habits of the Christmas rose as disquieting as the Stranger does. The similarity of their reactions serves to reinforce the link between these two "doubles." Finally, there are the learned associations connected with the Christmas rose. According to legend, Hercules—earlier the idol not only of Inspector Borg but of Strindberg himself—was cured of madness by the *Helleborus niger.* In Roman and medieval folk belief the plant was thought to ward off evil spirits.[59]

In *To Damascus* Strindberg must rely mainly on indirect "symbols" to express another important emotional reaction that he was able to present directly in *Inferno,* namely, his fear of demons and other malevolent powers. His symbolic material consists chiefly of relevant details that filled him with anxiety. In the second and fourth acts of the play, he constructs a scene that derives from the "ravine" at Klam (near the residence of Frida's grandfather), which he called "the Inferno landscape." The hovel with a broom and goat's horn (both thought to be the insignia of witches) as well as the smithy (reminiscent of Dante's *Inferno*) are only two of the many "symbolic" elements that Strindberg actually observed during his stay in Austria. The bird of prey that frightens the Stranger when he arises during the night is another symbolic manifestation of Strindberg's anxiety feelings during his visit in Klam. One remembers that he dreamed each night of an eagle tormenting him and spoke of an "invisible vulture" attacking him. Finally, the Stranger sees the devil in the pattern of the tablecloth, just as Strindberg saw him in the panel of the doctor's cabinet in Ystad.

In the same tablecloth Strindberg places a portrait of the "Werewolf," whose face later appears in the rock formations above the ravine. Of course, similar illusions abound in *Inferno,* where Strindberg reveals that he is purposely training himself to be a "seer." There, he perceives a "Turk's head" in the rocks above the ravine. In the play these details serve to make tangible the Stranger's guilty conscience after his abduction of the Lady. They are "the conscience, which rises up when one is hungry and tired, but subsides when one is satisfied and rested." Another, broader symbol for guilt feelings is the rumbling mill that the Stranger imagines he can hear. The same sensation occurs in *Inferno,* where it is interpreted as a reminder of God's effort to purify man: "It is the Lord's millwheel that grinds slowly, but exceedingly fine—and black." [60]

The directly religious symbols employed by Strindberg are more conventional than his indirect or private symbols. Most of them, like the Chapel of Saint Elizabeth, the garland of roses, and the Stations of the Cross, are drawn from the highly developed devotional practices of Roman Catholicism and have a meaning that is fixed by long usage. But even here, one finds personal and creative elements in his use of the symbols. The three masts of a ship that come to represent Golgatha in this play (Act IV, sc. iii) had already captured Strindberg's imagination in the 1870s and become the subject of a painting by him in 1894. Gunnel Sylvan, who first called attention to this painting, [61] signalizes the thematic importance of its sharply contrasting blacks and whites by recalling that when *To Damascus* was produced, Strindberg wanted the backdrop to show two mountains, one black and one white.[62] The same symbolic contrast may be found in the play itself, where the white mill stands opposite the black smithy. The sight of this contrast makes the Stranger think of an "old poem." In all likelihood he is thinking of the *Divine Comedy* with its dark funnel of Hell and its sunny mountain of Purgatory.

Finally, the chief function of the occult elements in the play is not really symbolic but technical. Strindberg had been deeply impressed by theories about the transmigration of souls that he found in the works of Carl du Prel and Stanislas de Guaita. Early in the 1890s he had already begun to believe in telepathy. Later, he imagined that during states of exaltation he was capable of being transported to strange and distant places. Even when he thought of himself as a pure scientist, Strindberg was interested in the possibilities of extrasensory experience, which is one of the basic features of a "naturalistic" occultism. Both telepathy and clairvoyance occur in *To Damascus.* The Lady's repeated entrances in the first scene are motivated by her feeling that the Stranger has "called out to her." Whenever anyone is talking about him, the Stranger can sense it from afar. Furthermore, when he meets the Mother, it appears that she has seen him before and "has almost been waiting for him." Before the Stranger accompanies the Lady to her home, he sees her family's kitchen in a kind of vision, just as Strindberg thought he had seen the landscape at Klam etched on the sides of a zinc bath before he ever left Paris. According to *Legends,* his mother-in-law in Austria had "actually seen" a figure like Strindberg behind the piano in her house in Austria at the very moment when he experienced his vision in Paris.

In the preface to *A Dreamplay,* Strindberg described *To Damascus* as his "previous dreamplay." Strindberg was quite capable of rejecting his earlier works in occasional pronouncements, but it was much more characteristic of him to attempt to invest them with new value by bringing them in line with his most recent efforts. His description of *To Damascus* as a "dreamplay" is about as accurate as his observation in 1894 that "The Romantic Sexton" and *By the Open Sea* were "symbolist" works. But this intimation of Strindberg's has

misled a whole school of Strindberg critics, who speak of Strindberg's "dreamplays" as a homogeneous group including *To Damascus*
(1898), *A Dreamplay* (1902), *The Chamber Plays* (1907), and possibly
even *The Great Highway* (1909). In assuming this position, such
critics gloss over the considerable differences that these plays show
in technique, mood, and content. The first part of *To Damascus* is
particularly subject to misinterpretation, if one chooses to regard it
solely in the light of the later plays.

The fact that critics have often overlooked the differences between
the various parts of the *To Damascus* trilogy has also contributed to
the proliferation of unfortunate generalizations. If one wishes to
regard a work of art as an autonomous entity, one must first determine whether or not the artist really created—or at least intended to
create—a work based on a unified conception. The three parts of *To
Damascus* were written at different times: the first part in the spring
of 1898, the second in the summer of the same year, the third part
three years later. Nothing indicates that when he finished the first
part, Strindberg intended to write a continuation. Thus, whereas
one can read the second part in the light of the first, and the third
part in the light of its two predecessors, one must in principle treat
the first part as independent drama, since it was planned and written
as such.

None of the notions about Strindberg's "dreamplays" is relevant
to the first part of *To Damascus*. In this play, Strindberg does not
record his dreams but (with one exception treated below) works with
real, waking experiences. In other words, instead of looking inward,
he looks outward toward reality. This reality is not the same, however, as the one that most people know. The Stranger's many doubles, the recurrent symbolic details—all such elements create a
strange impression that one may easily attempt to characterize by
resorting to the word "dream." Strindberg's experience of reality appears to be dreamlike, as he himself observed when he reported that
life was to him "like a dream." The reason for this reaction to life is
apparent: whereas most people project their subconscious conflicts
into their dreams, Strindberg also allowed them to be projected outward into his environment. Prompted by his neurosis, he saw life in

a dreamlike fashion. This, in fact, constitutes the essence of the autistically oriented mode of experience that emerged to dominate Strindberg's life during his Inferno crisis.

Therefore, what Strindberg presented in *To Damascus* is not a dream or a series of dreams; it is reality seen from a point of view reminiscent of that found in dreams. The statements made by Strindberg when he was writing the play indicate that he certainly did not conceive of it as a presentation of dreams. In a letter to his children on May 24, 1898, he observes that the play is "fantastic and brilliant," but at the same time he stresses that it "is set in the present against a fully real background." He had expressed himself more precisely in a letter to Geijerstam on March 17, 1898: "Yes, it is no doubt a poem with a terrifying half-reality behind it."

None of this precludes the possibility that Strindberg was more than willing for the spectator to regard the play as a dream. In the same letter to Geijerstam, Strindberg designates the dreamlike scene in the asylum as the center of the play. But neither in the scenes leading up to this climax nor in the scenes that follow can one trace any steady development, either from fantasy to reality or from reality to fantasy.[63] Whenever the bizarre, symbolic material assumes a more important place in the drama, the impression of unreality increases. Thus, the introductory scene with the pallbearers and the Beggar makes a markedly less realistic impression than do the succeeding scenes by the sea and along the highway. So much for the first half. In the second half, directly following the scene in the asylum, one finds the completely realistic conversation between the Stranger and the Mother in the Rose Room.

In the play, the scene in the asylum is described as a "fever dream." Certain technical details and theatrical tricks set it apart from the rest of the action and emphasize its unique status in the work. Sitting around a table are both of the Stranger's wives, his children, his parents, the Beggar, Caesar, the Doctor—indeed, everyone whom he has wronged or with whom he is still somehow involved. But the stage directions make clear that they are not the "real" characters who appear, only "people who resemble them," an effect that is achieved by the use of costume and make-up: "Beneath different colored veils, all of them are dressed in white. Their faces are waxen, pale as death; and there is something ghostly about their whole appearance and in their gestures." After a dialogue between the Stranger and the Confessor, culminating in the enumeration of all the Stranger's sinful acts, the Confessor pronounces the curse from Deuteronomy, and the ghostly congregation repeats in chorus: "Cursed shalt thou be!" The Stranger remains mute and appears to be unmoved.

Here once again Strindberg depicts the central experience of his conversion: the grinding, crushing pangs of conscience that finally reduce the sinner to despair and initiate his recovery. Because this development was entirely spiritual, it was especially difficult to present scenically. When Strindberg came to grips with this same problem in *Jacob Wrestles*, he could find no better device than the flying menu. One cannot help finding his innovation in *To Damascus* more adequate. The gripping asylum scene really makes a powerful impression on the spectator and provides the drama with a peripeteia that is both emphatic and effective.

He has achieved this effect by a completely different method from the one just analyzed. This scene has no basis in reality. It is related to Strindberg's experiences at the Saint-Louis Hospital in only the most superficial way. Perhaps he saw the refectory and the dining table or met the "Abbess" there, but only with his inner eye did he detect the grieving and anathematizing shades of persons living and dead, who still dominated his psychic life. Thus, one might say that the asylum scene is more "literary" than the rest of the play, for in many particulars it recalls the type of dramatic symbolism preferred by Maeterlinck and his followers. For example, scrims were held in high esteem by symbolist producers. Although Strindberg does not recommend the use of a scrim, he achieves the same effect by draping his characters in gauze transparencies. Both techniques produce the same impression of unreality. Another innovation is the stage set itself, which has many qualities of the stationary, decorative tableaux found in *Interior* and other one-act plays by Maeterlinck. Finally, Strindberg's use of a kind of chorus—an even more striking departure from his usual practice—suggests another link between

To Damascus and the symbolist theater; for groups are frequently more prominent than individuals in Maeterlinck's plays—as in *The Blind*—and collective scenes are rare in Strindberg.

One characteristic feature of Strindberg's symbolism is his constant repetition of symbolic motifs; indeed, they recur in the structure of the drama like themes in a musical composition. By means of such suggestive elements, past episodes are continually revived and reintroduced into the play, and these leitmotifs knit the play together into an organic whole. Thus, Strindberg's philosophy of recurrence, which he later attempted to express in the slogan "everything comes back," is closely allied with his symbolic technique itself. Already in the first part of *To Damascus* there is a speech that closely resembles this famous slogan: "Why does everything come back . . . both corpses, and beggars and madmen and human destinies and childhood memories?"

Quite apart from directly symbolic elements, all kinds of repetition play an important part in the drama. The Stranger constantly encounters unpleasant reminders of the past. When he meets the Doctor, he unexpectedly finds an old school friend; when he is shown to a hotel room, he discovers that he has previously occupied the same room. The Lady finds it difficult to converse with him because, as she confesses to her mother, she can never say "anything that he hasn't heard before." This theme of repetition is most strikingly illustrated in the asylum scene, where the Stranger is confronted with his entire past life. Thus, the phrase "everything repeats itself" covers two kinds of experience in *To Damascus*. On the one hand, the Stranger is unpleasantly reminded of his past; on the other, actual situations from his earlier experience are repeated.

The neurotic personality is much more prone than is the normal peronality to reduce the pattern of experiences to a set of stereotypes. Again and again he feels that he has become involved in the same situations, because instead of reacting objectively, he identifies the persons he meets with figures from childhood. It is probably also true that, as a result of this predisposition, he tends to act in such a way that he actually keeps on renewing the situations that bring him into conflict with his environment.[64] Strindberg clearly had a ten-

dency to experience life as a series of repetitions, and this tendency is
nowhere more evident than in his erotic relations. Frida Uhl reports
that in conversation he would sometimes use speeches previously
included in his works and that he confused some situations in his
second marriage with others he had depicted in *A Madman's Defense*.
Thus, when Strindberg synthetically conflates memories from his
first and second marriages and compresses several real-life episodes
into one story in *To Damascus,* he is by no means constructing a sort
of sophisticated and artificial puzzle. The tendency to experience life
on more than one level, to recognize old situations behind new ones,
was an integral part of his own day-to-day life.

It is correspondingly simple to isolate the psychological basis of
the other form of repetition used by Strindberg in this play. In *Inferno* one finds many counterparts to the Stranger's impression that
he is constantly being reminded of unpleasant things, of death, of
wicked deeds, of humiliating experiences. Because he was afraid of
his Polish friend, Strindberg continually heard someone playing
"Aufschwung," which was Przybyszewski's favorite piece; he ignored all other music that reached his ears. As soon as certain details
in the real world became saturated with symbolic meaning for him,
he imagined that he was encountering them with incredible
frequency and felt that he was being pursued by the very things he
wished to avoid. Every word in an innocuous conversation in *To
Damascus* pierces the Stranger "like an awl" and seems to him to be
full of allusions because he is—as the Lady rightly observes—"intensely vulnerable." This state of mind fosters his impression that he
is the victim of "small incidents that really do recur."

There is, however, yet another variant of the recurrence motif in
the first part of *To Damascus* which contributes to the form of the
play. In the second half of the play the scenes from the first half are
repeated in reverse order. Strindberg regarded this arrangement as
very important, and it appears that this disposition of scenes was actually his starting point when planning the play. In a couple of
early drafts, although there are fewer scenes, the second half of the
play is already the reverse image of the first half.[65] In a picturesque
letter to Geijerstam on March 17, 1898, Strindberg wrote: "The art

lies in the composition, which symbolizes the repetition that Kierkegaard speaks of. The action unrolls forward as it leads up to the asylum; there it hits the 'point' and then moves backward, kicking against the pricks, through the pilgrimage, the relearning, the ruminations, and then it starts anew in the same place at which the game ends and where it began."

In this form the recurrence motif expresses what is above all a moral idea. In one of his conversations with the Mother, the Stranger receives an account of what awaits him: he must do as children do when they have misbehaved—first "beg forgiveness," then "try to set things to rights." He must therefore return by the same path on which he has come, must retrace his steps in life and rectify all his injustices to others. This kind of penance was also a part of Strindberg's own program in 1887 and 1898.[66] In an undated letter to Geijerstam in November 1897, he speaks of "making a pilgrimage and rectifying all the wrongs" he had done. Nothing ever came of this proposed trip, but in his place he let the Stranger undertake a pilgrimage that led to his reconciliation with the Beggar, the Lady, and the Doctor. Since Strindberg did not believe in the efficacy of Christ's vicarious suffering for mankind, he felt that he himself ought to tread the path to Calvary, past the seven stations of suffering. As he explained to Geijerstam (Mar. 13, 1898), "the whole symbol of 'the journey' " is contained in the plan of the drama. "The journey" is simultaneously to Damascus and to Golgotha, at the end of which "the powers" give a sign of atonement by allowing the Stranger to fetch the money order that he has so long awaited.

Strindberg's idea of return or recurrence has nothing at all to do with Kierkegaard's "repetition," which happens to be one of the most obscure of all his ideas. For Kierkegaard, "repetition" was the most difficult and the most desirable of all experiences. It could not be realized in the aesthetic or ethical stages of man's life, but only in the religious stage, which very few people ever attain.[67] For Strindberg, repetitions were partly a torture, partly a moral duty. This concept—with its double aspect—is wholly personal and can only be understood in the light of Strindberg's need to feel that he had been put to the test and humbled. Yet in the agonizing, neurotic stereotypes he sees a promise of liberation, of atonement. He cries out, but in his outcry there is a note of optimism.

Letting the protagonist of *To Damascus* turn back to his point of departure was also a return for Strindberg—a return to a dramatic technique that he had used before. Gunnar Ollén points to this and to other features that align *To Damascus* with Strindberg's two earlier "pilgrimage plays" *Lucky Per's Journey* (1881) and *The Keys of Heaven* (1892).[68] In the letter to his children cited above, Strindberg characterizes *To Damascus* as "a new genre, fantastic and brilliant like *Lucky Per's Journey,* but with a contemporary setting and a fully real background." This description shows that Strindberg actually had his earlier fairy plays in mind when he wrote *To Damascus.*

Instead of "pilgrimage plays," one could also call these works "education plays," for all fairy plays trace a line of moral development. One finds this basic pattern in the folk tale and in *Peer Gynt.* The hero wanders through the world and then returns—richer in experience—to his point of departure. This was a very convenient genre for Strindberg to employ when he wished to give dramatic form to his religious crisis and conversion. He felt, just as he did when writing *Lucky Per's Journey,* that he had a moral experience to exhibit to his spectators. The most natural way of emphasizing this kind of experience is to let the protagonist, whom the action has transformed into a new person, return to his former milieu. Like *To Damascus, Lucky Per's Journey* also begins and ends with the same scenery. In *To Damascus,* however, the changes that have occurred in the character of the Stranger are further emphasized by a marked shift in the lighting: whereas the lights are concentrated on the café during the first scene, during the last one they are directed at the church.

Anyone wishing to interpret *To Damascus* ought to bear in mind the fact that Strindberg consciously reverted to the technique he had used in his earlier fairy plays. Viewing the play in this perspective, one is not so surprised by the unexpected encounters—between the Stranger and the Beggar, for example—or by the Lady's handy entrances at just the moments when she is most needed. People meet and are separated in exactly this way in a fairy play like *Lucky Per's*

Journey, where Lisa is always on hand to encourage Per whenever he feels downhearted. Generally speaking, the Lady in the first part of *To Damascus* has many qualities that suggest the good and wise fairy, and these qualities point back to the figure of Lisa in the earlier play. The scene in which the Beggar, after some beating about the bush, shows first the Stranger then the Lady the road they should take ("Follow the track!") also smacks strongly of the fairy tale. The hero of a folk tale is constantly meeting wise old men, old women, or elves of the same sort along his dangerous path through the world.

"Scenically," as Martin Lamm puts it, "the play's strength and its weakness lies in the fact that it is completely dominated by the figure of the Stranger." [69] The other figures in the play are simply not characterized to any significant degree. They react abruptly and without motivation. Although this kind of behavior may well enhance the illusion of capricious and complicated reality, it certainly does not make them easy to grasp. Throughout the play the Doctor is called "the Werewolf," but this side of him is never revealed to the spectator. According to the Stranger, the Old Man in the hunting lodge shows that he "is capable of nourishing a stout hatred," but to the spectator he appears to be only a tired old man who seeks comfort in religion. The Mother seems sympathetic in the scene in which she shows the Stranger the stations of the cross that he must follow, but in another scene she intrigues against his marriage. One could introduce many more such examples to illustrate the degree of inconsistency in Strindberg's illumination of his accessory figures.

The Lady is also something of an accessory character herself. After finishing the first part, Strindberg wrote to Geijerstam on March 17, 1898 and mentioned a "suggested change": "The Lady has not pronounced the curse; but by reading his book, she has eaten of the tree of knowledge; she begins to reflect, loses her 'unbewusste' or unconsciousness, discovers the difference between right and wrong, becomes filled with discord, and thereby loses her charm for him." Despite the fact that he reworked a scene in the third act—the scene in the Rose Room—and pushed her characterization in the direction that he outlines to Geijerstam, Strindberg never succeeded in making the Lady into a really independent character. When she and the Stranger find each other again after their separation, she resumes the role of an encouraging companion which she had played in the earlier scenes.

The people around the Stranger change in accordance with his own mood. He is the one who elicits the Lady's maternal instincts and transforms the Doctor into a werewolf; he is the one who fears the Mother at the same time that he feels the need to subordinate himself to her. The objective part of the play—plot and character development—is subject to the rules that govern the Stranger's neurotic strategy. One can take the Stranger's drawing in the sand at the beginning and end of the play as a symbolic expression of the relation that he bears to his environment. Indeed, in his essay entitled "Moi," Strindberg chose this very gesture to exemplify "the self's instinct to expand." [70] The subjective bias emerges with particular clarity in the first scene, where the Stranger provides the Lady with a name, an age, and a character of his own devising. Later the Mother gives a psychological interpretation of his attitude: "That is how in your self-made Eve you figure on destroying her entire progeny." The synthetic experience of life pushes one toward impersonality and abstraction: a woman becomes the Lady, a mother becomes the Mother. The Stranger prefers to imagine the Lady as "impersonal, nameless." The same process applies to all the other characters in the play. Since this tendency governed Strindberg's actual relations with people, one should not regard it as the expression of some kind of idealistic philosophy. Nor did Strindberg intend *To Damascus* to be a thoroughgoing "drame intérieur" of symbolist tradition. Therefore, it would be beside the point to ask the question: in whose consciousness does the drama occur? It is not possible to demonstrate that Strindberg wanted characters like the Mother or the Old Man to be regarded as pure figments of the imagination, as a few critics have suggested. [71]

The casualness with which Strindberg draws his secondary characters is, however, only the other side of a feature that serves to strengthen the dramatic effectiveness of the play. If one admits that the characters are inconsistently portrayed, one must also point out that in all likelihood Strindberg never intended to deepen his characterizations with an eye to making them "consistent" and "logically understandable." He had long criticized current concepts of character and had split his theatrical marionettes by endowing them with manifold impulses, drives, and attitudes. It was already apparent in his naturalistic plays that this kind of fragmentation increased the possibilities for intensifying dramatic situations. Situations, not characters, are quite obviously the essential ingredients in *To Damascus*. Because of Strindberg's neurotic tendency to experience repetitions, in his imagination people borrowed each other's features— their masks—according to his own relations to them. The figure of the Lady, for example, tends to become the abstract sum of all the women Strindberg had ever met, but for that very reason his dramatic situations become still more fraught with archetypal tension.

Standing at the center of the drama are the Stranger and the power that directs his destiny. In *Jacob Wrestles* this power was incarnated in a radiant imaginary figure; here it remains transcendent, and the artistic effect is strengthened. The most enduring memory that one carries away from a performance of the first part of *To Damascus* is this image of a soul in distress, wrestling with Something, with Someone above and beyond him.

The reader acquainted with the works that Strindberg wrote before *Inferno* will recognize this motif as a variation on some of his favorite themes. One can think of *By the Open Sea* (1890), "The Silver Marsh" (1892–1898), or even *The Father* (1887) and find parallels in all of these works: a protagonist who asserts himself with cold irony, with Promethean defiance, with jeering pride, but who is finally crushed and defeated—and who deep down is aware that he must be defeated. Tragic Titanism, Strindberg's personal variation on the superman motif, has also left its mark on *To Damascus*. Strindberg had always been sensitive to pressure from above—from his father and society, from morality and God. He had revolted against the pressure, but in dark moments he had anticipated his final capitulation. In his early poem about Loki, the "outsider" among the Old Norse gods, Strindberg rose up in youthful defiance against the authorities and ridiculed the rulers of Swedish society as withered Olympians. When the Stranger vents his wrath against "little bourgeois gods who parry sword thrusts with pinpricks from behind," one has a new variation of the young Strindberg's position: in the first case the bourgeois become gods, in the other the gods become bourgeois. This attitude of defiance was partly influenced by models that the youthful Strindberg had found in the works of some of the Titan worshipers among the romantics. Therefore, one finds certain features of Faust and Manfred in the characterization of the Stranger, as well as hints of romantic Luciferism in general.

These attitudes and the moods they create emerge with particular clarity in the first scene by the sea, where the Stranger, in a pantheistic rapture, plays with the idea that he himself is God. His ecstatic hymn of creation pulsates with an emotional power that makes one think of the young Goethe:

This is what it means to live! Yes, just now, at this very moment, I am alive! And I feel my self swelling, extending itself, becoming rarefied, becoming infinite: I am everywhere: in the sea that is my blood, in the mountains that are my skeleton, in the trees, in the flowers. And my head reaches up to heaven. I look out upon the universe which is my self; and I feel the whole power of the Creator in me, for it is my self. I would like to take the whole mass in my hand and knead it into something more perfect, more permanent, more beautiful . . . would like to see all creation and every created being happy: born without pain, live without sorrow, and die with quiet joy! [72]

The Titanism in *To Damascus,* however, is not tragic in the same sense as it is in *By the Open Sea.* This time the superman is forced to lay down his arms and to be rehabilitated in the moral order of the world. But he is no cowed and lifeless prisoner, dragged back the way he came behind the triumphal car of the Almighty. He bears his head high, and his defiance has not been quelled.

The Stranger is brought to his knees by the pangs of his own conscience, as illustrated by the scene in the asylum. The same kind of soul-searching analysis of one's past life that was central to Strindberg's Inferno crisis also occupies the center of this play. But just as Strindberg's Titanism entailed awareness of approaching defeat, so

276 Strindberg in Inferno

his submission contains an echo of defiance. The Stranger is so crushed by self-reproach that he thinks he has been "in hell," but his skepticism arises once again as soon as he catches his breath. On his journey back to the scene of his crimes, he tries out a new hypothesis concerning existence: let me see how things go if I think the best of people, instead of thinking the worst. As long as the play lasts, the hypothesis works rather well. The registered letter that the Stranger manages to fetch from the post office in the last scene should probably not be seen as a sign of "capitulation" on the part of the world order, but it does confirm the supposition that the Stranger is on the right path. Yet one feels that this pious mood has taken possession of only a part of the Stranger's being. His suspicion and his attitude of rebellion survive beneath the surface.

The road back is also the road forward. When Strindberg-the Stranger is left at the door of the church, he is a skeptical but shaken gentleman from the nineteenth century after Christ; and it is understood that his further wanderings will never lead him into the church. "Oh well! Of course, I can always pass through it, but I'll never stay!" He will not be found sitting in churches on the square or in expiatory chapels by the roadside. He will go forth to meet new anguish, new battles, and fearful new experiences of the problem of guilt and atonement, of life and coexistence.

Appendix, Notes, Bibliography, and Index

Notes

Translator's Preface to the Notes

The critical apparatus in Gunnar Brandell's original work was divided into two parts. On the one hand, he followed the standard Swedish practice of citing Strindberg's published works from John Landquist's critical edition, *Strindbergs Samlade Skrifter*, vols. 1–55 (Stockholm, 1912–1922), identifying the volume and page numbers after each citation in the body of the text. Since Landquist's edition is presumably unavailable to the readers of this translation, it seemed advisable to eliminate these references from the text. On the other hand, since in preparing this work Brandell went through a considerable body of hitherto unpublished material, which he identified or discussed in footnotes, it seemed essential to retain as many of the original footnotes as possible. Many of the letters that he found in various archives or scattered collections can now be easily located by reference to the dates in the new edition of Strindberg's correspondence, *Strindbergs Brev*, which first began to appear in 1948 under the editorship of Torsten Eklund. The part of the "Occult Diary" from which most of Brandell's citations are taken remains unpublished and is preserved in the manuscript department of the Royal Library in Stockholm. Also unpublished are the many drafts, manuscripts, and laboratory protocols that Brandell studied in the Strindberg Archives of the Nordic Museum, Stockholm. I have retained the Swedish form of referring to these archives, NMS (Nordiska Museets Strindbergsarkivalia), followed by the capsule number and often by a number in parentheses that refers to the section within the capsule. Whenever possible, Brandell dated and identified the paper on which a passage was written as a means of helping to fix its date of composition. Finally, since much of the Strindberg material that Brandell dealt with, including *Inferno* itself, was written in French, whenever Brandell included an extract in the text in Swedish translation, he followed it in the notes with Strindberg's (sometimes curious) French original.

1. Introduction and Background

1. Axel Herrlin, *Från sekelslutets Lund* (Lund, 1936), p. 140.

2. Martin Lamm, *Strindberg och makterna* (Stockholm, 1936), p. 30.

3. The best Swedish discussion of the supposed connection between fear and religion in Lévy-Bruhl, Ribot, Renan, and others is in the article "Fruktan" in Kinberg's *Psykologisk pedagogisk Uppslagsbok*, I, 574. In the light of Haeckel's thesis concerning the parallelism between ontogeny and phylogeny, identification of the religious concepts of the child and the savage appeared quite natural. In *Tjänstekvinnans son* (*The Son of a Servant*, 1886) Strindberg says, speaking of himself in the third person (as he does consistently in his autobiography), "He was an atheist, as children are, but like savages and animals in the dark he sensed the presence of evil spirits" (I, 18).

4. Lamm, p. 18.

5. *Ibid.*, p. 16.

6. Torsten Eklund, *Tjänstekvinnans son: en psykologisk Strindbergsstudie* (Stockholm, 1948), p. 20.

7. The mechanism whereby social morality is "interiorized" to form a superego or a conscience has been interpreted in different ways. Authorities agree, however, that moral demands are established in the childhood situation and reflect, more or less directly, the commandments and prohibitions of the parents, especially those of the father. In his *Samvetets uppkomst* (Stockholm, 1949), S. Wermlund summarizes modern discussions of this question; see especially ch. I and pp. 102 ff.

8. Eklund, p. 23.

9. According to Freud, the sense of guilt is an essential component in compulsive neuroses, but it can be either conscious or unconscious. In the latter case, neurotic actions assume the character of redemptive suffering. Cf. Freud's "Hemmung,

Symptom und Angst" in his *Gesammelte Werke* (London, 1947), XIV, 147: "Es gibt auch Zwangsneurosen ganz ohne Schuldbewusstsein; soweit wir es verstehen, hat sich das Ich die Wahrnehmung desselben durch eine neue Reihe von Symptomen, Busshandlungen, Einschränkungen zur Selbstbestrafung, erspart." At the same time, according to Freud, these actions imply "Befriedigungen masochistischer Triebregungen."

10. Eklund, p. 29.

11. That guilt feelings occupy such a central place in this introductory study certainly does not imply that I feel Strindberg's whole psychic constitution can be externally explained by means of this single component. Yet no literary study oriented toward deep psychology can overlook the necessity for careful documentation, and it must avoid interpretations that have little evidence (or at best very unclear evidence) to back them up, even though psychiatric evidence might tend to suggest that these interpretations are quite probable. Not only the nature of the material but also the scholar's situation in relation to his material serves to create a wide gap between the literary historian and the therapeutic psychologist. Nothing can alter the fact that the literary scholar must confine himself almost exclusively to those features of the psychic picture that are closest to the conscious mind; the degree of penetration he can attain by a carefully documented presentation depends to a certain extent on the level of insight that the author he is studying had into himself. In the case of Strindberg, guilt feelings have seemed to me, from certain points of view, to provide a suitable point of departure.

For my own part, I am convinced that various other psychological concepts besides the one employed in this work could be used to great advantage to illuminate the development of Strindberg's character. Like the probable homosexual component in his nature, neither his aggressiveness, nor his masochistic tendencies, nor his sexual anxiety and fear of castration can be totally explained as functions of his guilt feelings. Both primary and secondary guilt feelings do play a palpable role, however, in all of these connections. Moreover, this approach has the advantage that it can be directly supported by material based on clinical evidence from many other individuals besides Strindberg.

A factual matter reinforces this choice of method. Strindberg's sense of guilt was the psychic factor closest to the center of his Inferno crisis, as it was for all of his religious crises; it was also intimately connected with his erotic life and with his persecution ideas. Indeed, by placing his sense of guilt at the center of my investigation, I believe that I am able to show the coherent relation between the ideas and the mythological motifs that accompany his religious crises.

Consequently, this method does not preclude other psychological approaches, and I have no occasion to indulge in polemics against authors who have used other concepts than the one I have chosen. For Torsten Eklund, inferiority feelings and a need for self-assertion become Strindberg's central problems; Eklund's observations are striking, but his image of Strindberg becomes superficial in the very points that are presented here as essential: the moral and religious aspects of his development. The psychoanalytical authors, among whom special attention should be called to Karl Bachler (*August Strindberg: Eine psychoanalytische Studie*) and A. J. Uppvall (*August Strindberg*), seem to me to have a more profound understanding of the religious component in Strindberg's nature, particularly in light of his Oedipus situation; but their works suffer all along the line from faulty knowledge of the primary materials.

The weakness of previous psychological studies of Strindberg lies in the fact that all interpretations of Strindberg's character based on this approach neglect the dynamic aspect of his nature. They elucidate the components of Strindberg's psychic constitution and apply the results attained to his behavior in such a way that he emerges as monotonously the same from youth to old age. However, one cannot disregard Strindberg's striking capacity for regeneration. Just as in the case of the Inferno crisis, in dealing with Strindberg's development as a whole, one must use an approach that is flexible enough to account for the continuity as well as the development. Partly it must show how the conflict situations repeat themselves; partly how Strindberg, especially during his major crises, also rearranges the material provided by his life and experiments with it until he has arrived at new points of view. This is precisely the kind of approach that I have attempted to employ— somewhat sketchily in the introductory section, more thoroughly in the remaining chapters of this work.

The two most important psychiatrically oriented works on Strindberg, Karl Jaspers' *Strindberg und van Gogh: Versuch einer pathographischen Analyse* (Bern, 1922) and A. Storch's *August Strindberg im Lichte seiner Selbstbiographie* (Munich, 1921), are much more disposed to pay proper attention to the question of his development. Since that sort of presentation must be based largely on the author's correspondence and printed papers, both of these works are dated or hindered because of the fact that their authors were unfamiliar with most of the essential source material. Nonetheless, Storch's rather chaotically presented study still appears to contain the richest and most subtle psychiatric analysis of Strindberg's personality, even though it is often questionable in matters of detail. Jaspers' work, with all its symptomatology and diagnostics, is less useful to the literary historian; he appears radically to have underestimated the possibility of a "sympathetic" interpretation of Strindberg's psychoses. The extent to which his diagnosis, "periods of schizophrenia," is correct is a question that ought to be reexamined in the light of modern psychiatric findings. Nowadays, schizophrenia is hardly the unambiguous term it was for Jaspers, and Strindberg would really seem to be best described as a "borderline case."

Of course, earlier observers have noticed that guilt feelings are central for Strindberg. In his fruitful study of Strindberg's "guilt," *Strindbergs skuld: Madonnan och järnjungfrun* (Stockholm, 1927), Olle Holmberg has pointed out the connection between Strindberg's "guilt" and his "hatred." In this context one should also mention Ester Peukert's speculative monograph, *Strindbergs religiöse Dramatik* (Hamburg, 1929), because she has made an excellent case for the role that guilt feelings and pangs of conscience played in the Inferno crisis. Various other scholars have also touched on this emotional configuration in passing.

1973 Addenda by the Author: The Swedish psychiatrist Sven Hedenberg has corroborated the above statement. In his book *Strindberg i skärselden* (1961), he categorically refuted Jaspers' diagnosis. Instead of schizophrenia, one should consider a "psychogenic and constitutional psychosis," which includes serious psychic illness.

12. Eklund, p. 32.

13. "La chute, oui, la chute est immédiatement accompagnée des remords, et je me vois en costume de nuit, assis à la table le livre des prières devant moi, à la lueur faible de l'aube d'été. Honte et remords, malgré l'ignorance complète de la nature du péché. Innocent puisque inconscient, et tout de même coupable. Seduit et puis seducteur; repentirs et rechutes; doutes sur la véracité de la conscience qui accuse!"

14. Cf. also Strindberg's account in his essay entitled "Religious Renaissance" (1910), where he gives even greater emphasis to the melancholy aspect of his youthful pietism (*Talks to the Swedish Nation,* pp. 244 f.).

15. NMS 6 (14), Lessebo paper.

16. See Lamm, *Strindberg och makterna,* p. 18.

17. E. Rodhe, *Den religiösa liberalism: Nils Ignell–Viktor Rydberg–Pontus Wikner* (Stockholm, 1935), p. 208.

18. Lamm (*Strindberg och makterna,* pp. 38 f.) compared this statement with Strindberg's description of his Kierkegaardianism in *The Son of a Servant* and found that the latter was colored by his polemical irreligiosity at the time that he wrote his autobiography. Strindberg maintains in *The Son of a Servant* that he "did not know Kierkegaard was a Christian, but believed he was the opposite." Several months passed, however, between Strindberg's first reading of *Either/Or* and the student essay he wrote in Stockholm about Oehlenschläger's tragedy, *Hakon Jarl,* where he mentions Kierkegaard's *Training in Christianity.* It is not unlikely that during those months in Uppsala, when his impression of Kierkegaard was strongest, he really did not yet have a very clear understanding of the direction of this philosophy. In the meantime at the Royal Library in Stockholm he became acquainted with other works by Kierkegaard, including *The Concept of Dread* and *Repetition,*—as shown by the records of his borrowings from the library on Feb. 1, 1871—and then he understood that he was dealing with a Christian thinker.

19. For details of the short story, see later in this chapter, p. 50.

20. In Wilhelm Carlheim-Gyllensköld's collection of Strindbergiana at the Royal Library (Kungliga bibliotek) in Stockholm, capsule E, quarto 28.

21. Cf. Lamm, *Strindberg och makterna,* p. 40.

22. S. Kierkegaard, *Repetition: An Essay in Experimental Psychology,* trans. W. Lowrie (Princeton, N.J., 1946), pp. 111–113.

23. "Séduit la femme d'un autre," "un jeune célibataire debauché par une putain mariée." A similar passage turns up years later in *A Blue Book* (1907), p. 155, in the

essay "Nemesis humana." Cf. H. Jacobsen, *Strindberg og hans første Hustru* (Copenhagen, 1946), pp. 32 f.

24. See K. Smirnoff, *Strindbergs första hustru* (Stockholm, 1925), p. 130: "Le sens moral: il y a un amour qui n'est pas sensuel et qui ne s'achève ni veut être achevé par le mariage. *Notice* la difference exquise entre l'amour legitimé du mari, qui demande et celui de l'amant qui ne demande rien et qui néanmoins est coupable aux yeux du monde."

25. It seems to be generally agreed that through a process of retrospective analysis when writing *A Madman's Defense,* Strindberg assigned the origin of these ideas of jealousy to this early period of their intimacy. Cf. Jaspers, p. 21; Jacobsen, p. 32.

26. See esp. Bachler, p. 17.

27. *A Madman's Defense,* p. 45. Cf. Strindberg's letter to his publisher, K. O. Bonnier (Jan. 28, 1909); Erik Hedén, *Strindberg* (Stockholm, 1926), p. 19.

28. According to an entry in *The Occult Diary* (Feb. 14, 1901), Strindberg's third wife, Harriet Bosse, reminded him partly of his mother and his sister, Anna; partly of his second wife, Frida Uhl, and a woman he had known in Paris during the Inferno crisis, Mme. Lecain. Nor was Strindberg the only person to be struck by these outer signs of consistency in his erotic choices. Cf. Ruth Stjernstedt in the Christmas number of *Idun,* 1948.

29. In September 1872, Strindberg read *Manfred* for the second time and found it "great." Cf. his letter to Eugène Fahlstedt, one of his friends during his brief career as a student at Uppsala (Sept. 30, 1872). It was Fahlstedt who, years later, was to translate Strindberg's original French version of *Inferno* into Swedish.

30. Cf. Eklund, pp. 268 ff.

31. For the romantic Titanism in the figure of Master Olof, cf. Per Lindberg, "Tillkomsten av Strindbergs 'Mäster Olof' " (Stockholm, 1915), pp. 45 f.

32. Byron, *The Works: Poetry,* ed. E. H. Coleridge (London, 1903–1905), IV, 85 f.

33. M. Lamm, *Strindbergs dramer* (Stockholm, 1924–1926), I, 171; Eklund, p. 289.

34. Eklund, pp. 288 f. gives strong emphasis to this very point.

35. Lamm, *Strindbergs dramer,* I, 172.

36. Eklund, p. 438; Georg Brandes, *Naturalismen i England* (Copenhagen, 1900), pp. 541 ff.

37. For discussions of occultism in nineteenth century French literature, see A. Viatte, *Victor Hugo et les illuminés de son temps* (Montreal, 1942); M. Rudwin, *Les écrivains diaboliques de France* (Paris, 1937).

38. Wilhelm Carlheim-Gyllensköld, an intimate friend of Strindberg and an indefatigable collector of Strindbergiana, learned from Eugène Fahlstedt, who was on the editorial board of the *Nordisk familjebok* in the 1870s, that Strindberg had asked permission to write the article "The Devil," which was his only contribution to the encyclopedia. Once, according to Fahlstedt, Strindberg and his friends went up to

the Royal Library in Stockholm at night and Strindberg read aloud from "The Devil's Bible" by the light of phosphorous matches (Carlheim-Gyllensköld, *Strindbergiana,* capsule 21). In an essay in Stockholm's leading newspaper, *Dagens Nyheter,* on Jan. 6, 1929, Ruben G. Berg offers a different version of the genesis of this article.

39. Cf. Lamm, *Strindbergs dramer,* I, 194; Herrlin, *Från sekelslutets Lund,* pp. 156 f.; Eklund, p. 290.

40. Georg Brandes, *Søren Kierkegaard* (Copenhagen, 1899), p. 266.

41. Nathan Söderblom, *Svenskars fromhet* (Stockholm, 1933), p. 287.

42. Quoted from Erik Lie, *Erindringer fra et Dikterhjem* (Oslo, 1928), p. 122. Cf. also the letter to K. O. Bonnier (Dec. 17, 1883): "It is not the blows I receive, but those I strike that hurt me most, believe me."

43. Strindberg is thinking here of his friend, customs inspector Ossian Ekbohrn (1837–1911), whom he first met on the island of Sandhamn in the Stockholm archipelago in 1868. When Strindberg spent several months on Sandhamn in the autumn of 1873, they became close friends. When he returned to Sandhamn in 1889, he found that Ekbohrn was suffering from hypersensitivity, hypochondria, and megalomania. Strindberg attributed Ekbohrn's nervous condition to the isolated existence he had led for seventeen years on Sandhamn.

Delusions of persecution are here taken to be a projection of Strindberg's guilt feelings. Modern psychology applies a similar "sympathetic" interpretation to the psychotic contents of the schizophrenic's consciousness. The mechanism of projection can be observed both in "normal" personality types and in neurotic and schizoid types, and the concept of Strindberg's paranoid delusions (both before and during the Inferno crisis) employed here is not intended to represent a diagnosis of his illness. Cf., for example, a modern psychological handbook, *Encyclopedia of Psychology,* ed. Philip L. Harriman (New York, 1946), in the article "The Psychoses" where it deals with the schizophrenic personality: "His ego, extremely sensitive in the prepsychotic personality, is even more sensitive in the illness, and guilt feelings are rationalized into acceptable 'others-being-responsible' causes (delusions). The projection mechanism is strongly operative in the delusions and hallucinations" (p. 666).

44. Theodore Parker also makes this distinction between a conventional and a natural conscience. See his *Samlade skrifter,* trans. into Swedish by V. Pfeiff and A. F. Åkerberg (Uppsala, 1867–1875), IX, 8.

45. Strindberg's psychological portrait of Alrik Lundstedt was probably inspired by Schopenhauer, the first writer to give a clear description of "the flight into sickness." Cf. Eklund, pp. 296 f., where he cites the relevant passage from Schopenhauer.

46. In this context one might also cite Strindberg's curious novella, *Tschandala* (1888), which was inspired by unpleasant events that took place in the summer of 1888 during his stay at Skovlyst, the country estate of a shabby Danish noblewoman, Countess Frankenau. While there, Strindberg became involved in a quarrel

with the steward of the estate, Hansen, who was part gypsy. When Strindberg falsely reported Hansen to the authorities for theft, Hansen avenged himself by complaining to the police (with justice) that his sister had been seduced by Strindberg. Strindberg was so frightened by the possible consequences of this little affair that he fled to Berlin. Although Hansen was later sentenced to six months' imprisonment for attempted blackmail, Strindberg remained so terrified of him that he carried a revolver, even after his return to Sweden in 1889. Hansen figures in the novella as a thoroughly unscrupulous gypsy who is pitted against Strindberg's Aryan surrogate, Magister Törner, an intellectual superman who easily outwits his rival. Although the events in the novella correspond closely to the reality, Strindberg was careful to make Törner entirely innocent of the sexual lapse that had precipitated his own flight to Berlin. Although I omit this affair in the text here, it clearly shows how guilt feelings could activate Strindberg's persecution mania.

47. Lamm, *August Strindberg,* p. 207.

48. See Eklund, the chapter "Nietzscheanism and the Idea of the Superman in Strindberg." Eklund's research seems to demonstrate that the concept "Nietzscheanism" is generally ill-suited as a description of Strindberg's outlook at this time. The "Titanism of the intellectual aristocrat" comes closer to describing his real and rather contradictory position. Naturally, Nietzsche himself was also influenced by the contempt for the masses and the worship of the exceptional individual that he found in Schopenhauer and in various romantic writers. Many impulses are fused in the idea of the superman, and Strindberg was never exclusively devoted to Nietzsche. Concerning Byron, Nietzsche, and Gustaf Fröding, cf. S. Sjöholm, *Övermänniskotanken i Gustaf Frödings diktning* (Gothenburg, 1940), pp. 188 ff.

49. Hugo, *Les travailleurs de la mer,* in his *Oeuvres complètes* (Paris, 1911), the chapter "Homo edax," pp. 43 ff. Eklund in his "Strindbergs I havsbandet" (*Edda,* 1929) demonstrated the important influence of this work on *By the Open Sea.*

50. The short story, "The Silver Marsh," was written in its present form in the summer of 1898. On July 4, 1898, Strindberg sent it to F. U. Wrangel, editor of the magazine *Vintergatan,* noting that it had been conceived eight years earlier and that "its principal features were true." The manuscript later discovered at the Bonnier publishing firm is a neat copy on Bikupa paper (1894) and, as far as I can tell, gives no concrete evidence for deciding exactly when the work was first written.

Strindberg planned this story on several occasions. He first mentioned it in letters to K. O. Bonnier on July 13 and 29, 1890, where he envisages "The Silver Marsh" as a Christmas book "for the altar of the home." A description he gives two years later comes closer to the completed work, for this time Strindberg says he wants to write "a long subjective story about the Silver Marsh with no natural science, but lots of psychology and nature descriptions" (letter to Albert Bonnier, April 1, 1892). An undated letter from Strindberg to Bonnier in 1893 states that *La Nouvelle Revue* in Paris was going to publish the story, and the next year Strindberg informs Frida Uhl that the journal has announced publication of "The Silver Marsh" for January 15 (Dec. 3, 1894). This letter to Frida gives the impression that by then the story was finished and had been submitted to the journal; it is, however, based on an erroneous translation, for the original reads: "La nouvelle Revue a commandé das Silbermoor pour 15 Janvier, que tu traduiras en allemand." Thus, once again we are dealing with a projected, not a completed work. In the summer of 1898, when Strindberg resumed work on the story, he was not simply writing it out or translating it from French, for a letter from Strindberg to the young poet Emil Kléen suggests a much more comprehensive activity: "Am now writing about the Runmarö marsh and would love to talk it over with you" (July 1, 1898).

In all probability, Lamm was right in assuming (*August Strindberg,* p. 208) that the story was largely executed in 1898. On one point at least, the numerical speculations, one can find a firm connection between material in this story and the views he is known to have held in 1898, for he has borrowed one of the sentences in the story, "But the meter was a cosmic number, since it was one ten-millioneth of the quadrant of the earth," from one of his "alchemical" works, *Types and Prototypes in the Chemistry of Minerals,* datelined "Paris, March, 1898."

But Lamm seems too hasty in his judgment on the ending of the story, when he writes that here Strindberg, "in contrast to his later practice," lets the curator make a supervisory control that shows the hollowness of his numerical speculations (p. 209). By "later" he means the time during and after the Inferno crisis. But the story was written in 1898. Would Strindberg really have drafted a conclusion that was opposed to the belief he held at the time? Actually, Strindberg corroborates the curator's speculations by including a newspaper clipping about the treasure in the mountain on Runmarö, and the "supervisory control" that clears away the mirage should be interpreted as a maneuver of the powers that guard the marsh. That anyone who wished to penetrate nature's secrets should be prepared to be mocked and misled was a part of Strindberg's outlook in 1898, when he decided to give up "magic." Moreover, he was always—even during and after the crisis—half aware that such speculations were more a *jeu d'esprit* than a reality.

However, we have Strindberg's own word that he conceived the story at the beginning of the 1890s, and both its milieu and its events clearly belong to that period. That the conception should retain its vitality for him through so many years shows how essential the Titan motif was to his outlook throughout the 1890s.

51. Schopenhauer, *Parerga* (Leipzig, 1919), II, 688.

52. Cf. Lamm, *August Strindberg,* p. 200; Eklund, *Tjänstekvinnans son,* pp. 362 ff.

53. Borg originally considers it stupid to risk his life in small open boats, but after he becomes acquainted with Maria, he sails fearlessly about in his peter boat. Then he takes out his trusty pipe and comfortable dressing gown, accessories that seem more characteristic of Strindberg himself than of the refined decadent in the introductory chapters of the novel. After his first break with his fiancée, Borg

changes his hair style, having earlier combed his hair to suit her taste. This episode also occurs in *A Madman's Defense*, where Strindberg "removes the bangs she required me to wear." Inspector Borg, however, had worn his hair in just this coquettish fashion since the beginning of the book.

54. "Esseulé par son despotisme et ses tracasseries contre les insulaires qui le haissent cet homme vit avec sa femme sans commerce avec le monde. Il n'a pas parlé en six mois, et je fus pris de pitié avec mon ennemi, retrouvé comme un naufragé. Il parle, parle, cinq heures, dix heures, l'écume aux lèvres, le cerveau en feu. Il a pensé, il a philosophé, et il est inventeur d'une foule de choses déjà inventées. Mais je l'excite à s'épancher, et il fait une éruption pendant trois jours. Sa femme me confie à la dérobé qu'il a la manie des grandeurs . . . tiens! Ça y est! Il croit être un Napoléon relegué à l'île de St Helène. Il m'aime; se félicite d'avoir trouvé un égal (hein!) m'honore de la confiance de ses pensées secrètes et sacrées. Je fais l'humble, le comprenant, de ses vastes vus sur la vie et l'univers." NMS 6 (17), Bikupa paper, 1893.

55. B. Fr. Sanner ("Strindbergs väg ur ateismen," *Religion och Kultur,* 1935) has noticed this fear of isolation, which certain psychoanalysts would describe as "fear of the loss of an object." Sanner goes too far, however, in wishing to deduce the whole course of the crisis from the interchange between isolation and a sense of communion with God. According to him, the emptiness left by God when Strindberg became an atheist was filled by various surrogates—women, for example—and when the surrogate proved insufficient, Strindberg returned to his belief in God. It would be more correct to say that a relation to God became for him a surrogate for human relations, but this is only one of the psychological motifs of his conversion.

56. The insertion, which is nearly three pages long in Landquist's edition of Strindberg's collected works, was submitted to the publisher, K. O. Bonnier, on June 27, 1890, along with a letter containing the following notation: "Here is an insertion for the last chapter which should go in later—after the maid has set the lantern on the floor and left." Landquist does not say anything about this in the commentary.

57. "It seems to me that I am walking in my sleep, that life and poetry are fused" (letter to Axel Lundegård, Nov. 12, 1887), cited by Lundegård, *Några Strindbergsminnen* (Stockholm, 1920), p. 66. Other works that Strindberg wrote at this period, especially *The Keys to Heaven* (1892), contain many motifs similar to those I have analyzed here in *By the Open Sea*.

2. The Inferno Psychoses

1. "Je me suis fait le petit, le faible, sans le savoir, afin que tu fusses capable de m'aimer n'importe de quelle façon" (Mar. 22, 1893). Frida Strindberg, *Strindberg och hans andra hustru,* I, 242.

2. Frida Strindberg, II, 95.

3. Karl Jaspers, *Strindberg und van Gogh* (Bern, 1922), p. 11; Eklund, *Tjänste-kvinnans son*, p. 174.

4. In letters to them, Strindberg invited Bengt Lidforss (Feb. 28, 1894), Georges Loiseau (May 23, 1894), and Adolf Paul (April 3, 1894) to Ardagger (near Dornach, where his wife's grandparents lived). Cf. A. Paul, *Min Strindbergsbok* (Stockholm, 1930), pp. 152 f.

5. Frida Strindberg, II, 242.

6. Frida Strindberg, I, 156 f.

7. Frida Strindberg, II, 71.

8. "Une incompatibilité d'humeurs indéfinissable."

9. Frida Strindberg, II, 182.

10. Frida Strindberg, II, 183 f.

11. Frida Strindberg, II, 261.

12. "Mir is alles, Vergangenes und Gegenwärtiges zusammangeflossen wie im Traum, und das Leben macht mir Seekrank obgleich das Meer nicht" (undated, from Strindberg's journey between Hamburg and Rügen). Frida Strindberg, II, 46.

13. "Eine hohe schwarz angezogene Dame" (Feb. 7, 1895).

14. Cf. *A Madman's Defense*, p. 345, and Strindberg's one-acter, *First Warning*. Shortly after he moved into the Hôtel Orfila on Feb. 21, 1896, Strindberg began to keep the notebook that he called his "Occult Diary." It begins as a collection of quotations—many from the Bible—interlaced with chemical formulae, curious events, thoughts and accounts of his dreams. In the sixth chapter of *Inferno*, Strindberg publishes extracts from the diary for May and June 1896. Whereas the early section of the diary provided Strindberg with the raw material that he worked over in an attempt to find a pattern of meaning in his life, the part of the diary covering the period between May 31, 1900, and his last entry on July 11, 1908, contains a detailed account of Strindberg's complex relations with his third wife, Harriet Bosse. In 1963, Torsten Eklund published this latter portion of the famous diary, and the text has subsequently been translated into English by Mary Sandbach. The manuscript of the entire diary is a part of the Strindberg archives in the Royal Library in Stockholm.

15. "Ein Jahr alt, hässlich von Bier aufgeschwollen und rauchend Cigarette" (undated). Frida Strindberg, II, 373.

16. "Keine Gewissensbissen," "nur Abscheu und tiefe Sorge" (undated). Frida Strindberg, II, 373.

17. "Wo lebst Du, wo lebt die Kleine, was treibst Du, und was hoffst Du von deinem (mistake for 'diesem'?) elenden Leben?" Frida Strindberg, II, 393.

18. "Ne soyez pas mon ennemi! Seulement laissez-moi! Laissez-moi avec mes chagrins!" (undated). Frida Strindberg, II, 420.

19. "Donc nous cesserons jamais d'être en parenté! Toi et moi!" (undated, from Saint-Louis Hospital). Frida Strindberg, II, 396.

20. Frida Strindberg, II, 439 ff.

290 Notes to Pages 73–79

21. "L'argent me déniche; je peux acheter des livres, des objets appartenant à l'historie naturelle, un microscope entre autres qui me révèle les mystères de la vie."

22. According to a statement by Torsten Hedlund, datelined "Gothenburg, October, 1922" and preserved in the Hedlund Archives in the Municipal Library of Gothenburg, this money came from a wholesale grocer named August Röhss.

23. "Et je sens que cet homme est un de mes bienfaiteurs anonymes, qu'il m'a fait la charité et que je suis un mendiant qui n'a pas le droit de visiter le café. Mendiant! C'est le mot propre qui me sonne à l'oreille et me fait brûler les joues, de honte, d'humiliation et de rage."

24. Jean Lundin and Strindberg had been friends in youth, and Strindberg portrays Lundin as the "lieutenant" in The Red Room (1879). For Strindberg's account of his subsequent deterioration, see his remarks concerning "Carl *** " in his collection of stories Fair Haven and Foul Strand (1902), pp. 224 f.

25. "Heureux de ne point ressembler à ce buveur."

26. "Il me donne un sou comme à un mendiant! Mendiant! voilà le poignard que je m'enfonce à la poitrine! Mendiant! oui car tu ne gagnes rien et que . . ."

27. "D'un vice qui mène à la maison des aliénés."

28. "Mauvaise Société, alcool, veilles, chat noir, déséspoir et le reste, surtout paralysie." Frida Strindberg, op. cit., II, 344 ff.

29. "Und ohne Frau und Heimat gehe ich zu Grunde! Verurteilt zu trinken!"

30. K. Smirnoff, Strindbergs första hustru (Stockholm, 1925), pp. 345, 362.

31. W. Berendsohn in his Strindbergsproblem (Stockholm, 1946), p. 92, suggested the possibility of using Strindberg's letters and diary as a guide in delimiting the period of his illness.

32. Frida Strindberg, II, 258 f.

33. On this question, see Frida Strindberg, II, 256 f.

34. "Veuillez me regarder comme un malade et croyez que j'ai mes raisons suffisantes pour chercher la solitude."

35. "Fouetté par des Euménides."

36. "Un décrépitude naissante m'envahit peu à peu. Les mains noires et sanglantes m'empêchent de m'habiller et de soigner ma toilette. La peur de la note de l'hôtel ne me laisse plus de repos et je me promène dans ma chambre comme une bête dans la cage."

37. Cf. Frida Strindberg, II, 363 f.; Smirnoff, p. 344.

38. Frida Strindberg, II, 356. Frida Strindberg interprets Strindberg's reaction in connection with the "farewell letter" in the same way as here.

39. Frida Strindberg, II, 358.

40. "Une furie de me faire du mal," "suicide et assasin," "les remords."

41. "Ma Mère" (undated, from Saint-Louis Hospital). Frida Strindberg, II, 396.

42. "Pas un mot de reproche, pas de remontrances, ni d'exhortations."

43. "Je me dis que c'est une intrigue montée de ces dames Scandinaves dont la société j'ai refusée."

44. "Laissant livres et bibelots."

45. "Une éruption d'amour interverti," "une catastrophe réunissant deux coeurs, comme dans les romans les mains hostiles se recontrent au chevet d'un malade."

46. "Cependant, et afin de rompre un lien funeste je cherche l'occasion de remplacer mon affection par une autre, et aussitôt mes voeux malhonnêtes sont exaucés."

47. "Plus d'amour! le mot d'ordre des puissances est reçu."

48. "Mendiant, avec des obligations non accomplies vers ma famille, j'eus voulu entâmer une liaison compromettante pour une fille honnête."

49. These motifs recur later in *Crimes and Crimes* (1899).

50. "À observer des bagatelles negligées auparavant."

51. "Hermann" was in reality Paul Hermann, whose artistic pseudonym was Henri Héran. Cf. S. Bengtsson, "Vad Strindberg läste i Lund," *Svensk litteraturtidskrift* (1946), pp. 27 f.

52. "Une tête coupée fut rattachée au tronc d'un homme ayant l'air d'un acteur usé par l'ivrognerie. La tête commença à parler; j'eus peur et renversa un paravent en poussant un Russe devant moi pour me garder contre l'attaque de l'homme enragé."

53. "L'objet d'un courant électrique lancé entre les deux chambres voisines."

54. One can follow the "Aspasia" affair in Strindberg's correspondence with Bengt Lidforss and Adolf Paul. Guided by traditions emanating from Przybyszewski, M. Herman sketched a portrait of Strindberg's "Aspasia" in the chapter "Dagny Juel" in his *Un sataniste polonais: Stanislas Przybyszewski (de 1868 à 1900)*, (Paris, 1939). He seems, however, to have misunderstood the relationship between her and Strindberg. The best account of this affair in English is found in Evert Sprinchorn's extensive introduction to his translations of *Inferno, Alone, and Other Writings* (New York, 1968).

55. Strindberg himself said that he thought of "both of his wives as being the same size" (letter to T. Hedlund, July 9, 1896). It is not difficult to explain why he dreamed of this particular clock. In *Inferno* he mentions that he had earlier admired Carpeaux' "The Four Quarters of the Earth" in the park of the Observatoire in Paris, because one of the four female figures reminded him of his wife (p. 57). "Lie's clock," as he describes it in the book, was clearly similar to Carpeaux' group; there too, for example, the women were supporting a globe.

56. On the factual background of these events, see Herman, pp. 84 f.; Sprinchorn, pp. 71 ff.

57. G. Uddgren, *En ny bok om Strindberg* (Gothenburg, 1912), pp. 69 ff. Cf. what Maria Uhl, Frida's sister, tells about Strindberg's stay in Austria: when conversation came around to the political unrest in Vienna, Strindberg protested against the thought, obviously expressed by no one, that he was its instigator (interview with M. Uhl by K. de Pers in *Göteborgs Handels Tidning*, Jan. 31 and Feb. 8, 1924).

58. "C'est le rappel à la vie!—Je commence à renaître, au reveil d'un longue

mauvais rêve, et je comprends la bonne volonté du Maître sévère qui m'a puni de la main dure et intelligente."

59. "Et en même temps je ressentis vivement que tout ceci est fini, qu'il doit rester enseveli pour livrer la place à du nouveaux."

60. "Une lueur rose, mais rose incarnat."

61. "D'un printemps et d'un amour qui ne reviendra jamais, jamais!"

62. "Un poème, inspiré d'une âme qui n'existe qu'à demi sur la terre"; "la couche d'une vierge."

63. "Faute de mieux je suis obligé de prendre leur encre qui est rouge incarnat! Etrange tout de même! Un paquet de papier à cigarettes renferme entre les cent blancs une feuille rose! (Rose!) C'est l'enfer au petit feu."

64. "La nuit je fais ce rêve. Un aigle me picote la main en punition pour une cause inconnue."

65. "Les remords d'un côté, la crainte d'un autre."

66. Smirnoff, p. 362.

67. In a letter to Ola Hansson (Jan. 8, 1907) he writes: "Even so long afterwards I am unable to unravel life's tangled skein; but I remember, feeling guilty in Lund, expressing my remorse to both of you and begging your indulgence."

68. Smirnoff, pp. 364 f. Cf. N. Norman, "Strindberg i Lund," *Nittiotalsstudier tillägnade Olle Holmberg, Svensk litteraturtidskrift, tilläggshäfte,* 1943, pp. 79 f.

69. "Interné donc dans L. petite ville des Muses sans espoir d'issue, je livre la bataille formidable contre l'ennemi, moi.

"Tous les matins en me promenant sur le rempart sous les platanes, l'immense maison rouge des aliénés me rappelle le danger échappé, et l'avenir en cas de rechute. Swedenborg en m'éclairant sur la nature des horreurs survenus la dernière année, m'a délivré des electriciens, des magistes noirs, des envoûteurs, des jaloux faiseurs d'or, et de la folie. Il m'a indiqué la seule voie au salut: chercher les demons dans leur repaire, en moi-même et les tuer par . . . le repentir. Balzac l'aide de camp de prophète m'a enseigné dans Séraphita que le remords est une impuissance, il recommencera sa faute. Le repentir seul est une force, il termine tout."

3. Jacob Wrestles

1. "L'art de faire du mal au besoin," NMS 6 (17), Bikupa paper, 1893.

2. Frida Strindberg, *Strindberg och hans andra hustru,* II, 407.

3. According to a lecture by Julien Leclercq, reported in the Stockholm newspaper *Dagens Nyheter* (Nov. 10, 1897).

4. "C'est qu'une espèce de religion s'est créée en moi quoique je ne pourrais la formuler. Un état d'âme plutôt qu'une opinion fondée sur des théories; un pêle-mêle de sensations plus ou moins condensées en idées.

"Ayant acheté un paroissien romain je le lis avec recueillement; l'Ancien Testament me console et me châtie d'une manière un peu confuse, tandis que le Nouveau me laisse froid. Ce qui n'empêche pas qu'un volume de Bouddhisme exerce une influence plus forte que tous les autres livres sacrés, puisqu'il élève la souffrance positive au dessus de l'abstinence."

5. Cf. M. Lamm, *Strindberg och makterna* (Stockholm, 1936), pp. 15–18.

6. T. Eklund, who regards Strindberg's religion primarily as an "organ for his self-exaltation and his need to feel superior" (*Tjänstekvinnans son*, p. 212), cites these and similar statements from *Inferno* but overlooks the self-criticism they imply. On the whole, Eklund is unwilling to grant the seriousness of Strindberg's self-reproach (pp. 215 f.). If the underlying moral conflict is suppressed, the tension that informs Strindberg's whole Inferno period disappears and the crisis dissolves into a series of futile illusions of grandeur.

7. Strindberg quotes V. Rydberg, *Undersökningar i germanisk mytologi* (Stockholm, 1886–1889), II, 157, 164.

8. As early as 1875, however, Strindberg had borrowed Swedenborg's *Thoughts and Visions in Spiritual Matters* (Stockholm, 1858) from the Royal Library. In his *Svenska folket* (*The Swedish People*), (1881–1882) Strindberg nonchalantly asserts that since he has "not succeeded in forming any opinion" about Swedenborg's spiritual visions and religious activity, he is "leaving him to his fate—to be idolized and reviled."

9. "Cette époque avant la connaissance des doctrines de Swedenborg."

10. "Nous sommes déjà là bas! La terre c'est l'enfer, la prison construite avec une intelligence supérieure, où je ne puis faire un pas sans froisser le bonheur des autres, où les autres ne puissent rester heureux sans me faire de mal."

11. In NMS 9 (2), among other excerpts that Strindberg made from Swedenborg, are some notes he made on Bikupa paper (1893) concerning "Swedenborg's hells," in which he gives the correspondences with Klam point for point.

1973 Addenda by the Author: According to Stockenström, *Ismael i öknen*, p. 57, this is a mistake. These annotations are from 1897 and served as a preparation for *Inferno*. The work Strindberg studied in 1896 was not Pernetty's edition but a German book, based on a French presentation of Swedenborg's theology by Daillant de la Touche.

12. Schopenhauer, *Welt als Wille* (Leipzig, 1919), II, 663, 666 (translated here by John Moore). In *August Strindberg* (p. 275) Lamm pointed out that Strindberg paraphrases Schopenhauer's ideas. Cf. Schopenhauer, 666, and his *Parerga* (Leipzig, 1919), II, 324, where he refers to Luther, Pythagoras, and Origen. The learned apparatus turns up in Strindberg: the references to Pythagoras and Origen in a letter to Hedlund (Oct. 31, 1896) and the reference to Luther in the epilogue to *Inferno*. Thus, there is no doubt that Strindberg borrowed the idea from Schopenhauer. At the same time, he changed its sense to a certain extent. While Schopenhauer uses "hell" symbolically to represent a condition of maximal suffering, Strindberg is thinking of the concrete hell that one finds in various mythologies and, more especially, of the Christian hell. His descriptions are more palpable than Schopenhauer's and thus approach the Gnostic tradition, where the idea originated.

Schopenhauer was a Buddhist, not a Manichean. Even Buddhism can, in a sense, be said to conceive of the world as a hell, and it is described as such in a book that Strindberg had in his library, L. Riotor and G. Léofanti, *Les enfers bouddhiques* (Paris, 1895). But in this case the expression is metaphorical and implies a comparison with Christian doctrine. Strindberg took the parallel literally—at least during his crises.

As in the question of "the evil god," in his discussion of hell Schopenhauer has appropriated popular romantic notions, but used them primarily in a metaphorical sense. In Victor Hugo, for example, one can find the idea that the earth is hell expressed in a more palpable, mythological form, which comes much closer to Strindberg's concept. Thus, in the philosophical preface to *Les misérables,* he writes: "Mais quoi! cet immense monde que nous voyons et dont nous sommes, serait donc l'enfer? Ce monde-ci, oui. Mais nous ne voyons qu'un coin de l'infini; nous ne connaissons point tous les compartiments de l'Etre; il y a d'autres mondes. Mais alors les religions ont donc raison contre les philosophies, ce monde qui est sous nos yeux ayant le caractère de l'éternité, l'enfer est donc éternel? Distinguons. Eternel en soi, momentané en nous. Il est; on le traverse; on n'y souffre qu'un temps; on y entre et l'on en sort. Eternité, mais passage. Quant à lui, il est immanent et persiste; c'est en ce sens seulement qu'il est éternel. La permanence de mon cachot ne prouve pas la permanence de ma peine. Les théogonies ont confondu la durée de la prison avec la durée de l'emprisonnement" (*Oeuvres complètes* [Paris, 1908–1909], III, 342). Strindberg, however, could not have been familiar with Hugo's preface, which was not published until the twentieth century.

13. "Ceux de Dante, de la mythologie Grecque et Romaine et de la mythologie Germanique, portent à croire que les puissances se sont toujours servi de moyens à peu près analogues pour la réalisation de leurs desseins."

14. "Être persécuté par des élementaux, des élementaires, des incubes, des lamias désireux de m'empêcher de venir à bout du Grand Oeuvre alchimique. Instruit par les initiés je me procure un poignard de Dalmatie et je me figure être bien armé contre les mauvais esprits."

15. The article with Strindberg's corrections is preserved in NMS 20, "Les élementaux sont malins."

16. His personal contact with the occultists was certainly not extensive. The one he probably knew best was Jules Lermina, the littérateur, who could hardly be reckoned among the leading occultists in Paris. He was in touch with Fr. Jollivet-Castelot, the alchemist, but their exchanges were largely confined to their correspondence. He met Dr. Papus on at least a few occasions. A letter of his to Frida Uhl (see Frida Strindberg, II, 285) seems to imply that he had met Papus as early as 1894. This case, however, involves an error in proofreading or in translation, for the original reads, "Pabise de la réd. des Débats." Cf. A. Jolivet, *Le théâtre de Strindberg* (Paris, 1931), p. 221.

17. Dr. Papus' real name was Gérard Encausse. For information about him and the *fin-de-siècle* occultists, see the biographical section in Ph. Encausse, *Sciences occultes ou 25 années d'occultisme occidental: Papus, sa vie, son œuvre* (Paris, 1949).

18. In his historical study of symbolism, *Message poétique du symbolisme* (Paris, 1947), G. Michaud strongly emphasizes the importance of occultism: "On a tendance à sous-estimer d'ordinaire l'importance de ce facteur dans l'évolution du Symbolisme. Pourtant, c'est à l'heure où celui-ci cherchait à ses premières intuitions une justification et une unité philosophiques, où il sentait le besoin, non plus seulement de mots, mais d'une doctrine, que les traditions occultes revenaient en faveur. Le choc fut décisif, révélateur: ne fallait-il pas à cette génération d'insatisfaits et de poètes, mais de poètes chez qui le mysticisme n'avait pas fait taire l'esprit critique, quelque chose qui fût à la fois spiritualiste et scientifique, mystérieux et révolutionnaire? L'occultisme lui apportait tout cela, et bien autre chose encore. Il lui expliquait le sens et la raison de ses inquiétudes, il la confirmait dans ses espoirs. Surtout, il venait projeter une pleine lumière sur ce que pressentait la poésie française depuis Baudelaire, et qui, par une intuition quasi-miraculeuse, était devenu l'enseigne de la jeune école littéraire: le symbolisme universel et la métaphysique des correspondances" (p. 371).

19. Really Adolphe-Louis Constant (1810–1875). For further information, see P. Chacornac, *Éliphas Lévi, 1810–1875* (Paris, 1926); A. Viatte, *Victor Hugo et les illuminés de son temps* (Montreal, 1942), pp. 91 ff.

20. E. Lévi is said to have been "initated" into occult doctrine by the learned adventurer, Hoéné Wronski, whose work Strindberg learned about in 1894 from Littmansson. Cf. Chacornac, pp. 131 ff. On Wronski, see Viatte, pp. 81 f.

21. See J. Landquist, "Litteraturen och psykologien," in *Dikten, diktaren och samhället,* ed. A. Ahlberg (Stockholm, 1935), pp. 90 f.

22. Carl du Prel comes up in Strindberg's correspondence with Ola Hansson as early as October 23, 1891, and according to remarks in a letter that Strindberg wrote to E. Schering on July 4, 1904, he also discussed him in 1894 with his in-laws in Austria.

23. "Sûr que l'âme possède la faculté de s'étendre et que pendant le sommeil ordinaire elle s'étend beaucoup, pour, à la fin, dans la mort, quitter le corps et ne point s'éteindre."

24. See E. Briem, *Spiritismens historia* (Lund, 1922), esp. pp. 20, 107.

25. "L'âme se rétrécit par la peur et se transporte par la joie, le bonheur, le succès."

26. P. Mulford, *Vos forces et le moyen de les utiliser* (Paris, 1897), p. 7.

27. S. de Guaita, *Essais de sciences maudites* (Paris, 1890–1897), II:2, 405.

28. Guaita, II:2, 332.

29. "Espèce de Vatican formidable qui exhale des effluves de force psychique immensurables dont les effets se font sentir à distance, d'après le dire des théosophes."

30. Guaita, II:2, 301.

31. This passage occurs in Swedish in the French manuscript of *Legends.*

32. Lamm, *Strindberg och makterna,* p. 96.

33. Guaita, II:1, 541.

34. "Depuis plusieurs années j'ai pris des notes sur tous mes rêves et je suis arrivé à une conviction: que l'homme mène une existence double, que les imaginations, les fantaisies, les songes possèdent une réalité. Si bien que nous sommes tous des somnambules spirituels, que pendant le sommeil nous commettons des actes qui par leur nature différente nous poursuivent durant l'état de la veille avec la satisfaction ou la mauvaise conscience, ou la peur des conséquences. Et il me semble, par des raisons que je me réserve le droit d'exposer une autre fois, que la manie dite des persécutions est bien fondée sur des remords après les mauvaises actions commises pendant le 'sommeil' et dont les souvenirs brumeux nous hantent."

35. The original text of *Inferno* reads, "C'est passé ces cajoleries avec l'Éternel et je tiens au principe du Mahométan qui ne prie de rien que de la résignation de porter le fardeau de l'existence."

36. "Pas une des humiliations imaginables que je n'aie pas essuyées; et tout de même mon orgueil va toujours croissant en raison directe de l'abaissement! Qu'est-ce? Jacob luttant avec l'Éternel et sorti du combat un peu estropié mais remportant les honneurs de la guerre. Job, mis à l'épreuve, et persévérant de se justifier devant des peines infligées sans justice."

37. "Lese jetzt Swedenborg Arcana Coelestia und bin erschrocken. Es scheint mir alles wahr, und doch zu grausam von einem Gott der Liebe."

38. "Dans Arcana Coelestia les énigmes de ces dernières deux années s'expliquaient et avec une exactitude si puissante que moi, enfant de la fin du célèbre dix neuvième siècle, en garde une conviction inébranlable que l'enfer existe, mais ici sur la terre, et que je viens de passer par là."

39. "Ne mentionne que l'enfer et les châtiments, exécutés par les mauvais esprits, c'est dire les diables."

40. "L'enfer à perpétuité, sans espoir de fin, dénudé du mot consolateur."

41. "Ceci m'éclaire sur les intentions bienveillantes de l'invisible, sans me porter la consolation. Seulement après la lecture du Ciel et l'Enfer, je commence à me sentir édifié."

42. The wording in Pernetty's translation of Swedenborg (II, 274) is identical with Strindberg's citations in *The Occult Diary*, with the exception of "de mal faire" instead of Strindberg's "à mal faire." The second of the two quotations in *The Occult Diary* has not been transcribed by Lamm. Moreover, all of the citations from Swedenborg in the French version of *Inferno* (in the chapter entitled "The Redeemer") correspond nearly word for word with Pernetty, II, 274–275, 277–279. They have been somewhat condensed and paraphrased, but Pernetty's work is undoubtedly the source. Yet when Strindberg cited Swedenborg in *Legends,* he seems to have been using a text other than Pernetty's.

43. "Le sanctuaire est preparé, blanc et rose, et le Saint va prendre demeure chez son disciple appelé de leur pays natal afin de réveiller le souvenir d'homme né de femme le plus gratifié aux temps modernes."

44. "À Satan afin de mortifier la chair."

45. "Les opérations préparatoires à une vie spirituelle."

46. "L'espoir renaissant de trouver la paix du coeur, par le repentir et la stricte observance de pensées et d'actes."

47. "C'est alors seulement que je suis délivré du cauchemar qui me hantait depuis la première manifestation des invisibles."

48. "Dieu est l'amour; il ne gouverne pas des esclaves, c'est pourquoi il a accordé aux mortels le libre arbitre. Il n'existe pas de puissance du mal; c'est le serviteur qui fait la besogne en esprit correcteur. Les peines ne sont pas éternelles, libre à chacun d'expier avec patience le mal qu'il a commis."

49. Eklund (p. 226) thinks that only in the works written after publication of *Inferno* does one "catch a glimpse of the God of mercy, grace, and love," and he connects this change with Strindberg's "pecuniary and literary successes." Although Strindberg's mood was undoubtedly affected by financial success and critical acclaim, the statements cited above indicate that Eklund's interpretation is sharply oversimplified and that the categorical form of his judgment is wrong. To verify his theory, Eklund adduces a letter to Gustaf af Geijerstam (undated, October 1897) in which Strindberg says that his "belief in an invisible protector" has been strengthened by the favorable reception of *Inferno,* which had appeared the previous week. Yet Eklund does not cite what follows, where Strindberg writes, "You see? No confinement! No indictment!" In other words, he had feared that after his open confessions he might be sent either to prison or to a madhouse. Consequently, pecuniary or literary advances were not uppermost in his mind.

50. "Il y a un but dans ces souffrances inexplicables; l'amélioration et l'amplification du moi, l'idéal rêvé de Nietzsche, mais autrement compris."

51. "Alors le problème du mal se redresse, et l'indifférence morale de Taine tombe plate devant les exigences nouvelles."

52. "D'expier avec patience le mal qu'il a commis."

53. "De même, il existe des tentations malsaines. Des esprits malins éveillent au fond de l'âme tout le mal qu'il a commis dès son enfance et il est dénaturé dans un sens méchant. Mais les Anges révèlent le bon et le vrai chez le torturé. C'est là la lutte qui se manifeste sous le nom de remords."

54. "Déjà longtemps entamé un examen soigné de ma conscience, et fidèle à mon nouveaux programme de me donner tort devant le prochain, je trouve mon passé exécrable et je prends en dégoût ma propre personne."

55. "Avez-vous observé dans la solitude de la nuit ou au plein jour même, comment les souvenirs de la vie passée se remuent, ressuscités, un à un, deux à deux? Toutes les fautes commises, tous les crimes, toutes les bêtises en vous chassant le sang aux bouts des oreilles, la sueur aux cheveux, le frisson au dos. Vous revivez la vie vécue dès la naissance jusqu'au jour qu'il est; vous souffrez encore une fois toutes les souffrances souffertes, vous avalez tous les calices bus jusqu'à la lie tant de fois; vous vous crucifiez le squelette lorsqu'il n'y a plus de chair à mortifier; vous vous brulez l'âme lorsque le coeur est incinéré."

56. "Oui, ce n'est pas le mal, les crimes qui nous font honte, ce sont nos sottises!"

57. "Mais, dès que j'ai péché, quelqu'un m'attrappe sur le champ et la punition se présente avec une précision et un raffinement qui ne laisse plus de doute sur l'intervention d'une puissance correctrice."

58. "Mon épouse bien aimée"; "ma belle geôlière qui guettait jours et nuits mon âme, jalousait mes aspirations vers l'inconnu."

59. "Dans un accès d'orgueil legitime, saisi d'une furie de me faire du mal, je commets le suicide en expédiant une lettre infâme, impardonnable"; "suicide et assasin."

60. "Lese jetzt Bulwers Zanoni! Mit Entsetzen! Alles is da! Ich, Frida, weil er die Lebens-elixir getrunken! Er sucht immer seine Viola, und die flieht obschon sie ihn liebt! Les' mir das Buch! Fillide (Aspasia) ist auch da!"

61. "Inferno ist geplant, ich habe die Form gefunden, und will ihn jetzt schreiben."

62. "Si c'eût été l'orgueil non justifié qui m'avait fait fuir ces personnes, la punition aurait été logique, mais en ce cas où ma retraite fut amenée par une aspiration de purifier mon individualité de cultiver ma personne dans le recueillement du solitaire, je ne comprends pas la méthode de la providence."

63. "La punition quoique sévère et instantanée, administrée d'une main habile que je ne pus méconnaître, me parut insuffisante."

64. "Seul vice que les dieux ne pardonnent."

65. "D'ailleurs devant qui me plier? Devant les théosophes? Jamais! Devant l'Éternel, les puissances, la Providence je cède à mes mauvais instincts, toujours et tous les jours, si c'est possible. Lutter pour la conservation de mon moi contre toutes influences imposées par le désir de dominer d'une secte ou d'un parti, violà mon devoir, dicté par la conscience acquise par la grâce de mes protecteurs divins."

66. "Pour les psaumes pénitentiaux? Non. je n'ai pas le droit de me repentir, car ce n'est pas moi qui ai dirigé mes destinés; je n'ai jamais fait le mal pour le mal, seulement comme défense de ma personne. Le repentir, c'est critiquer la Providence qui nous inflige le péché comme une souffrance dans le but de nous purifier par le dégoût qu'inspire la mauvaise action."

"La clôture de compte avec la vie s'établit pour moi: faisons quitte à quitte! Si j'ai péché, parole d'honneur, j'en ai subi la peine suffisamment! pour sûr! Craindre les enfers! Mais j'ai traversé les mille enfers ici bas sans broncher. Assez pour m'éveiller le désir ardent de quitter les vanités et les fausses jouissances de ce monde que j'ai toujours détesté. Né avec la nostalgie du ciel, je pleurais comme enfant sur la saleté de l'existence, me trouvant étranger, depaysé entre mes parents et la societé. J'ai cherché mon Dieu depuis l'enfance et j'ai trouvé le démon. J'ai porté la croix de Jesus-Christ dans ma jeunesse, et j'ai désavoué un Dieu qui se contente de dominer sur des esclaves! qui aiment leurs fouetteurs."

67. "À ce moment où j'écris ceci j'ignore ce qui se passait cette nuit de Juillet lorsque la mort fondit sur moi."

68. "N'est-ce pas, que les dieux plaisantent avec nous autres mortels, et c'est pourquoi nous autres ricaneurs conscients savons rire aux moments les plus tourmentés de la vie!"

69. "Le soleil luit, la vie journalière va son train, la bruit des travailleurs égaie les esprits. C'est alors que le courage de faire la révolte se cabre! et que l'on jette le défi, les doutes vers le ciel.

"Or, la nuit, le silence, la solitude tombent, et l'orgueil se dissipe, le coeur bat et la poitrine se resserre! Alors à genoux, hors de la fénêtre dans la haie aux épines, allez chercher le médecin, trouvez un camarade qui veuille dormir chez vous!"

70. A clipping of the article, written in French, is preserved in NMS. I have been unable to establish its origin. One might guess, however, that it comes from *Le messager de Liège,* an occult journal to which Strindberg occasionally refers. Unfortunately, I have not had access to this journal.

71. "Sans faire amende honorable l'homme qui s'est révolté est reçu dans le conseil des Olympiens."

72. "Lance tes flèches fier Gaulois, vers le ciel, le ciel n'est jamais en reste!"

73. "Le prince de ce monde qui condamne les mortels aux vices et châtie la vertu avec la croix, le bûcher, les insomnies, les cauchemars, qui est-il? Le Punisseur auquel nous sommes livrés à cause de crimes inconnus ou oubliés, commis ailleurs! Et les esprits correcteurs de Swedenborg? Les anges-gardiens, qui nous protègent des maux spirituels! —Quelle confusion Babylonienne!"

74. "Est-ce à bon escient donc que j'ai baptisé mon livre par le nom *Inferno?*"

75. "Ma nostalgie au sein de l'Eglise Mère"; "m'humilier et me souiller."

76. Solesmes is a famous monastery that willingly received converted laymen. Huysmans stayed there in the autumn of 1897, and according to an article in *La Presse,* Sept. 6, 1897, it was in the library of Solesmes that he prepared his book *La cathédrale.*

77. "Lorsque ce livre sera imprimé la response doit être reçue. Et puis? Après— Une nouvelle plaisanterie des Dieux qui rient aux éclats quand nous pleurons à chaudes larmes?"

78. "Une décision, pas trop nette, j'avoue, de chercher une retraite dans le couvent."

79. "Suis-je donc toujours le jouet des invisibles?"

80. "Que la vie d'un homme puisse se présenter comme une blague!"

81. Herrlin, *Från sekelslutets Lund,* p. 148.

82. Lamm, *Strindberg och makterna,* p. 95.

83. Eklund, p. 437.

84. Although the gospel of Matthew (24:29) uses "powers" to mean metaphysical powers, the concept really appears to have originated with St. Paul. Several times in the Pauline epistles one finds formulas like "every rule and every authority and power" (I Cor. 15:24). Compare this with Strindberg's exclamation in the first part of *To Damascus:* "Powers, Authorites, principalities, ugh!" (p. 58). Sometimes St. Paul also speaks of "the worldly powers" or "the rudiments of the world" (Col.

2:8), which shows the same kind of vacillation that one occasionally finds in Strindberg: on the one hand, earthly authorities; on the other, heavenly rulers. St. Paul's expression has been interpreted as referring only to the angels, but people were also aware of satanic "powers." Thus, Thomas Aquinas speaks of both evil and good *potestates* (*Summa Theologiae*, I, Q. 63 art. 9 ad 3) and carefully divides the latter into a hierarchy that V. Rydberg summarizes in his *Medeltidens magi* (p. 7); at this point the Pauline concept is put to a new use. According to Larousse, for the French Catholic "les puissances célestes" still means the angels and other heavenly rulers, while "les puissances infernales" means the devils. More recently, the expression "the powers" has been used without any direct connection to its Christian significance. For other uses of the word in Swedish, see *Svenska Akademiens Ordbok*, "Makt," 12.

85. "Je fends en deux ma personnalité offrant au monde l'occultiste naturaliste, gardant en moi et soignant le germe d'un religieux sans confession."

86. "Les coupables, les assasins d'âmes, les empoisonneurs des esprits, les faussaires de la verité, les parjures!"

87. See NMS 6 (14), Lessebo paper. On the case of "Lundgren," see Lamm, *Strindbergs dramer*, II, 80 (footnote).

88. "Où est-il le Père du Ciel, le débonnaire qui savait sourire aux folies des enfants et pardonner après avoir puni?"

89. "Le patron qui tenait la maison en ordre surveillant les préposés afin d'empêcher des injustices."

90. "De toutes les passions funestes qui avilissent un prédicateur."

91. "Non; imiter l'Eternel, c'est impie, et malheur à lui qui s'en adjuge la faculté!"

92. "Et avec des souffrances, des remords d'un voleur qui s'en va avec la propriété d'autrui."

93. "Tout le mal, toutes les injustices, toute l'œuvre du salut n'est qu'une énorme épreuve, à laquelle il faut résister."

94. "Si le mal et les afflictions qui me frappent ne sont pas des châtiments, ils sont des épreuves à subir pour l'entrée à la classe. Je veux les interpréter comme telles et le Christ sera le modèle parce qu'il a bien souffert—quoique je ne comprends pas à quoi bon tant de souffrances si ce ne sont des repoussoirs qui doivent relever l'effet des félicités futures."

95. In Swedish in the manuscript.

96. In Swedish in the manuscript.

97. In Swedish in the manuscript.

98. "Mea culpa qui me fait rougir devant la devise de la médaille que je n'ai pas commandée moi-même."

99. "L'exemple du Sauveur qui a acquitté la femme adultère et le brigand."

100. "Sans faute devant soi même et toutefois torturé par les scrupules qui chassent le malheureux vers la religion qui ne pardonne ni ne console, en condamnant à la folie et à l'enfer—le pauvre innocent, la victime dépourvue de la force de résister

dans une lutte inégale contre la nature toute puissante. Cependant le brasier infernal est allumé pour brûler jusqu'à la tombe soit qu'il flambe tout seul sous les cendres, soit qu'il se nourrisse des combustibles d'une femme. Essayez d'éteindre ce feu par l'abstinence et vous verrez la passion se pervertir et la vertu châtiée d'une façon inattendue. Tâchez de tremper la bûche allumée dans du pétrole et vous aurez une idée de l'amour licite!"

101. "Tout est là! Toutes les horreurs, les péchés les plus secrets, les scènes les plus dégoûtantes où je tiens le rôle principal. . . ."

102. "Le jeune homme me devine et il baisse les paupières. —Vous devinez! Alors allez donc en paix et dormez bien!"

103. "Les voici les quatre mots qui valent les ordonnances des médecins. Ne fais plus cela. Libre à chacun d'interpréter le petit mot *cela* d'après sa conscience!"

104. "Grâce! Grâce! et je renonce à me justifier devant l'Eternel, et je cesse à accuser le prochain."

105. "J'apporte et je lis. Mais c'est Swedenborg et surtout Blawatsky, et quand je retrouve 'mon cas' partout je ne puis me céler que je suis un spiritiste."

106. Swedenborg was one of the writers who inspired Kardec, whose real name was H. L. D. Rivail. The second volume of Kardec's journal, *Revue Spirite,* which appeared in 1859, contains an article on Swedenborg. See Briem, p. 268.

107. "Pour moi en personne il paraît que le chemin de la croix me reconduit vers *la foi de mes aieux.*"

108. "C'est le Moyen-Age, l'âge de foi et de croyance qui approche en France, introduit par la chute d'un empire et d'un Augustulus, juste comme à la décadence de Rome et les invasions des Barbares, qui a vu Paris-Rome en flammes et les Goths se couronner au Capitole-Versailles. Les grands païens Taine et Renan sont descendus au néant emportant leur scepticisme; et Jeanne d'Arc est ressucitée—Tout est vénal; honneur, conscience, patrie, amour, justice, symptômes probants et réguliers de la dissolution d'une société où le mot et la chose vertu a été banni depuis trente ans.

"Est-ce Moyen-Age le déguisement des femmes primitives! Les jeunes hommes endossent le froc du moine se coupent les cheveux avec tonsure et rêvent le monastère; écrivent des légendes et font jouer des miracles, peignent des madones et sculptent des Christ, se laissant inspirer par le mysticisme du Magiste qui les ensorcèle de Tristan et Isolde, Parsifal et Graal.

. . .

"Le beau Moyen-Age où les hommes savaient jouir et souffrir, où la force et l'amour, la beauté en couleur en lignes et harmonies se révélèrent pour la dernière fois avant les noyades et les dragonnades de la Renaissance du paganisme dit protestantisme."

"The primitive women" in the translation is clearly a gallicism and means "medieval women." The costume he refers to is possibly some form of the so-called "reform dress." In the same piece (p. 347) he speaks of pilgrimages to Tilly-sur-Seine and of Rue Jean Goujon. The former is a place in Normandy, where the

Blessed Virgin appeared in April 1896. Of the numerous miracle plays written around 1890 by various young Frenchmen, the most famous one now is Claudel's *L'annonce faite à Marie* (1892).

109. "Le catholicisme fait son entrée solennelle et triomphante dans ma vie."

110. In Swedish in the manuscript.

111. "Depuis cette nuit, je me trouve plus dépaysé ici-bas qu'auparavant, et comme l'enfant, fatigué qui a sommeil je désire retourner à la maison, reposer la tête lourde sur le sein maternel, dormir sur les genoux d'une femme-mère, l'épouse chaste d'un Dieu énorme qui se dit mon père et que je n'ose approcher."

112. In Swedish in the manuscript.

113. "En portant ma croix moi-même, si possible, par un reste de fierté du mâle qui répugne devant la lâcheté à jeter ses fautes sur les épaules d'un innocent."

114. See the draft of *Jacob Wrestles* in NMS 6, Lessebo paper.

115. NMS 9 (2), Bikupa paper, 1895.

116. Naturally, Strindberg's religious development continued beyond that date. One can show, for example, that he was approaching a concept of Christ—albeit in an unorthodox form—between 1898 and 1899, that his pessimistic, Buddhistic moods returned around the time that he wrote *A Dreamplay* in 1901, and that he renewed his interest in occult speculation in connection with the composition of the so-called *Blue Books* between 1906 and 1908. Also, after 1900 he devoted himself to Swedenborg more intimately than he had before. Constant change is the essential feature of his religious concepts; they constituted, after all, not a doctrinal system but a system of attitudes and reactions. That I have nonetheless accepted the terminal date of his development which Strindberg himself insisted upon depends on the fact that his religious struggle was considerably more subdued after he had resumed his career as a writer. Anyone wishing to study his continuing religious development must analyze his enormous artistic output after 1900, where there are important problems that scholars have barely begun to deal with—among others, the problem of the great crisis that Strindberg called "Inferno II," which arose in connection with the dissolution of his relationship with Harriet Bosse.

117. NMS 6 (14), Bikupa paper, 1894.

4. A New Cosmos

1. NMS 6 (14), Bikupa paper, 1894, under the rubric of "Le vase de Bénarès."

2. Karl Groos, *Der Aufbau der Systeme* (Leipzig, 1924), p. 141.

3. See Victor Hugo, *Les travailleurs de la mer* (Paris, 1911), p. 9: "la vie universelle es là dans toute sa sérénité religieuse; nul trouble; partout l'ordre profond du grand désordre naturel." See also p. 13: "Ceci flotte et se décompose, ceci est stable et incohérent. Un reste d'angoisse du chaos est dans la création."

4. On April 21, 1894, Strindberg recapitulates his chemical past in a letter to Gustaf Lindström, a mineralologist.

5. NMS 19, draft. Essay dated 1887.

6. *Antibarbarus* deals exclusively with chemical speculations, but according to the original plan, it was to have covered much more than chemistry. NMS 30 contains a number of notes for the proposed contents of the work, which there bears the subtitle "Studies in the Theory of Knowledge." These notes are mostly written on Bikupa paper dated 1886 and 1889. Besides natural science, in that projected "Antibarbarus" Strindberg also intended to deal with psychology, jurisprudence, art and literary history, etc. Originally the chemical studies were merely one element in a plan for a revision of the philosophical outlook of the modern world and a massive attack on modern "barbarism" in general. The description of Inspector Borg's outlook in Chapter 3 of *By the Open Sea* can be regarded as a primary sketch of this vast plan.

7. NMS 23, letter paper and Lessebo paper. Cf. Strindberg's letter to Birger Mörner (Mar. 10, 1891); B. Mörner, *Den Strindberg jag känt* (Stockholm, 1924), pp. 38 ff.

8. Bengt Lidforss emphasized this point in an article in the *Nordisk Revy* in 1895: "For the Strindberg one encounters in *Antibarbarus* is essentially the same as the one who appears in *Tschandala* and in *By the Open Sea,* but the medium in which he moves is different" (p. 158).

9. NMS 24, M-D. Strindberg also studied the *Novum Organon* and the *De argumentis,* in Latin, as one can tell from some notes on draft paper in NMS 20.

10. Ola Hansson, *Kåserier i mystik* (Stockholm, 1897), the essay "Andliga producktionssätt."

11. For example, in an undated letter to K. O. Bonnier, written from Brünn, Austria, in 1893. In his *Naturens grundämnen i deras inbördes ställning till varandra* (Stockholm, 1875), Blomstrand wrote, "seen in this light, chemistry would also have its Darwinism and, consistently applied, it would accomplish its task more thoroughly than the Darwinism of zoology and botany" (p. 59). However, after considering the problem more carefully, Blomstrand rejects this hypothesis (p. 60) and assumes a doubtful position regarding the doctrine of biological descent (p. 67). Strindberg's dependence on Blomstrand and Haeckel on this point has been pointed out by Eklund, *Tjänstekvinnans son,* pp. 435 f.

12. E. Haeckel, *Der Monismus als Band zwischen Religion und Wissenschaft* (Leipzig, 1908), p. 17.

13. NMS 28, Bikupa paper, 1890.

14. NMS 32, Bikupa paper, 1890.

15. "Précipiter veut dire: reconstituer. Dissoudre veut dire: décomposer."

16. "La nullité de toute l'analyse spectrale."

17. The citations from Schopenhauer are taken from *Welt als Wille* (Leipzig, 1919), II, 50, 347, 348 (translated here by John Moore).

18. Schopenhauer, II, 358, 360 (translated here by John Moore).

19. "En somme, la chimie subventionnée travaille avec des conventions des à peu près, des licences qu'on voudrait qualifier de poétiques, et la théorie gouver-

nante, la théorie atomistique est fondée sur une hypothèse, l'existence de la particule indivisible, l'atome impondérable doué nonobstant d'un poids atomique."

20. NMS 28, M-D.

21. NMS 29, draft paper.

22. NMS 32, Bikupa paper, 1890.

23. NMS 33, draft paper.

24. NMS 28.

25. NMS 33, draft paper.

26. NMS 32, draft paper. In a letter to Bengt Lidforss on April 1, 1891, Strindberg formulated his theory that thunder results from the ignition of explosive gas. The idea appears to have been borrowed from Schopenhauer, who in old age propounded this thought (*Parerga* II, 132), which he himself characterized as "extravagant." Passing fancies like this that Schopenhauer threw out but was reluctant to defend were often the first ideas to attract Strindberg's attention. In his *Erinnerungen an Strindberg* (Leipzig, 1917), C. L. Schleich relates (p. 14) that Strindberg wanted to study the map of Europe on the reflecting ice of the moon. Strindberg gives expression to a variant of that thought in the fifth letter of *Antibarbarus* (NMS 15, Bikupa paper, 1893), where he speaks of "silicon glass." In *Parerga* (II, 139 ff.) Schopenhauer advanced the theory that the surface of the moon was composed of ice.

27. NMS 32, Bikupa paper, 1890.

28. Schopenhauer, *Welt als Wille,* II, 336 translated here by John Moore.

29. The crystals could also serve as examples of "integration" in the sense in which Herbert Spencer used the term. Cf. Herrlin, *Från sekelslutets Lund,* p. 9.

30. NMS 29, draft paper.

31. NMS 28, Bikupa paper, 1892.

32. Schopenhauer, II, 337 f.

33. "C'est une espèce de mémoire chez la matière que vous appelez brute tandis que moi je la considère comme vivante. Et comme vivante elle subit l'hérédité, héritant ses tendances." Quoted from the manuscript (not in Strindberg's hand) in NMS 35, draft paper.

34. "Un être vivant, un grand animal qui mange, digère, croît et aime."

35. This survey of the history of ideas concerning the "souls" of plants is based on Alf Nyman's presentation of this concept in his *Själsbegreppets förvandlingar* (Stockholm, 1943), pp. 77–130.

36. Schopenhauer, II, 333 f.; *Pflanzen-physiologie* (Leipzig, 1919), pp. 67 f. There can hardly be any doubt that Strindberg also studied the latter work, where in a note added to the third edition Schopenhauer observes that in tropical climates the bee gradually ceases to gather honey (p. 67). This anecdote is the basis of Strindberg's fable, "How the priest who believed in God becomes converted through the subtlety of the bee and dies in the bosom of his family in the true atheistic faith," which was written in the spring of 1885.

37. E. von Hartmann, *Verldsprocessens väsen,* trans. A. Stuxberg (Stockholm, 1877–1888), II, 73. Eklund (p. 435) has pointed out the parallel between Hartmann and Strindberg on this point.

38. In a letter to Strindberg on Sept. 13, 1893, Bengt Lidforss gave an account of Haberlandt's research on the nervous system of plants. Lidforss' essay in *Nordisk Revy* in 1895 (reprinted in his *Fragment och miniatyrer*) probably gives the best picture we have of the scientific discussions among members of the "Zum schwarzen Ferkel" circle to which both Strindberg and Lidforss belonged in Berlin.

39. NMS 24, M-D.

40. Haeckel's opinion of the work must have been the greatest disappointment to Strindberg. Although couched in very polite terms, it really expresses strong reservations: "Ich finde in Ihrer Schrift, *soweit ich sie verstehe,* Nichts, was nach meiner subjectiven Ansicht als absolut verkehrt oder 'verrückt' bezeichnet werden könnte" (I find nothing in your book—*insofar as I understand it*—that could, in my subjective opinion, be characterized as absolutely absurd or 'crazy'), letter dated May 28, 1895, preserved in the archives of the Bonnier publishing firm.

41. In the article about "L'affaire soufre."

42. C. Hemel, *Les métamorphoses de la matière* (Paris, 1894), p. 150.

43. See Lamm, *Strindberg och makterna,* p. 72; Eklund, pp. 203 f. See also Strindberg's letter to F. U. Wrangel on June 30, 1895: "But don't be frightened when you read them (i.e. the installments of the essay). They were some trial balloons I sent up to prepare the way for certain heterodox opinions of mine, especially in astronomy." In an earlier letter to the same friend (June 23, 1895), he says that "Deranged Sensations" is "very effective, beautifully executed, and was considered even in Paris to be ultramodern, even though I am regarded as old-fashioned in Sweden."

44. P. Verlaine, *Oeuvres posthumes* (Paris, 1911–1913), II, 8.

45. "N'est-ce pas l'insomnie et les débauches qui m'ont aiguisé les sens et les nerfs?

46. Frida Strindberg, II, 19 f.

47. "Ultrakrank." Undated letter in Frida Strindberg, II, 283.

48. "La cour de marbre forme le conduit d'une oreille, dont le pavillon est façonné des ailes du bâtiment."

49. E. Erckmann and A. Chatrian, *Contes fantastiques* (Paris, 1860), p. 132.

50. This draft, which exists in the manuscript of "Haze" ("Solrök") in the archives of the Bonnier publishing firm, is a prose variant of the poem one finds on pp. 99–101 in Strindberg's *Dikter och Sömngångarnätter.* It was published in the *Svea* annual for 1881. Because Landquist does not mention it in the critical apparatus of his edition of Strindberg's collected works, I include it here:

"They veered past the last skerry and headed for the open sea!

"The deck heaves and throbs and the wind pushes them along. He stood by the foresail and lapsed into speculations about the infinite nothingness hovering over the horizon of the sea; he felt as if he were being borne forth on sturdy arms right into the blue sky; his eye seeks a goal, but finds only water and air; he tries to locate a fixed point where he can rest, but finds none.

"Then at last his strained eyes fasten onto something; in the distance he sees a point, an unsteady white point. Wavering feebly above the hissing waves, it approaches. It comes closer, rises and falls, winds and flutters like a moth seeking the flame it is trying to flee.

"It is a butterfly, a white butterfly wandering like a will-o'-the-wisp out here in the sunshine in search of the unknown and turning back now toward land, which he will never reach—for now, the wave took him.

"He stands there once more on the heaving deck and gazes out over the water; they are moving forward toward the blue wall, the blue unknown, behind which—. Then a mischievous, mocking little thought creeps over him and says, 'if we hold to this course, we'll come to Riga; so we'd better turn back, if we're going to be home by evening.'

"On a pebbly feldspar beach grows a huge water hemlock. Who can say what it feeds on? But it is swollen with fat and with poison.

"At its root, now, in the midday sun a black adder lay asleep: but up at the top wild bees, bumblebees, and wasps were buzzing around the parasol-shaped corymb. The bumblees were gathering honey for their young, the wasps for themselves, the bees for pharmacies, but out of the same plant they were all sucking poison for their stings.

"It is a remarkable plant, that water hemlock."

In a manuscript fragment concerning "the influence of lines of perspective" (NMS 18, Bikupa paper, 1893), Strindberg gives another account of the same experience at the palace of Versailles that he uses in "Deranged Sensations," and this time he uses the term "agoraphobia." In the same fragment he mentions his habitual feeling of loneliness and abandonment on the open sea and adds: "Compare the impression that Birger Mörner and I had out on the plains of Scania, where we always felt anxious until we had crept back into Lund again."

51. "Je jette le masque du citoyen qui n'a jamais reconnu le contrat dit social, je laisse aller à la débandade les pensées révoltantes et je pense, pense . . . sans lâcheté, sans arrière-pensées. Et je vois d'une clairvoyance de sauvage, j'écoute, je flaire comme un peau-rouge."

52. The Svedberg, *Forskning och industri* (Stockholm, 1918), p. 81.

53. E. von Meyer, *Geschichte der Chemie* (Leipzig, 1914), pp. 340 ff.

54. NMS 29, extra superfine paper.

55. NMS 34, Bikupa paper, 1895.

56. Cf. Strindberg's correspondence with Fr. Jollivet-Castelot; for example, his letter of July 22, 1894. An early draft concerning alchemy is preserved in NMS 31, two pages on Bikupa paper, 1893, bearing the rubric "La construction de l'or."

57. "Utilisons le moment, sans cela nous aurons encore dix ans à subir."

58. Fr. Jollivet-Castelot, *Comment on devient alchimiste* (Paris, 1897), p. 389.

59. Jollivet-Castelot, pp. 297, 282, 298.

60. "Que cela signifie-t-il?"

61. "Serait-il que mon oeil se développe pour devenir un microscope solaire d'une force exorbitante?"

62. "Le soleil est lui-même une image virtuelle. De quoi? Quelques-uns disent: de la lumière universelle omniprésente, réfléchie par la sphère céleste."

63. "Il semble, mais ce n'est pas sûr, puisque tout ce monde semble illusoire."

64. C. du Prel, *Själsläran framställd ur synpunkten af menniskoväsendets enhet,* trans. A. F. Åkerberg (Stockholm, 1890), p. 92.

65. This letter, which was to have been the fifth section of *Antibarbarus,* is preserved in an incomplete manuscript in NMS 15 and 17, Bikupa paper, 1893.

66. Francis Bacon, *The Philosophical Works . . . Methodized . . . by P. Shaw* (London, 1733), II, 352.

67. P. F. P. Delestre, *Exploration du ciel théocentrique* (Paris-Lyon, n.d.), p. 14; Strindberg, *Prosa från 90-tal,* p. 299.

68. Delestre, p. 67. Another writer Strindberg refers to in this connection is a German named Dobler. In December 1892, Strindberg became acquainted with this man's book, *Ein neues Weltall,* which appears to have been written by a theosophist. In the fifth letter of *Antibarbarus,* Strindberg states that Dobler "believes that our system is closed and shows by means of synthesis that just as comet tails and certain double stars have been proved to be merely optic phenomena, one can also show that most planets are optic phenomena too."

69. Delestre, p. 94.

70. "Donc nous arrivons du ciel, et nous descendons vers les anthropomorphes. La vie, est-elle un développement à rebours?" NMS 6 (17), Bikupa paper, 1893.

71. "De la sorte il y aurait au moins deux créations et l'enfant entre trois et six ans représenterait une reminiscence de l'homme paradisiaque, et il nous serait encore une fois permis de nous servir de l'expression antédiluvienne quoique dans un sens plus beau."

72. H. P. Blavatasky, *Den hemliga läran* (Stockholm, 1895–1898), II, 398 ff.

73. NMS 33, Lessebo paper. In the Swedish manuscript of an essay entitled "On Cyclamen" in NMS 25, M-D—thus probably written while he was in Germany—Strindberg develops his theory that "Nature sometimes sketches before she draws or paints" and speaks of "God" in quotation marks.

74. Lamm, *Strindberg och makterna,* p. 64.

75. E. Haeckel, *Natürliche Schöpfungsgeschichte* (Berlin, 1873), pp. 59 f. (translated here by John Moore).

76. "Le Créateur, ce grand artiste qui se développe en créant, faisant des esquisses qu'il rejette, reprenant des idées avortées, perfectionnant, multipliant les formes primitives. Certes, c'est créé, à la main. Souvent il fait des progrès énormes en inventant les espèces, et c'est alors que la Science constate les lacunes, les chaînons qui manquent, s'imaginant que les espèces intermédiaires aient disparu."

77. Elias Fries, *Botaniska utflygter* (Stockholm, 1852), II, 183.

78. J. H. B. de Saint-Pierre, *Harmonies de la nature* (Paris, 1818), I, 113.
79. Saint-Pierre, III, 42.
80. NMS 29, Bikupa paper, 1895.
81. Saint-Pierre, I, 63, 67 f.
82. M. Lamm, *Swedenborg* (Stockholm, 1915), pp. 95 ff.
83. Swedenborg, *Les merveilles du ciel et de l'enfer de Des terres planétaires et astrales,* trans. A. J. Pernetty (Berlin, 1782), II, 57.
84. Saint-Pierre, II, 16 f.
85. C. L. Schleich, *Erinnerungen an Strindberg* (Leipzig, 1917), p. 9.
86. "Pardonnez mon silence puisque mes pensées sont ailleurs loin de la chimie et encore plus loin de l'occultisme. C'est que je suis revenu à l'art du théâtre sérieusement, c'est mon métier et je ne *dois* plus m'occuper de la magie, défendue par ma religion."
87. In the essay "Des arts nouveaux" in NMS 6 (17), Bikupa paper, 1893.

5. Toward a New Poetics

1. In his *August Strindberg* (Stockholm, 1948), pp. 210 ff., M. Lamm has assembled a number of illuminating statements concerning Strindberg and the literary programs proposed by Heidenstam and Levertin.
2. Ola Hansson, *Efterlämnade skrifter* (Hälsingborg, 1928–1931), IV, 23. Opinions differ about Hansson's own position in the development from naturalism to symbolism. Hansson, like Strindberg, counted himself a "naturalist" in the 1880s, but he later claimed that the articles he published between 1886 and 1888 in the periodical *Framåt* had introduced the new spiritualistic literary orientation to Sweden. In his *Ola Hanssons ungdomsdiktning* (Helsinki, 1930), pp. 231 ff., E. Ekelund studies Hansson's literary production during the 1880s against the background of European symbolism, and as a result of this juxtaposition he supports Hansson's pretentions to being the harbinger of the new literary style that emerged in Sweden in the 1890s. H. Levander objects to Ekelund's assessment of Hansson and insists that his definitive break with naturalism did not occur until 1891, when he wrote "Materialismen i skönlitteraturen." See Levander, *Sensitiva amorosa* (Stockholm, 1944), p. 257. Finally, S. Linder does not even think that essay represents a real break with naturalism and sees Hansson's mysticism as being "positivist and physiological, not transcendent." See Linder, *Ernst Ahlgren i hennes romaner* (Stockholm, 1930), pp. 307 f. However, in studying the actual facts in this development, one can hardly discern the sharp boundary between "physiological" and "transcendent" mysticism that Linder's argument presupposes. For Huysmans and Bourget, as for the succeeding generation of symbolists, the road to religious idealism led to a descent into the pit of half-conscious moods so widely cultivated during the period of "late naturalism." Applied to some phases of this development, the question, "Is this naturalism, or not?" cannot be answered with any degree of certainty, because

one is dealing with a trend which gradually slipped into an area of mysticism that is difficult to deal with precisely. In both Strindberg and Hansson, in the literary circle at Berlin's "Zum schwarzen Ferkel," and in the literary circles in Paris during the 1880s, one can observe the same cautiousness and the same sense that literature was in a state of transition.

3. For the link between the Kantian tradition and French *fin-de-siècle* idealism, see G. Michaud, *Message poétique du Symbolisme* (Paris, 1947), I, 200 ff., 223.

4. Hansson, *op. cit.*, IV, 23.

5. Maxime Herman, *Un sataniste polonais: Stanislas Przybyszewski* (Paris, 1939), p. 218.

6. S. Przybyszewski, *Totenmesse* (Berlin, 1893), pp. 17 f. (translated here by John Moore).

7. Herman (p. 61) feels that Hansson and Strindberg both had a greater influence on Przybyszewski than he had on either of them. Yet Przybyszewski was more radical in his subjectivism than either of the Swedish writers.

8. "C'est l'instinct de l'expansion du moi, la tendance de se poser comme l'axe du monde, le penchant de clôturer une motte de terre, de tracer un horizon autour de moi qui agit par la canne, rayon de ce cercle que chacun porte avec soi sans en pouvoir être dégagé." NMS 6 (17), Bikupa paper, 1893.

9. Ola Hansson, *Kåserier i mystik* (Stockholm, 1897), p. 44.

10. Michaud, p. 232.

11. For a lively and interesting discussion of the members of the "Zum schwarzen Ferkel" group, see Evert Sprinchorn's introduction to his translation of Strindberg's *Inferno, Alone and Other Writings* (Garden City, N.Y., 1968), esp. pp. 10–18, 37–47.

12. "France's camp" fails to capture the pun Strindberg intended when he wrote "France-riket" instead of "Frankrike," which is the Swedish name for "France." The pun may refer either to *Mercure de France,* the organ of the symbolists, or to Anatole France's paper, *Le Temps,* for Strindberg contributed to both. The context makes the latter alternative seem the most likely.

13. "L'existence du grand homme est un outrage permanent pour les petits," NMS 6 (17), Bikupa paper, 1893.

14. "Un phénomène intéressant: à étudier, non à imiter," NMS 6 (17), Bikupa paper, 1893.

15. Stellan Ahlström has called my attention to the fact that French criticisms of *The Father* after it was presented in Paris in December 1894 attacked Strindberg for, among other failings, his subjectivism.

16. The manuscript of "Des arts nouveaux! ou le hasard dans la production artistique" is preserved in NMS 6 (17), Bikupa paper, 1893. The essay was published in *Revue des Revues* in 1894 and bears the date Nov. 5, 1894. In the 1923 issue of *Samlaren,* T. Eklund reprinted this version of the essay, which was revised by Georges Loiseau, with the title "En obeaktad uppsats av Strindberg."

17. P. Martino, *Verlaine* (Paris, 1924), p. 192. For "neologism" in Baudelaire and Rimbaud, see Michaud, pp. 138 f.

18. "Une jouissance incroyable d'entendre un vieux morceau se rajeunir."

19. In this context Strindberg makes a statement about Max Nordau that shows how distant he had become from his former idol. In his magnum opus, *Degeneration,* Nordau had criticized most aspects of *fin-de-siècle* culture as manifestations of mental illness. He had also attacked Maeterlinck's "echolalia." Strindberg repays the criticism with interest: "Et cette bête dégénérée de critique, qui lui en impute l'aliénation mentale, rubriquant sa maladie avec le nom scientifique (!) Echolallie. — Echolallistes, tous les vrais poètes à partir de la création du monde. Exception: Max Nordau, qui rime, sans être poète. Hinc illae lacrimae!"

20. "Ce charmant pêle-mêle d'inconscient et de conscient."

21. "Un instant ce fut une vache; aussitôt deux paysans qui s'embrassaient; après un tronc d'arbre, puis . . . cette oscillation des impressions me fait plaisir . . . un acte de volonté et je ne veux plus savoir ce que c'est . . . je sens que le rideau du conscient va se lever . . . mais je ne veux pas . . . maintenant c'est un déjeuner champêtre, on mange . . . mais les figures sont immobiles comme dans un panopticon . . . ah . . . ça y est . . . c'est une charrue délaissée sur laquelle le laboureur a jeté son habit et suspendu sa besace! Tout est dit! Rien plus à voir! La jouissance perdue!"

22. Jules Huret, *Enquête sur l'évolution littéraire* (Paris, 1891), p. 60. Members of Strindberg's circle in Berlin were already familiar with this statement. Przybyszewski quotes it in his study of Munch. Cf. Herman, p. 218.

23. "Comme la nature capricieuse et sans but déterminé"; "la manière de créer de la nature."

24. On Baudelaire's aesthetics, see Michaud, I, 75 f. On "neologism" in Saint-Pol-Roux, see *Documents,* p. 17 f. In his *Själsläran,* trans. A. F. Åkerberg (Stockholm, 1890), p. 78, Carl du Prel makes a statement very similar to Strindberg's, to the effect that instead of imitating nature, the artist should, like nature, create out of his subconscious mind.

25. The paintings that Strindberg did in the early 1890s would no doubt throw a lot of light on the initial period of his crisis, but I am forced to pass over this source of material because the paintings cannot be analyzed in a satisfactory manner until they have been systematically catalogued and dated. Using the resources that are now available, G. Sylvan has written an essay, "August Strindberg som målare," in *Tidskrift för konstvetenskap* (1948), which gives an outline of the various periods during which Strindberg painted, including his symbolist period in 1894. Sylvan also isolates certain symbolist motifs that Strindberg retained over the years and thereby provides striking illustrations of the continuity I have frequently emphasized in this book between Strindberg's outlook in the 1870s and the 1890s. However, Sylvan appears to overemphasize the intellectual component in the paintings by Strindberg in 1894. When he painted these pictures, it was not Strind-

berg's intention to fill them with all the "content" that he later saw in them. As one can tell from the essay "On New Arts," his interpretations were subsequent rationalizations.

26. "Habitué à observer tout ce qui se passe dans mon âme, je me rappelle avoir été saisi d'une épouvante inusitée, tandis que des images se bousculaient, pêle-mêle, comme des conceptions d'un aliéné. Je vis le défenseur de Louis XVI, la guillotine derrière; je vis une grande rivière cotoyée de collines vertes, une jeune mère qui conduit une petite fille le long de l'eau; puis un monastère avec un retable d'autel par Velasquez; je suis à Sarzeau, dans l'Hôtel Lesage où il y a une édition polonaise du *Diable boiteux;* je suis derrière la Madeleine, rue Chauveau-Lagarde . . . ; je suis à l'Hôtel Bristol, à Berlin où je lance une dépêche à Lavoyer, Hôtel London: je suis à Saint-Cloud, où une femme en chapeau Rembrandt se tord sous le mal d'enfant: je suis assis au café de la Régence, où la cathédrale de Cologne est exposée en sucre brut . . . et le sommelier prétend que c'est bâti par M. Ranelagh et le maréchal Berthier."

1973 Addenda by the Author: As Sverker Hällen (*Ystads Allehanda* 19.9.1970) has shown, this piece of writing contains a "cryptogram," allusions intended as a warning to some of Strindberg's former friends in Paris who—so he believed—planned to murder him.

27. See "Dans la cimetière de * * *," in *Les rayons et les ombres.*

28. Cf. Michaud, pp. 108 ff.

29. "Je me crois en enfer, donc j'y suis." A. Rimbaud, *Oeuvres,* ed. P. Berrichon (Paris, 1945), p. 205.

30. In a letter to Marcel Réja on July 13, 1898, concerning Réja's *Ballets et variations.*

31. P. Gauguin, *Lettres de Gauguin* (Paris, 1946), p. 288.

32. *Ibid.,* pp. 288 f.

33. This fact was pointed out by W. Berendsohn in his *Strindbergsproblem* (Stockholm, 1946), pp. 88 ff. Berendsohn also draws attention to the biographical circumstances that Strindberg passes over in silence in his own account of the Inferno period.

34. NMS 6 (14), Bikupa paper, 1894.

35. André Chevrillon, *Dans l'Inde* (Paris, 1891), pp. 184 f.

36. NMS 6 (14), Bikupa paper, 1895.

37. The epilogue to *Legends* is not included in the manuscript owned by Kerstin Strindberg, which is preserved in the Royal Library in Stockholm.

38. For example, Lamm, *Strindberg och makterna,* p. 69; Eklund, *Tjänstekvinnans son,* p. 432; Berendsohn, p. 85.

39. See above, Chapter 3, pp. 130 ff.

40. See Jolivet, pp. 236 f.

41. NMS 6 (16), Lessebo paper.

42. "L'effet magique me fit penser que le Barberousse de France se fût éveillé,

que Saint-Louis célébrât le jour de sacre par une fête de gala à laquelle tous les monarques de la Terre étaient invités vêtus en bure du pénitent et desservant le repas à genoux."

43. "Le chemin de la Croix et peut-être les quatorze stations! si je ne me trompe."

44. Lamm, *August Strindberg,* p. 233.

45. "Un moment je reste affaissé devant le vaste sentier des larmes lorsque au dessous des arbres effeuillés une boule de lumière, s'approche portée sur deux ailes de buse. Elle s'arrête devant moi et à la hauteur de mes yeux et à la clarté répandue autour de la boule je vois un carton blanc et orné comme un menu. En dessus en caractères couleur de fumée je lis: 'Mange!' "

46 Lamm, *Strindbergs dramer,* II, 51.

47. In *August Strindberg* (p. 234), Lamm writes: "The play actually deals with the prehistory of the crisis, and for the protagonist of the play, the Stranger, that is only a little way on the road to Damascus." Lamm has clearly been misled by the surface action of the play, which does suggest the period before the crisis had begun. Strindberg has not "dealt with" any period of his life; he has written a play describing the process of conversion. Chapters 2 and 3 above show that the biographical background for the central scene, "In the Asylum," is the moral conflict that Strindberg began to experience in the spring of 1897. Lamm's statement implies that Strindberg himself had gone much further along the road to conversion than the Stranger does in *To Damascus.* As a matter of fact, the play represents the very act of submission that is such an essential part of the experience of conversion.

48. Passages in the manuscript that Strindberg later canceled indicate that theft was the offense he attributed to the Stranger.

49. "Veuf, solitaire, indépendant il a fait la rude école de la vie et des hommes qu'il méprise de ce dédain robuste et noble qu'amène une connaissance profonde de la nullité relative du tout, le propre moi y compris."

50. In this scene Strindberg originally used other material that clearly derives from the milieu he found when he stayed with Dr. Eliasson in Ystad. It is said that Eliasson used to shoot sparrows and cats, according to information supplied by Bruno Hoppe and published by Gunnar T. Pihl, under the signature "Pilot," in *Sydsvenska Dagbladet Snällposten* on Jan. 22, 1929. In the manuscript, Strindberg let the doctor shoot a cat on the garden wall, whereupon it fell, "but on the off-stage side of the wall," according to the stage directions. All of this was later canceled.

The episode of the stillborn child probably has no counterpart in Strindberg's actual experiences at Ystad; at least, Dr. Eliasson's friends believed him incapable of such a demonstration. However, Hoppe does report that Eliasson kept his own amputated finger in a matchbox and would from time to time show it to people.

51. A. Paul, *Min Strindbergsbok* (Stockholm, 1930), p. 64.

52. See Chapter 1, pp. 61–62.

53. A. Lundgren, "En Infernolegend," *Skånejournalisternas vårtidning* (May 1920).

54. In the manuscript, Strindberg's first formulation of the line was less effective: "He is great, but he is not Caesar."

55. Vagn Børge in *Strindbergs mystiske Teater* (Copenhagen, 1942), pp. 94 ff. Børge admits, however, that Strindberg's personal experiences played the decisive role.

56. The notation reads: "Pillow, Mandrake, Verlaine, Cushion, Cricket, Phonograph, Horsehair. Uhl, Aloys, Dornach. Thought-transference, Madhouse, God, Caesar (Shakespeare). The Death of Ahlberg." Strindberg was not alone in drawing the parallel between himself and Verlaine. When Strindberg was a patient at the Saint-Louis Hospital, the Paris newspapers published notices to the effect that no less than three poets were then languishing in charity wards: Laurent Tailhade, Paul Verlaine, and August Strindberg. See S. Ahlström, "När Strindberg 'erövade' Paris," *Göteborgs Handels Tidning* (July 7, 1950).

57. Lamm, *Strindbergs dramer,* II, 59.

58. "Comme cela sent la mort, aujourd'hui!"

59. On the history of the "Christmas rose," see, for example, N. Willie, "Vaarblomster i haven," *Kunst og Kultur* (1913–1914), pp. 162 f.

60. "C'est le moulin du Seigneur qui est lent à moudre mais broie fin—et noir!"

61. Sylvan, "August Strindberg som målare," p. 84.

62. *Ibid.,* p. 85.

63. Cf. Lamm, *Strindbergs dramer,* II, 55.

64. Cf. Freud, *Jenseits des Lustprinzips* (London, 1947), pp. 16 ff. Freud considers the compulsion to experience repetition—both by neurotics and by others—indicative of the existence of a "death wish" that is antagonistic to the libido.

65. In NMS 4 (3) and (28), both in Lessebo paper.

66. See Chapter 2, p. 95.

67. Cf. Jean Wahl's analysis of the concept of "repetition" in *Etudes kierkegaardiennes* (Paris, 1938), pp. 184 ff. In other contexts, however, one sometimes finds Kierkegaard making splenetic complaints about the monotony of life. At such times his statements seem very close to some of Strindberg's: "Strangely enough, it is always the same; at every age during his life one is busy, yet he never gets anywhere; indeed, he actually seems to go backwards" (*Samlede Værker,* [Copenhagen, 1901–1906], I, 19).

68. G. Ollén, *Strindbergs dramatik* (Stockholm, 1948), pp. 378 ff. Cf. Hedén, p. 287.

69. Lamm, *Strindbergs dramer,* II, 68.

70. See above, Chapter 5, p. 226.

71. As Vagn Børge suggests in *Strindbergs mystiske Teater,* pp. 81 f.

72. Cf. Flaubert, *La tentation de Saint Antoine,* ed. R. Dumesnil (Paris, 1940), p. 211: "Ô bonheur! bonheur! j'ai vu naître la vie, j'ai vu le mouvement commencer. Le sang de mes veines bat si fort qu'il va les rompre. J'ai envie de voler, de nager, d'aboyer, de beugler, de hurler. Je voudrais avoir des ailes, une carapace, une écorce, souffler de la fumée, porter une trompe, tordre mon corps, me diviser partout, être

en tout, m'émaner avec les odeurs, me développer comme les plantes, couler comme l'eau, vibrer comme le son, briller comme la lumière, me blottir sur toutes les formes, pénétrer chaque atome, descendre jusqu'au fond de la matière,—être la matière!"

Description of Works Written by Strindberg Between 1893 and 1898

These works are listed in their probable chronological order. In cases where manuscripts and drafts can be dated with relative certainty, the evidence for the date is given in right-hand margin. In other cases, I have chosen the date that seems most probable on the basis of general criteria, such as subject matter and the kind and date of the paper. I have not included the evidence to be found in letters or interviews. Nor have I tried to give exhaustive information concerning the dates of publication, printing, and reprinting of these works. The versions I cited in the text of this book are marked with an asterisk. I am indebted to Stellan Ahlström for several details in this description.

Zur Psychologie des Schwefels
Manuscript NMS 28, Lessebo bikupa   Dated Sellin, Rügen, June 8, 1893.
paper, 1892, pag. 1–4.

Zur Ontogenie des Schwefels. Erste Skizze
Manuscript NMS 28, Lessebo bikupa
paper, 1892, pag. 1–5. Variant of the
preceding text.

Was ist Kohlenstoff? (*Erste Skizze*)
Manuscript NMS 28, Lessebo bikupa
paper, 1892, pag. 1–6.

Dated Sellin, Rügen, July 12, 1893.

Antibarbarus I oder Die Welt für sich und die Welt für mich
* Preserved manuscript: fasc. I Lessebo
bikupa paper, 1892, pag. 1–7 NMS
30, *pag*. 9–19 NMS 32; fasc. II Lessebo
bikupa paper, 1892, pag. 20–39 NMS
30; fasc. III draft paper, pag. 50–61
NMS 30, pag. 40–46 NMS 33, pag.
47–49 NMS 44; fasc. IV M-D paper,
pag. 65–73 NMS 30. Written entirely
in Swedish.

According to information on the title
page of the 1905 Swedish edition, this
ms. was composed at Brünn, Austria;
hence, it can be dated October-
November 1893. The fragment of fasc.
I is dated Brünn, Nov. 24, 1893.

Antibarbarus. Révision générale des Sciences Naturelles
Manuscript NMS 30, Lessebo bikupa
paper, 1893, pag. 1–3. Resumé in
French of fasc. I. Printed in Berlin,
1894. Cited from the Swedish manuscript as far as it goes, otherwise from
Landquist's edition of Strindberg's
works.

Världen för sig och världen för oss
* Fragmentary manuscript, Lessebo bikupa paper, 1893, irregular pag. 1–52,
whereof pag. 1–8 NMS 15, pag. 16–20
NMS 15, pag. 21–23 NMS 19, pag.
24–37 NMS 15, pag. 38–39 NMS 19,
pag. 27–47 NMS 17, pag. 48–52 NMS
15.

In a letter to B. Lidforss on Dec. 26,
1893, Strindberg speaks of this "fifth
letter" of *Antibarbarus*.

Le Monde pour soi et le Monde pour nous
Manuscript NMS 15, draft paper, pag.
1–13. Not in Strindberg's handwriting.
Signed: Fra Giovanni. Variant of the
preceding.

Paralipomènes à Le Monde per se et le Monde pour nous
Manuscript NMS 15, same paper and handwriting as preceding, pag. 1–3. Completion of the preceding.

Vivisections II
* Manuscript NMS 6, Lessebo bikupa paper, 1893.

Probably written July-October 1894. Cf. letters to Littmansson and Loiseau cited below, undated letter to Thyselius (written from Dieppe), and the letter to B. Mörner of Oct. 8, 1894.

The work contains the following essays:
Moi, pag. a–f.

Written at the end of July 1894 (letter to Littmansson, July 22, 1894).

L'Homme à venir, pag. g–p.

Finished Oct. 6, 1894, at the latest (letter to Loiseau on that date).

D'où nous sommes venus, pag. q–v.

Les Barrabas, fragment, pag. 1–2.

La genèse d'une Aspasie, pag. 1–10.

Des arts nouveaux ou Le hasard dans la production artistique, pag. 5–15. Publ. in *Revue des Revues,* 1894.

Dated Nov. 5, 1894, in *Revue des Revues.*

Qu'est-ce que le Moderne? pag. 16–20. Publ. in *L'Echo de Paris,* Dec. 20, 1894, and under the title "Die Modernen" in *Das Magazin für Literatur,* 1895.

According to Frida Strindberg (II, 312), this essay was written in September 1894.

Cristaux de remplacement, pag. 21–31. Publ. in *La Plume,* Dec. 15, 1894.

Finished no later than Aug. 8, 1894 (cf. letter to Littmansson on that day).

Où est-elle? pag. 32–34.

Nemesis divina (suite), pag. 35–45.

Les pervers, pag. 46–55.

Written at the end of July 1894 (cf. letter to Littmansson, July 29, 1894).

L'origine d'un Style, pag. 56–63.

Hérédité encore une fois, pag. 64–67.

Finished no later than Oct. 6, 1894 (cf. letter to Loiseau on that day).

Le caractère un rôle? pag. 100–111.

Le mensonge, fragment, unpag.

Césarine
Publ. in *Le Figaro littéraire,* Sept. 30, 1894.

According to Frida Strindberg (II, 313), this essay was written in September 1894.

Marionetter
Publ. in *E'Echo de Paris,* Jan. 2, 1895, and in *Das Magazin für Literatur,* 1895.

Nouvel avant-propos
In: Le plaidoyer d'un Fou. Paris 1895.

Dated Paris-Passy, October 1894.

Misogynie et gynolâtrie
Publ. in *Gil Blas,* July 24, 1895.

Reference to a conversation with Henri Becque suggests that this essay was written in the autumn of 1894.

Sensations détraquées
* Manuscript in the Royal Library, Stockholm, Lessebo bikupa paper, 1893, pag. 1–15, 1–14. Publ. in *Le Figaro littéraire* in three installments: Nov. 17, 1894; Jan. 26, Feb. 9, 1895.

According to a notation on the ms., written October-December 1894.

Le Barbare à Paris
Publ. in *Gil Blas,* Aug. 8, 1895.

Probably written in December 1894. Cf. S. Ahlström, "Barbaren i Paris," *Ord och Bild* (1947).

Le soufre est-il un corps simple?
This article, publ. in *Le Petit Temps,* Jan. 30, 1895, was not written by Strindberg himself but contains a summary of his research.

L'affaire Soufre
* Manuscript NMS 35, draft paper, unpag. (5 sheets). Not in Strindberg's hand. Publ. in *Le Figaro,* Feb. 12, 1895.

Dated Feb. 12, 1895.

Lettre à Gauguin
Cited from the Landquist edition of Strindberg's works.

Preface to the catalogue of Gauguin's exhibition at the Hôtel Drouot, Feb. 18, 1895.

Öppet brev till Berthelot om svavlet
Manuscript in French NMS 30, draft paper, unpag. (4 sheets). Not in Strindberg's hand.

Dated Feb. 28, 1895.

L'avenir du soufre
Publ. in *La Science française,* Mar. 15, 1895.

Introduction à une chimie unitaire (Première esquisse)
Manuscript NMS 30, Lessebo bikupa paper, 1893, pag. 1–26. Printed by *Mercure de France* in Paris, 1895.

Written spring of 1895 (cf. letter to Dubosc, May 27, 1895).

L'iode comme un dérivé de houilles
Manuscript NMS 35, Lessebo bikupa paper, 1893, pag. 1–4. Publ. in *Le Temps,* May 14, 1895.

Dated May 21, 1895 (cf. letter to B. Mörner, May 22, 1895).

Nouvelle Synthèse d'Iode
Manuscript NMS 35, Lessebo bikupa paper, 1894, pag. 1–4.

According to the text, written while *Introduction à une chimie unitaire* was "sous presse," i.e., during the summer of 1895.

Sur l'Iode: Paralipomena

Manuscript NMS, draft paper, pag. 1–6.

The title places this article last in the series of essays on iodine written in 1895; it might also be assigned to the beginning of 1897.

La construction de l'or

Manuscript fragment NMS 31, Lessebo bikupa paper, 1893, pag. 1–2.

Probably written in the summer of 1895 (cf. letter to Jollivet-Castelot, *Bréviaire alchimique,* p. 13).

Etudes funèbres

Publ. in *Revue des Revues,* July 15, 1896. * Publ. in Swedish tr. under the title "På kyrkogården" in 1897. Here called "In the Cemetery"; sometimes translated into English as "Graveyard Reveries."

Written during the autumn, probably in 1895. The five-week trip to a foreign country that Strindberg mentions is probably his trip to Ystad, Sweden, in the summer of 1895.

Sylva Sylvarum

Manuscripts:

Ad Zoïlum. NMS 30, draft paper in French, unpag. (1 sheet).

Written near the end of 1895.

La Tête de Mort (Ch. 4). NMS 30, Lessebo bikupa paper, 1894, in French, pag. 1–9.

* *Dödskallefjäriln. Försök i rationell mysticism.* NMS 22, Lessebo bikupa paper, 1894, in Swedish, pag. 1–11. Five more pages of the same work are in NMS 9, Lessebo paper, pag. 1–5.

Corps simples, chimie simpliste. NMS 30, Lessebo, in Swedish, pag. 61–67. French counterpart in NMS 30, draft paper, pag. 1–6, not in Strindberg's hand. Manuscript variant: *Min Verld och Min Gud,* NMS 30, Lessebo bikupa, 1894,

pag. 1–3. Draft of "Introduction."
Sylva Sylvarum was publ. in Paris in
1896 in book form. The articles, except for the Introduction, were later
reprinted in their Swedish versions in
Jardin des Plantes II (Gothenburg,
1896). My citations are based on this
Swedish text (printed by Landquist),
augmented by the ms. of "Dödskallefjäriln" and the French text of the
Introduction publ. in Paris.

Om Cyclamen
Manuscript NMS 25, M-D paper, pag.
10–15. Publ. in summary form in *Le
Petit Temps,* Dec. 29, 1895.

Cf. letter to W. Molard, Dec. 30,
1895: "Instead of printing my
rigorously scientific 'Cyclamen,' *Le
Temps* printed their own inept remarks
about my article, which is unknown to
the reader."

Ett minne från Sorbonne
Publ. in *Göteborgs Handels Tidning,*
Mar. 5, 1896.

Dated Paris, February 1896.

*Om Ljusvärkan vid Fotografiering. Betrak-
telser med anledning af X-strålarne.*
Publ. in *Göteborgs Handels Tidning,*
Mar. 11, 1896.

Dated Paris, Feb. 20, 1896.

Stenarnes suckan
* Manuscript fragment, Lessebo bikupa
paper, 1894, pag. 1–12 NMS 23, pag.
13–26 NMS 29. Publ. in *Jardin des
Plantes* I (Gothenburg, 1896).

Dated Paris, March 1896.

En blick mot Rymden
* Manuscript at Bonnier's publ. firm,
draft paper, pag. 1–5. Publ. in *Initiation,* April 1896, in French, under the
title "Un regard vers le Ciel."

Pourquoi le fer seul indique le nord
Publ. in *Initiation,* April 1896. Manuscript variant in NMS 20, Lessebo paper, pag. 1–5.

L'analyse spectrale
* Publ. in *Initiation,* May 1896. Manuscript variant in NMS 18, Lessebo bikupa paper, 1892, pag. 1–3.

Le ciel et l'œil
Publ. in *Initiation,* May 1896.

Sur la photographie en couleurs directes
Publ. in *Initiation,* May 1896.

La distance du soleil de la terre
Publ. in *Initiation,* May 1896.

Järneken
Publ. in *Jardin des Plantes* II (Gothenburg, 1896).

Probably written in the spring of 1896 and sent to T. Hedlund later than the other essays in *Jardin des Plantes* (cf. letter to Hedlund, May 15, 1896).

Paralipomena och upprepningar
Publ. in *Jardin des Plantes* II (Gothenburg, 1896).

See above.

L'horizon et l'œil
Publ. in *Initiation,* June 1896.

Les étoiles fixes
Publ. in *Initiation,* June 1896.

L'exposition d'Edward Munch
Publ. in *La Revue Blanche,* June 1, 1896.

L'irradiation et l'extension de l'âme
* Publ. in *Initiation,* July 1896. Later publ. in *Legends.* Manuscript draft:

Lifskraften, NMS 9, Lessebo bikupa paper, 1893, pag. 1–2, in Swedish.

La terre, sa forme, ses mouvements
Publ. in *Initiation,* September 1896.

All of the articles in *Initiation* were probably written between February and July 1896, at the time of Strindberg's close contact with the circle connected with the journal.

Guldets synthes förklarad af guldextraktionen ur kopparkis genom Faluprocessen
Publ. as a brochure (Gothenburg, 1896).

Submitted Aug. 18, 1896 (cf. letter to T. Hedlund on that date).

Gold-Synthese
Manuscript NMS 31, Lessebo bikupa paper, 1895, pag. 1–8. Publ. as a brochure (Grein, 1896).

Dated Sept. 3, 1896.

Synthèse d'or
Publ. in *Hyperchimie,* November 1896.

Dated Saxen, Sept. 15, 1896.

Nutidens Guldmakeri
Manuscript NMS 29, Lessebo bikupa paper, 1894, pag. 1–6. Publ. as a brochure (Stockholm, 1896).

Dated Klam, Oct. 26, 1896.

Solrosen
* Manuscript at Bonnier's, draft paper, pag. 1–5. Only p. 5 in Strindberg's hand. Manuscript variant in French: *Le grand soleil,* NMS 25, draft paper, pag. 1–4. Publ. in *Tryckt och otryckt,* IV, 1897.

Dedicated to M. Guymiot in connection with his article in *Initiation* in September 1896. According to an undated letter to Hedlund, Strindberg completed his study of the sunflower (*solros*) in November 1896.

Skånska landskap med utvikningar
* Publ. in *Tryckt och otryckt,* IV, 1897. Manuscript fragment at Bonnier's, draft paper, pag. 1–4.

Written at the end of 1896 or beginning of 1897: ". . . this morning on the fourth day of Christmas . . ."

La synthèse de l'Iode
Publ. in *Hyperchimie*, January 1897.
Manuscript variant in Swedish: *Jodens Synthes Förklarad ur Extraktionmetoderna*, NMS 35, draft paper, pag. 1–7.

Dated Lund, January 1897.

Swedenborg i Paris
Publ. in *Holmia*, 1898.

Written in February 1897 (Cf. letter to K. O. Bonnier, undated, [February 1897]).

Notes et observations sur la Chimie actuelle
Publ. in *Hyperchimie*, April 1897.

Le Pain de l'avenir
Publ. in *Hyperchimie*, April 1897.

Inferno
* Manuscript in the Municipal Library of Gothenburg, Lessebo bikupa paper, 1893 and 1895, pag. 1–406. Publ. in Swedish translation, Stockholm, 1897.

Dated May 3–June 25, 1897. Epilogue composed later.

Légendes
* Manuscript in the Royal Library, Stockholm (belongs to Kerstin Strindberg), Lessebo bikupa paper, 1895, pag. 1–250. Publ. in Swedish translation in *Legender*, Stockholm, 1898.

According to the *Occult Diary*, written between Sept. 22 and Oct. 17, 1897.

Coram populo (Jakob brottas)
* Manuscript in the Royal Library, Stockholm (belongs to Kerstin Strindberg), Lessebo bikupa paper, 1895, pag. 1–178. In French up to p. 109, thereafter in Swedish. Publ. in Swedish in *Legender*, Stockholm, 1898.

According to the *Occult Diary*, started in November 1897. A comparison with entries in the diary seems to indicate that the work was abandoned before the end of the year. The latest episodes dealt with occurred at Christmas time in 1897.

Deklaration på svenska (no title)
Manuscript NMS 9, Lessebo bikupa paper, 1895, pag. 1–4.

Dated Nov. 24, 1897.

Le télescope désiré
Publ. in *Hyperchimie,* February and May
1898.

Till Damaskus
* Manuscript in the Royal Library,
Stockholm, Lessebo bikupa paper,
1895, pag. 1–279. Publ. as the first
part of *Till Damaskus,* I–II, Stockholm,
1898.

According to the *Occult Diary,* this first
part of the *To Damascus* cycle was written between Jan. 19, and Mar. 16,
1898.

Typer och prototyper inom mineralkemien
* Manuscript NMS 34, Lessebo bikupa
paper, 1895, pag. 1–94. Publ. in
Stockholm, 1898.

Dated Paris, March 1898.

Efterskrift (to *Legendes*)
Publ. in *Legender,* Stockholm, 1898.

Dated Lund, Apr. 23, 1898.

Silfverträsket
* Manuscript at Bonnier's, Lessebo bi-
kupa paper, 1894, pag. 1–53. Publ. in
Vintergatan, 1898.

Finished in July 1898 (cf. letter to E.
Schering, July 5, 1898).

Till Damaskus, II
* Manuscript at the Royal Library,
Stockholm, Lessebo bikupa paper,
1895, pag. 1–237. Publ. in *Till Damaskus,* I–II. Stockholm, 1898.

According to the *Occult Diary,* finished
on July 17, 1898.

Les gîtes aurifères de la France
Publ. in *Hyperchimie,* October 1898.

Les nombres cosmiques
Publ. in *Hyperchimie,* November and
December 1898.

Advent
Manuscript in the Royal Library, Stockholm, Lessebo bikupa paper, 1895,
pag. 1–240. Publ. in *Vid högre rätt,*
Stockholm, 1899.

Written between November and December 1898.

Bibliography

Ahlström, S. "Barbaren i Paris," *Ord och Bild* (1947).

————. "När Strindberg 'erörade' Paris," *Göteborgs Handels Tidning* (July 7, 1950).

Bachler, K. *August Strindberg: Eine psychoanalytische Studie.* Vienna, 1931.

Bacon, Francis. *The Philosophical Works . . . Methodized . . . by P. Shaw.* 3 vols. London, 1733.

Balzac, H de. *Séraphita. Oeuvres complètes.* Ed. M. Bouteron et H. Longnon. Vol. 31. Paris, 1927.

Bengtsson, S. "Vad Strindberg läste i Lund samt några Strindbergsbrev," *Svensk litteraturtidskrift* (1946).

Berendsohn, W. A. *Strindbergsproblem: Essäer och studier.* Stockholm, 1946.

Berg, R. G. "August Strindberg som medarbetare i Nordisk Familjebok," *Dagens Nyheter* (Jan. 6, 1929).

Blavatsky, H. P. *Den hemliga läran,* trans. from 3rd English ed. 2 vols. Stockholm, 1895–1898.

Blomstrand, C. W. "Naturens grundämnen i deras inbördes ställning till hvarandra," *Ur vår tids forskning.* Vol. 14. Stockholm, 1875.

Brandes, Georg. *Søren Kierkegaard. Samlede Skrifter.* Vol. 2. Copenhagen, 1899.

————. *Naturalismen i England. Samlede Skrifter.* Vol. 5. Copenhagen, 1900.

Briem, E. *Spiritismens historia.* Lund, 1922.

Brunetière, F. *La science et la religion.* Paris, 1895.

Bulwer, E. G. *Zanoni. The New Knebworth Edition of the Novels and Romances of Edward, Lord Lytton.* Vol. 15. London, n.d.

Byron, Lord. *The Works. Poetry.* Ed. E. H. Coleridge. Vols. 1–7. London, 1903–1905.

Børge, V. *Strindbergs mystiske Teater: Aestetisk-dramaturgiske Analyser med særlig Hensyntagen til Drömspelet.* Copenhagen, 1942.

Chacornac, P. *Eliphas Lévi: 1810–1875.* Paris, 1926.

Chevrillon, A. *Dans L'Inde.* Paris, 1891.

Delestre, P. F. P. *Exploration du ciel théocentrique.* Paris-Lyon, n.d.

Diderot, D. *La religieuse. Oeuvres complètes.* Ed. J. Assézat. Vol. 5. Paris, 1875.

Divoire, F. *Les deux idées: Faut-il devinir mage?* Paris, 1909.

Ekelund, E. *Ola Hanssons ungdomsdiktning.* Helsinki, 1930.

Eklund, T. "En obeaktad uppsats av Strindberg," *Samlaren* (1923).

———. "Strindbergs I havsbandet," *Edda* (1929).

———. *Tjänstekvinnans son: En psykologisk Strindbergsstudie.* Stockholm, 1948.

Encausse, P. *Sciences occultes ou 25 années d'occultisme occidental: Papus, sa vie, son oeuvre.* Paris, 1949.

Erckmann, E., & A. Chatrian. *Contes fantastiques.* Paris, 1860.

Flaubert, G. *La tentation de Saint Antoine. Oeuvres complètes de Flaubert.* Ed. R. Dumesnil. Paris, 1940.

Freud, S. *Jenseits des Lustprinzips. Gesammelte Werke chronologisch geordnet.* Vol. 13. London, 1947.

———. *Hemmung, Symptom und Angst. Gesammelte Werke chronologisch geordnet.* Vol. 14. London, 1948.

Fries, E. *Botaniska utflygter: En samling af strödda tillfällighetsskrifter.* Vol. 2. Stockholm, 1852.

Gauguin, P. *Lettres de Gauguin à sa femme et à ses amis.* Ed. M. Malingue. Paris, 1946.

Groos, K. *Der Aufbau der Systeme.* Leipzig, 1924.

Guaita, S. de. *Essais de sciences maudites.* 3 vols. Paris, 1890–1897.

Hamsun, K. *Sult. Pan. Victoria. Samlede Værker.* 2nd ed. Christiania & Copenhagen, 1918.

Hansson, O. *Kåserier i mystik.* Stockholm, 1897.

———. *Efterlämnade skrifter i urval.* Ed. Hjalmar Gullberg. 5 vols. Hälsingborg, 1928–1931.

Harriman, P. L. (ed.). *Encyclopedia of Psychology.* New York, 1946.

Hartmann, E. von. *Verldsprocessens väsen eller Det omedvetnas filosofi.* Trans. A. Stuxberg. 2 vols. Stockholm, 1877–1878.

Hedén, E. *Strindberg: En ledtråd vid studiet av hans verk.* Stockholm, 1926.

Hemel, C. *Les métamorphoses de la matière.* Paris, 1894.

Herman, M. *Un sataniste polonais: Stanislas Przybyszewski (de 1868 à 1900).* Paris, 1939.

Herrlin, A. *Från sekelslutets Lund.* Lund, 1936.

Holmberg, O. "Strindbergs skuld," in his *Madonnan och järnjungfrun.* Stockholm, 1927.

Hugo, V. *Les Rayons et les Ombres. Oeuvres complètes. Poésie,* vol. 2. Paris, 1909.

———. *Les misérables. Oeuvres complètes. Romans,* vols. 3–6. Paris, 1908–1909.

———. *Les travailleurs de la mer. Oeuvres complètes. Romans,* vol. 7. Paris, 1911.

Huret, J. *Enquête sur l'évolution littéraire.* Paris, 1891.

Huysmans, J. K. *A rebours.* Paris, 1884.

———. *En route.* Paris, 1895.

Haeckel, E. *Generelle Morphologie der Organismen.* 2 vols. Berlin, 1866.

———. *Natürliche Schöpfungsgeschichte.* 4th rev. ed. Berlin, 1873.

———. *Die Perigenesis der Plastidule oder die Wellenzeugung der Lebenstheilchen.* Berlin, 1876.

———. *Der Monismus als Band zwischen Religion und Wissenschaft.* Leipzig, 1908.

Jacobsen, H. *Strindberg og hans første Hustru.* Copenhagen, 1946.

Jaspers, K. *Strindberg und van Gogh: Versuch einer pathographischen Analyse.* Bern, 1922.

Jolivet, A. *Le théâtre de Strindberg.* Paris, 1931.

Jollivet-Castelot, F. *La vie et l'âme de la matière.* Paris, 1894.

———. *Comment on devient Alchimiste.* Paris, 1897.

Kardec, A. (pseud. for H. L. D. Rivail). *Le livre des esprits contenant Les principes de la doctrine spirite.* Paris, 1857.

Kierkegaard, S. *Samlede Værker.* Ed. A. B. Drachmann, J. L. Heiberg, and H. O. Lange. 14 vols. Copenhagen, 1901–1906.

Landquist, J. "Litteraturen och psykologien," in A. Ahlberg et al. *Dikten, diktaren och samhället.* Stockholm, 1935.

Lamm, M. *Swedenborg: En studie öfver hans utveckling till mystiker och andeskådare.* Stockholm, 1915.

———. *Strindbergs dramer.* 2 vols. Stockholm, 1924–1926.

———. *Strindberg och makterna.* Stockholm, 1936.

———. *August Strindberg.* 2nd rev. ed. Stockholm, 1948.

Levander, H. *Sensitiva amorosa: Ola Hanssons ungdomsverk och dess betydelse för åttiotalets litterära brytningar.* Stockholm, 1944.

Levertin, O. *Konflikter: Nya noveller.* Stockholm, 1885.

Lidforss, B. "Strindberg som naturforskare," *Nordisk Revy* (1895).

Lie, E. *Erindringer fra et Dikterhjem.* Oslo, 1928.

Lindberg, P. "Tillkomsten av Strindbergs 'Mäster Olof,' " *Skrifter från Stockholms högskolas litteraturhistoriska seminarium.* Vol. 1. Stockholm, 1915.

Linder, S. *Ernst Ahlgren i hennes romaner: Ett bidrag till det litterära åttiotalets karakteristik.* Stockholm, 1930.

Linné, C. von. "Anteckningar öfver nemesis divina," ed. E. Fries, in *Inbjudningsskrift till . . . philosophiska promotion.* Uppsala, 1848.

Lundegård, A. *Några Strindbergsminnen knutna till en handfull brev.* Stockholm, 1920.

Lundgren, A. "En Infernolegend," *Skånejournalisternas Vårtidning* (May 1920).

Maeterlinck, M. *Théâtre.* 2 vols. Brussels–Paris, 1901–1902.

Martino, P. *Verlaine.* Paris, 1924.

Mattsson, G. (ed.). *Psykologisk pedagogisk uppslagsbok.* 4 vols. Stockholm, 1943–1946.

Maupassant, G. de. "Le Horla," *Oeuvres complètes.* Vol. 18. Paris, 1909.

Meyer, E. von. *Geschichte der Chemie von den ältesten Zeiten bis zur Gegenwart.* 4th rev. ed. Leipzig, 1914.

Michaud, G. *Message poétique du Symbolisme.* 3 vols. and Documents. Paris, 1947.

Michelet, Jules. *La mer.* Paris, 1861.

Michon, J. H. *La religieuse par l'abbé —— auteur du Maudit.* 2 vols. Paris, 1864.

Mulford, P. *Vos forces et le moyen de les utiliser.* Paris, 1897.

Mörner, B. *Den Strindberg jag känt.* Stockholm, 1924.

Newman, E. *Gemenskaps– och frihetssträvanden i svenskt fromhetsliv 1809–1855. Lund, 1939.*

Nordau, M. *Entartung.* 2 vols. Berlin, 1892–1893.

Norman, N. "Strindberg i Lund," *Nittiotalsstudier tillägnade Olle Holmberg,* suppl. vol. of *Svensk litteraturtidskrift* (1943).

Nyman, A. *Själsbegreppets förvandlingar: Fyra allmänfattliga kapitel jämte ett inlägg om växtbesjälning.* Stockholm, 1943.

Ollén, G. *Strindbergs dramatik: En handbok.* Stockholm, 1948.

Oseen, C. W. *Atomistiska föreställningar i nutidens fysik.* Stockholm, 1919.

Parker, Theodore. *Samlade skrifter.* Trans. V. Pfeiff & A. F. Åkerberg. 10 vols. Uppsala, 1867–1875.

Paul, A. *Min Strindbergsbok: Strindbergsminnen och brev.* Stockholm, 1930.

Péladan, J. *Coeur en peine. La décadance latine, Ethophée.* Vol. 7. Paris, 1890.

——. *Comment on devient mage.* Paris, 1892.

Pers, K. de. "August Strindbergs äktenskap med Frida Uhl" (interview with Maria Uhl), *Göteborgs Handels Tidning* (Jan. 31, Feb. 4, Feb. 8, 1924).

Peukert, E. *Strindbergs religiöse Dramatik.* Hamburg, 1929.

Pihl, G. T. "Strindbergs vän och hjälpare i orons och guldmakeriets tid: Några ord om den originelle Ystadsdoktorn Anders Eliasson," *Sydsvenska Dagbladet Snällposten* (Jan. 22, 1929).

Poe, E. A. *The Works of Edgar Allan Poe.* Ed. E. C. Stedman and G. E. Woodberry. New York, 1914.

Prel, Carl du. *Själsläran framstäd ur synpunkten af menniskoväsendets enhet.* Trans. A. F. Åkerberg. Stockholm, 1890.

Przybyszewski, Stanislas. *Totenmesse.* Berlin, 1893.

Réja, M. *Ballets et variations.* Paris, 1898.

Rimbaud, A. *Oeuvres: Vers et prose.* Ed. P. Berrichon. Paris, 1945.

Riotor, L., and G. Léofanti. *Les enfers bouddhiques.* Paris, 1895.

Rochas d'Aiglun, A. de. *Les états profonds de l'hypnose.* Paris, 1892.

———. *L'extériorisation de la sensibilité, étude expérimentale et historique.* 2nd ed. Paris, 1895.

———. *L'extériorisation de la motricité, recueil d'expériences et d'observations.* Paris, 1896.

Rodhe, E. *Den religiösa liberalismen: Nils Ignell—Viktor Rydberg—Pontus Wikner.* Stockholm, 1935.

Rosenius, C. O. *Samlade skrifter.* 4 vols. Stockholm, 1896.

Rudwin, M. *Les écrivains diaboliques de France.* Paris, 1937.

Rydberg, Viktor. *Medeltidens magi.* 2nd ed. Stockholm, 1865.

———. *Undersökningar i germanisk mythologi.* 2 vols. Stockholm, 1886–1889.

Saint-Martin, L. C. de. *Des Erreurs et de la Vérité ou Les Hommes rappelés au principe universel de la Science.* 2nd ed. Salomopolis [Paris], 1781.

Saint-Pierre, J. H. B. de. *Harmonies de la nature. Oeuvres complètes mises en ordre . . . par L. Aimé-Martin.* Vols. 8–10. Paris, 1818.

Sanner, B. Fr. "Strindbergs väg ur ateismen," *Religion och kultur* (1935).

Schleich, C. L. *Erinnerungen an Strindberg nebst Nachrufen für Ehrlich und von Bergmann.* Leipzig, 1917.

Schopenhauer, A. *Sämmtliche Werke.* Ed. J. Frauenstädt. 2nd ed. 6 vols. Leipzig, 1919.

Sjöholm, S. *Övermänniskotanken i Gustaf Frödings diktning.* Gothenburg, 1940.

Smirnoff, Karin. *Strindbergs första hustru.* Stockholm, 1925.

Storch, A. *August Strindberg im Lichte seiner Selbstbiographie.* Munich, 1921.

Strindberg, A. "Djefvul," in *Nordisk familjebok.* Vol. 3. Stockholm, 1880.

Strindberg, A. *Bréviaire alchimique: Lettres d'August Strindberg à Jollivet-Castelot.* Paris, 1912.

———. *Samlade skrifter.* Ed. J. Landquist. 55 vols. Stockkholm, 1912–1919.

———. *Samlade otryckta skrifter.* Ed. W. Carlheim-Gyllensköld. 2 vols. Stockholm, 1918–1919.

———. *En dåres försvarstal.* Trans. from the French original by J. Landquist and E. Staaff. Stockholm, 1925.

———. *August Strindbergs och Ola Hanssons brevväxling 1888–1892.* Stockholm, 1938.

———. *August Strindbergs brev.* Ed. T. Eklund. Stockholm, 1948 to date.

Strindberg, Frida. *Strindberg och hans andra hustru.* 2 vols. Stockholm, 1933–1934.

Svedberg, T. *Forskning och industri: Naturvetenskapliga essayer.* Stockholm, 1918.

Swedenborg, E. *Les merveilles du ciel et de l'enfer et Des terres planétaires et astrales.* Trans. A. J. Pernetty. 2 vols. Berlin, 1782.

———. *Arcana Coelestia.* Trans. C. Deleen. 3 vols. Stockholm, 1832–1842.

———. *Delitiae sapientiae de amore conjugali.* Trans. C. Deleen. Stockholm, 1852.

————. *Den sanna kristliga religionen.* Trans. C. Deleen. 2nd ed. 3 vols. Vexiö, 1840–1852.

————. *Tankar och syner i andeliga ämnen.* Stockholm, 1858.

————. *Apocalypsis revelata.* Trans. C. Deleen. 3 vols. Stockholm, 1858–1863.

————. *Drömmar 1744 jemte andra hans anteckningar.* Ed. G. E. Klemming. Stockholm, 1859.

Sylvan, G. "August Strindberg som målare," *Dikt och konst: Tidskrift för konstvetenskap* (1948).

Söderblom, N. *Svenskars fromhet.* Stockholm, 1933.

Taub, H. *Strindberg als Traumdichter.* Gothenburg, 1945.

Uddgren, G. *En ny bok om Strindberg.* Gothenburg, 1912.

Uppvall, A. J. *August Strindberg, a Psychoanalytic Study.* Boston, 1920.

Wahl, J. *Etudes kierkegaardiennes.* Paris, 1938.

Verlaine, P. *Oeuvres posthumes.* 2 vols. Paris, 1911–1913.

Wermlund, S. *Samvetets uppkomst: En socialpsykologisk studie.* Stockholm, 1949.

Viatte, A. *Victor Hugo et les illuminés de son temps.* Montreal, 1942.

Wille, N. "Vaarblomster i haven," *Kunst og Kultur* (1913–1914).

Index of Names

Agassiz, Louis, 209-210
Ahlström, Stellan, 309n15
Albertus Magnus, 173
Almquist, C. J. L., 33
Aristotle, 170, 173, 176, 178, 181, 183,
185, 193, 207, 208
"Aspasia" (Dagny Juel), 86, 87, 90, 93,
132, 291n54
Atterbom, P. D. A., 95

Bachler, Karl, 282n11
Bacon, Francis, 165-167, 176, 201, 216
Balzac, Honoré de, 97, 103, 105, 125, 249
Barbey d'Aurévilly, Jules, 39
Barrès, Maurice, 111, 115
Baudelaire, Charles, 39, 189, 232, 234
Becque, Henri, 229
Bengtsson, Simon, 291n51
Berendsohn, Walter A., 290n31, 311n33
Berg, Ruben G., 284n38
Bergh, Richard, 67, 189
Bergson, Henri, 183
Bernard, Claude, 182
Berzelius, J. J., 220
Beskow, Gustaf Emanuel, 11

Björnson, Björnstjerne, 5
Blavatsky, H. P., 110, 111, 149, 206
Blomstrand, C. W., 169, 303n11
Böhme, Jacob, 111
Bonnier, Karl Otto, 45, 46, 53, 61, 166,
167, 285n42, 286n50, 288n55, 303n11
Børge, Vagn, 312n55, 313n71
Bosse, Harriet, 67, 284n28, 289n14
Boullan, Jean-Baptiste, 111
Bourget, Paul, 224, 225, 308n2
Brandes, Edvard, 54
Brandes, Georg, 19, 20, 38, 41, 55, 140,
224
Briem, Efraim, 295n24
Brunetière, Ferdinand, 185
Buffon, G.-L., L. de, 211
Bulwer-Lytton, E. G. E., 132, 133
Byron, Lord, 22, 32, 34, 37, 38, 39, 40,
157, 286n48

Calvin, Jean, 153
Carlheim-Gyllensköld, Wilhelm, 25,
283n20, 284n38
Charcot, J.-M., 112
Charpentier, Georges, 228

Chatrian, Alexandre, 40, 191
Chevrillon, André, 237, 243, 244
Christiernsson, Gustaf, 24
Crookes, William, 192
Cuvier, Georges, 210, 211

Dante Alighieri, 106-107, 263
Darwin, Charles, 162, 168, 182, 183, 196
Dehmel, Richard, 227
Delestre, P. F. P., 202
Diderot, Denis, 146, 147
Didon, Père, 101
Dionysius the Elder, 191
Divoire, Fernand, 138
Dobler, 307n68
Driesch, Hans, 183

Ekbohrn, Ossian, 61, 254, 285n43
Ekelund, Erik, 308n2
Eklund, Torsten, 4, 7-9, 36, 38, 40, 57,
    67, 140, 148, 161, 286n48, 289n14,
    293n6, 297n49, 281n11, 303n11,
    309n16
Eliasson, Anders, 91, 105, 122, 253, 254,
    312n50
"Elisabeth," 25, 29
Elmblad, Per Magnus, 10
Erckmann, Emile, 40, 191
Essen, Betty von, 38
Essen, Siri von, 25-29, 30, 31, 37, 38, 47,
    48, 49, 56, 62, 67, 68, 69, 70, 77, 78,
    94, 252, 253

Fahlstedt, Eugène, 40, 284nn29, 38
Fechner, Gustav Theodor, 181, 184
Fénelon, François, 214
Flaubert, Gustave, 143, 147, 313n72
France, Anatole, 228, 309n12
Freud, Sigmund, 280n9
Fries, Elias, 211, 212
Fröding, Gustaf, 286n48

Gauguin, Paul, 81, 185, 228, 230, 234,
    235, 241, 242, 248
Geijerstam, Gustaf af, 62, 94, 156, 163,
    190, 266, 269, 270, 272, 273, 297n49
Goethe, J. W. von, 33, 168, 177, 178, 211

Goncourt, E. and J., 225, 229
Görres, J.-J., 111
Grétor, Willy, 76
Grimm, Bröderna, 107
Groos, Karl, 162
Guaita, Stanislas de, 110, 111, 115, 116,
    117, 118, 221, 264

Haberlandt, Gottlieb, 183, 305n38
Haeckel, Ernest, 164, 168, 169, 170, 174,
    177, 179, 180, 183, 184, 205, 209, 210,
    303n11, 305n40
Hamsun, Knut, 73, 142, 247
Hansson, Ola, 57, 62, 119, 163, 165, 167,
    177, 224, 225, 226, 227, 257, 292n67,
    295n22, 308n2, 309n7
Hartmann, Eduard Von, 34-37, 116, 168,
    181, 183, 184, 218, 239
Hedlund, Torsten, 44, 49, 73, 79, 81, 82,
    83, 84, 85, 88, 89, 90, 91, 93, 95, 96,
    100, 101, 102, 103, 104, 105, 106, 107,
    108, 109, 110, 112, 119, 122, 123, 125,
    134, 140, 142, 157, 158, 166, 186, 187,
    194, 195, 204, 206, 208, 217, 218, 219,
    220, 240, 244, 245, 246, 249, 290n22,
    293n12
Heidenstam, Verner von, 166, 167, 223
Heijkorn, Edla, 12
Hello, Ernest, 111
Hemel, Claude, 187
Hericaut, 116
Hering, Ewald, 180
Herman, Maxime, 225, 291n54, 309n7
Hermann, 83, 119, 248, 291n51
Herrlin, Axel, 1, 40, 41, 140, 141
Hervieu, Paul, 229
Hesiod, 107
Hoffmann, E. T. A., 40, 55, 225
Holmberg, Olle, 282n11
Hoppe, Bruno, 312n50
Hugo, Victor, 33, 52, 58, 59, 162, 238,
    294n12
Humboldt, Alexander von, 211
Huret, Jules, 233
Huysmans, J. K., 39, 111, 151, 152, 224,
    225, 229, 299n76, 308n2

Ibsen, Henrik, 16, 47, 259
Ingersoll, Robert, 51

Jammes, Francis, 235
Janet, Pierre, 116
Jaspers, Karl, 67, 282n11
Jollivet-Castelot, Fr., 187, 194, 195, 196,
    220, 221, 294n16, 306n56
Jørgensen, Johannes, 152
Josephson, Ernst, 60

Kant, Immanuel, 53
Kapff, Dr., 11
Kardec, Allan (H. L. D. Rivail), 125,
    149-150, 301n106
Kierkegaard, Mikael, 41
Kierkegaard, Sören, 16, 17, 18-22, 33, 38,
    40, 41, 50, 55, 102, 270, 283n18,
    313n67
Kjellberg, Isidor, 47
Kléen, Emil, 93, 287n50
Klemming, G. E., 5, 6, 46

Laforgue, Jules, 240
Lamm, Martin, 2, 3, 36, 37, 41, 45, 57,
    106, 107, 118, 140, 141, 161, 208, 217,
    250, 251, 260, 272, 287n50, 296n42,
    308n1, 312n47
Landquist, John, 279, 288n55, 305n50
Langen, Albert, 76
Lecain, Mme., 81, 87, 88, 131, 284n28
Leclercq, Julien, 292n3
Lermina, Jules, 294n16
Levander, Hans, 308n2
Levertin, Oscar, 51, 52, 223
Levi, Eliphas (A.-L. Constant), 110, 111,
    138, 197
Lidforss, Bengt, 85, 86, 93, 94, 124, 163,
    164, 165, 166, 167, 175, 176, 184, 201,
    289n4, 291n54, 303n8, 304n26, 305n38
Lie, Erik, 285n42
Lie, Jonas, 20, 45, 50, 73, 87, 88
Linck, Josef, 17
Linder, Sten, 308n2
Lindström, Gustaf, 302n4
Linnaeus, 40-42, 158, 181, 211
Littmansson, Leopold, 20, 39, 59, 73, 75,

76, 77, 94, 100, 104, 179, 182, 184,
    185, 186, 187, 188, 195, 228, 231
Loiseau, Georges, 289n4, 309n16
Lucas, Louis, 187
Lugné-Poe, A. M., 76
Lundegård, Axel, 288n57
Lundin, Jean, 74, 256, 290n24
Luther, Martin, 138, 153, 293n12
Lyell, Charles, 207

Maeterlinck, Maurice, 229, 230, 232, 234,
    235, 236, 238, 258, 259, 267, 268,
    310n19
Mallarmé, Stéphane, 111, 228, 233, 236,
    240, 242
Martino, Pierre, 231
Maupassant, Guy de, 140, 142, 224, 247
Melanchton, Phillipp, 153
Mendelieff, D. I., 169, 192
Michaud, Guy, 222, 227, 239
Michelet, Jules, 187
Michon, J. H., 147
Molard, William, 248
Moleschott, Jakob, 162
Mörner, Birger, 86, 187, 202, 229, 303n7,
    306n50
Munch, Edvard, 84, 86, 87, 227
Musset, Alfred de, 238

Nansen, Fridtjof, 202
Nerval, Gérard de, 238
Nietzsche, Friedrich, 57, 58, 60, 100, 129,
    146, 147, 182, 189, 286n48
Nordau, Max, 57, 58, 201, 310n19
Nordenskjöld, A. E., 202
Nyman, Alf, 304n35

Öhrwall, Hjalmar, 163
Oken, Lorenz, 169, 181
Olin, Johan Axel, 10
Ollén, Gunnar, 271
Origen, 293n12
Owen, Samuel, 11
Ovid, 206

Papus, Dr. (Gérard Encausse), 89, 109,
    110, 112, 117, 197, 221, 294nn16, 17